Islamic Laws of
Fasting

Islamic Laws of
Fasting

ACCORDING TO THE RULINGS OF GRAND
AYATULLAH SAYYID ALI AL-HUSSEINI AL-SISTANI

I.M.A.M.
IMAM MAHDI ASSOCIATION OF MARJAEYA

Imam Mahdi Association of Marjaeya, Dearborn,
MI 48124, www.imam-us.org
©2022 by Imam Mahdi Association of Marjaeya
(I.M.A.M.), Inc.
All rights reserved.
Printed in the United States of America

ISBN-13: 978-0-9997877-6-2

Contents

I.M.A.M.'s Foreword.. ix

Part One: Fasting in Islam 1

Fasting in Islam..2
- Fasting in Previous Nations 3
- The Definition of Fasting....................................4
- Its Significance, Status, and Reward....................4
- Characteristics and Advantages of Fasting and the Holy Month of Ramadan.............................12
- The Wisdom of Legislating Fasting and Its Benefits..21
- Fasting Levels...28

Part Two: Rules of Fasting..................................... 33

Rules of Fasting...34
- Fasting Etiquette 34

Types of Fasting...45
- Unlawful Fasting 45
- Detestable Fasts...47
- Recommended Fasts 47
- Obligatory Fasting...49

Conditions for the Obligation of Fasting and Its Validity 56
- First: Sanity (Aql) and Consciousness (not to be insane, unconscious, or intoxicated)..................56
- Second: Being at the Age of Religious Obligation (Bulugh) 58

Contents

- Third: Capability, Tolerance, Hardship, and Security from Harm 61
- Forth: Establishing the Beginning of the Month of Ramadan 68
- Fifth: Not Traveling..............90
- Sixth: The State of Purity 104
- Seventh: Intention 109

Fast-Nullifiers 118
- First & Second: Eating and Drinking..............119
- Third: Sexual Practices..............124
- Fourth & Fifth: Deliberately Remaining in the State of Janabah, Haydh, or Nifas until Fajr ...127
- Sixth: Deliberately Causing Thick Dust or Smoke to Reach the Throat 132
- Seventh: Applying Liquid Enema 134
- Eighth: Deliberately Ascribing False Things to Allah and the Infallibles 135
- Ninth: Deliberately vomiting..............136
- Tenth: Immersing the Head under Water..............137

Making Up Missed Fasts and Offering Kaffarah and Fidyah 138
- The Intention of Making Up a Missed Fast (Qada)..............139
- Obligation to Offer Kaffarah in Addition to Making Up the Missed Fast 140
- Cases Only Requiring Qada without Kaffarah.142
- Cases Requiring Qada with Kaffarah..............143
- Making Up Fasts on Days When Fasting Is Recommended 145
- Keeping a Missed Fast on Behalf of a Deceased Person 146

Contents

- The Amount of Fidyah and Kaffarah and Their Disbursement......148
- Time of Offering Fidyah......152

Fasting on Behalf of Someone Else......153
- Voluntarily Fasting on Behalf of Someone Else......153
- Fasting for Hire......154

Rulings on Fasting Errors......155
- Deficient Intention......155
- Mistakes Related to Fast-Nullifiers......155
- Mistakes in Imsak......158
- Mistakes in Fulfilling the Conditions of Qada and Kaffarah......159
- Mistakes in Performing an On-time or Makeup Fast......160

Spiritual Retreat......163
- Conditions of Spiritual Retreat......163
- Conditions to Avoid on Spiritual Retreat......165
- Summary......166

The Fitra Alms Tax (Zakat al-Fitra)......168
- Fitra Alms Tax......168
- When Does Fitra Alms Tax Become Obligatory and When Must It Be Paid?......169
- Who Must Pay the Fitra Alms Tax?......170
- The Form of Fitra Alms Tax......171
- The Amount of Fitra Alms Tax......171
- Location of Fitra Alms Tax Spending......172

Eid al-Fitr......173
- Eve of Eid al-Fitr......174
- The Day of Eid al-Fitr......175

Contents

- Eid prayer..178
- Details to pay attention to on the day of Eid..180

Glossary 185

I.M.A.M.'s Foreword

In the name of Allah, the Most Gracious,
the Most Merciful

May peace and blessings be upon Prophet Muhammad
and his immaculate and pure progeny

The success of any project must begin with the support of God. Moreover, the project must have a reason for its initiation, a desired outcome, an intended goal, and be different from existing literature. Thus, we begin by explaining what distinguishes this work from others and what makes it more than a mere addition to other publications.

There are several reasons for preparing this booklet.

- A lack of authoritative jurisprudential material in English that is accurate in content, professionally translated [from Arabic], and restructured and carefully edited to ensure linguistic suitability
- A lack of simple and straightforward jurisprudential material in English, presented with complete and detailed explanations of the Islamic legal terms related to fasting, in a way that is suitable for youth and teenagers
- Details about the rules of fasting and the conditions related to them currently exist in many places (books, pamphlets, or websites). This makes it difficult for the duty-bound person (*mukallaf*) to

find an accurate, all-encompassing, and easy-to-access booklet that contains all the details and rulings of fasting in one place.

- The absence of a resource that considers the appropriate order and hierarchy of the rulings of fasting. For example, many of the existing texts begin with an explanation of the intention for fasting and delve into its details (such as requirements, timing, or annulling) before even presenting the conditions that obligate someone to fast. Similarly, some texts start by covering what invalidates the fast, such as eating and drinking, before explaining the conditions of fasting, such as knowing when it starts and ends. In addition, discussion of the crescent and the beginning of the month of Ramadan often occurs at the end of these books, as if its sighting only concerns the declaration of Eid and not when the month of Ramadan starts. For these and many other reasons, this booklet endeavors to rearrange the rulings of fasting, present them in an objective manner, and explain them step-by-step.

This booklet contains two parts.

- The first part describes the importance and greatness of fasting and the benefits it has on the individual, family, and society. It also discusses the reward God Almighty has promised in the hereafter for those who fast. It attempts to demonstrate the importance and virtue of the month of Ramadan and the honorable occasions and significant events that take place in it. Thus, believers must appreciate the significance of this temporary opportunity so they can avail themselves of it in the best way possible.

- The second part explains the rulings of fasting from A to Z. It describes the rulings in detail and includes additional related topics that a fasting person must know. These include the rules of *tayammum*, which a duty-bound person must know so they can purify themselves when the time to do so is very short, the rules of the traveler, whether to religiously consider a person a frequent traveler, and when to fast during travel. Other rules in this book cover sighting of the crescent and the means of establishing unity or multiplicity of horizons; *itikaf* (spiritual retreat) and its importance because unfortunately, it has become an almost abandoned form of worship; and *zakat al-fitra*, which jurisprudential books usually mention in the chapter on *zakat* rather than in the chapter of fasting. As such, this booklet includes everything the duty-bound person needs to know about fasting and the rules concerning its proper execution, God-willing. The booklet concludes with some recommendations about the social aspect of the month of Ramadan and discusses the joyous occasion of Eid, its gatherings, and visits. Unfortunately, by celebrating Eid in a sinful manner and engaging in acts of disobedience, many of these gatherings are the cause of spoiling believers' deeds, which they worked for during the month. This could cause the believers to lose the rewards and effects of fasting, denying them from reaping any benefit they should receive on that blessed day.

In describing the rulings of this booklet, we relied on authoritative jurisprudential sources like the revised 1439 editions of *Al-taliqah ala al-urwah al-wuthqa, Minhaj al-salihin,* the revised 1441 edition of *Al-masail al-muntakhabah, Tawdih al-masail jami* in Persian (published in 1435), and the booklet *Al-siyam junnatun min al-nar* (1426). All these books are available electronically on the official website of His Eminence al-Sayyid al-Sistani. In addition to all these sources, the booklet updates the rulings (if necessary) based on the latest questions and answers (*istifta*) published on the official website up until the publication of this booklet.

Developing this booklet began with collecting the titles of chapters and arranging them thematically. Then the material was written in that thematic order and according to what was adopted from *Minhaj al-salihin.* As mentioned above, the text also includes rulings from other books and resources, such as recent questions and new jurisprudential explanations. Furthermore, it was necessary to develop new titles that make it easier for the reader to reference and search for topics or rulings (e.g., mistakes in fasting, obligation to make up missed fasts, *kaffarah*), since the objective of this booklet was to present the material in an easy to follow and well-prioritized format.

Eminent scholars, who oversaw preparing the booklet and maintaining the accuracy of the content, reviewed the first draft. They carefully reviewed, edited, and revised it to ensure that the explanations of the rulings and topics were clear and that they did not cause any confusion or misinterpretation. The final Arabic version was then translated into English. After the translation process, the English text was evaluated and reviewed to confirm that it exactly matched the content presented in the Arabic text. Finally, the content was linguistically checked to ensure it flowed in English and suited the lay reader's understanding, especially the youth.

As such, we would like to thank and extend our sincere appreciation to all employees and volunteers of this blessed organization who contributed to the preparation, processing, review, editing, and dissemination of this booklet, especially Sayyid M. B. al-Kashmiri, Sayyed Muntadher al-Jaberi, and Dr. Shaykh Mehdi S. Hazari. We particularly recognize and thank His Eminence Ayatullah Shaykh Ali al-Dihneen (may God protect him) for reviewing the contents of this booklet and making sure that they are consistent with the edicts of His Eminence Grand Ayatullah Sayyid al-Sistani. We would also like to let the respected readers know that Part 1 of this booklet was prepared by I.M.A.M.'s team, it was not taken or adapted from the works of His Eminence.

We ask Almighty God to accept this work and make it a means for attaining nearness to Him and ascendence on the ladder of perfection, acknowledging that perfection is God's alone. Thus, because we are prone to fault and negligence, we would be grateful if the honorable readers could share any suggestions or notes so they may be considered for future editions of the booklet. We ask you all to remember us in your supplications, and we ask God Almighty to accept this trivial work of ours, hoping for its addition to our good deeds. Most importantly, praise be to God Almighty.

I.M.A.M.

In the name of Allah, the Most
Gracious, the Most Merciful

 *Believers, fasting
has been made mandatory for you
as it was made mandatory for the
people before you, so that you may
have fear of God.*

(The Quran 2:183)

Part One

Fasting in Islam

Fasting in Islam[1]

Fasting is one of the most important obligations in Islam. God says, "Believers, fasting has been made mandatory for you as it was made mandatory for the people before you, so that you may have fear of God."[2] Prophet Muhammad (peace be upon him and his progeny) included fasting among the pillars of Islam. Hadiths report that Prophet Muhammad (pbuh&hp) said, "Islam is built on five [pillars]: testifying that there is no god but Allah, establishing prayers, paying zakat, fasting in Ramadan, and performing pilgrimage to the House of Allah for those who are capable of doing so."[3] Additionally, there are many narrations from the Imams of Ahl al-Bayt (pbut) that emphasize the importance of fasting. Narrations tell us that Imam al-Baqir (p) said, "Islam is built on five [pillars]: praying, zakat, fasting, hajj, and *wilayah;* and the most important pillar is wilayah."[4] Therefore, fasting in the month of Ramadan is an essential and necessary part of Islam, and whoever denies it has denied Islam.

---

1. This part of the booklet was prepared by I.M.A.M. so that the content is comprehensive and exhaustive from a theoretical and not just jurisprudential perspective. It is not from the writings attributed to al-Sayyid al-Sistani.

2. The Holy Quran 2:183, Muhammad Sarwar translation (MS).

3. al-Sarkhasi, *al-Mabsut*, vol. 2, p. 149.

4. al-Kulayni, *al-Kafi*, vol. 2, p. 18.

Fasting in Previous Nations

Several rulings in the *sharia* date back to legislations promulgated by divine religions, with changes in their implementation or expansion on their conditions, in the era before Islam. For example, the Quranic story of Luqman, the Wise, mentions prayer, "My son, be steadfast in prayer. Make others do good. Prevent them from doing evil. Be patient in hardship. Patience comes from faith and determination."[5] Similarly, hajj is mentioned in the Quran in the story of Abraham and Ishmael, "We made the house (in Mecca) as a place of refuge and sanctuary for men. Adopt the place where Abraham stood as a place for prayer. We advised Abraham and Ishmael to keep My house clean for the pilgrims, the worshippers and for those who bow down and prostrate themselves in worship."[6] The same applies to fasting, "Believers, fasting has been made mandatory for you as it was made mandatory for the people before you, so that you may have fear of God."[7] It is clear from this verse that fasting was legislated for previous nations as well, even if it was implemented in a more general manner and did not include the details found in Islamic law. In addition to this, there are supplications from Imam Ali ibn Hussain Zayn al-Abidin al-Sajjad (p), which include one for the farewell of the month of Ramadan. He says, "Through it (i.e., fasting in the month of Ramadan), You preferred us over other nations and chose us for its excellence

---

5. The Holy Quran 31:17, MS.

6. The Holy Quran 2:125, MS.

7. The Holy Quran 2:183, MS.

over people of other creeds. We fasted by Your command in its daytime, and we stood in prayer with Your help in its night."[8]

The Definition of Fasting

Linguistically, fasting is to abstain from something. In Islamic terminology, fasting is the act of abstaining from a set of fast-nullifiers with the intention of attaining nearness, submission, and obedience to God Almighty.

Its Significance, Status, and Reward

The Holy Quran stipulates the obligation of fasting, its status, the reason for its legislation, and its conditions in more than one verse. Some of these verses include:

- "Believers, fasting has been made mandatory for you as it was made mandatory for the people before you, so that you may have fear of God."[9]
- "God has promised forgiveness and great rewards to the Muslim men and the Muslim women, the believing men and the believing women, the obedient men and the obedient women, the truthful men and the truthful women, the forbearing men and the forbearing women, the humble men and the humble women, the alms-giving men and the alms-giving women, the fasting men and the fasting women, the chaste

---

8. Imam Zayn al-Abidin, *al-sahifah al-sajjadiyyah*, supplication 45.

9. The Holy Quran 2:183, MS.

men and the chaste women, and the men and
women who remember God very often."[10]

- "The month of Ramadan is the month in which
the Quran was revealed; a guide for the people,
the most authoritative of all guidance and a
criterion to discern right from wrong. Anyone of
you who knows that the month of Ramadan has
begun must start to fast. Those who are sick or on
a journey have to fast the same number of days at
another time. God does not impose any hardship
upon you. He wants you to have comfort so that
you may complete the fast, glorify God for His
having given you guidance, and perhaps you give
Him thanks."[11]

In addition to the verses from the Holy Quran, many
Qudsi hadith,[12] prophetic hadith, and noble narrations[13]
show the status and importance of obligatory fasting.
The most important narration is Prophet Muhammad's
famous sermon. Imam al-Rida, his fathers, and Amir
al-Muminin narrate that the Messenger of Allah
addressed us one day and said:

"O People!
"Indeed, the blessed month of Allah has arrived
with blessings, mercy, and forgiveness for you.

---

10. The Holy Quran 33:35, MS.

11. The Holy Quran 2:185, MS

12. The Qudsi hadith are words of God Almighty, but they are not
the Quran. Prophet Muhammad (pbuh&hp) relayed these
traditions to the people.

13. The noble narrations are narrated from the infallibles of the
Ahl al-Bayt (pbut) from Prophet Muhammad (pbuh&hp).

A month that is considered the best of months by Allah. Its days are the best of days, its nights are the best of nights, and its hours are the best of hours. It is a month in which you are invited to be the guests of Allah. In this month you are considered to be people worthy of the grace of Allah. In this month, each breath you take glorifies Allah, your sleep is worship, your deeds are accepted, and your prayers are answered. "So, ask Allah, your Lord, with sincere intentions and pure hearts, to aid you in fasting and reciting His Holy Book. The unfortunate one is he who is denied Allah's forgiveness during this great month. Through your hunger and thirst, remember the hunger and thirst that you will experience on the Day of Judgment. Give charity to the needy and poor, honor your old, show kindness to your young ones, maintain relations with your kin, guard your tongues, look away from that which is not permissible for your sight, close your ears to that which is forbidden to hear, show compassion to the orphans of other people so compassion may be shown to your orphans. "Repent to Allah for your sins and raise your hands and ask Allah during times of prayer, for these are the best of times; Allah looks at His servants with mercy, answering their supplications, answering their call if they called, and granting their prayers if they asked. "O People! Indeed, your souls are tied to your deeds, so free them with repentance. Your backs are heavy with sins, so lighten them with long prostrations. Know that Allah swears by His Might that He does not punish those who pray and prostrate, and He will not frighten them with the fire of the day when people stand before the Lord of the worlds.

"O People! One who gives food to a believer to break his fast, is given the reward of freeing a slave and his past sins will be forgiven."

Some people listening to the sermon said, "O Prophet of Allah, not all of us are able to invite those who are fasting"

The Prophet (pbuh&hp) said, "You could avoid hellfire with even a piece of date or a drink of water.

"O People! One who attains good morals during this month will be able to pass the sirat on the day that feet will slip. The one who forgives his slaves in this month Allah will forgive him on Judgment Day. The one who abstains from evil in this month, Allah will save him from His anger when he meets Him. The one who honors an orphan in this month, Allah will honor him when he meets Him. The one who maintains relations with his kin in this month, Allah will shower him with His mercy when he meets Him. The one who cuts ties with his kin, Allah will cut His mercy from him when he meets Him. Whoever performs a recommended prayer in this month, Allah will keep the fire of Hell away from him. Whoever performs one obligatory prayer, Allah will give him the reward of seventy prayers prayed in other months. Whoever increases his prayers (salawat) on me in this month, Allah will increase his scale of goods deeds when other people's scales become light. The one who recites one verse from the holy Quran in this month, will be

given the reward of reciting the whole Quran
during other months.
"O People! The doors of heaven are open during
this month, so ask your Lord not to close them for
you. The doors of hell are closed, so ask your Lord
not to open them for you. Shaytan is imprisoned
during this month, so ask your Lord not to let him
have power over you."
*Amir al-Muminin, Imam Ali bin Abi Talib (peace be
upon him) said, "I stood up and said, 'O Messenger of
God! What is the best worship in this month?'* The
Prophet (pbuh&hp) said, **'O Aba al-Hasan, the best
worship in this month is to abstain from that
which is forbidden by God Almighty.'** *Then he [the
Prophet] cried and I said, 'O Messenger of God! What
makes you cry?'* He said, **'O Ali, I cry because of
what will happen to you in this month. You will
be praying to your Lord, and a wretched person—
the brother of the one who slaughtered the camel
of Thamud—will strike you on your head,
drenching your beard with blood.'** *Amir
al-Muminin said, 'O Messenger of God, will my death
keep my religion safe? He [the Prophet] said,* **'Yes, it
will keep your religion safe.'** *Then the
Prophet (pbuh&hp) said,* **'O Ali, the one who kills
you has killed me, and the one who hates you has
hated me, and the one who curses you has cursed
me. This is all because you are from me; your soul
is my soul, and your clay is my clay, God
Almighty has created you and I, and He has
chosen you and I. He chose me as His prophet and
chose you as His imam. He who denies your
imamah has denied my prophethood. O Ali, you
are my successor, the father of my sons, and the**

husband of my daughter. You are the successor after me in my ummah (nation), during my life, and after my death. Your command is my command, and your prohibition is my prohibition. I swear by the One who has sent me as His prophet and made me the best of His creation, that you are the proof of God on His creation, the trustee with His secret, and the successor amongst His servants."[14]

Additionally, some of the most important noble narrations from the Prophet Muhammad (pbuh&hp) and his progeny (pbut) are presented here for further enlightenment and enrichment about the many dimensions of fasting, its virtue, and the benefit of the blessed month of Ramadan.

Traditions state that Prophet Muhammad (pbuh&hp) has said, "If the servant knew what Ramadan contained [of blessings] he would wish that Ramadan lasted for a year."[15]

It has been narrated that Imam Ali (p) has said, "How many fasting people do not gain anything from their fasting except thirst. And how many fasting people do not gain anything from their standing for prayer at night except exhaustion, their acts are empty sleep and meaningless eating."[16]

---

14. al-Majlisi, *Bihar al-anwar*, vol. 93, p. 356; *Uyun al-akhbar*, vol. 1, p. 295–297.

15. al-Majlisi, *Bihar al-anwar*, vol. 93, p. 346.

16. al-Majlisi, *Bihar al-anwar*, vol.93, p.294.

It has been narrated that Lady Fatimah al-Zahra (p) said, "What does a fasting person do with their fasting if they do not protect their tongue, hearing, eyesight and body parts [from that which is forbidden]?"[17] In response to someone who asked about the wisdom behind the legislation of fasting, it is narrated that Imam Hussain (p) said, "So the rich man can taste the pain of hunger and thereby give to the poor."[18] Imam Zayn al-Abidin (p) says in his supplication, which he recited at the beginning of the month of Ramadan, "And help us to fast its days by restraining our body parts from acts of disobedience and by using them for that which pleases You; so that we do not use our ears to listen to idle talk, and we do not hurry with our eyes to look at diversion. And so we do not stretch our hands toward that which is forbidden, and we do not stride with our feet toward that which is prohibited. And so our bellies hold only what you have made lawful, and our tongues speak only what You have exemplified. And so we undertake nothing but that which brings us close to Your reward, and so we pursue nothing but what protects us from Your punishment."[19] Narrations also show that Imam Muhammad al-Baqir (p) said, "The fasting of the one who disobeys the imam is not valid. The fasting of the servant who has not returned [to his master] is not valid until he returns. The fasting of the disobedient woman is not valid until she repents. The fasting of the disobedient child is not valid until he

---

17. al-Majlisi, *Bihar al-anwar*, vol. 93, p. 295.

18. al-Qurashi, *The Life of Imam Hussayn*, vol. 1, p. 155.

19. *al-sahifah al-sajjadiyyah*, supplication 44.

obeys [his parents] and pleases them."[20] It has also been narrated that Imam al-Sadiq (p) said, "When you fast, your hearing, sight, private parts, and tongue should all be fasting. You should divert your gaze from that which has been forbidden for you to look at. You should not listen to what has been forbidden. You should protect your tongue from lying and obscenity."[21] It has been narrated by Imam Musa al-Kadhim (p) that he said, "To break your brother's fast by inviting him to food is better than your own fast."[22] Additionally, a detailed narration containing a long dialogue with Imam al-Rida (p) indicates that in response to being asked, "Why did God command fasting?" he said, "So they [the people] can experience the pain of hunger and thirst, and thereby understand the poverty of the hereafter. And so the fasting person can be fearful, lowly, satisfied [with what they already have], rewarded, deliberate, and patiently aware of the hunger and thirst that afflict them, so they deserve the reward of having suppressed their desires. And so that this would be a reminder to them in the immediate future, a reckoning for what God has obligated them to do, a guide for them in the future, and so that they know the severity of the affliction on the poor in this world and [as a result] do what God has ordained for them in their money.[23] So if it were asked, why was fasting obligated in the month of Ramadan and not other months? It would be said, 'Because the month of

---

20. al-Majlisi, *Bihar al-anwar*, vol. 93, p. 295

21. al-Majlisi, *Bihar al-anwar*, vol. 93, p. 295.

22. al-Majlisi, *Bihar al-anwar*, vol. 93, p. 317.

23. Shaykh al-Saduq, *Uyun akhbar al-Rida*, vol. 1, p. 123.

Ramadan is the month in which the Quran was sent and truth was distinguished from falsehood, as God says, "The month of Ramadan is one in which the Quran was sent down as guidance to mankind, with manifest proofs of guidance and the Criterion,"[24] and it is the month of Prophet Muhammad (pbuh&hp), and in it is the Night of Power (*qadr*) which is "better than a thousand months"[25] and "Every definitive matter is resolved on it."[26] Which is the pinnacle of the year and through it the rest of the year is determined, good or bad, harm or benefit, immediate sustenance or delay, this is why it is known as the Night of Power."[27]

The sources contain additional narrations for those interested in reading more.[28]

Characteristics and Advantages of Fasting and the Holy Month of Ramadan

1. Solely for God and He Accepts It

Many acts of worship become sullied because of showing off and a lack of sincerity in their performance, except for fasting, which is private worship between the servant and their Lord. A Qudsi hadith narrates that God

---

24. The Holy Quran 2:185, Ali Quli Qarai (AQQ).

25. The Holy Quran 97:3, MS.

26. The Quran 44:4, AQQ.

27. Shaykh al-Saduq, *Uyun akhbar al-Rida*, vol. 1, p. 123.

28. There are many hadith sources and large encyclopedias, such as *al-Kafi* by Shaykh al-Kulayni; *Wasail al-Shia* by al-Hurr al-Amili; *Bihar al-anwar* by Shaykh al-Majlisi and more.

Almighty said, "Fasting is for Me and I give the reward for it."[29] God Almighty specified this worship solely for Himself and considered it accepted in advance.

2. Its Proven Benefits

God Almighty says in the Holy Quran, "However, fasting is better and will be rewarded. Would that you had known this!"[30] Thus, fasting has innumerable benefits.

3. Continuous worship

Fasting is one of the rare acts of worship that God accepts and rewards regardless of the state of the servant, even if they are sleeping. A noble hadith narrates that the Messenger of God (pbuh&hp) said, "The fasting person worships God even if they are sleeping on their bed, as long as they do not backbite another Muslim."[31] Likewise, the Prophet (pbuh&hp) said in his sermon welcoming the month of Ramadan, "Your sleep in it is worship, and each of your breaths during it glorify God."

4. Answered supplications

It has been narrated by Imam al-Sadiq (p), through his fathers and from the Messenger of God (pbuh&hp) that he said, "There are four people whose prayers are answered, and the doors of the heavens open [for their

---

29. al-Majlisi, *Bihar al-anwar*, vol. 93, p. 249; Ibn al-Arabi, *al-futuhat al-makkiyya*, vol.1, p. 258.

30. The Holy Quran 2:184, MS.

31. al-Shaykh al-Saduq, *Thawab al-amal*, vol. 1, p. 75, hadith 1.

supplications] until they reach the Throne. They are: the supplication of parents for their children, the supplication of the oppressed against their oppressor, the supplication of the one performing *umrah* until they return [home], and the supplication of the fasting person until they break their fast."[32]

5. Patience and willpower

Fasting is the best way to enhance the virtue of patience and strengthen willpower. God Almighty says, "Believers, help yourselves (in your affairs) through patience and prayer; God is with those who have patience."[33] In the interpretation of this verse by the Ahl al-Bayt (pbut), narrations state that Imam al-Sadiq (p) said, "Patience in this [verse] is referring to fasting."[34] Therefore, fasting is the ultimate means of strengthening a person's patience and willpower by refraining from what God has made permissible (i.e., during the daytime). Therefore, a person who can demonstrate patience by controlling their desires during the daytime can do so at night as well, and if they are able to do it for a week, then they would be able to do it for a month, or two months, and so on until it becomes a natural part of their disposition and makes the attributes of patience and willpower an integral part of their being.

---

32. al-Majlisi, *Bihar al-anwar*, vol. 93, p. 356; *Uyun al-akhbar*, vol. 1, p. 295–297.

33. The Holy Quran 2:153, MS.

34. al-Majlisi, *Bihar al-anwar*, vol. 93, p. 254.

In Islam, the description of patience above does not mean that the person should be in a state of humiliation, dejectedness, or marginalization. God forbid that some people would think that this is Islam's intent. Rather, it is a process that helps us to ensure that we reach the desired outcome by teaching us to control the self and discipline our emotions and tendencies and then know when to move and act appropriately. A narration from Amir al-Muminin (p) supports this when he said, "The patient one will reach victory, even if it takes a long time."[35]

6. Forgiveness and a great reward

Among the benefits of fasting is the chance to earn God's forgiveness and a great reward, which is indicated by the apparent meaning of the holy verse, "God has promised forgiveness and great rewards to the Muslim men and the Muslim women, the believing men and the believing women, the obedient men and the obedient women, the truthful men and the truthful women, the forbearing men and the forbearing women, the humble men and the humble women, the alms-giving men and the alms-giving women, the fasting men and the fasting women, the chaste men and the chaste women, and the men and women who remember God very often."[36]

---

35. al-Sharif al-Radi, *Nahj al-balagha*, vol. 2, p. 183.

36. The Holy Quran 33:35, MS.

7. Innumerable Rewards

It was previously mentioned that the meaning of patience in the verse, "Believers, help yourselves (in your affairs) through patience and prayer; God is with those who have patience."[37] God Almighty has also said, "God will recompense the deeds of those who have exercised patience, without keeping an account."[38] Based on this, the fasting person earns rewards that are innumerable and unmeasurable. This is one of the rare acts of worship for which God Almighty promises such an immense reward.

8. A barrier from fire

Imam al-Sadiq (p) through his fathers narrates that the Messenger of God (pbuh&hp) said, "Fasting the month of Ramadan is a haven from hellfire."[39] Thus, fasting is a barrier to the fire because it eradicates sins, strengthens piety, brings the servant closer to heaven, and keeps them away from hellfire. No other act of worship has been described in this manner, except charity.

9. A gate of paradise reserved for those who fast

It is known that heaven has eight gates, and God Almighty has assigned one gate to those who fast due to its importance and significance. It has been narrated

---

37. The Holy Quran 2:153, MS.

38. The Holy Quran 39:10, MS.

39. al-Majlisi, *Bihar al-anwar*, vol. 93, p .342.

that the Messenger of God (pbuh&hp) said, "There is a gate in heaven called *al-Rayyan,* only those who fast enter from it. It is called al-Rayyan because enduring thirst is more difficult than enduring hunger. Hence, when those who fast enter from that gate, they are greeted with never having to feel thirst again."[40]

10. The revelation of divine books

The month of Ramadan has a loftier status than all other months because it is when God revealed all the divine books to His prophets and messengers, and even though there were other months that were sacred before the advent of Islam. These months have a special status and unique distinction for the performance of acts of worship and obedience. They include four months mentioned in the Holy Quran: Rajab, Dhu al-Qidah, Dhu al-Hijjah, and Muharram. God says, "According to the Book of God, from the day He created the heavens and the earth, the number of months is twelve, four of which are sacred. (This is part of the law) of the religion. Do not commit injustice against your souls during the sacred months but fight all the pagans just as they fight against all of you. Know that God is with the pious ones."[41]

Several noble hadiths narrated from the Imams of the Ahl al-Bayt (pbut) discuss the revelation of scriptures in Ramadan. For example, narrations indicate that Imam al-Sadiq (p) said, "The Quran was revealed in its entirety and all at once in the month of Ramadan to

40. al-Majlisi, *Bihar al-anwar*, vol. 93, p. 252.

41. The Holy Quran 9:36, MS.

17

Bayt al-Mamur (built house), then it was gradually revealed over twenty years." Then the Imam (p) said, "The Prophet said, 'Prophet Ibrahim's scriptures were revealed on the first night of the month of Ramadan, and the Tawrat was revealed after the sixth day of the month of Ramadan, and the Injil was revealed after the thirteenth night of the month of Ramadan, and the Zabur, was revealed after the eighteenth day of the month of Ramadan, and the Quran was revealed on the twenty-third day of the month of Ramadan.'"[42]

God chose the month of Ramadan from among the other months for its virtue. This is also evident if we connect the arrival of the Holy Quran all at once to *Bayt al-Mamur* (the built house) as is indicated in the reported hadith of Ahl al-Bayt (pbut) and what is interpreted by the commentators about the verses, "We revealed the Quran on the Night of Destiny."[43] and "That We have revealed the Quran on a blessed night to warn mankind."[44] which demonstrate that it was revealed to the heart of the honored Prophet Muhammad (pbuh&hp) in the Night of Power during the holy month of Ramadan. Hence, it is a month of special significance, blessing, and divine legislation, due to the revelation of the Holy Quran and the other divine books.

---

42 al-Kulayni, *al-Kafi*, vol. 2, p. 629.

43. The Holy Quran 97:1, MS.

44. The Holy Quran 44:3, MS.

11. The Nights of Destiny

Commentaries of the Holy Quran unanimously indicate that what is meant by "night" in the verses, "We revealed the Quran on the Night of Destiny."[45] and "That We have revealed the Quran on a blessed night to warn mankind."[46] is the Night of Power, or the night in which God revealed it all at once as a whole book to the heart of the Prophet Muhammad (pbuh&hp). However, God has willed that the exact date of this night is unknown, except to Him. The night is hidden amongst other nights of the month of Ramadan and is known to only God and the righteous and sincere servants that He chose. There are many narrations reported from the Prophet Muhammad (pbuh&hp) and his Ahl al-Bayt (pbut) about the Night of Power being in the last ten nights of the month of Ramadan. Furthermore, we have narrations that tell us it is one of three nights of those last ten, specifically the nineteenth, twenty-first, or twenty-third night. Many narrations also emphasize the order of significance and importance of these nights and what God decrees for His servants of lifespan, sustenance, success, and blessings therein. One of these narrations is by Imam al-Sadiq (p) who is reported to have said, "God decrees [people's fates] on the nineteenth night of the month of Ramadan, destines it for them on the twenty-first, and finalizes it for their [upcoming] year on the

---

45. The Holy Quran 97:1, MS.

46. Quran 44:3, MS.

twenty-third night. God does with His creation what He chooses."[47]

As such, God Almighty has broadened [the potential] and singled out this blessed month over other months with this additional virtue by decreeing mercy, forgiveness, and blessings for His servants on more than one of its blessed nights. This means that we must be aware of the importance of these nights and their recommended worship.

12. The last ten days and spiritual retreat (itikaf)

The lives of the noble Prophet Muhammad (pbuh&hp) and the Ahl al-Bayt (pbut) indicate that the last ten nights of the month of Ramadan have a special status and virtue and require greater attention and devotion to worship. The Prophet and the Ahl al-Bayt commemorated these ten nights with worship, especially by practicing itikaf or spiritual retreat, which is a desirable act of worship at any appropriate time during the year and highly recommended in the last ten days of the month of Ramadan. It is reported that the Commander of the Faithful described that the Prophet (pbuh&hp) "Would wake up (i.e., remind) his family during the last ten days of Ramadan"[48] and that "If the ten days began, [the Prophet] would become preoccupied [with worship] and he would ask his

---

47. Ibn Tawus, *Iqbal al-amal*, vol. 1, p.150.

48. al-Kashani, *Zubdat al-tafsir*, vol. 1, p. 477.

family to do the same."[49] He is also reported to have stated that "If the ten days started the Prophet would retreat [for worship] into the mosque, and a tent of fur would be set up for him, he would roll up his clothes, and put away his bed."[50]

Another indication of the virtue and reward of itikaf in these ten days of the month of Ramadan is a hadith from Imam al-Sadiq (p) by way of his forefathers that the Prophet (pbuh&hp) said, "Performing a spiritual retreat [for worship] in the last ten days of the month of Ramadan is equal [in reward] to performing hajj twice and umrah twice."[51]

The Wisdom of Legislating Fasting and Its Benefits

No one knows the reason behind divine laws except for the Legislator Himself, God Almighty, and whoever God approves of from the prophets, the messengers, and their pure successors. Therefore, many of the obligations are performed with a specified intention of worship, due to a person's conviction and certainty in God Almighty, and His message as promulgated by His prophets, messengers, and their deputies, and the desire to live in a manner that is obedient to His commands. God Almighty in His holy book and the Messenger (pbuh&hp) and the Ahl al-Bayt (pbut) in

---

49. al-Kashani, *Zubdat al-tafsir*, vol. 1, p. 477.

50. al-Naraqi, *Mustanada al-Shia*, vol. 10, p. 544.

51. al-Saduq, *Man la yahthuruh al-faqih*, vol. 2, p. 188.

their narrations have nevertheless made a part of the wisdom behind legislating fasting clear. The sections that follow contain narrations that describe this wisdom and the benefits and effects of fasting.

1. Strengthening One's Piety

The verse of fasting clearly states that the purpose and wisdom behind legislating it is the attainment of piety. God Almighty says, "Believers, fasting has been made mandatory for you as it was made mandatory for the people before you, so that you may have fear of God."[52] Piety is a developed internal ability that prevents one from committing sins, even detestable or *makruh* acts, and from practicing pleasures and desires beyond what is permissible. Therefore, fasting is one of the most important means to help a person attain piety and strengthen it through controlling desires.

2. Ensuring Sincerity

It has been narrated that the Commander of the Faithful, Imam Ali (p), said, "God has obligated fasting to test the sincerity of His creation."[53] It has also been narrated that the pure and infallible Lady Fatimah al-Zahra (p) said in her famous sermon in which she described the philosophy behind some of God's legislations, "And fasting has been imposed by God as an affirmation of sincerity."[54] Perhaps this is because

---

52. The Holy Quran 2:183, MS.

53. *Nahj al-balagha*, sermon 192, hadith 252.

54. *Bihar al-anwar*, vol. 4, p. 368, hadith 96.

fasting is an intimate, discreet type of worship between the servant and their Master, far from hypocrisy and showing off.

3. A Reminder to Be Grateful

After God Almighty mentions the virtue of the month of Ramadan and the fact that fasting is obligatory for those who are not sick or traveling, He reminds us of another reason for the legislation of fasting, and that is to be thankful. God says, "The month of Ramadan is the month in which the Quran was revealed; a guide for the people, the most authoritative of all guidance and a criterion to discern right from wrong. Anyone of you who knows that the month of Ramadan has begun, he must start to fast. Those who are sick or on a journey have to fast the same number of days at another time. God does not impose any hardship upon you. He wants you to have comfort so that you may complete the fast, glorify God for His having given you guidance, and that, perhaps, you would give Him thanks."[55] Therefore, it is incumbent upon us to be especially grateful for the bounties He has bestowed in this month, for the guidance He has blessed us with, and for all His other countless blessings. We should show our gratitude for these blessings through our words and actions, and by using His blessings only to do what He commanded us to do, because if we do, God will preserve these blessings [for us] and increase them as He says in the verse, "If you give thanks, I shall give you greater (favors)."[56]

---

55. The Holy Quran 2:185, MS.

56. The Holy Quran 14:7, MS.

4. Cultivating Wisdom and Contentment

The hadith of *Miraj*, or the ascension, narrates that Prophet Muhammad (pbuh&hp) asked God, "Oh my Lord, what does fasting cultivate in us?" God Almighty said, "Fasting cultivates wisdom, and wisdom confers understanding, and understanding leads to certainty, and if a servant is certain [in God], they will not worry about themself, whether they wake up [to the day] in difficulty or ease."[57] How many people search endlessly for ways to attain wisdom, morals, and perfection to become an image of perfection and strength yet are unable to do so? Moreover, how many people look for ways to reduce their greed and bridle their insatiable pleasures yet are unable to do so? This narration shows that wisdom and contentment with the decree and destiny of God are embedded in the virtue of fasting. As such, fasting is the best way to obtain wisdom and contentment with what God has ordained for His servants, and they are so needy for it.

5. A Reminder of the Hereafter

As mentioned earlier, Prophet Muhammad (pbuh&hp) is reported to have said, "Through your hunger and thirst, remember the hunger and thirst that you will experience on the Day of Judgment."[58] Moreover, he said about the legislation of fasting, "There is no

---

57. al-Majlisi, *Bihar al-anwar*, vol. 74, p. 27.

58. A question may arise about the type of hunger and thirst a person will experience on the Day of Judgment. Perhaps it is argued that if the resurrection is physical and not just spiritual, then hunger and thirst will be of a physical nature, even if food or drink is not offered during judgment.

believer who fasts the month of Ramadan with anticipation [of its effects] that God gives them seven characteristics: the first is the melting off of all *haram* that has built up [from sinning], the second is they become closer to God's mercy, the third is. . .the fourth is God eases their pangs of death, the fifth is safety from hunger and thirst on the Day of Judgment, the sixth is God grants them safety from hellfire, and the seventh God feeds them from heaven's pleasant food."[59] The thirst and hunger of a fasting person reminds them of their lengthy stand in the presence of God until the person says, "'What kind of record is this that has missed nothing small or great?' They will find whatever they have done right before their very eyes."[60] Therefore, fasting is nothing but a period of training that trains and readies a person to overcome inevitable difficulties so that they may be prepared for the hereafter with more good deeds.

6. Encouraging Empathy

It is narrated from Imam al-Rida (p) that he said the reason for legislating fasting was, "So that they (people) know the pain of hunger and thirst, and they get a taste of the poverty of the hereafter. . .and that they know the hardships faced by the poor and impoverished in this world, so they offer to them what God Almighty has obligated from their money (of charity and alms)."[61] God Almighty says, "They are

---

59. al-Shaykh al-Saduq, *Ilal al-sharai*, vol. 2. p. 379.

60. The Holy Quran 18:49, MS.

61 al-Shaykh al-Saduq, *Ilal al-sharai*, p. 270.

those who assign a certain share of their property for the needy and the deprived."[62] Narrations also indicate that Imam al-Hasan al-Askari (p) said in reply to a question about the reason behind fasting, "So the rich taste hunger and in turn help the poor."[63] Imam Hussain (p) is reported to have said something similar, "So the rich taste hunger and respond by giving generously to the impoverished."[64] As previously mentioned, the Holy Prophet (pbuh&hp) said in his sermon, "'O People! One who feeds a believer at the time of *iftar* in this month will be rewarded as if they freed a slave and their past sins will be forgiven.' Some people then asked, 'O Messenger of God, not all of us are able to invite those who are fasting.' He said, 'Fear [and save yourselves from] the hellfire with even a piece of date or a drink of water.'" These are all teachings that make people aware of their humanity and social responsibility toward the hungry and toward the needy brothers and sisters in their community. If people were to feel the pain of hunger and thirst and experience the hardships that the needy go through, they would become motivated to do good and share with others the blessings and sustenance that God has bestowed upon them. Indeed, the month of Ramadan is the month of empathy.

---

62. The Holy Quran 70:24–25, MS.

63. al-Majlisi, *Bihar al-anwar*, vol. 96, p. 368.

64. al-Majlisi, *Bihar al-anwar*, vol. 96, p. 368, hadith 4; p. 369, hadith 50; p. 375.

7. A Sense of Belonging and Order

Any person with a sound intellect who examines this world carefully, from its smallest atoms to its largest galaxies, would see that this universe is based on organization and a very accurate system. Many verses in the Holy Quran speak of this precise system. God Almighty says, "He has created all things with precisely accurate planning."[65] "We have made the day and night each as evidence (of Our existence). The night is invisible, and the day is visible so that you may seek favors from your Lord and determine the number of years and mark the passing of time. For everything We have given a detailed explanation."[66] and "According to the Book of God, from the day He created the heavens and the earth, the number of months are twelve, four of which are sacred."[67] Just like many other verses throughout the Holy Quran, this one shows us the precise system of time that God has decreed for us, the acts of worship that He has designated for each time, and then finally declaring that "Anyone of you who knows that the month of Ramadan has begun, he must start to fast."[68] All of these verses highlight and remind "those who commemorate God while standing and sitting, or resting on their sides and who think about the creation of the heavens and the earth"[69] that we live according

---

65. The Holy Quran 25:2, MS.

66. The Holy Quran 17:12, MS.

67. The Holy Quran 9:36, MS.

68. The Holy Quran 2:185, MS.

69. The Holy Quran 3:191, MS.

to a precise system of governance determined by a great divine wisdom and will, which makes a pondering, reflective human feel as though they are a part of a greater universe and that God Almighty has honored them with reason and choice, unlike all other creatures, to cultivate it and use it to ascend and reach perfection and ultimately God. Thus, humankind should organize their time and daily affairs if they want success in this temporary life and the other permanent one.

Fasting is an act of worship that teaches us organization and how to live and act within the established divine system. As such, it gives us a feeling of belonging because everyone begins and breaks their fast at a specific time, all the while remembering God Almighty and glorifying Him in the day and night.

Hadiths narrate that Amir al-Muminin Ali ibn Abi Talib (p) stated in his will to his sons al-Hasan (pbut) and al-Hussain as he neared departure from this world, "I advise you and all of my children, my family, and those who hear my will to fear God and organize your affairs."[70] Therefore, we must see the blessed month of Ramadan as an opportunity to rearrange our priorities, our way of life, and to restore order.

Fasting Levels

Each type of worship has different levels based on the awareness and perception of the servant performing it

---

70. *Nahj al-balagha*, https://www.al-islam.org/articles/letter-father-son-last-will-ali-ibn-abi-talib.

and the extent to which they draw closer to God Almighty through it. Fasting is not an exception, since it also has different levels. Traditions report that Imam Ali (p) said, "Fasting of the heart is better than the fasting of the tongue, and fasting of the tongue is better than the fasting of the stomach."[71] This hadith indicates that there are three levels of fasting as explained in the sections below.

Fasting of the Stomach

The fast of the stomach involves abstaining from food and drink. It is the jurisprudential fast, which means it is obligatory for anyone who meets the conditions requiring fasting. If the duty-bound person (mukallaf) makes an intention to refrain from fast-nullifiers seeking nearness to God Almighty by abstaining from eating, drinking, sexual intercourse, and other things throughout the days of the month of Ramadan, then they have performed and fulfilled their obligation. With this type of fasting, only God knows whether the fast was a source of benefit or reward for the person or whether He even accepted it, because it could have just been a state of hunger and thirst for the person [and not done in a true spirit of worship]. Therefore, this is the lowest level of fasting.

Fasting of the Body Parts

This second level of fasting is more honorable than the first. It is the fasting of a person's body parts achieved by controlling and refraining from using them in

---

71. *Gurar al-hikam wa durar al-kalim*, p. 424, hadith 80.

anything detestable (makruh) or forbidden. This includes keeping the tongue from arguing, backbiting, and useless speech, the eyes from looking at anything forbidden, the ears from hearing anything forbidden, the nose from voluntarily smelling things that should be avoided like the *rayahin*,[72] and the hands from touching anything forbidden. Narrations from Imam al-Baqir (p), from his fathers, state that the Messenger of God (pbuh&hp) said to Jabir ibn Abdullah, "O Jabir, this is the month of Ramadan, a person who fasts during the day, rises at night for worship, controls their stomach and private parts, and restrains their tongue, leaves their sins [behind] just as they leave and end the month." Jabir said, "O Messenger of God, how beautiful is this hadith!" to which the Prophet replied, "O Jabir, and how difficult are these conditions [to fulfill]."[73] It has also been narrated that Imam al-Sadiq (p) said, "If you fast, let your hearing, sight, hair, and skin also fast."[74] We can call this level of fasting the moral fast.

Fasting of the Heart

Fasting of the heart is the highest level of fasting—the fasting of those with true understanding [of God]. In this level of fasting, the servant does not even think about practicing detestable acts, let alone forbidden

---

72. Rayahin are pleasant-smelling plants that appear to make the person who smells them feel satiated and not feel hunger. Therefore, smelling them obviates the purpose of fasting. God knows best.

73. al-Kulayni, *al-Kafi*, vol. 4, p. 87.

74. al-Kulayni, *al-Kafi*, vol. 4, p. 87.

ones. For example, if the time for iftar comes, this person starts by saying the name of God and does not eat with greed and rapacity. Moreover, they only eat the amount of food and drink that is necessary to strengthen their body after making sure it is halal, pure and free from any suspicions [of prohibition]. Therefore, it is imperative for a person to practice this level of fasting to reap the best results from the month of Ramadan, gain the greatest benefits, and achieve the highest status. This has already been mentioned in the hadith narrated from the Prophet (pbuh&hp) during *Isra* and Miraj when he asked God Almighty, "'Oh my Lord, what does fasting cultivate in us?' God Almighty said, 'Fasting cultivates wisdom, and wisdom confers understanding, and understanding leads to certainty, and if a servant is certain [in God], they will not worry about themself, whether they wake up [to the day] in difficulty or ease.'" Therefore, a person must practice fasting of the heart to reach high levels of wisdom, knowledge, certainty, and satisfaction with God's decree and destiny. If they do so, they will be the personification of "People, who can neither be diverted by merchandise nor bargaining from worshipping God, saying their prayers and paying religious tax. They do these things, for they are afraid of the day when all hearts and eyes will undergo terrible unrest and crisis."[75] This level of fasting could be called the fasting of those who have true understanding of God. We ask God Almighty to help us reach that rank.

---

75. The Holy Quran 24:37, MS.

Part Two

Rules of Fasting

Rules of Fasting

Fasting Etiquette

There are many recommended acts related to fasting listed below.

- Concealing the recommended or *mandub* fast from others except if asked about it. The recommendation is for a person to break such a fast if another believer invites them to eat. Narrations report that Imam al-Sadiq (p) said, "If one visits his brother [in faith] while observing a recommended fast and thereafter breaks it [upon being offered food or drink] without letting him (i.e., the host) know that he was fasting, God will record one year's worth of fasts as a reward for him."[76]

- Taking a nap. Reports state that the Holy Prophet (pbuh&hp) said, "The sleep of a fasting person is worship, and his [every] breath is [a form of] glorification (*tasbih*)."[77] Narrations also show that Imam Musa al-Kadhim (p) said, "You should take naps because God feeds the fasting person and pours water for him (i.e., as a relief from hunger and thirst) in his sleep."[78]

---

76. al-Hurr al-Amili, *Tafsil wasail al-Shia* , vol. 10, p. 152.

77. al-Hurr al-Amili, *Tafsil wasail al-Shia*, vol. 10, p. 136.

78. al-Hurr al-Amili, *Tafsil wasail al-Shia*, vol. 10, p. 136.

- Providing iftar for a fasting believer, even if it is something small like a date, as reported in the sermon cited above given by the Prophet (pbuh&hp) on the last Friday of the month of Shaban. Imam Abu al-Hasan Musa [al-Kadhim] (p) also reported, "[The reward of] providing iftar for your brother to break his fast is better than [the reward of] your own fast."[79]

- Eating a predawn meal *(suhur)* or something before the time of *fajr*. Narrations state that the Prophet (pbuh&hp) said, "My people should not forsake suhur, even if it means [eating] a part of a date."[80] and "Have suhur even if it is only a drink of water, may the blessings of God be upon those who observe suhur."[81]

- Reciting the special supplication when breaking the fast. Imam Jafar al-Sadiq (p) narrates that the Holy Prophet (pbuh&hp) used to recite the following upon breaking his fast, "O Allah we fasted for Your sake, and broke our fast by Your sustenance, so accept it from us, thirst has gone, the arteries are moist, and the reward is what remains."[82] Narrations also report that Imam al-Sadiq (p) said, "The supplication of a fasting person is accepted at the time of breaking their fast."[83]

---

79. al-Hurr al-Amili, *Tafsil wasail al-Shia*, vol. 10, p. 139.

80. al-Hurr al-Amili, *Tafsil wasail al-Shia*, vol. 10, p. 143.

81. al-Hurr al-Amili, *Tafsil wasail al-Shia*, vol. 10, p. 144.

82. al-Hurr al-Amili, *Tafsil wasail al-Shia*, vol. 10, p. 147.

83. al-Hurr al-Amili, *Tafsil wasail al-Shia*, vol. 10, p. 148.

- Performing *maghrib* prayer at its prescribed time before breaking the fast. Reports state that Imam al-Baqir (p) said, "'During Ramadan you [should] pray and then break your fast, unless you have joined [a group of] people who wait for you [to eat with them], then do not oppose them [in making them wait for you to pray first], break your fast then pray. Otherwise, pray first.' [The narrator said] I asked, 'Why is that?' The Imam (p) replied, 'That is because you are faced with fulfilling two duties simultaneously, breaking your fast and praying, so start by performing the better of the two, which is prayer.' The Imam (p) then said, 'You pray while fasting and it is recorded as such, thus concluding with fasting is more beloved to me.'"[84]

- Breaking the fast with lukewarm water and dates. Reports state that Imam al-Sadiq (p) said, "The Messenger of God (pbuh&hp) used to break his fast with *tamr* during the time of [just ripening] dates, and with *ratab* (i.e., fully ripened dates) during their season," and he also said, "If a person breaks their fast with lukewarm water, it purifies their liver, and washes away the sins from the heart, and strengthens the sight and pupils."[85]

- Being diligent in observing moral virtues and refraining from vices. In a long narration by Imam al-Sadiq (p): "When you fast, safeguard your tongues from lying, lower your gazes [unlawful lustful gazes], do not dispute, do not envy [each

---

84. al-Hurr al-Amili, *Tafsil wasail al-Shia*, vol. 10, p. 150.

85. al-Hurr al-Amili, *Tafsil wasail al-Shia*, vol. 10, p. 157.

other], do not backbite, do not quarrel, do not lie, do not endeavor [towards falsehood], do not disagree, do not become angry, do not insult [each other], do not swear [at each other], do not call each other names, do not argue, do not act ignorantly, do not oppress [others], do not act foolishly, do not reprimand [each other], do not neglect the remembrance of God and performance of prayer, keep silent, observe forbearance, patience, and truthfulness, avoid evil people, false statements, lying, slandering, disputing, negative suppositions [about other believers], avoid backbiting and gossiping, and remain cognizant of the hereafter while waiting out the remaining days [of your lives]."[86]

- Reciting the supplication for greeting the month of Ramadan. Narrations report that Imam al-Baqir (p) said, "When the Messenger of God (pbuh&hp) looked at the crescent of the month of Ramadan, he directed his face towards the qiblah and recited, 'O Allah, let the crescent shine on us with security, faith, safety, Islam, encompassing good health, abundant sustenance, repulsion of ailments, [good fortune] reciting of the Quran, and assistance in [sincerely] performing prayer and observing fasting. O Allah, safeguard us for [the month of] Ramadan, make it a safe haven for us, and accept [our actions during] it from us, until it is complete and You have forgiven us.' Then he would turn to the people and say, 'O Muslims, when the crescent of the month of Ramadan appears, the devils will be

---

86. al-Hurr al-Amili, *Tafsil wasail al-Shia*, vol. 10, p. 166.

shackled, the doors of the sky, the doors of paradise and the doors of mercy will be opened, the gates of [hell] fire will be closed, and the supplications will be answered. Allah will set [deserving] people free from hell fire during every [night of] breaking the fast, while the [divine] caller will ask, "Is there any beseecher? Is there anyone seeking forgiveness? O Allah, give everyone who spends and strives in your way perpetuation [of goodness] and give every denier deterioration such that if the crescent moon of Shawwal appears the believers are called to claim their prizes, so it is the day of the prize.'"[87] Then Imam al-Baqir (p) said, 'By the One who holds my life in His hands, this prize is not [mere] *dananir* and *dinars*.'"

- Reciting the supplication for the beginning of the holy month of Ramadan, which is the forty-fourth supplication of *Al-sahifah al-sajjadiyyah* by Imam Ali ibn al-Hussain al-Sajjad (p).

- Reciting the supplication for the farewell of the holy month of Ramadan, which is the forty-fifth supplication of *Al-sahifah al-sajjadiyyah* by Imam Ali ibn al-Hussain al-Sajjad (p).

- Spending the nights of the holy month in worship, prayers, remembrance of God, and reciting the Quran.

---

87. Ibn Babawayh al-Qummi, *Fadail al-ashhar al-thalathah*, p. 80.

Night Prayer (Salat al-Layl)

The night prayer is a *sunnah* (i.e., a recommended act), and the sharia stipulates that it was among the acts of worship that were obligatory for the Prophet (pbuh&hp). Almighty God says, "O you wrapped up in your mantle! Stand vigil through the night, except a little [*of it*], a half, or reduce a little from that or add to it, and recite the Quran in a measured tone. Indeed, soon We shall cast on you a weighty word. Indeed, the watch of the night is firmer in tread and more upright in respect to speech, for indeed during the day you have drawn-out engagements. So, celebrate the Name of your Lord and dedicate yourself to Him with total dedication."[88] Almighty God also says, "Maintain the prayer [*during the period*] from the sun's decline till the darkness of the night, and [observe particularly] the dawn recital. Indeed, the dawn recital is attended [by angels]. And keep vigil for a part of the night, as a supererogatory [devotion] for you. It may be that your Lord will raise you to a praiseworthy station. And say, 'My Lord! Admit me with a worthy entrance, and bring me out with a worthy departure, and render me a favorable authority from Yourself.'"[89]

Thus, the holy Prophet (pbuh&hp) never got tired of remembering God Almighty and praying to Him, as he used to weep [in awe of Him] until he would faint. Someone asked him, "'O Messenger of God, did God Almighty not forgive you for what has passed of your

---

88. The Quran 73:1–8, AQQ.

89. The Quran 17:78–80, AQQ.

sin[90] and what is to come?' He said, '[Even so], should I not be a grateful servant?'"[91]

Therefore, a believer who is seeking nearness to God, especially in the month of Ramadan, should follow the way of the holy Prophet (pbuh&hp), for Almighty God says, "In the Apostle of Allah there is certainly for you a good exemplar, for those who look forward to Allah and the Last Day, and remember Allah greatly."[92] By following the way of the Prophet (pbuh&hp), a believer is granted a high position, about which Almighty God says, "Indeed the God-wary will be amid gardens and springs, receiving what their Lord has given them, for they had been virtuous aforetime. They used to sleep a little during the night, and at dawns they would plead for forgiveness."[93] The holy Prophet (pbuh&hp) is reported to have said, "[Archangel] Gabriel kept on reminding me of the [importance of] night prayer to the extent I felt that the righteous ones of my community would not sleep [at night]."[94] It is also reported that the Prophet (pbuh&hp) said, "When a servant remains [awake and] alone with his master [Almighty God] in the middle of the dark night and

---

90. Sin in this narration does not indicate that the Prophet (pbuh&hp) had committed or would ever commit a sin, because he is infallible according to our belief. Therefore, it has a different significance, as explained in the books of Quranic exegesis.

91. al-Majlisi, *Bihar al-anwar*, vol. 10, p. 40.

92. The Quran 33:21, AQQ.

93. The Quran 51:15–18, AQQ.

94. Shaykh al-Saduq, *al-amali*, p. 257.

whispers to Him ˉin supplication], He [God] shall secure the light [of guidance] in his heart, . . .then the Most Majestic says to His angels, 'My angels, look at my servant, he is up ˑn the middle of the dark night [worshipping Me] while the idle are heedless and the negligent are asleep, bear witness that I have forgiven him.'"[95] In another narration by Imam al-Sadiq (p), he says "The night prayer brightens the face, makes the fragrances pleasant, and draws sustenance [to the worshipper]."[96] There are many more narrations about the importance and merits of the night prayer.

TIME OF NIGHT PRAYER

The time of nighˑ prayer starts at the beginning of the night, although it is better to perform it after midnight, and the closer it is tc dawn (i.e., prior to fajr) the better.

TIME OF MIDNIGHT

Midnight is the half-way point between the time of sunset and dawn (fajr).

METHOD OF NIGHT PRAYER

Night prayer is composed of eleven units in the following sequence:

1. Four separate two-unit prayers[97] performed with the intention of supererogatory night prayer (*nafilat al-layl*).

---

95. Shaykh al-Saduq, *al-amali*, p. 354.

96. Shaykh al-Saduq, *Thawab al-amal*, p. 41.

97. Each two-unit prayer is performed just like fajr prayer.

2. Two-unit prayer with the intention of *shaf* prayer.

3. One-unit prayer with the intention of *witr* prayer.

    o   It is permissible to perform only shaf and witr, or just even witr alone.

    o   Night prayer may be performed while walking or riding (i.e., in a vehicle), and it is permissible to choose to perform it in a sitting position (even if the person can perform it in a standing position).

    o   It is recommended to perform *qunut*[98] in the unit of witr before bowing down *(ruku)*.

    o   There is no specific invocation or supplication required in the qunut. Yet, in the witr prayer, the recommendation is to seek forgiveness for forty believers (by saying O Allah forgive so-and-so), and then say, "I seek forgiveness from Allah, my Lord, and to Him I repent" seventy times, then "This is the position of one who seeks refuge in You from the fire" seven times, and then "I seek pardon" three hundred times.

    o   It is permissible and [actually] recommended for a person who missed the night prayer to make it up during the day.

---

98. Qunut is the act of raising one's hands in supplication to God Almighty and placing them in front of the face with palms facing the sky and with both hands kept next to each other.

Detestable Acts (*Makruhat*) during Fasting

The following are detestable for a person who is fasting:

- Traveling in the month of Ramadan is detestable, except if the person travels for umrah. Moreover, it is especially detestable if undertaken to evade fasting, even though traveling is permissible in and of itself.[99]

- Engaging in intimate interaction (e.g., touching) with one's lawful spouse if the husband is confident of not ejaculating and the wife is confident that she will not reach sexual climax.

- Applying eyeliner (*kohl*) like musk or something similar such that its taste or smell reaches the throat.

- Bathing in a sauna if there is fear of weakness [from the heat or humidity].

- Drawing blood[100] if it causes weakness.

- Applying medicine in the nose such that it does not reach the throat.

- Smelling plants with pleasing fragrances.

- Moistening the clothes (i.e., with water) to cool the body if, for example, the month of Ramadan falls in the summer.

- Inserting solid enema.

---

99. Umrah is recommended all year round especially in the months of Rajab, Shaban, and Ramadan.

100. For example, to donate blood or sell it to a sick person.

- Dental treatment or extraction and anything that causes the mouth to bleed.

- Brushing the teeth with a moist stick (*siwak*).

- Rinsing the mouth (i.e., with water) for other than *wudu*.

- Engaging in sexual intercourse for a traveler that does not have to observe a fast.

- Immersing the head under water; although it does not nullify the fast, it is very detestable.

Types of Fasting

Fasting is divided into four types: Unlawful, obligatory, recommended, detestable

Unlawful Fasting

Fasting is unlawful in the following cases:

1. Fasting on the day of Eid al-Fitr and the day of Eid al-Adha.
2. Fasting on the days of *tashriq* for a pilgrim in Mina.[101]
3. Fasting on the day of doubt with the intention of it being the first day of the month of Ramadan. The day of doubt is when it is not known whether it is the last day of Shaban or the first of the month of Ramadan.
4. Fasting beyond sunset (*sawm al-wisal*), such that the person fasts all day and continues into and through the night to the next dawn or fasts two consecutive days without breaking the fast at night. However, there is no problem in delaying breaking the fast until the following night if it (i.e., the extended period beyond the first day) is not done with the intention of fasting.
5. Fasting of the wife performed for recommended purposes or an unspecified obligatory fast if it conflicts with her husband's matrimonial rights.

---

101 Mina is a valley southeast of Mecca where pilgrims perform certain rituals on the day of Eid.

Based on obligatory precaution,[102] a wife must not perform a recommended fast if her husband forbids her, even if it does not conflict with his matrimonial rights.

Fasting on the Day of Ashura

Fasting on the tenth of Muharram, which is the day on which the Umayyads rejoiced over their killing of Imam al-Hussain (p), is an innovation (*bida*) if it entails rejoicing [over the killing of Imam al-Hussain (p)].

It is not prohibited to fast on the tenth of Muharram per se, meaning it would be permissible if a person fasts on that day [not for rejoicing the killing of Imam Hussain (p)]. However, its reward would be less when compared to refraining from eating and drinking until after *asr* prayer and then drinking some water.

Fast of silence

A fast of silence is forbidden and considered an innovation (*bida*) if one does so with the intention of it being an act of worship to seek nearness to God Almighty. As for merely observing silence, it is permissible, and in some cases it is praiseworthy.

---

102. This is a ruling that is obligatory to follow based on precaution. According to Sayyid al-Sistani, in such verdicts, one may follow the next most knowledgeable jurist after him.

Detestable Fasts

Fasting is detestable in the following cases:

1. Fasting on the Day of Arafah[103] for someone who fears that it will weaken them for performing supplication.
2. Fasting on the Day of Arafah if there is a doubt about the new moon, such that it may be the day of Eid.
3. Fasting of a guest without the permission of his host if it is a recommended or an unspecified obligatory fast.
4. Recommended (*mustahabb*) fasting of a child without the permission of their father.

Recommended Fasts

Fasting is a highly recommended act of worship in Islam. Narrations have described it as a haven from hell fire and a charity of the body; that the good deeds of a person who observes a fast will be accepted; their prayers will be answered; the angels will supplicate for them until they break their fast; and there are many other merits and benefits.

There are many recommended fasts. The following are some of them:

1. Fasting three days of each lunar month, and the best method for doing so is to fast the first and last Thursdays of the month, and the first

---

103. The ninth of Dhu al-Hijjah.

Wednesday that falls in the second ten days of the month.

2. Fasting every Thursday and Friday if they do not coincide with Eid.
3. Fasting on the birthday of the Prophet (pbuh&hp), which is the seventeenth of Rabi al-Awwal based on the most well-accepted opinion.
4. Fasting on the day of al-Mabath,[104] which is the twenty-seventh of Rajab.
5. Fasting on the day of the spreading of the earth (*dahwu al-ard*), which is the twenty-fifth of Dhu al-Qidah.
6. Fasting on the Day of Arafah for someone who does not fear that it will weaken them for supplication and if there is no doubt about the new moon.
7. Fasting on the day of Ghadir, which is the eighteenth of Dhu al-Hijjah.
8. Fasting on the day of Mubahalah, which is the twenty-fourth of Dhu al-Hijjah.
9. Fasting the first, third, and seventh of Muharram.
10. Fasting the entire month of Rajab.
11. Fasting the entire month of Shaban.

NOTE: If a person who is observing a recommended fast or is fasting in the month of Ramadan, mistakenly commits a nullifier their fast remains valid.

If a person is observing a recommended fast when his believing brother/sister invites him to eat, it is recommended that they break their fast as a way of accepting their brother/sister's invitation and bringing

---

104. The anniversary of the beginning of the Prophetic mission.

pleasure to their heart. However, the invitation must be serious and not just appetizers, such as tea and light fare, that people usually offer their guests when they visit. The inviting person can be a person's spouse, sibling, friend, or any other believer.

Six days fast of Shawwal

Some oft-cited narrations suggest that it is recommended to fast six days in the month of Shawwal. However, these narrations are not authentic. Therefore, if a person chooses to observe either consecutive or separate fasts in Shawwal with the intention of *raja*,[105] they should begin doing so three days after the day of Eid, because there are authentic narrations that a person should not be fasting during the first three days of Eid since those days are meant for eating and drinking.

Obligatory Fasting

There are ten types of obligatory fasts, some of which are essentially obligatory[106] and others that become obligatory due to certain conditions. Traditions report that Imam Ali ibn al-Hussain al-Sajjad (p) mentioned

---

105. Intention of raja is the performance of an act of worship reported in an unauthentic narration, with the hope that God Almighty desires it.

106. Fasting is one of the pillars of Islam, meaning that one who does not believe that fasting is part of the religion is not considered a Muslim.

various types of fasting in a long narration reported by al-Zuhri.[107]

1. Fasting the blessed month of Ramadan based on the Quranic verse, "So let those of you who witness it fast [in] it."[108]
2. Fasting two consecutive months as an expiation for *dhihar*[109] based on what God says: "Those who repudiate their wives by dhihar and then retract what they have said, shall set free a slave before they may touch each other. This you are advised [to carry out], and Allah is well aware of what you do. He who cannot afford [to free a slave] shall fast for two successive months before they may touch each other. If he cannot [do so], he shall feed sixty needy persons. This, that you may have faith in Allah and His Apostle. These are Allah's bounds, and there is a painful punishment for the faithless."[110]
3. Fasting two consecutive months[111] as an expiation for deliberately breaking a fast during the month of Ramadan without a valid excuse.
4. Fasting two consecutive months as an expiation for mistakenly killing someone if the killer is

---

107. al-Kulayni, *al-Kafi*, vol. 4, p. 83.

108. The Quran 2:185, AQQ.

109. Dhihar is when a husband makes a statement to his wife falsely claiming that she is like his mother in terms of being sexually impermissible to him.

110. The Quran 58:3–4, AQQ.

111. One has the option to either fast two consecutive months or feed sixty poor believers.

unable to free a slave based on God stating, "A believer may not kill another believer, unless it is by mistake. Anyone who kills a believer by mistake should set free a believing slave, and pay blood-money to his family, unless they remit it in charity. If he belongs to a people that are hostile to you but is a believer, then a believing slave is to be set free. And if he belongs to a people with whom you have a treaty, the blood-money is to be paid to his family and a believing slave is to be set free. He who cannot afford [to pay the blood-money], must fast two successive months as a penance from Allah, and Allah is all-knowing, all-wise."[112]

5. Fasting three consecutive days as an expiation for breaking an oath if the person is unable to feed the poor based on God saying, "Allah shall not take you to task for what is frivolous in your oaths; but He shall take you to task for what you pledge in earnest. The atonement for it is to feed ten needy persons with the average food you give to your families, or their clothing, or the freeing of a slave. He who cannot afford [any of these] shall fast for three days. That is the atonement for your oaths when you vow. But keep your oaths. Thus does Allah clarify His signs for you so that you may give thanks."[113]

6. Fasting ten days as a *fidyah* for a pilgrim who is unable to cut his hair because of physical pain on the head based on God stating, "Complete the hajj

---

112. The Quran 4:92, AQQ.

113. The Quran 5:89, AQQ.

and the umrah for Allah's sake, and if you are prevented, then [make] such [sacrificial] offering as is feasible. And do not shave your heads until the offering reaches its [assigned] place. But should any of you be sick, or have a hurt in his head, let the atonement be by fasting, or charity, or sacrifice."[114]

7. Fasting ten days for a pilgrim performing *hajj al-tamattu* who cannot find an animal to sacrifice based on God stating, "And when you have security—for those who enjoy [release from the restrictions] by virtue of their umrah until the hajj—let the offering be such as is feasible. As for someone who cannot afford [the offering], let him fast three days during the hajj and seven when you return; that is [a period of] ten complete [days]. That is for someone whose family does not dwell by the Holy Mosque. And be wary of Allah, and know that Allah is severe in retribution."[115]

8. Fasting as an atonement for deliberately hunting and killing while in the state of *ihram* based on God stating, "O you who have faith! Do not kill any game when you are in pilgrim sanctity. Should any of you kill it intentionally, its atonement, the counterpart from cattle of what he has killed, as judged by two fair men among you, will be an offering brought to the Kabah, or an atonement by feeding needy persons, or its equivalent in fasting, that he may taste the untoward consequences of his conduct. Allah has excused what is already

---

114. The Quran 2:196, AQQ.

115. The Quran 2:196, AQQ.

past; but should anyone resume, Allah shall take vengeance on him, for Allah is all-mighty, avenger."[116] One must estimate the value of the animal which he hunted and then convert it to *sa* of wheat, and fast a day for each half sa.[117]

9. Fasting for the fulfillment of a vow (explained later).

10. Fasting as part of a spiritual retreat (itikaf), which is obligatory in some cases (explained later).

Fasting in Fulfillment of a Vow

Fasting for the fulfilment of a vow is permissible and valid. When a duty-bound person makes a vow to fast three days in gratitude to God Almighty upon fulfillment of a specific need or makes a vow to fast three days as a punishment if they commit a sin like backbiting, then they must fast [as vowed] if it occurs. The vow may be specific such as fasting three days in the beginning of the month, the end of the month, the middle of the month, or [even] three days consecutively such as Wednesday, Thursday, and Friday. The vow can be unspecified, for example, if the vow is to fast any time during the year. Therefore, it is important to note the following details:

- Fasting, whether obligatory or recommended, is invalid if performed by a traveler who must shorten their four-unit prayers, except if they make a general vow to fast, meaning their

---

116. The Quran 5:95, AQQ.

117. It is a unit of weight that is equal to 6.6 pounds (three kilograms).

intention was to observe the fast irrespective of whether they are in a state of traveling or not.

- A person who has lapsed (*qada*) fast(s) from the month of Ramadan may vow to fast; however, they must make up the lapsed fast before fulfilling the fast of vow, even if specified.

- If a person vows to fast on a specific day, such as the first of Rajab, they must make the intention to fast before dawn (fajr) of that day. If they deliberately delay the intention, their fast is invalid. If they forget about the [specified] fast for that day and remember before *dhuhr* and do not commit a fast-nullifier, they make the intention to fast and their fast for that day is valid. However, if they remember after dhuhr, then based on obligatory precaution, they must abstain from fast-nullifiers for the rest of the day with a [general] intention[118] of nearness to God and then make it up later.

- If a person vows a specific fast and the day of fulfillment arrives and they do not fulfill it, they must make it up.

- If a person must perform an unspecified fast for a fulfilled vow, they may do so on the last day of Shaban (the day of doubt). However, if they later come to know that it was the first day of the

---

118. The general intention or *qurbah al-mutlaqah* is made when a person seeks to fulfill an obligation among several possibilities, like fasting on the last day of Shaban with the intention of doing so according to the de facto condition as known by God, or by making an intention of hesitancy such that it would be for Shaban if it turned out to be the last day of Shaban and the month of Ramadan if it turns out to be so.

month of Ramadan, their fast would count as part of Ramadan, and they would have to make up the vowed fast later.

- If a person vows to fast on a specific day and deliberately does not fulfill it, they will have committed a sin and must make up the fast. Moreover, they must perform an expiation (kaffarah) for the broken vow. However, there is no expiation requirement if they do not fulfill the vow due to a legitimate excuse such as illness or menstruation. In that case, they must only make up the fast.

- It is permissible for a person to observe a recommended fast even if they must perform a fast for a fulfilled vow.

Conditions for the Obligation of Fasting and Its Validity

There are several conditions for the obligation of fasting and its validity listed below.

First, Sanity (Aql) and Consciousness (not to be insane, unconscious, or intoxicated)

- Sanity is an essential condition for acts of worship. Hence, a person who has lost their sanity for any reason does not have to perform any obligatory act of worship, although they may have to make them up in certain cases (explained below).
- The obligation for all acts of worship is revoked for a person who is essentially (i.e., permanently) insane.
- The obligation of fasting is revoked for a person who is temporarily insane,[119] involuntarily loses consciousness, or unintentionally becomes intoxicated throughout the entire day (e.g., before

---

119. Insanity (e.g., mental disability) from the perspective of religious law is determined based on common understanding (*urf*) or by referring to the *ahl al-khibra* (the experts in the field), such that the mind of the person is not able to properly function, and therefore they cannot understand or fulfill religious requirements.

dawn until after sunset), and no qada is necessary. However, if the person intends to fast before dawn, and during the day one of the aforementioned situations occurs (for part of the day), they must continue fasting for the rest of the day based on obligatory precaution. They must make up the fast for that day if they do not continue fasting.

- Based on obligatory precaution, it is not permissible for a person who must fast the month of Ramadan to take anesthetics or sedative drugs that cause loss of consciousness for an unnecessary surgery. In the event they do so, but thereafter wake up during the day, then based on obligatory precaution, they must refrain from fast-nullifiers (if they had made an intention to fast) and make up the fast.

- If a person misses the time of making the intention to fast due to losing their sanity, losing consciousness, or becoming intoxicated, but thereafter wakes up during the day, they must refrain from fast-nullifiers and make up the fast. However, if they made the intention to fast before dawn, the fast would be valid, although, based on obligatory precaution,[120] they should make it up.

---

120. This is a ruling that is obligatory to follow based on precaution. According to Sayyid al-Sistani, in such verdicts, one may follow the next most knowledgeable jurist after him.

Second, Being at the Age of Religious Obligation (*Bulugh*)

Age of religious obligation is a condition for fasting to be obligatory for a person, although it is not a condition for its validity. As such, the fast of a discerning child[121] (*mumayyiz*) is valid and rewarded by Almighty God.

Age of religious obligation for males

A male becomes religiously duty-bound if one of the following occurs:

- Growth of thick pubic hair between the lower abdomen and the private parts
- Ejaculation of semen
- Completion of fifteen lunar years[122]

Note: underarm and chest hair and the deepening of the voice are not signs of bulugh.

---

121. A child who is close to the age of bulugh and understands the meaning of bulugh and religious obligations, meaning that they intend the performed acts and discern between what is valid and what is invalid.

122. Fifteen lunar years is equivalent to fourteen years seven months and fifteen days of the solar calendar (Gregorian calendar.)

Age of religious obligation for females

A female becomes religiously duty-bound upon completion of nine lunar years.[123] Therefore, she must observe her religious duties on the first day of her tenth lunar year.

Fasting during the first years of bulugh

The following are rulings for the first years of bulugh:

- If a person does not fast the month of Ramadan after having reached bulugh and subsequently does not remember the exact number of days they missed, they should make up the minimum number of days (i.e., that they think they missed) and pay kaffarah for intentionally breaking a fast for each day missed (unless they were certain that they did not have to fast at that time—then they only must make up the fasts without paying a kaffarah). Additionally, based on obligatory precaution, they must offer a kaffarah for delaying the make-up (qada) fast [beyond the next month of Ramadan], which is to give 750 grams of food to a poor person for each day missed.
- If a girl does not fast because she assumes that she only becomes duty-bound at menarche, then she must make up the days she did not fast, but no kaffarah is necessary in her case.
- If a girl in the first year(s) of bulugh does not fast due to severe physical weakness in her body, a [true] inability to bear fasting for the entire day,

---

123. Nine lunar years is equivalent to eight years, eight months and twenty days of the solar calendar (Gregorian calendar.)

because it is very hot, or similar difficult conditions, then she must make up the missed fasts, but no kaffarah is due.

- If fasting causes serious harm to a girl who is religiously duty-bound or she deems it veritable and highly likely (i.e., that she would suffer harm), then she does not have to fast. However, she must make it up later. On the other hand, if she is unable to fast due to, for example, the length of the day or intensity of heat, despite taking the necessary nutrition before dawn (suhur) and resting during the day, then she must fast for the sake of general nearness to God.[124] When she reaches a stage of unbearable fatigue and needs to eat or drink, she may do so. However, she must limit eating and drinking to the minimum extent that lifts the hardship, based on obligatory precaution, and not eat and drink to fullness. Thereafter, she should continue to abstain from fast-nullifiers for the rest of the day and make up the fast later.[125]

---

124. Without considering it an obligatory fast, rather abstinence of eating and drinking for the sake of nearness to God.

125. It is important to train the child to fast in months other than the month of Ramadan, even for part of the day, because this can help the body become used to fasting. Also, it is worthy to note that the permissibility of eating and drinking only as much as necessary does not necessarily apply during the entire blessed month. Thus, for example, the child can become accustomed by fasting one day and skipping the next.

Third, Capability, Tolerance, Hardship, and Security from Harm

Capability and tolerance

There are many things to consider about the capability and tolerance of a person for fasting.

- Fasting is not valid if a person knows that it will cause illness, or they fear that they will become ill due to weakness.
- Fasting of an ill person is not valid if they suffer harm from it to the extent that it is usually unbearable, whether it is due to worsening of the illness, delaying recovery, or increasing pain. This ruling applies for a person who has certainty, or even any rational conjecture that usually leads to true and reasonable fear [that fasting would lead to harm]. An ill person who does not suffer harm by fasting must fast.

The criterion of capability and tolerance

Weakness is not a valid reason to avoid fasting in the month of Ramadan per se, unless it amounts to unbearable hardship. In such a case, it is permissible not to fast, however, the person must make it up later.[126] Also, it is permissible for a person not to fast if

---

126. The same ruling applies for young boys and girls who are at the age of religious obligation but are unable to fast due to the weakness of their bodies (that is, the child cannot fast on account of their physical incapability). In this case, they do not need to

it causes them weakness that prevents them from working and it is their only source of earning a livelihood (i.e., there is no alternative). The same applies if the worker is unable to continue fasting because of extreme thirst. However, in both cases, the worker must eat or drink only to the minimum extent necessary, based on obligatory precaution, and thereafter continue abstaining from nullifiers until the end of the day.

Harm

Consideration is also given to whether the fasting will cause harm to a person.

- The obligation to fast is revoked if a person is certain that doing so will cause them unbearable serious harm or even if they deem it to be veritable and highly likely, and it is forbidden for them to fast in such a case.
- Fasting is revoked if it results in worsening of [an existing] illness, a delay in recovery, or causes a new illness.
- If a person fasts believing that it will not cause them harm, but they [later] realize otherwise, then fasting for them is problematic (i.e., based on obligatory precaution, it is invalid).
- The fast of a person who knows or fears serious harm is invalid unless they intended to fast for the sake of general proximity to God and later realized that the fast did not cause any harm.

---

fast. However, they must make it up later even if in the winter season.

- It is permissible for a person to break their fast if they are certain or strongly think it is likely that fasting will cause them serious harm based on a doctor's recommendation. Otherwise, it is not permissible to break a fast even if the doctor recommends it.
- A person must fast if they are certain or strongly think it is likely that fasting will not cause them serious harm, even though a doctor advises them not to. On the other hand, a person may break their fast if they are certain or strongly think it is likely that fasting will cause them serious harm, even though a doctor says that it will not.

Criteria of harm

Serious harm means anything that leads to death, damage of organ(s), or bodily weakness that results in the inability to carry out [essential] daily living activities, such that people commonly accept it as being unbearable. Therefore, change of mood, blurry vision, headache, and similar symptoms, usually alleviated shortly after breaking the fast, are not considered serious harm.

Those who are excused from fasting

Certain individuals are excused from fasting during the month of Ramadan: the elderly, a pregnant woman approaching the time of delivery, a nursing mother with little breast milk, a person suffering from polydipsia, an ill person, and those who cannot fast due to unbearable hardship. The following is a detailed explanation of each of these groups:

THE ELDERLY

- An elderly person, who is not capable of fasting or for whom fasting causes difficulty, does not have to fast.
- An elderly person who is not capable of fasting does not have to offer a kaffarah.
- An elderly person who can fast, but it causes them difficulty, does not have to fast. However, they must offer a fidyah of one portion of food for each day,[127] and it should be two portions of food based on recommended precaution. They must make up the fast later.

A PREGNANT WOMAN WHO IS CLOSE TO TIME OF DELIVERY

- A pregnant woman who is close to delivery (i.e., in her eighth or ninth month) is excused from fasting if she fears harm to herself or her unborn child, and it may be obligatory for her to break her fast if it entails serious harm to either of them. She must make up the fast and offer a fidyah for each lapsed day. If she delays making up the fasts until the following month of Ramadan for another reason like due to nursing her child, she must offer another fidyah for delaying the lapsed fasts, which is to feed a poor person for each day missed.
- A pregnant woman who is not close to delivery (from the first to the end of the seventh month) is excused from fasting if she fears harm to herself

---

127. A portion of food is equal to 1.65 pounds (750 grams).

or her unborn child or if it causes her unbearable hardship. However, she must make it up later and she does not have to offer a kaffarah. If she delays making up the fasts until the following month of Ramadan, even if it is due to nursing her child, she must pay a kaffarah for delaying the lapsed fasts based on obligatory precaution, which is to feed a poor person for each day missed.

- It is permissible for a pregnant woman to consume what is necessary for medical examinations in the month of Ramadan if the examination is necessary and cannot be administered at night, after the month of Ramadan, or if it is not possible to break her fast by traveling the legal distance, but she must make it up later.

A NURSING WOMAN WITH LITTLE MILK

- A nursing woman with little breast milk is excused from fasting if it is harmful for her or the newborn if there is no other way, like a wet-nurse or formula milk, to feed the child (i.e., this breast feeding is the only way to feed the newborn). Otherwise, it is not permissible for her to break the fast. However, she must make up the fast and offer a fidyah.

- Based on obligatory precaution, the mother may not break her fast if there is a way to hire a wet nurse, who can feed the child, or by other means such as using baby formula.

AN ILL PERSON

- A duty-bound person is excused from fasting if it causes them illness, worsens an existing illness, delays recovery, or results in another illness.
- If a person experiences critical health symptoms that require immediate treatment while fasting during Ramadan, such as low blood sugar and the need for insulin medication, they may break their fast.

HARD LABOR WORKERS

- If fasting prevents a person from working a job which is their only source of securing a livelihood, for example, by causing weakness because of which they are unable to perform their tasks, or unbearable thirst, they must still fast if they can change their job or take a break from work throughout the month of Ramadan and rely on savings or borrowed money that they can repay later. Otherwise, they are excused from fasting. However, based on obligatory precaution, they must eat and drink the minimum amount necessary to lift the hardship that prevents them from working, and they must make up the missed fasts. They do not have to offer any kaffarah.
- Working in hard labor jobs (e.g., construction, bread baking, cooking) during the hot summers does not permit a person to break their fast. Rather, the worker must fast, and if during the day they reach a point where they fear harm or unbearable hardship due to extreme thirst, then they may drink water to the extent necessary to relieve the hardship, continue to refrain from

fast-nullifiers until the end of the day, and make up the fast later.

- It is permissible for those who work in a profession (e.g., pilot) that requires staying hydrated to drink water to the extent necessary if work in the month of Ramadan is essential to secure a livelihood, such that they would encounter unbearable hardship if they did not. In such a case, they must make up the missed fasts, but they do not have to offer any kaffarah.

- It is permissible for a person who works in delicate occupations and tasks that require full consciousness, awareness, and readiness (e.g., guard, security guard, soldier) and is unable to take leave, even for some days of the month of Ramadan, to eat and drink only to the extent necessary if fasting poses harm to them, causes them to fall short in fulfilling their tasks, and subjects them to termination. Based on obligatory precaution, they must eat and drink to the minimum extent necessary to fulfill their duties, continue to refrain from fast-nullifiers until the end of the day, and make up the fast later.

A PERSON WHO SUFFERS FROM POLYDIPSIA

- A person who suffers from polydipsia is excused from fasting and they are not required to offer a fidyah if they are unable to fast, but if fasting causes them unbearable hardship they must offer a portion[128] of food to the poor as fidyah, and

---

128. A portion of food is equal to 1.65 pounds (750 grams).

based on a recommended precaution, they should offer two portions.

- If a person needs to drink water to avoid illness or prevent worsening of an illness, such as a severe headache or dehydration that leads to hemorrhoids, and there is no other way to obtain hydration, such as eating water-filled vegetables and fruits like cucumbers and watermelon before fajr (dawn), then they may break their fast and make it up later.

- If a fasting person becomes extremely thirsty such that they fear harm or will be subject to unbearable hardship if they do not drink water, then they may drink water but based on obligatory precaution, it must not be more than necessary. Also, they must refrain from fast-nullifiers for the rest of the day if this fast is during the month of Ramadan (i.e., respecting the holy month), and they must make up the fast later. If it is an obligatory fast in other months they do not have to refrain from fast-nullifiers.

Forth, Establishing the Beginning of the Month of Ramadan

Among the conditions that establish the obligation of fasting for the month of Ramadan is witnessing the start of the holy month. Almighty God says, "So let those of you who witness it fast [in] it."[129] Therefore, if a duty-bound person witnesses the start of the month,

---

129. The Quran 2:185, AQQ.

they must fast it in its entirety "so that you may complete the number."[130]

Determining the beginning and end of the lunar month

Confirming the sighting of the crescent moon of the ninth month of the lunar year establishes the beginning of the blessed month of Ramadan, and the month ends with the sighting of the crescent of the tenth month, which is the month of Shawwal. Lunar months are sometimes twenty-nine days and at other times thirty. Confirming the sighting of the crescent of Shawwal ends the month of Ramadan, and the next day is the first of Shawwal, which is Eid al-Fitr. Fasting is not permissible on the first of Shawwal.

WAYS OF ESTABLISHING THE START OF LUNAR MONTHS

The criterion for the beginning of a lunar month is the appearance of the crescent moon on the horizon such that the naked eye can see it if not obstructed by clouds and other obstacles (such as mountains or trees). One of the following ways establishes the beginning of the lunar month:

1. Knowledge [of the appearance of the crescent, which leads to certainty] attained by sighting the crescent with the naked eye (i.e., by the person

---

130. The Quran 2:185, AQQ.

themselves) and not via an optical aid (e.g., a telescope).[131]

2. Knowledge [of the appearance of the crescent] received from multiple eyewitness accounts (i.e., from various people or *tawatur*) such that one derives certainty or confidence of the crescent sighting.

---

131. This is one of the controversial issues among jurists. The juristic opinion which asserts that an optical aid cannot confirm the [new] crescent is based on the following points. First, God states, "They question you concerning the new moons. Say, 'They are timekeeping signs for the people and [for the sake of] hajj." (Quran 2:189, AQQ) This verse addresses people in general and directs them to use the crescent as a reference point for the start of the religious months, and it does not just address those who have knowledge of astronomy, which was available and used in the pre-Islamic era. Secondly, the criteria for applying religious rulings are based on common understanding (urf) and practice. Consider, for example. the religiously prescribed limit known as *hadd al-tarrakhuss* or where the traveler shortens their prayer or breaks their fast, which is the distance outside of the traveler's hometown where they can no longer see its buildings nor hear the *adhan* (call to prayer) or the residents of the town can no longer see the traveler. The criterion is that the residents of the hometown cannot see the traveler with the naked eye, otherwise, the simplest binoculars could see them. If that was the case, the prescribed limit would likely become the same as the religiously required distance that makes a person a traveler. Similarly, if a duty-bound person washes their white shirt to purify it of blood and the color disappears, then they would consider it to be pure and suitable for prayers. However, what if they were to place the shirt under a microscope and see small red particles? Would they then consider the shirt impure? Jurists say the criterion is the unaided vision [of an ordinary person], and therefore, they would not even regard the vision of someone with extraordinary vision, who sees things from afar [as the standard], because it is beyond the normal capacity of common people, which shapes a religiously accepted common view.

3. The spread of common news (*shaya*) such that the person becomes certain of the crescent sighting.
4. Any rational means by which a person becomes certain of the appearance of the crescent [and its sighting by the naked eye].
5. The passing of thirty days from the first of Shaban so there is no doubt that the next day is the first of the month of Ramadan or the passing of thirty days from the first of the month of Ramadan, which means the next day is the first of Shawwāl.
6. The testimony of two just men that they sighted the crescent, provided that a comparable opposing testimony does not contradict them, even if in principle. Therefore, if two just men testified that they sighted the crescent and [at the same time] two other just men testify to the contrary (i.e., that they did not see the crescent), and the sky was clear with no obstacle to sighting it, then this means does not establish the first of the month.

   o It is permissible to act according to the report of a non-Muslim on the sighting of the crescent with the naked eye if one becomes certain and content by the report.
   o Crescent sighting is not established by the testimony of women,[132] the testimony of one

---

132. This ruling, like all others, is a binding obligation the wisdom behind which is unknown (i.e., it is only known to God and those He chooses to inform). Some might assume that Islam considers women to be incompetent or underestimates women's abilities, which is an invalid judgment raised against Islam from time and time. The Holy Quran has clearly stated that human beings have dignity irrespective of their gender, and God created them equal and distinguished them from each other based on their piety, despite their different practical roles. In addition, while the

just man who swears an oath [that he truly sighted it], nor the statement of astrologers.[133] It also cannot be established by its disappearance after twilight to indicate that it is for the second night; by seeing it before *zawal* or dhuhr time such that it would be considered the day of the new month; nor by the ruling of a qualified jurist (al-hakim al-shari) even if it is not known that the he is mistaken unless contentment is achieved by means of his ruling that the crescent has been sighted.

---

testimony of women is not considered in establishing the crescent sighting, it is legislated, [sometimes] through the testimony of one woman in other matters, such as proving crimes that pertain (e.g., directed at) to women. On the other hand, the testimony of a woman is sometimes half that of a man, as would be the case in some general matters. Hence, there is no single ruling by which a person can judge the religion (i.e., by ascertaining the appropriateness of a rule or not). It is also important to note that if contentment is achieved from the testimony of women then a person may act upon it.

133. It is important to differentiate between astrologers and astronomers. The latter are experts in astronomy and are capable of [scientifically] predicting the possibility of sighting the crescent according to their specialization and professional experience. Moreover, a duty-bound person may attain contentment from their statement and act accordingly [to visually sight the moon]. As for the astrologers, they apparently base their astronomical information on suspicions and attempt to predict the unknown, which Islam forbids.

UNITY AND MULTIPLICITY OF HORIZONS

The following points explain the concept of the unity of horizons:

- The beginning of the lunar month in every area[134] is based on sighting the crescent there.
- If there is confirmation of the crescent sighting in an area, it becomes established for other areas that share the same horizon. This means the actual sighting of the crescent in that area guarantees it will be visible in the other areas unless there are clouds or other similar obstructions. In other words, if the altitude (i.e., above the horizon) and luminosity of the crescent in two adjacent areas are close, then they would be considered to have the same horizon. This closeness is usually [within] one to two degrees depending on the geographical location and according to the season.

ADDITIONAL DETAILS ABOUT THE ESTABLISHMENT OF THE CRESCENT AND THE ISSUE OF UNITY AND MULTIPLICITY OF HORIZONS

More details follow concerning the crescent and unity of horizons:

- If a duty-bound person acquires [veritable] knowledge or becomes content, albeit through

---

134. Area, as used in this booklet, refers to the jurisprudential term *balad*, which describes a particular place where the crescent must be sighted. This could be a city, metropolis (large city) or general area. The details of this are determined from place to place based on *urf* or common understanding. Thus, it could apply to only a metropolis in one place; a city and its suburbs in another; or even two or three cities in yet other places.

experience and repeatedly encountering the same conditions, that the crescent on the local horizon has the features (e.g., size and altitude) that make it visible with the naked eye, then they must act according to their knowledge and certainty even if it is not visible due to clouds, fog, or any other natural obstacle.

- Two areas are considered to have the same horizon if sighting the crescent in the first area guarantees sighting it in the second one absent natural obstacles such as clouds or mountains. This is established if the crescent in the second area has the same or more prominent features to the first in terms of size, altitude above the horizon at sunset, and angular distance from the sun as determined by accurate astronomical calculations.

- If the area in which the duty-bound person resides is located west of the area where the crescent sighting occurred, and the two areas are close in latitude (i.e., vary only by one or two degrees), then sighting is also established for that area to the west if the luminosity is ascertained. However, this is not a general condition [applied in every circumstance], because establishment of sighting for adjacent areas, even with relatively close latitude and longitude, may vary in different seasons.

- A person who is content about the crescent sighting must act accordingly [in beginning the next month]. However, if they do not achieve contentment, then they must act upon other criteria explained in this booklet.

- A person's contentment is not sufficient for others to act upon.
- It is not sufficient to rely on a single person who claims to have sighted the crescent if others who are proficient in knowing its position and have sharp vision cannot do so, provided the sky is clear and there is no likelihood of something obstructing the view.
- A person may rely on the information provided by an astronomer who reports on the visibility of the crescent on the horizon with the naked eye if they derive contentment from it. For example, if astronomers report that the crescent is not born yet and that it is still in the stage of *mahaq* (just a few hours old), then this could instill contentment that the crescent is not present on the horizon such that the naked eye can see it.
- The main criteria that influence the sighting of the crescent are its size (i.e., magnitude of illumination), its altitude over the horizon, and its angular distance from the sun. For example, if the sighting of the crescent is established in an area at sunset and its size is 4 percent, its altitude is eight degrees, and its distance from the sun is twenty-five degrees, then it is certain that it will be visible (unless there is an external obstruction) in the area if the criteria are not less than those guaranteeing visibility.
- The criterion for establishing the beginning of the lunar month is the presence of the crescent on the horizon such the naked eye can see it unless clouds or other such obstacles obstruct it. Therefore, it is not sufficient to establish the first of the lunar month if the birth of the crescent and

its presence on the horizon occur, but it is not visible or is only visible with an optical aid. Based on this, astronomical information reporting the birth of the crescent and its transition from the stage of mahaq is not useful in establishing the beginning of the new lunar month, even if it is based on definitive mathematical calculations, unless a person derives contentment from it in certain cases which are explained in detail in books of jurisprudence. Astronomers' reports about the visibility of the crescent with the naked eye depend on two factors: (1) astronomical calculations about the position of the crescent in terms of its age, degree of elevation from the horizon, angular distance from the sun, and other factors that affect its sighting, and (2) astronomical observations of the crescent that verify the minimum conditions required to sight it with the naked eye (i.e., by characterizing its age, altitude, and distance from the sun). Astronomers differ on these criteria, however. For example, some astronomers posit that it is possible to sight the crescent when it is at fourteen hours, while others state that the minimum age [for visibility] is sixteen hours, still others state eighteen hours, and some state even more. Similarly, some astronomers claim that it is [only] possible to sight the crescent when it is at an altitude of four degrees above the horizon at sunset, while others state that the minimum altitude required to see it is five degrees, or six degrees, and even other altitudes. This is the case for all the factors that affect crescent visibility. As such, it is not feasible for a duty-bound person to act according to astronomical data substantiating the possibility of sighting the crescent in an area when there is uncertainty of doing so with the naked eye. This is because religious texts indicate that one cannot rely on opinion and speculation in the matters of the crescent. Traditions state that Imam al-Baqir (p) said, "If you sight the crescent then fast, and if you sight it [the following month] then break your fast, and these practices are not established by opinion or speculation but with actual sighting."[135]

ISTIFTA (RESPONSE TO JURISPRUDENTIAL QUESTIONS)

A group of believers in North America inquired about a ruling mentioned in *Minhaj al-Salihin* and other sources that the unity of the horizons only occurs for two places if the sighting in the first land guarantees sighting of the crescent in the second land unless dust or clouds obstruct visibility.

Based on the figure below, experience (i.e., repeated measurements) indicates that the naked eye can see the crescent moon in the orange and dark yellow areas if conditions are ideal, such as having clear skies. On the other hand, it has been repeatedly confirmed that the crescent can be seen clearly and easily in the red areas, such that the person can be certain of seeing it based on the astronomical calculations.

---

135. al-Tusi, *Tahthib al-ahkam*, vol. 4, p. 156.

Question
According to the criteria mentioned in *Minhaj al-Salihin* and scientific proof, as well as through practical experience in sighting the crescent in the red areas in the figure below, is it appropriate to include all of the areas that are within the red, without paying attention to those parts [immediately] adjacent to the dark yellow areas, as having the same horizon (i.e., unity of horizons) such that, for example, as long as the crescent sighting has been proven religiously in the city of Los Angeles, then it will also be established in Miami and Ecuador?

Answer by the office of His Eminence al-Sayyid al-Sistani (may God prolong his life)

If it is proven that the crescent moon in the areas that fall close to the edge of the red zone has an altitude and size that is close to the crescent in the areas beyond it (i.e., outside of the red zone), in which the crescent moon was indeed sighted with clarity, then contentment is usually attained that such a relationship between the two areas exists (i.e., guarantee of visibility). In contrast, contentment is not achieved for those areas in which it may be expected that the crescent is smaller in size or lower in altitude such that it is not possible to sight it with the naked eye, even if astronomers make the claim that it is indeed possible.

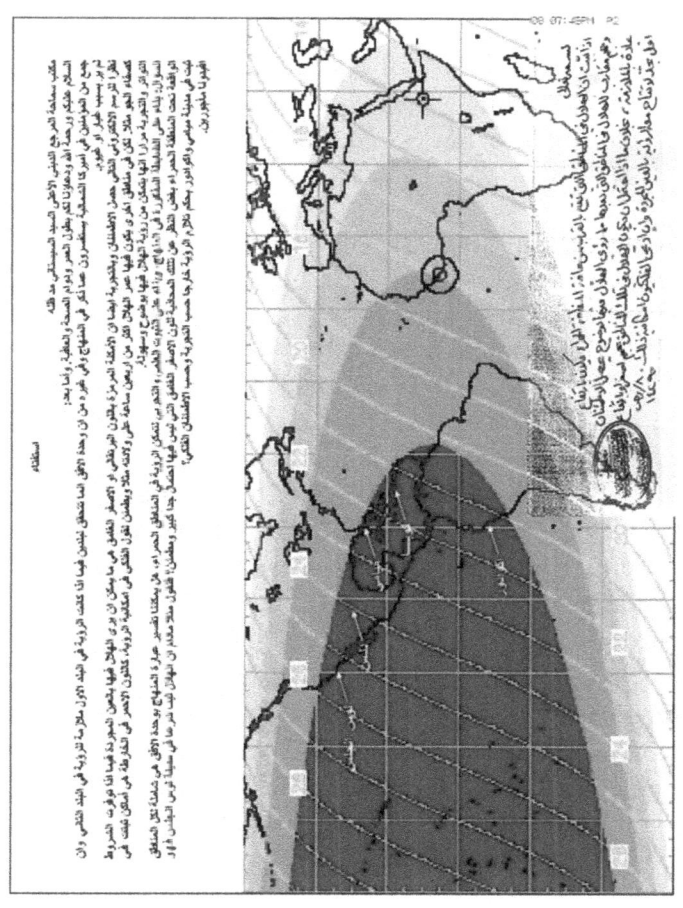

A PRACTICAL MODEL FOR DETERMINING THE UNITY OF HORIZONS

A release issued by the office of His Eminence Grand Ayatullah Sayyid al-Sistani (may Allah prolong his life) announced that the beginning of the month of Ramadan 1431 A.H. had been proven in the Holy City of Najaf, Iraq, and some countries close to it at sunset on Wednesday, August 11, 2010. As a result, the office of

His Eminence issued a statement specifying the horizon of Najaf and all other cities that share it (i.e., unity of horizon), beginning with Australia and ending with the United States. Below is a copy of the statement:

In the name of Allah, the Beneficent, the Merciful

The office of His Eminence Sayyid al-Sistani in the Holy City of Najaf announces to the gracious believers that it has been proven to His Eminence (may Allah prolong his life) that tomorrow, Thursday, is the first day of the blessed month of Ramadan in most Islamic countries such as Iraq, the remaining Arab countries, Iran, Pakistan, Indonesia, Malaysia, as well as India, Australia, the African nations, the nations of South America, the United States, and areas of southern Canada. As for most regions of Europe such as Britain, Ireland, France, Germany, Italy, Belgium, Holland, the Scandinavian nations, and most regions of Canada, the first day of the holy month will be the day after tomorrow, Friday. We ask Allah Almighty to make it a month of goodness and blessings for all Muslims.

The seal of the office of Sayyid al-Sistani
The Holy City of Najaf / The eve of Thursday,
Ramadan 1, 1431

بسم الله الرحمن الرحيم

يعلن مكتب سماحة السيد السيستاني في النجف الاشرف المؤمنين الكرام
انه تحقّت لدى سماحته دخول ظهور انجم عند (الخميس) هو اول ايام شهر
رمضان المبارك في معظم الدول الاسلامية كالعراق وسائر الدول الخليجية
وايران وباكستان واندونيسيا وماليزيا وكذلك في الهند واستراليا و
الدول الامريكية ودول امريكا الجنوبية والولايات المتحدة والجزء من جنوب
كندا . واما في اغلب مناطق اوربا كبريطانيا وايرلندا و فرنسا والمانيا و
ايطاليا وبلجيكا وهولندا والدول الاسكندنافية ومعظم اجزاء كندا فان
يوم بعد غدٍ (الجمعة) سيكون اول ايام الشهر الفضيل . نسأل الله
تبارك وتعالى ان يجعله شهر خير وبركة لجميع المسلمين .

ليلة الخميس ٨ رمضان ١٤٣١ هـ

If we refer to what the [astronomical] sources that track the conditions of the crescent published, including charts that depict the areas in which the crescent is visible if the conditions are clear (see below), we will see that all the areas designated in green have been included in the statement and it is consistent with the edict on the unity of horizons included in his manual of [Islamic] practice.

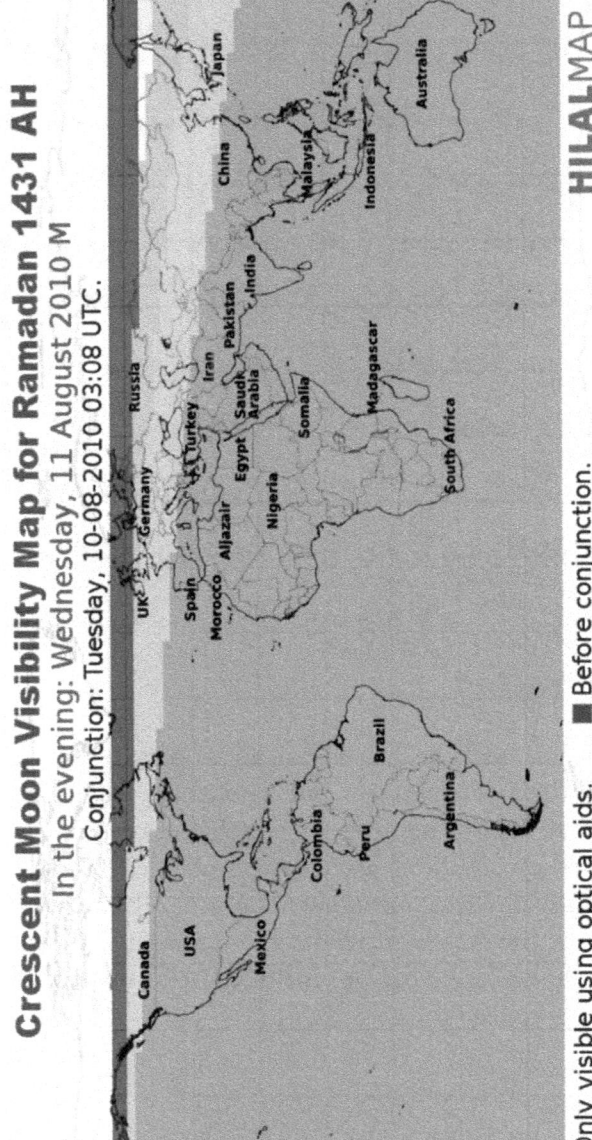

Crescent Moon Visibility Map for Ramadan 1431 AH
In the evening: Wednesday, 11 August 2010 M
Conjunction: Tuesday, 10-08-2010 03:08 UTC.

■ Only visible using optical aids.   ■ Before conjunction.
▨ May need optical aids.   ■ Moon has set.
▨ Easy for naked eye sighting.   ☐ Moon over the horizon, not visible.

HILALMAP
www.al-habib.info
(Criterion: Odeh 2006)

ANOTHER PRACTICAL MODEL FOR DETERMINING THE UNITY OF HORIZONS

Similarly, the office of His Eminence al-Sayyid al-Sistani confirmed the sighting of the crescent of the month of Ramadan 1433 A.H. in Najaf, Iraq, and some nearby cities at sunset on Friday, July 20, 2012. As a result, the office of His Eminence issued a statement specifying the horizon of Najaf and all other cities that share it (i.e., unity of horizon), beginning with Australia and ending with the United States. Below is a copy of the statement.

بسم الله الرحمن الرحيم

يعلن مكتب سماحة السيد السيستاني في النجف الاشرف للمؤمنين الكرام انه قدست لديه سماحته دام ظله ان غداً السبت هو اول ايام شهر رمضان المبارك في العراق وسائر الدول العربية وفي الدول الاسلامية المجاورة لها كما هو الحال في استراليا ومونزلندا والدول الامريكية والولايات المتحدة ودول امريكا الوسطى و الجنوبية . واما في بريطانيا والمانيا وفرنسا واطاليا و صوصاً الدول الاروبية وفي حفظكم فانه يكون يوم الاحد اول ايام الشهر الفضيل ، نسأل الله تعالى ان يجعل شهركم ومركم لجميع المسلمين انه سميع مجيب .

ليلة ١ // رمضان
١٤٣٣

Once again, this confirms that the statement includes all the areas designated in green (below).

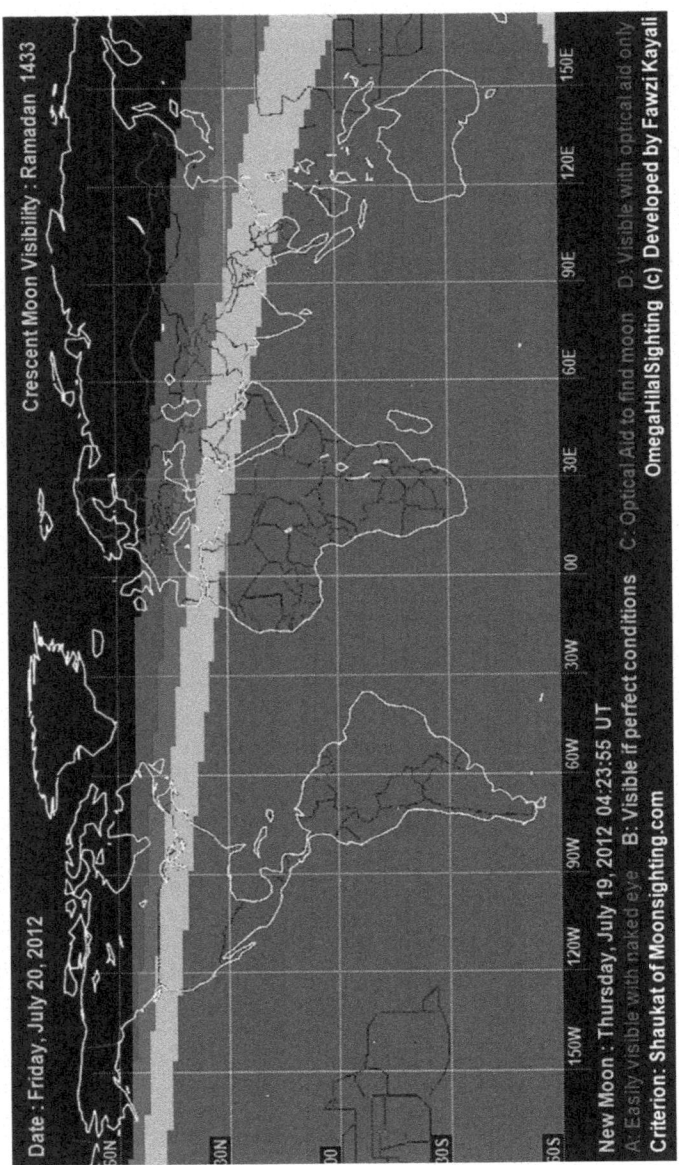

A CONTEMPORARY ISSUE RELATED TO FASTING, TRAVELING, AND DIFFERENT HORIZONS

If sighting of the crescent of the month of Ramadan occurs in the hometown of a duty-bound person who must fast while traveling (e.g., a frequent traveler), but they have traveled to another town which has a different horizon where the crescent has not been confirmed, then they do not have to fast that day. On the other hand, if sighting the crescent of the month of Shawwal occurs in their hometown but they have traveled to another town with a different horizon where the crescent has not been confirmed, then they must abstain from fast-nullifiers for the rest of that day and make it up later, both based on obligatory precaution.

Determining the beginning and end of the day according to Islamic law

After confirming the beginning of the month of Ramadan, a duty-bound person must ascertain the times of *imsak* or when to stop eating and drinking and the times of iftar or when to break the fast to ensure that their fasting is correct. Almighty God says, "Eat and drink until the white streak becomes manifest to you from the dark streak at the crack of dawn. Then complete the fast until nightfall."[136] It is clear from this holy verse that it is permissible to eat and drink until dawn, after which one must fast until the disappearance of the redness in the eastern sky (twilight).

---

136. The Quran 2:187, MS.

DETERMINING TIME OF DAWN (FAJR)

The following points contain detailed explanations about determining the time of dawn:

- One must abstain from fast-nullifiers when the white streak becomes manifest and distinguished from the dark streak as stated in the Holy Quran. This is known as true dawn (*al-fajr al-sadiq*). True dawn has a horizontal brightness on the horizon that is clearly apparent and emanates from the direction of sunrise and increases in intensity. This distinguishes true dawn from false dawn, which is a column of light that appears on the horizon, ascends vertically to the sky, diminishes, and weakens until it disappears.

- The means for establishing the time (of fajr) is either by [veritable] knowledge or contentment that it has set in or by using any rational means.

- The schedules and timetables issued by astronomers (for sunset, for example) are based on estimations and they cannot be relied upon unless the person derives contentment [from them] that the time has set in. Similarly, the sound of the adhan or call to prayer, heard from mosques and other Muslim places of worship, cannot be relied on unless the duty-bound person derives contentment that the time has set in.

- It is permissible for a person to practice *istishab* or consider it is still night and therefore continue eating and drinking until they know or are content that dawn has set in. However, it is better to abstain before that time (i.e., as a precaution) and delay dawn prayer slightly [to ensure the time of prayer has set in].

- It is permissible for spouses to practice istishab or consider it is still night and engage in intercourse if they are content that they will have enough time to perform the ritual bath (*ghusl*) before dawn sets in.

- It is not sufficient to resort to assumption (*dhan*) when determining the time of dawn, even if the duty-bound person has a personal excuse, like blindness or imprisonment, which prevents them from knowing it. As such, even if there is a natural obstruction (e.g., clouds) which prevents the determination of the time, the person must delay their prayer based on obligatory precaution until they are content that the time has arrived.

DETERMINING SUNSET TIME (MAGHRIB)

The following points describe how to determine the time of maghrib:

- The time of breaking the fast is when the redness in the eastern sky disappears, even if a person knows that the sun has set based on obligatory precaution.[137]

- The exact hour and minute when the eastern redness disappears varies from place to place and

---

137. This is a controversial issue among Imami Twelver jurists. For those people who wish to break their fast at sunset without waiting for the eastern redness to disappear, especially to join others in fast-breaking, and they do not believe that it is necessary to wait until the disappearance of the eastern redness if they are certain that the sun has set, then they may emulate the next most learned jurist who does not require waiting until the disappearance of the eastern redness.

time of year. Therefore, determinations must be made accordingly.

- If a person breaks their fast before sunset due to *taqiyya* or fear of serious harm to themselves, their property, or their dignity, then it becomes obligatory upon them to break their fast anyway, but they must make up the fast later and do not have to pay kaffarah.[138]

- If the time for maghrib prayer sets in for the duty-bound person's city while they are taking off in an airplane and heading west to a destination where the sun has not set, they do not need to wait for maghrib to occur at their destination [and therefore continue fasting], although the recommendation is to refrain from fast-nullifiers until sunset at the destination.

FASTING IN THE POLAR REGIONS

In the polar regions, the night becomes very short and sometimes there is no night at all. Similarly, days can be very short and sometimes there is no day at all. Based on these conditions, the duty-bound person must observe the following rulings:

- In the polar regions where the night is short and it is not completely dark, dawn starts when the light begins to increase on the horizon after its decrease in an observable way. Thus, the fasting

138. It is not justifiable for people to break their fast before the legal time in public iftar gatherings because they are joining other Muslims who break their fast earlier. This is not permissible even if it is to achieve unity with other Muslims. The religious rulings must be observed within their prescribed limits.

person must refrain from fast-nullifiers (i.e., imsak) right before that time and [thereafter] pray the fajr prayer but before sunrise. It is permissible to break the fast (i.e., iftar) at sunset if there is no eastern redness or if its redness persists. Hence, [when the days are very long (e.g., twenty-two hours)] the duty-bound person must fast the entire day if possible. However, if they experience severe hunger or thirst that is not bearable, then it is permissible for them to eat or drink the minimum amount necessary and abstain from anything more based on obligatory precaution, and they must make up the fast later. If eating and drinking the minimal amount is also not possible, then the obligation of fasting is revoked; however, they must make it up later.

- In the polar regions, fasting is not possible at times when there is no night or no day (i.e., there would be no way to delineate the start and end of the fast). In such cases, it is necessary for the person to move to another place where there is dawn and sunset so they can fast the month of Ramadan if possible. The other option is to wait for another time of the year in which they can make it up. If the person is not capable of making it up, even by moving to another place, they only have to offer a fidyah for each day they could not make up.

- If the night decreases to only a few hours and the level of light from sunset to sunrise does not change, then based on obligatory precaution, the person must fast from sunrise to sunset with the intention of raja, which means fasting with the hope that God desires it in this special case and make it up later. If the duty-bound person is not capable of doing so, they must travel to another place where there is dawn and sunset so they can fast the month of Ramadan if possible, or they can make it up later in the year. If the person is not capable of making up the fast, even if they travel to another place, they only have to offer a fidyah for each day they missed.

Fifth, Not Traveling

Almighty God says, "The month of Ramadan is one in which the Quran was sent down as guidance to mankind, with manifest proofs of guidance and the Criterion. So, let those of you who witness it fast [in] it, and as for someone who is sick or on a journey, let it be a [similar] number of other days. Allah desires ease for you, and He does not desire hardship for you, and so that you may complete the number, and magnify Allah for guiding you, and that you may give thanks."[139] Accordingly, one of the requirements of a valid fast is that the duty-bound person is not traveling, such that they must shorten their four-unit prayers, with certain exceptions.[140] What follows are detailed rulings which

---

139. The Quran 2:185, AQQ.

140. Among the exceptions are the following:
   - Fasting three days out of a total of ten as an atonement for not being able to offer a sacrifice in hajj
   - Fasting eighteen days in place of offering an animal sacrifice as an atonement for departing Arafat before sunset
   - Observing a fast to fulfill a vow to fast while traveling
   - Reports indicate that it is recommended for a person who has a need and wants it to be fulfilled to travel to the holy city of Medina and reside there for three days, Wednesday,

a duty-bound person who is traveling must know and observe, whether before, during, or after travel, to ensure that their fasting is valid.

Intending to travel

Recanting the intention to fast or being hesitant to fulfill it invalidates it. This will be explained in the section on the intention of fasting. Therefore, one who intends to travel must note the following:

- If the person travels before dhuhr prayer, it is permissible for them to break the fast. Rather, it is obligatory to break their fast based on obligatory precaution if they intended to travel the previous night.
- If the person travels after dhuhr prayer, they must continue fasting based on obligatory precaution especially if they did not make the intention to travel from the previous night.
- If the person decides to travel after the time of dhuhr prayer, even if they intended to do so the previous night, he must continue his fast based on obligatory precaution.

If a traveler returns to their hometown or enters a town where they will reside for ten days,

- the person must fast that day based on obligatory precaution if they enter the town before dhuhr

---

Thursday, and Friday; observe fasts; and spend the time in the holy shrine of the Prophet (pbuh&hp) engaged in remembrance of God. Then God will fulfill their need.

and they have not committed a fast-nullifier (e.g., eating), and the fast will be valid;

- the person does not have to fast if they enter the town after the time of dhuhr prayer, and it would not be valid if they do fast based on obligatory precaution. Rather, they must make it up later; and
- the criterion for whether the traveler has reached the town before dhuhr or after dhuhr is entering the town itself and not just reaching the outer limit or hadd al-tarrakhuss.

Five conditions

One of the conditions for the validity of fasting is not to be traveling, so it would be invalid if the fasting person travels. However, the invalidation of fasting [due to travel] is contingent upon five conditions:[141]

1. THE TRAVEL MUST BE LAWFUL.

A traveler must not shorten their four-unit prayers nor break their fast if the conditions of their travel include:

- distress to the parents, which would occur [due to the parents' legitimate concern for the person (e.g., harm)] if they embark upon the travel, since Islam prohibits causing distress to one's parents;
- a wife embarking on travel without the permission of her husband, unless the purpose of her travel is to fulfill an obligatory pilgrimage (i.e., once the criteria for her obligation are fulfilled) or visiting her kin if

---

141. The traveler must fastif one or more of the five conditions is not met.

the obligation of maintaining ties with them requires traveling, if doing so does not entail a forbidden act that would revoke the duty;

- traveling to commit an unlawful act (e.g., murder, adultery, robbery, unlawful trade) or visiting an oppressor for the purpose of aiding them in their oppression;
- being indebted to someone and traveling to flee from them; and
- hunting for amusement.[142] However, if the purpose of hunting is to secure a livelihood, then the traveler must shorten their prayers and break their fast.

2. THE PERSON MUST INTEND TO TRAVEL THE RELIGIOUSLY PRESCRIBED DISTANCE THAT WOULD MAKE THEM A TRAVELER AND MAINTAIN THAT DISTANCE.

The distance is equivalent to eight *farsakh*, which is 44.5 km or 27 miles one-way, or four farsakh [22.25 km or 13.5 mi] for each leg of a two-way or round-trip.

a. The religiously prescribed distance is calculated starting from the outer boundary of a town. However, in very large cities, the distance is calculated from the outer boundary of a given locality or even a particular neighborhood if the common view or urf [of the residents] is that a person is a traveler from that point.

b. The traveler must reach the outer limit or hadd al-tarrakhuss (as described above) before they can

---

142. Sayyid al-Sistani does not prohibit this form of hunting.

shorten their prayer or break their fast. This is usually the point outside the hometown where the buildings are no longer visible to the naked eye, which is approximately three to five km or two to three miles.

3. TRAVELING MUST NOT BE A [REGULAR] PART OF WORK OR THE NATURE OF THE WORK

Traveling must not be a [regular] part of work or the nature of the work, such as the jobs of a pilot, navigator, or taxi driver (NOTE: the taxi driver must shorten their prayer if they work locally and travel past the religiously prescribed distance). Similarly, this includes when a person's profession necessitates travel on a frequent basis, such as a physician who travels more than the religiously prescribed distance to different hospitals or a teacher who travels to different universities to teach. Such individuals must always perform full prayers and fast the month of Ramadan even if their travel does not repeat in certain months if they are considered a frequent traveler, moreover, their travel does not only have to be for work. A person, who is [only] required to travel for their work occasionally and the nature of their work does not include regular travel, must shorten their prayer and break their fast when traveling beyond the religiously prescribed distance.

4. THE TRAVELER MUST NOT PASS THROUGH AN AREA WHICH INTERRUPTS THEIR TRAVEL OR WHERE THEY ARE NO LONGER CONSIDERED A TRAVELER.

In the following instances, the person must pray full prayers and observe the fast of the month of Ramadan:

- Hometown of origin (*al-watan al-asli*): A person's birthplace, which can usually be the residence of their parents and remains their home unless they permanently abandon it as a place of residence (i.e., never plan to live there again). Therefore, if the person reaches their hometown during a trip and stays in it for a short while (it is not enough to just pass through it), they must perform full prayers and observe the fast if it is the month of Ramadan.

- Domicile of [temporary] stay (*watan al-iqamah*): A place where the person intends to reside for ten full days. Therefore, if a person reaches a place where they intend to stay for ten days they must pray full and fast because they are no longer a traveler and must note the following:

    o The ten days are calculated from the time the person enters the town during the day until the same time on the eleventh day when they intend to depart and to begin the journey away from where they were staying. However, if they arrive anytime during the night, the ten days must be calculated from the time of fajr of the following day to sunset (maghrib) of the tenth day.

    o The prayers are shortened as soon as they cross the boundary of the temporary domicile (i.e., upon departure) where they resided for ten days; it is not necessary for them to wait until they reach the outer limit (hadd al-tarrakhuss) [as they would if they were departing their home].

o Residing in one place for the entire duration of ten days. However, there is no problem in leaving for a couple of hours during the day to go to the outskirts of town.

o A place where a person remains for thirty days but is undecided about staying or leaving is also considered a temporary domicile. In such a case, they must begin performing full prayers and observe the fast of the month of Ramadan on the thirty-first day [and beyond].

- Long-term stay (LTS) (*watan al-itikhadhi*): A place where a person plans to stay long-term for work, school, summer or spring vacations, or similar purposes, even if they do not own property or a home there. Except for the first month of stay during which time the person must perform both full and shortened prayers and fast the month of Ramadan and make up those fasts based on obligatory precaution if one of the following criteria related to their stay in that place applies:

o Remain there for six hours during every trip, in twenty-two days every month, for four years

o Remain there for eight hours during every trip, in twenty days every month, for four years.

o Remain there for twelve hours during every trip, in fifteen days every month, for five years.

o Remain there for twelve hours during every trip, in twenty-two days every month, for three years.

o Remain there for twenty-four hours during every trip, in seven to eight days every month, for four years.

- o Remain there for twenty-four hours during every trip, in fifteen days every month, for three years.
- o Remain there for twenty-four hours during every trip, in twenty-two to thirty days every month, for one and a half years.

The following table contains more clarification.

	Hours each day	Days each month	Number of years	Ruling
1	24 hours	22-30 days	1½	LTS
2	24 hours	15 days	3	LTS
3	24 hours	7-8 days	4	LTS
4	24 hours	6 days	less than 5	LTS does not apply
			greater than or equal to 5	Observe precaution[143]
5	24 hours	4 days	less than 7	LTS does not apply;
			greater than or equal to 7	Observe precaution
6	12 hours	22 days	3	LTS
7	12 hours	15 days	5	LTS
8	12 hours	6 days	less than 7	LTS does not apply;
			greater than or equal to 7	Observe precaution
9	8 hours	20 days	4	LTS
10	6 hours	22 days	4	LTS

---

143. Obligatory precaution in this matter means performing both full and shortened prayers as well as fasting the month of Ramadan and making it up later.

5. THE PERSON MUST NOT BE A FREQUENT TRAVELER.

The person must not be a frequent traveler or someone who has no permanent residence, such as a nomad with no permanent home or a person who lives in a mobile home. These are individuals who travel [frequently] beyond the religiously prescribed distance for any reason and not necessarily for work or profession. This includes, for example, frequent visits to check on one's parents, visits to the holy shrines, visiting believers, travel for amusement, or a patient who goes to the hospital frequently for long-term treatment. A person who is considered a frequent traveler must always pray full prayers and fast in the month of Ramadan no matter where they are. A person is considered a frequent traveler if they

- plan to travel ten days every month for a period of six months in one year;[144]
- plan to travel ten days every month for a period of three months each year for two years or more;[16]
- plan to travel 8-9 days every month for a period of six months in one year. However, in this case they should shorten their prayers as well as pray in full, and fast (if in the month of Ramadan) as well

---

144. If the person is hesitant and does not feel certain that their status is that of a traveler (*musafir*), someone who is a frequent traveler, or is residing (*muqim*) when they settle in the new location where they have arrived, then they must observe precaution for the first two weeks or however long it takes them to become certain, by praying shortened prayers and full prayers, and by fasting (if in the month of Ramadan) as well as making it up later. This also applies for LTS.

as make it up later based on obligatory precaution.

- If the person travels less than these three scenarios, they must shorten their prayers and break their fast.

The table below contains more clarification.

	Overall duration	Number of days or trips	Ruling
1	Six months in one year or three months every year for two years or more	10 days each month	Frequent traveler
2	Five months in one year or 2½ months every year for two years or more	9 days in a month and 11 days in the following month (repeated in that sequence)	Frequent traveler
3	Five months in one year or 2½ months every year for two years or more	8 days in a month and 12 days in the following month (repeated in that sequence)	Frequent traveler
4	Five months in one year or 2½ months every year for two years or more	7 days in a month and 13 in the following month (repeated in that same sequence)	Frequent traveler
5	Five months in one year or 2½ months every year for two years or more	9 days in one month	Observe precaution (i.e., pray a shortened prayer as well as a full prayer, and observe a fast and make it up later).
6	Five months in one year or 2½ months every year for two years	8 days in one month	Observe precaution (i.e., pray a shortened prayer as well as a

	Overall duration	Number of days or trips	Ruling
	or more		full prayer, and observe a fast and make it up later).
7	Five months in one year or 2½ months every year for two years or more	6 days in one month and 14 in the following month (repeated in that sequence)	Observe precaution (i.e., pray a shortened prayer as well as a full prayer, and observe a fast and make it up later).
8	Five months in one year or 2½ months every year for two years or more	5 days in one month and 16 in the following month (repeated in that sequence)	Observe precaution (i.e., pray a shortened prayer as well as a full prayer, and observe a fast and make it up later).
9	Five months in one year or 2½ months every year for two years or more	4 days in one month and 16 in the following month (repeated in that sequence)	Not a frequent traveler
10	Five months in one year or 2½ months every year for two years or more	7 days or less every month	Not a frequent traveler
11	Five months in one year or 2½ months every year for two years or more	10 days or more every month	Observe precaution (i.e., pray a shortened prayer as well as a full prayer, and observe a fast and make it up later).
12	Five months in one year or 2½ months every year for two years or more	9 days or less every month	Not a frequent traveler
13	Four months in	12 days or more	Observe

	Overall duration	Number of days or trips	Ruling
	one year or two months every year for two years or more	every month	precaution (i.e., pray a shortened prayer as well as a full prayer, and observe a fast and make it up later).
14	Four months in one year or two months every year for two years or more	11 days or less every month	Not a frequent traveler
15	Three months in one year or 1½ months every year for two years or more	15 days or more every month	Not a frequent traveler
16	Three months in one year or 1½ months every year for two years or more	14 days or less every month	Not a frequent traveler
17	Two months in one year or one month every year for two years or more	22 days or more every month	Not a frequent traveler
18	Two months in one year or one month every year for two years or more	21 days or less every month	Not a frequent traveler

Rulings for people who follow others in their travel (e.g., wife, child, servant, soldier)

A person who is associated with the traveler (in terms of traveling with them) such as the wife who follows her husband, children who follow their father, an employee who follows their employer (e.g., servant), a prisoner transferred from one place to another by the person responsible for them, or the soldier who follows his commander wherever he goes in his mission should adhere to the rules that apply to the person they are following. This includes shortening their prayer and breaking their fast, or praying a full prayer and fasting, whether they chose to travel with them or had to do so, if the follower knows that the individual or group (as in the case of the army) they are following will travel the legal distance. When in doubt, they must pray a full prayer and continue to fast if it is the month of Ramadan. However, based on recommended precaution, the person should inquire about the distance they have traveled.

If the person who follows another decides to separate from them before reaching the religiously prescribed distance or is hesitant to do so, then they must continue to pray full prayers and observe fasts. The same applies if they are determined to separate from the person they are following upon fulfillment of certain conditions, such as a woman becoming divorced from her husband. The same ruling applies if there is a high probability of an impediment to the continuation of travel, such as a security hindrance. In general, if the person intends to travel the legal distance, but assumes there is a rational possibility that something will impede their travel, then they must pray full prayers and continue to fast, even if later they come to know that there was no impediment.

University students, ambassadors, and consuls

University students who reside outside of their hometowns during the period of their study, ambassadors, consuls, and similar individuals who settle outside their country or town of origin must consider the place where they have settled as their home if it is considered as such by common view. Therefore, their fasting would be valid and they must pray full prayers. However, during the first month of their settlement, they must combine shortening their prayers and praying in full as well as fasting the month of Ramadan and making it up based on obligatory precaution.[145]

Fasting of people with temporary occupations

Those with temporary occupations, such as managers of hajj caravans, those contracted to perform temporary tasks that involve traveling (e.g., security investigators), and those who temporarily reside outside their countries for certain periods and in their countries for the rest of the year fall under one of the following categories in terms of the rulings about their prayer and fasting:

---

145. If a person finds this precaution difficult, they may follow the next most learned jurist or intend to reside in the new place for ten days without leaving. Thus, they can observe a fast from day one and pray in full [and not have to make up the fast and pray shortened prayers as well]. Thereafter, they can switch their intention to residing for the period of their study.

Travel period	Ruling
Three months or more, for two years or more	Pray full prayers and fast
Two months or less	Pray a shortened prayer[146]
More than two months but less than three	Based on obligatory precaution combine performing shortened and full prayers, and fasting the month of Ramadan as well as making it up later.

Sixth, The State of Purity

Being in the state of purity is an obligation when one wants to perform obligatory prayers, fasting, or tawaf.

Ritual impurity due to *janabah* (sexual intercourse), *haydh* (menstruation), or *nifas* (postnatal bleeding)

The following are points related to ritual impurity:

- A fasting person, male or female, must be in a state of purity from janabah, haydh, or nifas before fajr sets in.
- If a fasting woman experiences bleeding from menstruation or postnatally, even if it is a few minutes before maghrib, her fast becomes invalid and she must make it up later.

---

146. However, anytime they intend to reside for ten days, not leave the town, and remain there after the ten days without initiating new travel, they must pray a full prayer and fast even if they are there for less than two months.

- If a woman must observe the rulings of *istihadha* (non-menstrual blood) and refrain from the acts that are not permissible for a woman in the state of nifas (after just giving birth) on account of adhering to precaution, then she must make up the fast of that day based on obligatory precaution.
- It is permissible for a woman to use means to delay her monthly menstrual cycle to fast the entire month of Ramadan if it does not cause her serious harm.

Performing tayammum in place of *ghusl*

A person must perform a ritual bath (ghusl) before dawn (fajr) to purify from janabah, menstruation (haydh), or postnatal bleeding (nifas). However, if there is not enough time to do so before fajr, then they must perform tayammum (dry ablution).

CONDITIONS AFFECTING PERMISSIBILITY OF PERFORMING TAYAMMUM IN PLACE OF GHUSL

The following conditions affect the permissibility of tayammum in place of ghusl:

- Cases when tayammum is warranted in place of ritual purification with water are as follows:

  o If there is not enough time to perform a ritual bath (ghusl) before fajr. For example, if there were only a few minutes left before dawn and there was not enough time to perform a ritual bath (ghusl), the person must perform tayammum immediately for their fast to be valid, and thereafter perform a ritual bath (ghusl) for dawn prayer.

o   If there is not enough water to perform a ritual bath (ghusl) and the person tries to acquire it but is incapable of doing so or there is not enough time to do so

o   If using water causes a person unbearable hardship; for example, if it results in infecting a wound or causes some other serious illness or harm which is usually unbearable

- If a person can use ice by melting it and performing ablution (wudu) or they are able to wipe the face and hands in a manner that is considered washing and wipe the head and feet with the moisture that remains on the palms, then they must do so and not perform tayammum.

THINGS WITH WHICH ONE CAN PERFORM TAYAMMUM

The following things are acceptable for performing tayammum:

- It is permissible to perform tayammum with anything considered to be earth, whether it is soil, sand, a clump of dirt, pebbles, or rocks. However, the recommended precaution is to use soil if possible. Moreover, it is necessary for whatever one uses to cling to (i.e., rub off onto) the skin based on obligatory precaution. Thus, tayammum is not valid with a smooth stone that has no dirt or dust on it.

- It is not permissible to perform tayammum with something usurped. However, if a person is compelled to remain on usurped land, they may perform tayammum on it, but instead of striking the earth they must [just] place their palms on it.

- It is permissible to perform tayammum with dust that has collected on clothes, carpet, or something similar if it is considered fine dust and has mass based on common view or urf.
- If it is not possible to perform tayammum with any of the above-mentioned substances, then the person must do so with anything that has dust on it. If the latter is also not possible, then the fasting will be valid. As for the prayer at that time, they will need to make it up later [once they are able to perform ritual purification].

HOW TO PERFORM TAYAMMUM IN PLACE OF GHUSL

The instructions that follow explain the performance of tayammum:

- The method of performing tayammum is to strike or place the palms of the hands on the earth and do so all at once based on obligatory precaution. Then, the person must wipe the entire forehead, based on obligatory precaution, from the hairline to the eyebrows and the bridge of the nose, including the temples. Then, they must wipe the whole of the back of the right hand, from the wrist to the tip of the fingers, with the palm of the left hand, and the whole of the back of the left hand, from the wrist to the tip of the fingers, with the palm of the right. It is not sufficient to wipe the left hand before the right based on obligatory precaution.

- One strike on the earth is sufficient for a valid tayammum, whether it is in place of ablution (wudu) or a ritual wash (ghusl), although the person should strike the earth once for wiping the face and a second time for wiping the hands based on recommended precaution. In fact, it is even better to strike the earth once to wipe the face and hands, and then strike it a second time to wipe the hands [again].
- If there is a barrier (e.g., a cast) over the part being wiped, which cannot be removed, then the person should wipe over that barrier. If the palm itself has a barrier on it, the person should wipe with an uncovered part of the palm.

CONDITIONS OF TAYAMMUM

The list below explains the conditions for valid tayammum.

- One must have an intention of nearness to God for tayammum, just like wudu and ghusl, and based on obligatory precaution, the intention should be made at the same time the hands strike or are placed on the earth.
- It is not necessary to intend to perform tayammum in place of ablution (wudu) or the ritual bath (ghusl); rather it suffices if it is for nearness to God.
- Tayammum lifts the state of impurity (hadath) if it does not become nullified (e.g., by urinating).
- A person must perform tayammum without the assistance of someone else and do so in close succession (i.e., without interruption) and in the

correct sequence. Based on obligatory precaution, wiping should occur from top to bottom. Tayammum becomes invalid if not done in the proper sequence and its completion is interrupted, even if this occurs due to ignorance or forgetfulness. However, it is valid if there is no interruption and they [immediately] restart the tayammum and use the correct sequence.

- The hair [from the scalp] that falls on the forehead must be lifted to wipe directly on the skin of the forehead, whereas the person should wipe over the hair that grows on the forehead if it is not longer than normal; otherwise it must be removed.

- Any rings worn on the fingers (i.e., that constitute a barrier) must be removed during tayammum.

- If a person doubts whether there is a barrier such as nail polish or glue on one of the parts of tayammum, then they must examine themselves to the extent that they become certain or content that it is not there.

Seventh, Intention

Fasting the holy month of Ramadan becomes compulsory if all the previously mentioned conditions are met. At that point, it is necessary to establish the intention to fast seeking nearness to God which is an essential requirement in many acts of worships. Narrations tell us that the Prophet (pbuh&hp) said, "Verily [the significance of] actions are by intentions,"[147] and Imam

---

147. al-Majlisi, *Bihar al-anwar*, vol. 67, p. 212.

Zayn al-Abidin (p) is reported to have said, "No act [of worship is valid] without an intention."[148] Hence, it is imperative for a person who wishes to fast to recognize and be attentive to the importance of intention and its effect on this holy act of worship.

Intention of seeking nearness to God

The intention of fasting is characterized by deliberateness in seeking nearness to God,[149] which means that a person intends to abstain from certain acts (i.e., fast-nullifiers) out of obedience and submission to God, the Exalted. Therefore, if a person abstains from fast-nullifiers (e.g., eating and drinking) due to lack of desire,[150] only with the goal of taming carnal desires,[151]

---

148. al-Kulayni, *al-Kafi*, vol. 2, p. 84.

149. There are three types of acts when it comes to intention:
- Acts that require intention of nearness to God, such as praying and fasting
- Acts that require intention, but without delineating it as nearness to God, like conducting transactions (e.g., buying, selling, renting, marriage, and divorce) Acts that do not require an intention nor delineation of nearness to God, such as purifying an impure object. For example, if a person has a shirt that has become impure and it accidentally falls under the rain or in water, then it becomes pure even though they did not intend to purify it.

150. Like someone who does not desire food at all and does not eat except when necessary (i.e., they eat something simple at night) or someone who does not feel the desire to have sex during the day at all.

151. Like someone who practices yoga or engages in certain spiritual practices that may require abstaining from food, drink, and sex for long hours, noting that Islam forbids some of these spiritual practices.

or only to protest something,[152] then it does not constitute a valid fast. Therefore, the intent of abstaining must solely be out of obedience and submission to God, the Exalted, and it must not be to show off, because this would invalidate the fast.

Continuity of intention

It is necessary to maintain a continuous intention during the entire period of fasting, in addition to abstaining from the fast-nullifiers, out of obedience and submission to God, the Exalted. This means that the person should have full awareness of their obligation and never hesitate in continuing the fast with that intention.

Time of intention

What follows are some rulings related to the time of one's intention:

- The time of intention differs based on the type of fasting. There are three major types:

  o Fixed and specified obligatory fasts[153] such as the fasts of the month of Ramadan. The intention must be made prior to fajr based on obligatory precaution. It is also permissible for

---

152. For example, someone who goes on a hunger strike in a prison for a political position.

153. The fixed and specified obligation has a specified time, such as fasting the month of Ramadan, which would not be valid in Shaban or Shawwal (i.e., it must be during the month of Ramadan, from the first day until the last).

the duty-bound person to make the intention each night to fast the following day or from the first night and before fajr of the first day to fast the entire month.

o Extended and unspecified obligatory fasts[154] such as the missed fasts of the month of Ramadan. A person can make the intention until before dhuhr sets in as long as they have not committed any fast-nullifiers. If dhuhr sets in, and the person has not made the intention to fast, even if they wished to do so, their fast would be invalid based on obligatory precaution.

o Recommended fasts. The time for making the intention extends all the way until moments before maghrib if the person has not committed a fast-nullifier during that day.

• If a person does not make the intention to fast because they forgot or were ignorant of the rule, or they forgot or were ignorant of the fact that the month of Ramadan had begun, and they came to know or remember before dhuhr, they must make the intention to fast and it would be valid if they have not committed a fast-nullifier. However, if they remember or come to know after dhuhr sets in, then based on obligatory precaution they must abstain from fast-nullifiers for the rest of the day with the intention of absolute nearness to God[155]

---

154. The extended and unspecified obligation does not have a specified time, such as making up the missed fasts from the month of Ramadan. These may be made up any time during the year.

155. Absolute nearness (*al-qurbah al-mutlaqa*) means that a person intends to abstain from fast-nullifiers for the sake of absolute

and make up the day later. Also, precaution must be observed by intending to fast and continuing the fast with hope that it is desired by God.

- If a person fasts to make up a fast that they believe is missed, then they may break it anytime during the day, before dhuhr or after, if they choose.

Changing intention

It is not permissible to change the intention from one type of fast to another, such as changing from making up a missed day of the month of Ramadan to a vowed or recommended fast, because this is a breach of the intention and doing so invalidates the fast. However, if the person makes an intention to end the fast, and right before noon intends a different fast, it would be valid if they did not commit a fast-nullifier.

The intention of fasting the last day of Shaban

The following are rulings concerning fasting intention for the last day of Shaban:

- It is permissible to fast the last day of Shaban with an intention, whether recommended or obligatory, of it being what is known (i.e., last day of Shaban or first of the month of Ramadan). This means that the person should make an intention for a recommended fast if it is the last day of

---

nearness to God and not with a specific intention of it being an obligatory fast.

Shaban and an obligatory fast if it is indeed the first day of the month of Ramadan.

- It is invalid and not permissible to fast the last day of Shaban with an intention of it being the first day of the month of Ramadan without establishing that the latter has started, even if it turns out to be the former.
- If a person fasts the last day of Shaban as a recommended or make-up fast, or to fulfill a vow, and they find out later that it is the first of the month of Ramadan, their fast will count as part of Ramadan, and if they come to know before dhuhr they must change their intention to a fast for the month of Ramadan.
- If a duty-bound person wakes up with the intention of not fasting thinking that it is the thirtieth of Shaban (Day of Doubt), and they come to know that it is the first day of the month of Ramadan before dhuhr, then they must make the intention and fast the first of the month Ramadan if they have not committed a fast-nullifier. If they find out that it is the first of the month of Ramadan before dhuhr but they committed a fast-nullifier, then they must abstain from any further fast-nullifiers for the rest of the day based on obligatory precaution and make up the day later. On the other hand, if they find out after dhuhr and they have not committed any fast-nullifiers, then based on obligatory precaution they must fast with the intention of raja[156] and make it up

---

156. The intention of absolute nearness means to intend complying with one of the possible obligations.

later. If they find out after dhuhr, but they committed a fast-nullifier, then they must abstain from any further fast-nullifier for the rest of the day and make up the fast later based on obligatory precaution.

Sleep, insanity, unconsciousness, and intoxication

The rulings for situations when one is not in full possession of one's faculties are as follows:

- Sleeping all day from fajr until maghrib while fasting does not invalidate the intention if the person made the intention to fast before fajr (even the night before).
- The rulings for insanity, unconsciousness, and intoxication are different from sleep. A person who has a mental impairment or who passes out involuntarily and later becomes mentally cognizant or wakes up, respectively, during the day must abstain from fast-nullifiers with the intention of (dhimmah). If they do not, then they must make up the day later.
- A person who voluntarily becomes intoxicated or purposefully does something to pass out (not sleep) must complete the fast for that day and make it up later if they made the intention to fast before fajr.

The intention of raja is to perform an act hoping that it is desired and accepted by God (rather than not) in cases of uncertainty of whether the act is obligatory (i.e., legislated), thus, it is performed with the hope of it being so.

- If a person is voluntarily induced into a coma for the entire day, such as someone who is going to have surgery, then they must make up the fast of that day based on obligatory precaution.

Hesitancy of intention

The following rulings involve hesitancy of intention to fast:

- It is obligatory to maintain the intention of fasting until the end of the day. Therefore, if a person intends to break their fast or becomes hesitant about continuing it for any reason, then it becomes invalid based on obligatory precaution even if they return to their previous intention of fasting. Moreover, the person must abstain from fast-nullifiers until the end of the day and make up the fast based on obligatory precaution.
- A person's fast remains valid if they become hesitant because they doubt the validity of their fast.
- If a person observes an unassigned fasting such as making up a missed day from the month of Ramadan, and intends to break their fast or becomes hesitant as to whether they will continue to fast, their fast is valid if they return to their original intention of fasting before dhuhr sets in.

Intention of fasting for a traveler

Refer to the previously mentioned rulings on the conditions of valid fasting of a traveler.

If all the aforementioned conditions of a valid fast are fulfilled, in addition to making the intention to fast out of obedience to God, the duty-bound person must learn the fast-nullifiers that must be avoided. These fast-nullifiers are explained in the next section.

Fast-Nullifiers

The significance behind the worship of fasting is to abstain from certain things out of obedience and submission to God; these are known as fast-nullifiers (*mufattirat*).

Before getting into the details of the fast-nullifiers, it is important to point out that a fast is invalid only if a person knowingly and willfully commits a fast-nullifier. Therefore, if a person commits a fast-nullifier unintentionally or due to forgetfulness, their fast remains valid, irrespective of the type (fixed and specified, recommended, etc.).

If someone deliberately eats, drinks, or engages in sexual intercourse, whether they know they are fast-nullifiers or not, their fast is invalid. However, the fast is not invalid if the person commits one of the other fast-nullifiers out of inculpable ignorance[157] of the

---

157. A person who is inculpably ignorant has a valid excuse for not knowing the ruling, whereas someone who is culpably ignorant does not. For example, an inculpably ignorant person is someone who might have relied on a certain jurisprudential source for a given ruling and found out later that they were wrong [in their understanding of the ruling] or they emulated a qualified jurist not knowing that the jurist had changed his ruling. Similarly, a person is considered inculpably ignorant if they think that a prohibited act is permissible on account of living far away from a religious environment. In contrast, a culpably ignorant person is someone who fails to learn the rulings that are relevant to the fulfilment of their religious duties such as praying, fasting the month of Ramadan, avoiding backbiting, consumption of alcoholic beverages, and adultery; or someone who believes that something is permissible due to being negligent in learning [the rules].

ruling. On the other hand, a person's fast is invalid if they commit a fast-nullifier due to willful negligence in learning the ruling. As for an inculpable ignorant who is hesitant about a nullifier, they must not [even] intend to commit it because this is contrary to the intention of abstaining from all the fast-nullifiers.

The fast of a person forced to eat, drink, or engage in sexual intercourse is invalid, and they must make it up later unless they were stripped of their will (i.e., physically forced) such that water was forced down their throat, then their fast is valid. However, if they are forced to commit any of the other fast-nullifiers, then they should complete their fast and make it up later based on recommended precaution.

First & Second: Eating and Drinking

Knowingly eating or drinking invalidates a person's fast, even if it is a very small amount (e.g., the food that remains between the teeth, medicine, or gum). On the other hand, the fast is not invalid if a person mistakenly or forgetfully eats or drinks something, even if it is a lot.

Rinsing the mouth

Rinsing the mouth is recommended for ablution (wudu), yet the person should ensure that water is not swallowed. However, the fast remains valid if water enters the esophagus inadvertently, provided the rinsing was for ablution (wudu), otherwise it would become invalid.

Rinsing the nose

It is permissible to aspirate water through the nose for the purposes of rinsing if the person is certain that it will not enter the esophagus. The fast is invalid if the water enters the esophagus; however, the person must continue abstaining from fast-nullifiers for the rest of the day and make up the fast later.

The use of asthma inhalers does not invalidate fasting if there are no medicinal particles that enter the esophagus. If use of the inhaler is necessary [for the person's health] and it is known that the medicinal particles will enter the esophagus, then it is permissible to break the fast. However, it must be made up later if possible.

Swallowing saliva

Swallowing saliva that collects in the mouth, when a person purposely smells a fragrance or remembers a certain taste, does not invalidate a fast irrespective of the quantity of saliva.

Tasting food

Tasting food while cooking, preparing, or chewing it for a toddler does not invalidate a fast if the person does not swallow it and provided they spit [any remnants out] three times afterwards.

Phlegm and mucus

Swallowing one's own phlegm or mucus does not invalidate the fast; however, it is a recommended precaution not to do so.

Chewing gum

Chewing gum does not invalidate a fast, even if the person can taste its flavor, if it does not have particles like sugar that dissolve, spread with the saliva, and are swallowed, unless it is so minute that it disintegrates and disappears with chewing and does not go down the esophagus as particles. In any case, a person must avoid chewing gum unless they are certain not to swallow any particles.

Moisturizing the lips

It is permissible for a fasting person to use lip moisturizers or balms, and it does not invalidate the fast.

Fragrances, eyeliner, and body lotion

The following are rulings about fragrances and some cosmetics:

- There is no problem if a fasting person applies eyeliner even if they taste it in their mouth, nor is there a problem with using fragrances, even if they are strong. However, it is detestable (makruh) to smell fragrant plants like flowers.
- Applying creams or lotions to moisturize the face and body or applying deodorants does not invalidate a fast.

Brushing the teeth

The following rulings concern care of the teeth:

- It is permissible for a fasting person to use a toothbrush and other things to clean their teeth during the day provided they do not swallow anything during the cleaning process. Moreover, there is no problem if there are little particles that disintegrate and dissolve in the saliva. However, after brushing their teeth, the person must spit out all the rinse water (e.g., by spitting three times) to ensure that nothing goes down the esophagus.
- It is not necessary for a person who intends to fast to floss their teeth after eating, even if there is a chance that not doing so will result in swallowing the food that is inadvertently stuck between the teeth. However, if they know that leaving food debris in the mouth will result in it entering the esophagus, then they must floss it out.

Dental treatment and blood from the gums

These rulings cover other dental treatments:

- It is permissible for a fasting person to get dental treatment during the day if they can ensure that nothing (e.g., water or medicine) enters their esophagus. However, the fast is invalid if something accidently enters, and it must be made up. On the other hand, if they are uncertain that nothing will enter their esophagus, they must not undergo dental treatment during the day and instead seek it at night or after the month of

Ramadan, if it is not an urgent or immediately needed treatment.

- If a person suffers from bleeding gums, the blood enters their esophagus while sleeping, and they are unable to prevent it, then their fasting remains valid. However, if during the day the person swallows the blood that mixes with saliva due to severe difficulty in spitting it out, then their fast is invalid, they must abstain from fast-nullifiers for the remainder of the day, and make it up later.

Using medicine

What follows are edicts on using medicine while fasting:

- Injecting medicine into the veins or the muscle does not invalidate a fast, even if the person is not in dire need of it and it alleviates hunger and thirst.
- Applying medicine [such as drops] into the eyes or ears does not invalidate a fast, even if its color or taste reaches the mouth.
- Any treatment that does not enter the esophagus and is not considered food or drink does not invalidate a fast (e.g., if medicine is applied to a wound or to the private parts).
- It is permissible to take a medicinal pill for necessary treatment during the day; however, the fast becomes invalid and must be made up later. Moreover, if the person cannot make up the missed fast [because the need for taking the medicine continues until the following month of

Ramadan], then they only must offer a fidyah of feeding one poor person for each day.

Use of energizers

There is no problem with injecting supplements into the vein, even if they provide energy. However, if food and drink are delivered to the stomach through some other means, such that it is considered eating or drinking, then the fast is invalid.

Medical imaging

Ultrasound examinations and other such imaging that take images of the inside of the body do not invalidate a fast provided that no substances (e.g., contrast dye) enter the esophagus in the process.

Third: Sexual Practices

Intercourse

The following are rulings on sexual intercourse and fasting:

- Sexual intercourse invalidates fasting for both participants, whether it is vaginal or anal, and even if it is with other than a person. It becomes invalid as soon as penetration occurs, even if the person does not reach sexual climax and ejaculation and even if they do not intend to ejaculate. Similarly, masturbation also invalidates fasting regardless of whether the act is permissible (e.g., stimulation by a person's lawful spouse).

- The fast of a person who intends to engage in sexual intercourse during the day is invalid because it constitutes breaking the intention to fast the entire day. Therefore, even if they do not engage in sexual intercourse, they must abstain from fast-nullifiers and make up the fast later. However, they do not have to offer a kaffarah.
- Fasting does not become invalid if a person intends to engage in foreplay with their spouse and penetration occurs unintentionally.

Masturbation

These rulings concern masturbation and fasting:

- Masturbation, as defined by religious law, is the act of climaxing and it is either permissible or prohibited.
  - o Permissible masturbation is when a person stimulates their spouse to reach sexual climax.
  - o Prohibited masturbation is when a person uses their own hand or some other means to reach sexual climax, even if it is by imagining.
- Both permissible and prohibited forms of masturbation invalidate a fast if it reaches sexual climax or even if the person intends to reach climax and they do not.
- The fast remains valid if a person accidently reaches sexual climax or ejaculates but they did not intend to do so and were [previously] confident that it would not occur.

- If a person masturbates knowing that it invalidates the fast or does not know due to culpable ignorance,[158] they must make up the fast and offer kaffarah.

- If a person willfully masturbates but does not reach sexual climax or ejaculate, their fast is invalid, they must abstain from fast-nullifiers for the rest of the day and must make up the fast later.

- If a person accidently reaches sexual climax or ejaculates after [only] engaging in foreplay with their spouse when they were not certain that it would not occur [by continuing to do so], then their fast is invalid and they must make it up later. In this case, they must also offer kaffarah if they knew that this act would invalidate the fast. However, they do not have to offer kaffarah if they were inculpably ignorant about the ruling. In contrast, a culpably ignorant person must offer a kaffarah based on obligatory precaution if they

---

158. A person who is inculpably ignorant has a valid excuse for not knowing the ruling, whereas someone who is culpably ignorant does not. For example, an inculpably ignorant person is someone who might have relied on a certain jurisprudential source for a given ruling and found out later that they were wrong [in their understanding of the ruling], or they emulated a qualified jurist not knowing that the jurist had changed his ruling. Similarly, a person is considered inculpably ignorant if they think that a prohibited act is permissible on account of living far away from a religious environment. In contrast, a culpably ignorant person is someone who fails to learn the rulings that are relevant to the fulfilment of their religious duties such as praying and fasting the month of Ramadan; avoiding backbiting, consumption of alcoholic beverages, and adultery; or someone who believes that something is permissible due to being negligent in learning [the rules].

were unsure of the ruling; otherwise, they do not need to do so.

- If a person masturbates knowing that it is unlawful but confident that it does not invalidate their fast, they do not have to offer kaffarah, and this rule applies to both men and women.

Fourth & Fifth: Deliberately Remaining in the State of Janabah, Haydh, or Nifas until Fajr

Janabah

These next rulings concern remaining in janabah:[159]

- A *mujnib* who is unable to perform a ritual bath (ghusl) or dry ablution (tayammum) is absolved of that obligation and their fast is valid.
- The fast of a person who willfully becomes mujnib during a night in the month of Ramadan knowing the time is too short to perform a ritual bath (ghusl) or dry ablution (tayammum) is invalid. If they can perform tayammum (i.e., there is enough time), then they must do so and their fast will be valid. However, their fast is invalid if they have sufficient time and do not perform tayammum, and they must make up the fast and offer kaffarah.

---

159. Ritual impurity that results from sexual intercourse, sexual climax, or ejection of semen. A mujnib is a person in the state of janabah.

- A mujnib must perform dry ablution (tayammum) before dawn if they are unable to perform a ritual bath (ghusl) during the night of the month of Ramadan due to illness. They do not need to remain awake until fajr if they do so. However, they are considered deliberately remaining in janabah until fajr if they do not perform dry ablution (tayammum).

- Nothing is required of a person who becomes mujnib after assuming there is enough time, but then realizes that there is not enough time to perform even dry ablution (tayammum). Thus, they should continue their fast. However, they should perform ghusl before praying fajr.

- A person must make up the fast(s) if they realize after a day or even a few days in the month of Ramadan that they forgot to perform a ritual bath (ghusl), but they do not have to offer kaffarah.

- There is no difference between men and women in janabah rulings. A woman becomes in the state of janabah either by penetration or when she reaches sexual climax.

Menstruation (haydh) and postnatal bleeding (nifas)

The following are edicts on menstruation and postnatal bleeding during fasting:

- The rulings of janabah apply to menstruation and postnatal bleeding. Therefore, a fast of the month of Ramadan, or its qada based on obligatory precaution, is invalid if a woman who has ended menses or postnatal bleeding does not perform a ritual bath (ghusl) before dawn. The fast of a woman is valid if her menstruation or postnatal bleeding ends, even if she is still bleeding, but does not have enough time to perform a ritual bath (ghusl) or dry ablution (tayammum) or she finds out after fajr that her menstruation or postnatal bleeding had ended.

- Unlike for the state of janabah, a woman's fast is valid (i.e., there is no qada) if she ends menstruation or postnatal bleeding but forgets to perform a ritual wash (ghusl) before dawn and realizes after a day or more.
- All types of non-menstrual bleeding (istihadha) do not invalidate the fast, and unlike prayer, performing a ritual bath is not a condition of the fast's validity.

Sleep of a person who is in the state of janabah, haydh, nifas until fajr in the nights of the month of Ramadan

What follows are rulings about sleeping at night while in the state of janabah during the month of Ramadan:

- If a person becomes in the state of janabah at night during the month of Ramadan and sleeps before performing a ritual bath (ghusl),
  - o the ruling of deliberately remaining in the state of janabah applies if they willfully do not perform the ritual bath (ghusl) before fajr. They must make up the fast and offer kaffarah
  - o the ruling of deliberately remaining in the state of janabah applies if they are unsure that

they will wake up to perform a ritual bath (ghusl) before fajr [and do not do so] based on obligatory precaution. They must make up the fast and offer kaffarah

- If a person sleeps intending to perform a ritual bath (ghusl) before fajr after becoming in the state of janabah during a night in the month of Ramadan,

    o the fast is valid if the person does not wake up from their first [and only] bout of sleep and they were confident [before sleeping] that they would wake up before fajr [to have time to perform ghusl] due to an alarm clock or on account of habitually doing so. However, they must make up the fast based on obligatory precaution if they were not confident about waking up.

    o they must make the fast up if they slept knowing they were in the state of janabah, woke up from their first bout of sleep before fajr, went back to sleep again [without performing ghusl], and then woke up after fajr. However, they do not have to offer kaffarah

    o they must make the fast up if they woke up twice before fajr but went back to sleep [without performing ghusl] each time and thereafter woke up after fajr

    o in all three cases, the person should offer kaffarah based on recommended precaution if they were not confident about waking up.

The same rulings apply to a woman who experiences sexual climax or becomes in the state of janabah during the night.

- The sleep in which a person has a nocturnal emission at night is considered the first bout of sleep. Hence, if they wake up and go back to sleep again, it would be the second bout of sleep.
- A person in the state of janabah must make up the fast if they sleep heedless of the need to perform ghusl and not about having to fast the next day.
- If a person who is in the state of janabah is not confident that they will wake up in time [to perform ghusl] before dawn, they must not go to sleep based on obligatory precaution. They must make up the fast based on obligatory precaution if they sleep and wake up after fajr, and offer kaffarah based on a recommended precaution.
- The rulings concerning the first, second, and third bouts of sleep for janabah do not apply to a woman who has ended menstruation or postnatal bleeding. Her fast is valid provided she is not negligent in performing a ritual bath (ghusl) before fajr. Her fast is invalid if she is neglectful about waking up before dawn to perform a ritual bath (ghusl), even if this was her first bout of sleep.

Waking up after fajr in the state of janabah or having an emission [during sleep] during the day

The following are decisions about becoming janabah involuntarily:

- A fast is not invalid if a person wakes up in the morning in the state of janabah [after not being so when they went to sleep], even if their sleep extends past fajr.
- A person's fast is valid if they have an emission while sleeping during the day and they do not have to perform a ritual bath (ghusl) for their fast to be valid. However, they must perform ghusl for prayer.
- A man who involuntarily becomes janabah during the day may urinate to clear the urethra (*istibra*) of any remaining semen. However, if he performs a ritual bath (ghusl) before istibra, the recommended precaution is to delay istibra until after maghrib, even if he knows that no semen will come out, provided that delaying it does not result in harm.

Sixth: Deliberately Causing Thick Dust or Smoke to Reach the Throat

These rulings concern dust or smoke during fasting:

- The fast of a person who deliberately causes thick dust or smoke to enter their throat is invalid based on obligatory precaution. However, there is no problem if the dust is thin, like dust rising in the air due to sweeping, movement, or something similar.
- A fasting person must avoid smoking (cigars, pipes, and hookahs) and the smoke that comes from burning firewood.
- A fasting person must avoid thick dust, especially when exposed to it during work. Examples include

demolishing old buildings; working in flour plants or cement factories; transferring bags of flour or cement; and other similar sources of exposure.

- A fasting person must prevent thick dust from reaching the throat when encountering a sand storm, even if by wearing a face mask.

The use of an inhaler

The rulings about using inhalers are as follows:

- It is permissible to use an inhaler to treat asthma if it enters the windpipe. However, the fast is invalid if its droplets collect in the mouth and enter the esophagus. If a fasting person needs to use an inhaler that invalidates a fast, they must make it up later, and they do not have to make up the fast if the illness continues until the next month of Ramadan, but they must offer a fidyah.
- It is permissible for a person with asthma to use vapor inhalants as treatment if the steam and whatever medicine it contains does not enter the esophagus, because that will invalidate the fast. It is permissible to use vapor inhalants if necessary [for treatment]; however, the person will need to make up the fast if possible (i.e., as determined by the persistence of the illness).
- Steam does not invalidate fasting unless it turns into water droplets in the mouth and is then swallowed.

Smoking

The following are rulings about smoking:

- Smoking is considered heavy smoke. Therefore, it invalidates the fast based on obligatory precaution irrespective of whether a person can stop [during the month].
- If a person smokes during the day, they must abstain from all fast-nullifiers for the remainder of the day with the intention of hoping that this is what God has ordained and then make up the fast based on obligatory precaution.
- A fasting person must avoid using electronic cigarettes (liquid that contains nicotine and fruit flavors converted into vapor upon inhalation) based on obligatory precaution, and it would invalidate the fast if the vapor droplets collect in the mouth and enter the esophagus in a way that would be customarily considered drinking.

Seventh: Applying Liquid Enema

The rulings concerning liquid enema are as follows:

- Applying liquid enema invalidates the fast even if it is necessary for treating an illness. However, there is no problem in using a solid enema, or a liquid enema that does not ascend past the anus.
- Fasting is valid if a woman applies liquids such as vaginal creams or solid enema in her private [reproductive] area and there is no problem with the insertion of medical instruments for the purpose of examination.

Suppositories

The use of solid suppositories does not invalidate fasting, however, it is not permissible to use suppositories that melt immediately after being placed in the anus.

Surgery and treatment of fistulas and hemorrhoids

Applying ointments and medicines to treat fistulas, hemorrhoids and similar ailments does not invalidate fasting.

Eighth: Deliberately Ascribing False Things to Allah and the Infallibles

These edicts concern ascribing false things to Allah and the infallibles (pbut) and how this affects fasting:

- A fast is invalid based on obligatory precaution if a person ascribes a false statement to or lies about God Almighty, the holy Prophet (pbuh&hp), or one of the twelve holy Imams (pbut), irrespective of whether the information is relevant to religious or worldly matters.
- The fast of a person is valid if they ascribe something to God or one of the infallibles with the belief that it is true but realize afterwards that it was false. However, if they ascribe something with the belief that it was false and found out afterwards that it was true, then their fast is invalid.
- A fasting person must not report a hadith by saying "The infallible said..." and ascribe it to one

of the infallibles (pbut) if they do not have any evidence of its authenticity because this would be considered a form of lying. In all cases, it is better to quote a hadith by saying "It is reported that the infallible (p) said..." rather than "The infallible (p) said..."

- When conducting an *istikhara*, it is not permissible to report that something good or something evil will happen and attribute it to God, the Exalted, because this is a form of prognosticating the unseen and is considered falsely ascribing things to God, the Exalted. Instead, if a person wishes to perform an istikhara they should say for example, "The apparent meaning of the verse suggests that the matter is good, God willing" or "The apparent meaning of the verse suggests that the matter is not good."

Ninth: Deliberately vomiting

The following are rulings about vomiting and fasting:

- Fasting becomes invalid by deliberately vomiting, even if there is a need for it such as treatment. However, involuntarily vomiting does not invalidate fasting.
- Fasting does not become invalid by vomiting due to an illness or a natural bodily cause as opposed to if it is just spontaneous.
- It is permissible for a fasting person to burp, even if they think it is possible that something (i.e., food or drink) will come up with it. However, if they are certain that something will come up,

then they must avoid burping based on obligatory precaution.

- The fast remains valid if a person burps and some food or drink is regurgitated to the mouth and then involuntarily enters the esophagus. However, if it reaches the mouth and the fasting person voluntarily swallows it, then their fast is invalid based on obligatory precaution, they must make it up later, and they must offer kaffarah.
- If a fasting person knowingly swallows something at night that will cause them to vomit the [next] day, then their fast is invalid in the event they do so.

Tenth: Immersing the Head under Water

Several jurists have mentioned that immersing the head under water, such as in swimming, invalidates a fast; however, this is not established, although it is highly detestable.

Making Up Missed Fasts and Offering Kaffarah and Fidyah

A duty-bound person who has missed fasts of the month of Ramadan must fulfill the following duties in terms of making up the fast and offering kaffarah or fidyah:

- A person must make up missed fasts of the month of Ramadan later.

- If a person is sick before or becomes sick during the month of Ramadan, and their sickness continues until the following month of Ramadan, they do not have to make up the fast even if they eventually recover from the illness after a year or even several years. However, they must offer fidyah for each day they missed.

- It is not permissible for a person who has a missed fast (qada) of the month of Ramadan to observe a recommended fast until they make up the missed one. On the other hand, if the person must fast due to kaffarah or if they were hired to fast on behalf of a deceased person, then they may observe a recommended fast according to certain conditions mentioned in more detailed books.

- It is not obligatory to make up the missed fast immediately nor to do so in the order missed. It is also not necessary to specify which fast a person is making up, rather it is acceptable just to make an intention to do so for one of the fasts missed from the month of Ramadan for the sake of attaining nearness to God, the Exalted. However, if a person does not make up their missed fasts until the next month cf Ramadan, whether intentionally or out of negligence, they must offer fidyah,[160] which is a portion of food for one poor person for each day missed. The fidyah is for delaying the make-up fast, and they must make it up as well. However, if they delay making up the fasts, but not out of negligence, they must offer a fidyah based on obligatory precaution in addition to making the fast up.

* A person who has become honored by converting to Islam does not have to make up any fasts that they did not keep prior to becoming a Muslim.
* A Muslim, who is not a Twelver Shia, does not have to make up their fasts that they kept according to their sect if they later become a Twelver Shia.

The Intention of Making Up a Missed Fast (Qada)

As mentioned in the previous sections, it is sufficient for the intention of fasting in the month of Ramadan to do so for the sake of attaining nearness to God. As such, if a person wants to make up a missed fast, they must make an intention of qada for the sake of attaining nearness to God, the Exalted. Similarly, if a person is hired to keep a fast on behalf of someone who is

---

160. A portion of food (mudd) is equivalent to 1.65 pounds (750 gm).

deceased, they must make the intention to fast to fulfill the duty on their behalf.

Obligation to Offer Kaffarah in Addition to Making Up the Missed Fast

- Kaffarah is obligatory upon a person who deliberately invalidates their fast by eating, drinking, engaging in sexual intercourse, masturbating, [willfully] remaining in the state of janabah until fajr in the month of Ramadan, invalidating their qada fast after dhuhr with one of the first four fast-nullifiers, or breaking an assigned vow.[161]

- Kaffarah is obligatory for a person who knows that committing a fast-nullifier will invalidate their fast. The same rule applies based on obligatory precaution if the person is culpably ignorant and hesitant [about a particular fast-nullifier].

- The kaffarah for deliberately breaking a fast in the month of Ramadan is either to fast two months consecutively or to feed sixty poor people by offering one *mudd*[162] of food to each one. If a person deliberately breaks their fast with something unlawful, such as eating or drinking

---

161. Fasting for an assigned vow includes such things as vowing to fast the last three days of the month to fast in the holy city of Medina with the intention of remaining there for ten days.

162. A portion of food (mudd) is equivalent to 1.65 pounds (750 grams).

something impure, or masturbating, then they should offer a combined kaffarah (i.e., fast two months and feed sixty poor people) based on recommended precaution.

- If a person is not capable of offering kaffarah, then they must seek forgiveness from God. They should offer the kaffarah based on obligatory precaution if they become capable of doing so later.
- If a person breaks a make up fast (qada) for the month of Ramadan after dhuhr they must offer a kaffarah of feeding ten poor people a mudd of food each, and if they are incapable of doing so, they must fast three days, which do not have to be consecutive.
- If a person breaks a fast for an assigned vow, they must offer kaffarah. For example, if the person vowed to fast on a certain Thursday, or the fifteenth of Shaban or the Day of Mabath and they broke their fast on that day, they must offer a kaffarah of feeding ten poor people one mudd[16] of food each or provide clothing for ten poor people. Otherwise, the person must fast three days consecutively if they are incapable of offering the kaffarah.
- If a person commits a fast-nullifier more than once on a given day, they do not have to offer more than one kaffarah.
- If a man forces his wife to have sexual intercourse during the day in the month of Ramadan, he must offer two kaffarah based on obligatory precaution. However, if the husband has a valid excuse not to fast and forces his wife to have sexual intercourse,

he has committed a sin, and he does not have offer kaffarah. As for the wife, she does not have to offer a kaffarah in either case.

- If a person knows that they invalidated their fast [by committing one of the fast-nullifiers], and they are uncertain whether it requires making up the fast only or making up the fast and offering kaffarah, then they do not have to offer kaffarah.
- If a person knows that they missed several days of fasting but they are not certain of the exact number, they only need to pay kaffarah (in addition to making up the fast) for the number of days they are certain about (e.g., they doubt if they missed six or nine days and they are certain that it cannot be less than five, then they must go with five).
- It is not necessary to offer a kaffarah immediately, rather one can delay it if doing so does not amount to negligence.

Cases Only Requiring Qada without Kaffarah

It is obligatory for a person to fulfill a qada fast without kaffarah in the following cases:

1. If a person sleeps in the state of janabah until fajr.
2. If a person invalidates their fast by hesitating in their intention [during the day] without committing a fast-nullifier.
3. If a person forgets to perform a ritual bath (ghusl) for janabah for one or more days.
4. If a person commits a fast-nullifier after fajr without checking that it had occurred. However, if

they knowingly commit a fast-nullifier after dawn, they must make up the fast and offer kaffarah. A person may eat and drink if they doubt whether fajr has set in.

5. If a person commits a fast-nullifier before the time of maghrib with the assumption that maghrib has set in. They may not commit a fast-nullifier if they doubt whether maghrib has set in, and if they do, they will have committed a sin and must make up the fast and offer kaffarah.

6. If a person places water or any other liquid in their mouth for the purpose of washing, cooling, reducing thirst, or even without a purpose, and they accidently swallow it, they must make up the fast, irrespective of whether this was a fast of the month of Ramadan or some other.

7. Emission of semen due to unintentional sexual arousal that is not customary for the person in cases other than with one's wife. However, if foreplay preceded emission, then the person must make up the fast and offer kaffarah, even if they did not intend to do so or it was not customary for them if they assumed a high possibility of the emission of semen.

Cases Requiring Qada with Kaffarah

As mentioned in several other sections, the following cases require making up the fast and offering kaffarah:

1. If a person deliberately and knowingly invalidates their fast in the month of Ramadan by eating, drinking, sexual intercourse, and masturbation. This does not apply to someone compelled.

2. If a person knows that masturbation invalidates fasting in the month of Ramadan or was culpably ignorant and hesitant[163] that it invalidates fasting, they must make up the fast and offer kaffarah.
3. If a person deliberately becomes in the state of janabah during the night of the month of Ramadan when there is not enough time to perform a ritual bath (ghusl) before fajr, they must make up the fast and offer kaffarah if they could perform dry ablution (tayammum) and they do not do so.
4. If a person doubts whether the time of maghrib has set in, they must not break their fast. If they break their fast, they will have committed a sin and they must make up the fast and offer a kaffarah.
5. If a person ejaculates semen due to touching or kissing even if they did not intend to do so, and it was not something that usually occurs, they must

---

163. A culpably ignorant person is one who does not have a valid excuse for not knowing the ruling. For example, a culpably ignorant person is one who fails to learn the rulings that are relevant to the fulfilment of his religious duties, such as praying, fasting the month of Ramadan, avoiding backbiting, avoiding consumption of alcoholic beverages, avoiding adultery, or believing that something is permissible by being negligent in learning. An inculpably ignorant person is one who has a valid excuse for not knowing the ruling, and the culpable ignorant person does not. An example of an inculpably ignorant person is one who relied on a qualified jurist and found later that the jurist was not qualified or who acted according to the ruling of the qualified jurist not knowing that the jurist had changed his ruling. In addition, this could include a person who because of living far from a religious environment became certain that an act was permissible, when it was unlawful.

make up the fast and offer kaffarah unless they assumed that touching or kissing would not cause it to happen. In the latter case, they must only make up the fast.

Making Up Fasts on Days When Fasting Is Recommended

The following rulings concern what to do when recommended fasts and make-up fasts coincide:

- It is not permissible for a person to observe a recommended fast if they have missed fasts from the month of Ramadan.
- It is permissible for a person to observe a recommended fast if they also must observe a kaffarah fast for deliberately breaking their fast in the month of Ramadan.
- If a person observes a qada fast for the month of Ramadan during the months when fasting is recommended, such as Rajab, Shaban, the twenty-seventh of Rajab, or the fifteenth of Shaban, with the hope of also receiving reward for fasting those days, God, the Exalted, will reward them for it. It is also permissible to combine multiple intentions for a fast in one day. For example, a person may make an intention to make up a fast from the month of Ramadan and one of the following recommended fasts if they choose to keep the fast on that day, and they will be rewarded for it:
  - Intention to fast a day in the month of Rajab
  - Intention to fast three days in the month of Rajab

o   Intention to fast the thirteenth, fourteenth, and fifteenth of Rajab
o   Intention to fast the first and last Thursday of Rajab
o   Intention to fast Thursday and Friday in the month of Rajab

Keeping a Missed Fast on Behalf of a Deceased Person

The following are rulings for fasting on behalf of a deceased person:

- Based on obligatory precaution, the *wali* or guardian of the deceased, who is the eldest son, must perform [or hire someone to perform] any missed obligatory acts of worship (i.e., prayer, fasting) that his father had not performed due to a valid excuse and could have made up, but did not. It is not obligatory for the son to perform the father's obligatory worship if the latter did not perform them deliberately, performed them improperly due to culpable ignorance, or had an excuse such as sickness, or if the son is not aware that his father had missed them. The same ruling applies to a person's mother based on recommended precaution.

- If the son knows that his father missed some acts of worship (e.g., prayer or fasting) but is not certain whether he made them up during his life, then he must perform them on his behalf based on obligatory precaution.

- The son does not have to make up missed acts of worship for the deceased father if the details are in doubt or not known. If the son does not know the exact number of missed fasts, he must only perform the minimum he is certain of. In any case, if the son knows that his father missed some acts of worship but is not certain whether he made them up during his life, then he must perform them on his behalf based on obligatory precaution.

- If the eldest son was not at the age of religious obligation (bulugh) or he was insane at the time of his father's death, then it is not obligatory for him to perform his father's missed acts of worship when he becomes the age of religious obligation or becomes sane.

- The son does not have to make up fasts the father was hired for or otherwise responsible to keep on behalf of someone else but were missed.

- It is not obligatory to observe a qada on behalf of a deceased person immediately. Instead, it is permissible to delay it if doing so does not amount to negligence.

- The eldest son does not have to observe qada on behalf of his father if he is disqualified from inheriting from his father because he killed him or because he is a non-Muslim.

- If another person voluntarily observes a qada on behalf of the deceased or if the eldest son hires them and they fulfill the qada, then the son no longer must observe it.

- If the deceased does not have a wali (i.e., a son at the age of religious obligation) or in the event it is not obligatory for the son to observe the qada on his behalf, it is not obligatory for the heirs to use the estate to hire someone to fulfill it. Although, the inheritors should do so based on a recommended precaution if it does not affect the shares of any minor children.

- If the deceased has missed fasts, it is permissible to offer a mudd of food for each day they missed in place of observing the fast on his behalf, and it is permissible to take it from the estate with the consent of all heirs. Then the wali no longer must make it up.

The Amount of Fidyah and Kaffarah and Their Disbursement

As mentioned previously, fidyah is feeding one poor person for each day missed on account of sickness, and kaffarah is feeding sixty poor people for deliberately breaking a fast in the month of Ramadan, feeding ten poor people for deliberately breaking a qada fast after dhuhr, and feeding one poor person for each day of qada delayed until the following month of Ramadan. The following points explain these circumstances in detail:

- The obligatory feeding for kaffarah or fidyah can be either by giving the unprepared food to the poor person(s) [for them to prepare] or by making the meal and feeding them directly such that they are satisfied (i.e., not hungry anymore), and it is permissible to give the unprepared food to some poor people and feed a meal to others. There is no specific amount considered necessary for satisfaction. Instead, it is [any] food made readily available and enough [to satiate their hunger], whether it is a little or a lot. As for giving unprepared food to the poor, the least allowable is a mudd, and it is better to offer two.

- In both cases, whether giving unprepared food or feeding, the person must satisfy the entire number of sixty or ten (based on the type of kaffarah) different poor people. It is not sufficient to feed thirty or five poor people twice, or to offer two mudd to each person. However, it is not obligatory to do it at the same time. Therefore, it will suffice if a person feeds sixty poor people at separate times and places.

- Feeding requires giving the poor person one complete meal of food, although it is better to offer two meals: lunch and dinner.

- It is sufficient to feed the poor any meal that is commonly eaten by people such as cooked food and bread made from wheat or barley, even if offered without something to dip it in (e.g., yogurt). However, it is better to include something liquid or solid to dip the bread in, and it is better if it is of high quality.

- If a person chooses to give food instead of feeding, they can give anything that is commonly called food, whether cooked or not, made from wheat, barley, or their flour; or rice, corn, dates, raisins; and other such items.

- Giving the poor person the food makes them the owner of it and the giver has then discharged their obligation in offering the kaffarah. Moreover, they do not have to make sure the poor person eats the food, rather the recipient can sell it.

- Children and adults are equal in terms of receiving a mudd of food. Hence, a poor child receives a full mudd just like the adult, although the child's portion must be given to their guardian. On the other hand, if a person chooses to expiate by feeding the poor (i.e., giving prepared meals), they must consider two children for each adult, and in such a case they do not require the permission of the guardian if feeding the child does not violate the guardian's rights (of guardianship, custody, etc.).

- It is permissible to give several mudd of food to one poor person or to feed one poor person several times for different kaffarah. For example, if a person deliberately breaks their fast for the entire month of Ramadan, they may feed sixty specified poor people thirty times, or offer thirty mudds of food to each of the sixty poor people, even if there were other deserving poor people present.

- If a person cannot find sixty poor people or ten poor people in their town, they must feed or give food to [deserving people in] another town, and if this is also not possible, they must wait.

- The definition of a poor person is someone who does not possess the means to meet their expenses for a full year, whether in terms of possessing the resources or the means to acquire them. They must be a Muslim, and based on obligatory precaution, they must be a Twelver Shia. However, in the event a person cannot find a Twelver Shia, it is permissible for them to give the kaffarah to non-Shia Muslims who are weak. Moreover, it must not be given to those people for whom one is responsible (i.e., for their expenses) such as parents, children, the permanent wife (not a temporary one), and it is permissible, and perhaps better, to give to any other relatives.

- A poor person does not have to be just; however, the kaffarah must not be given to someone who does not perform their obligatory prayers, drinks wine, or sins openly based on obligatory precaution.
- Giving the monetary value of food or clothing to the poor does not suffice. Instead, when it comes to feeding, the person must offer food, either by feeding the poor person [directly] or giving them ownership of the food. However, there is no problem in giving the monetary equivalent to the poor person and delegating them to purchase food on behalf of the person offering the kaffarah after which they would take possession of it. Still, the obligation of the kaffarah is not fulfilled unless the poor person purchases food with the money.
- If a person is incapable of offering a kaffarah, or even part of it, they must offer what they can, even if it is to feed less than sixty poor people. Moreover, if the person is not able to offer anything, they must seek forgiveness from God. However, they must offer the kaffarah based on obligatory precaution if they become capable of offering it later.
- If a person is not capable of fasting three days, which is the alternative kaffarah for breaking a qada fast after dhuhr, then they must seek forgiveness from God.
- It is permissible to delay offering the kaffarah if doing so does not amount to negligence in fulfilling the obligation, although one should offer it without delay based on recommended precaution.

- It is permissible to delegate someone else to offer the kaffarah by authorizing them to pay it using the money of the delegator. At the time of delegation, the delegator must make the intention to offer the kaffarah, which they delegated to their deputy to offer it on their behalf for the sake of attaining nearness to God, the Exalted.

Time of Offering Fidyah

These rulings explain the time to offer fidyah:

- The elderly, pregnant women approaching birth, nursing women with little milk, and people who suffer from polydipsia as explained in the previous sections may break their fast and offer fidyah after the month of Ramadan. It is also permissible to offer the fidyah for each day after maghrib during the month of Ramadan.
- A person who has a chronic illness and knows that they will not be capable of fasting the month of Ramadan must not offer fidyah until time passes and they establish that they are in fact unable to make up the fast (i.e., they must wait until the following month of Ramadan before offering the fidyah).
- A pregnant woman or a nursing woman who is not capable of fasting due to its harm to her or her child must not offer fidyah before the month of Ramadan. Rather, she must wait while her pregnancy or nursing (i.e., that which prevented her from fasting) continues and after the days in which she could not fast pass; then she must offer a fidyah.

Fasting on Behalf of Someone Else

It is permissible to fast on behalf of another person who is dead, whether voluntarily or for hire. It may sometimes be necessary, as in the case of the eldest son making up the fasts his deceased father missed in the month of Ramadan. The son or hired person must make an intention to fast to fulfill the duty of the deceased.

Voluntarily Fasting on Behalf of Someone Else

The following rulings concern voluntary fasting for another person:

- It is not permissible for a person who has missed (qada) fasts of the month of Ramadan of their own to volunteer to fast on behalf of someone else.
- It is permissible for a person who must perform a kaffarah fast for deliberately breaking their fast in the month of Ramadan to voluntarily fast on behalf of someone else.
- Fasting voluntarily on behalf of someone is not permissible if it causes distress to a person's parents, which would occur [out of concern for their child] if they perform it.
- It is not permissible for a wife to voluntarily fast based on obligatory precaution if her husband forbids her from doing so, even if her fasting does not interfere with his rights.

Fasting for Hire

These rulings explain fasting for hire:

- It is permissible for a person who has missed (qada) fasts of the month of Ramadan of their own to fast for hire on behalf of someone else.
- Merely hiring someone to fast on behalf of a deceased person does not fulfill the obligation unless the hired person performs the fast correctly.
- It is not permissible for a discerning child to fast on behalf of a deceased person based on obligatory precaution.
- Fasting for hire is not permissible if it causes distress to a person's parents, which would occur [out of concern for their child] if they perform it.
- It is not permissible for a wife to fast for hire based on obligatory precaution if her husband forbids her from doing so, even if it does not interfere with his rights.

Rulings on Fasting Errors

This section provides details about circumstances that can invalidate a fast and how to correct them appropriately. Most of this section was presented in some form in earlier sections, but it is discussed more comprehensively here.

Deficient Intention

If the duty-bound person does not make an intention to fast, delays it past its required time, or invalidates it somehow (e.g., showing off [*riya*]), they must make up the day later even if they did not commit any fast-nullifiers.

Mistakes Related to Fast-Nullifiers

If a duty-bound person deliberately commits one of the fast-nullifiers or remains in the state of janabah until dawn and was not compelled to do so, then in addition to having committed a sin, they must make up the fast for that day.

However, if a person unknowingly or mistakenly commits a fast-nullifier, their fast is valid and they do not have to do anything apart from the cases described below:

- The fast of a person who commits a fast-nullifier, such as eating, drinking, engaging in sexual intercourse, or remaining in the state of janabah until the end of the night (i.e., until fajr) out of forgetfulness and unaware that they must fast is valid in all cases.

- The fast of a person is invalid if they eat, drink, or engage in sexual intercourse out of ignorance that these acts invalidate it, and they must make it up later even if they are inculpably ignorant. Examples of this include the following:

  o A person eats something that is not usually edible or drinks medicine believing that it does not invalidate a fast and that only normal food (and not medicine) invalidates a fast.

  o A person is content that the sun has set and the eastern redness has disappeared, so they eat or drink and then realize that the sun has not set. However, the obligation to make up the fast is based on obligatory precaution if their reason for being content that the sun had set was darkness in the sky or something similar.

  o A person doubts whether fajr has set in, considers that it is still night, continues to eat or drink, and later it becomes apparent to them that fajr had set in. However, the fast is valid if the person investigates and concludes that fajr has not set in, and as a result, eats or drinks and later realizes that their eating or drinking occurred after dawn.

- If a person commits a fast-nullifier other than eating, drinking and sexual intercourse, or if they remain in the state of janabah until fajr, then their fast is valid if they are inculpably ignorant. This could be a person who grew up in an unreligious environment and believed firmly, for example, that masturbation does not invalidate a fast, or for instance, relied on the ruling of a qualified jurist that smoking does not invalidate a fast and realized later that the ruling was incorrect. As for remaining in the state of janabah until fajr, if the person was certain that it would not have invalidated a fast, then they do not have to make it up, even if they were culpably ignorant.

- If a person unintentionally commits any fast-nullifiers, such as forcibly opening their mouth and spraying water in, or rinsing their mouth for ablution (wudu) or just to cleanse it and accidentally swallowed the water, then their fast is valid except for these two cases:

  o Rinsing the mouth to alleviate thirst and accidently swallowing the water. The fast is invalid and must be made up later.
  o Engaging in foreplay with their spouse without intending to ejaculate but not being confident that it will not occur. The fast must be made up if ejaculation occurs accidently.

- If a person is forced to eat, drink, or have sexual intercourse and they do so fearing harm, or they initiate committing one of these acts fearing a person might harm them if they do not, then their fast is invalid and they must make it up. As for committing fast-nullifiers other than eating, drinking, and sexual intercourse, their fast is invalid based on obligatory precaution.

- If a person remains in the state of janabah until fajr because they could not perform a ritual bath (ghusl) or dry ablution (tayammum), whether it is because they have no water or dirt, or out of fear, then their fast is valid.

Mistakes in Imsak

If a person invalidates their fast by committing one of the fast-nullifiers or remains in the state of janabah until fajr, they must abstain from committing any fast-nullifier for the rest of the day according to the following details:

- If a person deliberately remains in the state of janabah until fajr, they must abstain from fast-nullifiers for the entire day and based on obligatory precaution and they must make their intention of doing so for the sake of attaining absolute nearness to God without specifying it as fast for the month of Ramadan or abstaining from fast-nullifiers to respect the holy month.
- If a person deliberately ascribes falsehoods to God, the Exalted, or His messenger (pbuh&hp), or if they inhale thick dust or smoke, then they must abstain from fast-nullifiers for the rest of the day based on obligatory precaution with the hope that God desires it, which means that God could desire it as a fast of the month of Ramadan or [merely] abstaining from fast-nullifiers to respect the holy month.
- If a person invalidates their fast with any other fast-nullifier not mentioned in the previous bullet, then based on obligatory precaution they must abstain from fast-nullifiers for the rest of the day to respect the holy month hoping that God desires it.

Mistakes in Fulfilling the Conditions of Qada and Kaffarah

If a person invalidates their fast by eating, drinking, sexual intercourse, or masturbation they must make up the fast and offer a kaffarah if they meet the following conditions:

- They must make up the fast if one of the four fast-nullifiers was committed intentionally and willfully, not like the case of a person who rinses their mouth to alleviate their thirst and accidently swallows the water or someone who engages in an act that causes sexual arousal and accidently ejaculates (even if they were not confident of not ejaculating), in which case the person does not need to offer kaffarah. However, if an act of sexual arousal involves foreplay or kissing, they must offer kaffarah in addition to making up the fast.
- The person is not compelled to commit a fast-nullifier due to being threatened. Thus, if they commit one of the fast-nullifiers out of fear then they only must make up the fast and do not have to offer kaffarah.
- The person is not certain that the act is a fast-nullifier. Thus, they do not have to offer kaffarah if they commit an act that they are certain is permissible, whether they assumed that fasting was not obligatory for them because of their young age or that God does not consider that act to be a fast-nullifier. Hence, kaffarah is not obligatory in these cases, whether the person's assumption is due to inculpable or culpable ignorance, such as a person who neglected

learning the religious rulings and, as a result, assumed that a certain act was not a fast-nullifier.

Mistakes in Performing an On-time or Makeup Fast

Anyone who must fast the month of Ramadan and neglects it or does not perform it in the correct manner according to Islamic laws, with or without a valid excuse, must make it up by fasting the number of days missed after the end of the month of Ramadan. A person who does not have to fast the month of Ramadan because they do not meet one of the conditions of its obligation, and thus, does not fast, does not have to make it up unless it is one of the following situations:

- If a person does not fast because it is harmful to them, they must make it up if fasting later is no longer harmful. This is the case unless it is a harm related to their health and it persists until the following month of Ramadan; then they do not have to make up the fast, but they must offer fidyah.

- A woman who does not fast certain days of the month of Ramadan due to its coinciding with menstruation or postpartum bleeding must make up the fasts.

- If a person does not fast in the month of Ramadan because it causes severe unbearable hardship, then they must make it up afterwards if they are able to do so without its continuing to cause them hardship.

- If a person does not fast certain days of the month of Ramadan due to being a traveler, who must shorten their prayers, then they must make up the fast after the month of Ramadan.

Rulings of Making Up a Fast

What follows are some rulings related to making up a fast:

- It is not obligatory to make up a missed fast immediately; however, it is not permissible to delay it out of negligence or considering it unimportant. In the event a person delays making up their missed fast until the arrival of the next month of Ramadan for any reason, then they must offer kaffarah [of feeding one poor person for each day] in addition to making it up. Moreover, they would only offer the kaffarah once and do not repeat it if they delay their make-up fast for several years.

- It is not obligatory to make up the missed fasts of the month of Ramadan in the order missed; instead, the person can make up any day they wish [in any order].

- A person has until the time of dhuhr to make their intention to perform a make-up fast and it must be for what they missed in the month of Ramadan.

- It is not permissible for a person who is observing a make-up fast to break it after dhuhr; doing so counts as a sin, and they must make up the fast later. If a person invalidates their make-up fast by eating, drinking, sexual intercourse, or masturbation, they must offer a kaffarah of feeding ten poor people, and if they are not capable of doing so, then they must fast for three days.

- If a person knows that they have missed fasts from the month of Ramadan but are unsure of the number, they may make up the minimum that they are certain of.

- If a person knows that they have missed fasts from the month of Ramadan but are unsure if they made them up, they must [act as if they did not and] make them up to ensure fulfilment of their obligation.

Spiritual Retreat

Spiritual retreat (itikaf) is a recommended (mustahabb) ritual act of worship, which helps to refine and purify the self and results in a person becoming closer to God, the Exalted. It is the act of remaining in the mosque (masjid) for the purpose of worship, prayer, remembrance of God, fasting, and similar acts of devotion. It is valid any time when fasting is permissible, and it is better in the last ten days of the month of Ramadan.

Conditions of Spiritual Retreat

Spiritual retreat is valid under the following conditions:

1. Sanity
2. Intention of nearness to God, the Exalted
3. Fasting. A spiritual retreat is invalid without fasting. Therefore, if a person is traveling and fasting is not permissible, they cannot engage in spiritual retreat.
4. The minimum duration for a spiritual retreat is three days, including the two nights in between. There is no problem in including the first or the fourth night in the intention of spiritual retreat.
5. It must be performed in one of the following four mosques: al-Masjid al-Haram (Mecca), Masjid al-Medina, Masjid al-Kufa, or Masjid al-Basra. It is

also permissible to observe it in the central mosque[164] of a town.[165]

- o It is not permissible to perform a spiritual retreat in a central mosque where the imam is not just based on obligatory precaution.

6. Permission. It is necessary to obtain permission from whom it is required, such as the parents if the child wishes to perform a spiritual retreat, which might cause them distress (i.e., out of compassion for the child). Also, the wife must obtain her husband's permission before she can perform a spiritual retreat. if he does not permit her to remain in the mosque without his consent or it is with his consent but doing so interferes with his marital rights, then the retreat would not be valid.

7. To remain in the mosque where the person originally embarked on a spiritual retreat. Therefore, if they leave without a valid excuse, their spiritual retreat is invalid even if they were ignorant of the ruling or had forgotten it.

- o It is permissible for a person who has embarked on a spiritual retreat to leave the mosque in some cases, such as for a dire necessity; if they are forced; to use the restroom; or to perform an obligatory ritual wash (ghusl) for janabah,

---

164. A mosque is a place essentially endowed to God for the purpose of performing prayers.

165. The central mosque is the main mosque of a town, which is usually the largest one and is not assigned to a certain group or family, rather it is for everyone irrespective of their color and ethnic background and is designated for the five daily and Friday prayers.

menstruation (haydh), irregular bleeding (istihadha), or for touching a dead body. However, if the person can perform a ritual bath (ghusl) inside the mosque, they must not leave based on obligatory precaution if the occurrence does not prevent a person from remaining in the mosque such as touching a dead body or irregular bleeding (istihadha), and if it is for janabah they must perform it in the mosque based on obligatory precaution. It is also necessary to preserve the purity of the mosque when performing a ritual bath (ghusl al-janabah) and make sure not to rush it in a way that causes the mosque to become impure.

o It is permissible for a person who has embarked on a spiritual retreat to leave the mosque to perform Friday prayer; to attend a funeral procession and funeral prayer; and to wash, shroud, and bury a deceased person. It is also permissible to leave to visit the sick.

o A person engaged in a spiritual retreat must not leave the mosque even to perform laudable things based on obligatory precaution unless they are necessary. If they must leave, then based on obligatory precaution they must take the shortest route and return as quickly as possible.

Conditions to Avoid on Spiritual Retreat

A person who embarks on a spiritual retreat must avoid the following:

1. Engaging in debates and arguments on religious or worldly matters to defeat the other party or

demonstrate one's own prowess. However, there is no problem in arguing for the sake of proving the truth and to turn the opponent away from something that is wrong. The criterion for this is based on intention.

2. Buying, selling, and trading in general based on obligatory precaution. However, there is no problem in buying and selling what the person needs during the spiritual retreat such as water, food, or other needs if there is no way for them to delegate someone else to do that on their behalf or to transfer it by other than buying and selling.

3. Smelling fragrances in general, particularly natural scents (rayahin),[166] for the purpose of seeking pleasure. It is permissible if it is not for pleasure.

4. Masturbation[167] based on obligatory precaution.

5. Sexual intercourse, including touching and kissing with lust, based on obligatory precaution.

Summary

The following are a few additional points about the validity of a spiritual retreat:

- If one of the previously mentioned acts that invalidate a spiritual retreat occurs inadvertently (mistakenly), the spiritual retreat remains valid.

- If a person invalidates their fixed and specified spiritual retreat, which they had to fulfill due to a

---

166. Rayahin is the plural of rayhan, which is any plant that has a natural fragrance. [al-Sistani, *Minhaj al-Salihin*, vol. 1, p. 384].

167. This refers to lawful masturbation between spouses.

vow, then they must make it up based on obligatory precaution. If the spiritual retreat was not fixed and specified, it must be repeated. If the spiritual retreat was recommended and a person invalidates it after completion of two days, they must make it up. Otherwise, there is no required make-up retreat if they invalidate it before the completion of two days. Moreover, making up a missed spiritual retreat does not have to be immediate; it can be delayed if it does not amount to negligence.

The Fitra Alms Tax (Zakat al-Fitra)

Alms tax (zakat) is one of the obligatory acts of worship that God, the Exalted, mandated, and He joined it with prayers in many verses: "Certainly, the faithful have attained salvation —those who are humble in their prayers, who avoid vain talk, who carry out their [duty of] zakat,"[168] and "Felicitous is he who purifies himself, celebrates the Name of his Lord, and prays."[169]

Numerous authentically transmitted and honorable prophetic traditions state that zakat is one of the pillars of Islam, and if a person neglects to pay any part of it, they shall die as if outside of the circle of Islam.[170]

Fitra Alms Tax

The duty-bound person must make an intention to pay zakat al-fitra out of obedience and seeking nearness to God, the Exalted; must set it aside on the night of Eid; and pay it to the deserving recipient on the day of Eid.

---

168. The Quran 23:1–4, AQQ.

169. The Quran 87:14–15, AQQ.

170. Reports state that Imam Muhammad al-Baqir (p) said, "Islam is built on prayer, alms, fasting, pilgrimage, and guardianship [of Ahl al-Bayt], and nothing will be emphasized like guardianship." [al-Kulayni, *al-Kafi*, vol. 2, p. 18, and vol. 3, p. 505].

When Does Fitra Alms Tax Become Obligatory and When Must It Be Paid?

If the conditions of fitra alms tax are met by maghrib on the night before Eid, it becomes obligatory for the duty-bound person, and it is required even if the conditions are met after maghrib based on obligatory precaution. Therefore, it must be set aside and paid before Eid prayer based on obligatory precaution for a person who plans to perform the prayer. If the person does not set aside the fitra alms tax until dhuhr (or later), then they must pay it with an intention of absolute nearness[171] to God based on obligatory precaution.

- If a duty-bound person sets aside the fitra alms tax during the prescribed time, it is permissible to delay paying it if they need to wait and find a poor recipient or for similar reasons.
- If a duty-bound person sets aside the fitra alms tax, they must not change it without the permission of the qualified jurist (al-hakim al-shari). If a person delays paying the fitra alms tax and it is subsequently lost or damaged, they must pay it again to the deserving poor if possible.
- It is permissible to pay zakat al-fitra during the month of Ramadan to those people who are deserving or to an agent (*wakil*) who will execute it according to religious rules.

---

171. Absolute nearness means that a person intends to pay the fitra alms tax for the sake of nearness to God and without specifying it as *ada* (performed within the prescribed time) or qada (performed after its prescribed time).

- It is sufficient for the head of the household to set aside the fitra alms tax on behalf of their dependents on the night of Eid according to the establishment of the month of Shawwal by their jurist, even if the dependents do not consider the next day as Eid based on a different jurist.

Who Must Pay the Fitra Alms Tax?

Every sane person who has reached the age of religious obligation (bulugh) whose annual finances are secured through available assets, wealth, or ability to earn must pay the fitra alms tax on behalf of themselves and their dependents, whether they must support them or not, and whether they are near or far, Muslim or non-Muslim, young or old.

- Fitra alms tax is not obligatory for a child; insane or unconscious person;[172] or the poor.
- If a person gets married before the night of Eid, and his spouse is considered a dependent[173] at that time, he must pay fitra alms tax on her behalf.

---

172. A poor person is one who does not possess the means to meet his annual expenses either all at once or gradually, such as in the form of monthly payments.

173. This varies in terms of traditions and customs. Conducting the marriage ceremony (nikah) per se does not make the wife a dependent before she moves with her husband to his home. After marriage, some cultural traditions require that she remains with her family for a while, therefore she is dependent on her family, and at other times she is independent from them and a dependent of her husband..

- It is not obligatory to pay the fitra alms tax on behalf of a newborn child unless it was born before maghrib of the night before Eid.
- It is obligatory for the host to pay fitra alms tax for a guest who stays in their house, but it is not necessary if the guest is only invited for iftar.
- If a dependent person's fitra alms tax becomes obligatory for someone else, they do not have to pay it themselves. However, if the person who must pay it does not do so out of disobedience or forgetfulness, the dependent must pay it based on obligatory precaution if they meet the conditions of obligation.
- If the head of the household is poor, their dependents must pay their own fitra alms tax if they meet the conditions of obligation, and even if the poor head of household pays it, they must still pay it based on obligatory precaution.

The Form of Fitra Alms Tax

The way to apply fitra alms tax is to cover the cost of common food commodities such as rice, wheat, dates, corn, and macaroni. It must not be poor quality based on obligatory precaution, and it is permissible to pay the monetary value instead, which is the price of the food at the time of payment and in the place where the zakat is being used and not the price in the duty-bound person's location or when it became obligatory for them.

The Amount of Fitra Alms Tax

The amount of fitra alms tax is one *sa* of food, which is equivalent to 6.6 pounds (three kilograms).

Location of Fitra Alms Tax Spending

- The fitra alms tax must be paid to poor believers (i.e., Twelver Shias) who do not possess the means to cover their annual expenses based on obligatory precaution. If there are no poor Twelver Shias in the area where a person lives, they can pay it to other poor Muslims.
- A non-Sayyid cannot give their fitra alms tax to a Sayyid; however, a Sayyid can give it to both Sayyids and non-Sayyids.
- It is permissible for a duty-bound person to pay their fitra alms tax directly to the poor. However, the recommended precaution is to pay it to the qualified jurist who can appropriately distribute it or to his authorized representative.
- It is not permissible to transfer the fitra alms tax outside the area in which a person resides if there are deserving poor people there based on obligatory precaution.
- Based on a recommended precaution the fitra alms tax should be paid to the qualified jurist.

Eid al-Fitr[174]

Eid al-Fitr is one of the most important holidays in Islam. God Almighty has assigned special acts (pbuh&hp) of worship for it, some are obligatory while others are recommended, and there are even forbidden acts like fasting on this special day. As such, God Almighty attests to it, "To respect the symbols of God is the sign of a pious heart."[175] The eve of Eid al-Fitr is also a night of virtue. The eve and day of Eid al-Fitr mark the end of the holy month and a completion of the blessed acts of worship and obedience performed throughout it, as God Almighty states, "So that you may complete the fast, glorify God for His having given you guidance, and that, perhaps, you would give Him thanks."[176] The Holy Prophet Muhammad (pbuh&hp) and his pure Ahl al-Bayt (pbut) highly regarded the eve and day of Eid al-Fitr, paid close attention to their significance, and urged people to wisely occupy themselves with worship, prayer, and supplication during that period. Prophet Muhmmad (pbuh&hp) is narrated to have said, "Indeed, God has a favorite in everything He has created. As for His favorite eves, they are the eve of Friday, the eve of the fifteenth day of the month of Shaban, the Night of Power, and the eves of the

---

174. This last chapter of the booklet was prepared by I.M.A.M. so that the content is comprehensive and exhaustive from a theoretical and not just jurisprudential perspective. It is not from the writings attributed to al-Sayyid al-Sistani.

175. The Holy Quran 22:32, MS.

176. The Holy Quran 2:185, MS.

two Eids."[177] He also said, "The heart of a person who observes the night of Eid and the night of the fifteenth of Shaban in worship will not die on the day that other hearts will die."[178] Lastly, it has been narrated from Imam Musa al-Kadhim (p) that Imam Ali (p) said, "I like for a man to occupy himself with nothing but worship on four nights of the year: the night of Eid al-Fitr, the night of Eid al-Adha, the night of the fifteenth of Shaban, and the night of the first day of Rajab."[179]

Eve of Eid al-Fitr

It is obligatory to take out zakat al-fitra and separate it from the rest of one's money if the eve of Eid al-Fitr arrives, as previously mentioned.

There are several recommended things to do on that night.

- Appreciate the blessing of completing the fasts of the month of Ramadan and the grace bestowed by God Almighty.
- Learn and understand the rulings of zakat al-fitra and the details of its obligation; the way to determine its amount and pay it; and those who are deserving recipients. These are important details so the duty-bound person can discharge their obligation appropriately.
- Perform a ritual wash or *ghusl*.

---

177. al-Majlisi, *Bihar al-anwar*, vol. 94, p. 78.

178. al-Majlisi, *Bihar al-anwar*, vol. 88, p. 132.

179. al-Hurr al-Amili, *Wasail al-Shia*, vol. 8, p. 109.

- Say *takbir* after the maghrib prayer in accordance with God saying, "So that you may complete the fast, glorify God for His having given you guidance, and that, perhaps, you would give Him thanks."[180] Perform takbir by saying: "*Allahu akbar, Allahu akbar, la ilaha illallahu wallahu akbar, Allahu akbar, wa lillahil hamd, Allahu akbar ala ma hadana, walahul shukru ala ma awlana.*" Narrations from Imam al-Sadiq (p) recommend saying it after maghrib and isha prayer on the eve of Eid al-Fitr, and before the Eid prayer.[181]
- Pray the two-unit prayer for the eve of Eid and an additional ten units. Books of supplications and worship contain the details for both prayers.
- Observe the eve of Eid with worship and devotion to God Almighty. Imam Ali al-Sajjad (p) used to worship the whole night until sunrise and connect it to the Eid prayer. He would say, "The importance of this night is not less than the importance of the Night of Destiny."[182]

The Day of Eid al-Fitr

The day of Eid is a day of joy for the believers knowing that they completed the month of Ramadan and are now pure from sins, hoping that God has accepted all their good deeds and worship and that they have gained His satisfaction with the start of a new year. It is narrated that the noble Prophet (pbuh&hp) said, "On

---

180. The Holy Quran 2:185, MS.

181. Ibn Tawus, *Iqbal al-amal*, vol. 1, p. 459.

182. Ibn Tawus, *Iqbal al-amal*, vol. 1, p. 464.

the first day of the month of Shawwal, a caller calls from the heavens announcing, 'O believers, claim your rewards.' He continued, 'O Jabir, the rewards of God are not like the rewards of these worldly kings.' Then he said, 'It [the day of Eid] is the day of reward.'"[183] Other narrations state that he said, "On the day of Eid al-Fitr God Almighty dispatches the angels all over the land, and they will descend and roam the alleys and call in a voice that all of God's creation, from humans to jinns, will hear. They will say, 'O nation of Muhammad, come to your Lord, the Generous One Who gives abundantly and forgives even the great.' If they go out to pray, God Almighty says, 'O my angels, what is the compensation for a worker who finishes his work?' The angels say, 'Our Lord, Our Master, their compensation is that you pay them for their work.' God Almighty will say, 'My angels, bear witness that I am compensating those who fasted in the month of Ramadan and worshiped in its nights with My forgiveness and satisfaction.' God Almighty will say, 'My servants, ask Me! For I swear by My might and My majesty that anything you ask of Me today for your hereafter I shall give you, and anything you ask of Me for this world I shall consider. By My might, I will conceal your faults if you know I am watching you and I will not embarrass you or reveal your sins in front of those in attendance [in the hereafter]. Depart with all your sins forgiven by Me. You have sought my satisfaction; therefore, I am pleased with you.' The angels will then ascend and joyfully celebrate what God has given the people of this nation when they break their fast at the end of the

---

183. Ibn Tawus, *Iqbal al-amal*, vol. 1, p. 481.

month of Ramadan."[184] Therefore, the day of Eid al-Fitr is a day of reward, and we should not be negligent of the Glorified One who is offering these rewards. We should observe the day and its recommended acts with due diligence to reap God's best rewards. Some of these acts are

- to recall the meaning of Eid, which is a day of joy and a celebration of fulfilled promises. It is God Almighty's promise to forgive and reward His servants and grant them a pure rebirth from their sins;
- to perform a ritual bath (ghusl) that is followed by supplications as mentioned in supplication books;
- to recite the prayer of tabia, when going out for the Eid prayer. It begins, "Allahumma man tahaya fi hadhal yaum wa taba aw ada wa istadda liwafadatin ila makhluqin raja rifdihi wa jaizatihi wa nawafilihi." "O God, whoever prepares, gets ready, and seeks aid from another creature with the hope of gaining his aid;"
- to recite Dua al-Faraj for Imam al-Mahdi (may God hasten his reappearance);
- to eat breakfast before going out to the Eid prayer, and offer breakfast to the believers if possible;
- to wear nice clothes and apply perfume;
- to go out to the Eid prayer shortly after sunrise;
- to pay zakat al-fitra to those entitled to it before the prayer;
- to pray outside under the sky;

---

184. al-Saduq, *Fadail al-ashhur al-thalath*, p. 127–128.

- to recite the ziyarah of Imam al-Hussain specified for the two eids;
- to read Dua al-Nudbah; and
- to read the supplication of Imam Zayn al-Abidin al-Sajjad that he recited after his Eid prayer, which is the forty-sixth supplication from *Sahifah al-Sajjadiyyah*.

Eid prayer

Eid prayer is obligatory in the presence of the infallible Imam and recommended in the era of occultation, or ghayba. It is permissible to perform Eid prayer, which is a two-unit prayer, either individually or in congregation. The person should recite Surat al-Fatihah and another short surah (preferably Surat al-Ala) in the first unit. Then, they should perform five takbirs with a qunut (to raise hands for a prayer) between each takbir. The following dua is recited in the qunut:

"اللّهمّ أَهْلَ الكِبْرِياءِ وَالعَظَمَةِ، وَأَهْلَ الجُودِ وَالجَبَرُوتِ، وَأَهْلَ العَفْوِ وَالرَّحْمَةِ، وَأَهْلَ التَّقوى وَالمغْفِرَةِ، أَسْأَلُكَ بِحَقِّ هذا اليَوْمِ الّذي جَعَلْتَهُ لِلْمُسْلِمِينَ عِيْداً، وَلِمُحَمَّدٍ صَلّى الله عَلَيْهِ وَآلِهِ ذُخْراً وَمَزِيداً، أَن تُصَلِّيَ عَلى مُحَمَّدٍ وَآلِ مُحَمَّدٍ، وَأَنْ تُدْخِلَني في كلّ خَيْرٍ أَدْخَلْتَ فِيهِ مُحَمَّداً وَآلَ مُحَمَّدٍ، وَأَنْ تُخْرِجَني مِنْ كلّ سُوءٍ أَخْرَجْتَ مِنْهُ مُحَمَّداً وَآلَ مُحَمَّدٍ صَلَواتُكَ عَلَيْهِ وَعَلَيْهِمْ. اللّهمّ إِنِّي أَسْأَلُكَ خَيْرَ ما سَأَلَكَ عِبادُكَ الصَّالِحُونَ، وَأَعُوذُ بِكَ مِمّا اسْتَعاذَ مِنْهُ عِبادُكَ الصَّالِحُونَ"

"Oh Allah, You are the Lord of glory and greatness, and the Lord of magnanimity and omnipotence, and the Lord of forgiveness and mercy, and the worthiest of being feared and the Lord of forgiveness. I ask You in the name of this day, which you have made an Eid (celebration) for Muslims and an increasing honor and treasure for Muhammad, peace be upon him and his progeny. I ask You to send Your blessings upon Muhammad and his progeny, and to include me in everything you have included Muhammad and his progeny in, and to exclude me from everything you have excluded Muhammad and his progeny from, peace and blessings be upon them all. Oh Allah, I ask you for the best of all that which Your righteous servants have asked you for, and I seek Your protection from all the evil that Your righteous servants have sought protection from."

After the fifth takbir, the person should complete the ruku (bowing), sajdatayn (prostrations), get up for the second unit, and read Surat al-Fatihah and another short surah (preferably Surat al-Shams). Then the person should perform another four takbir and qunut between each takbir; recite the same dua mentioned above; complete ruku and sajdatayn; and finally complete tashahhud, taslim and end the prayer.

After finishing the prayer, it is recommended to do tasbih al-Zahra.

After the prayer, it is recommended for the imam of the congregational prayer to deliver two sermons separated by taking a seat for a short while. In the first sermon, he should praise, glorify, and thank God Almighty and remind the believers of simple matters that are good. In the second sermon, he should praise God and send peace and blessings upon the Prophet and his family in the best manner. He should end the sermon by praying for the believers and their deceased ones and finally end with a short surah from the Holy Quran.

Details to pay attention to on the day of Eid

The day of Eid is a day of joy and happiness for receiving the rewards of God as mentioned in previous narrations from Prophet Muhammad (pbuh&hp). However, many believers forget the greatness of this day and what is expected from them [in recognizing this greatness]. They overlook the fact that they must safeguard the acts of obedience and worship they performed throughout the holy month. The believer should be aware that Satan uses this day as an opportunity to pull people into his traps again. It is narrated that Imam Hasan al-Mujtaba (p) once looked at people laughing and playing on the day of Eid al-Fitr and said to his companions, "God Almighty has made the month of Ramadan a race for his creation in which they compete to win His satisfaction by obeying and worshiping Him. Some people will win, and others will stay back and lose. One wonders at these people who are laughing and playing on a day in which the winners are rewarded and the losers are disappointed. I swear by God, if the veil was lifted for them, then the one who won would be busy with his reward, and the one who lost would be busy with his sins and disappointment."[185]

---

185. Ibn Tawus, *Iqbal al-amal*, vol.1, p. 468.

Therefore, we must follow the verse, "Believers, save yourselves and your families from the fire"[186] and protect ourselves, families, and communities from falling into any of Satan's traps on the blessed day of Eid. This warning is especially timely now when falling into sin and disobedience and ignoring religious obligations are easy. Accordingly, the following list of recommendations will help safeguard us from falling into sins and disobedience:

- Observe modesty in clothing and appearance. Believing men and women are not supposed to display their bodies in an attractive manner under any circumstance in addition to safeguarding their intentions [of being modest]. Nowadays, many young men and women are unfortunately distorting the concept of *hijab*, restricting it only to women and displaying immodest fashion and aesthetics in the name of the Islamic veil. This results in misleading others, falsifying religious beliefs, and tempting those who are ignorant.
- Be wary of extravagance and wasting food and drink because Islam forbids it. Moreover, it has bad consequences, because it negates the positive effects of fasting and its philosophy of consciously remembering the hunger and thirst of others, especially the poor, so that we empathize with them and act charitably.
- Take out the obligatory zakat al-fitra on the night of Eid al-Fitr and pay it to those who deserve it before performing the Eid prayer. The obligation to remember the poor, show compassion, and help

---

186. The Holy Quran 66:6, MS.

them satisfy their most basic needs is a lesson for us to strengthen our humanity and foster empathy. It is an act of worship that draws us closer to God, and it is not less rewarding than prayer or remembrance, for God says, "Lasting happiness will be for those who purify themselves, remember the name of the Lord, and pray to Him."[187] Therefore, the believers, especially those with means, should give more for the sake of social solidarity and to lift the needy out of their hardships. If they do so, God will bless them and their wealth, bounty, and livelihoods for their virtue, righteousness, and generosity. They will also receive the prayers of the needy and impoverished people whom they helped.

- The recommendation to wear nice clothes and perfume, and pray in congregation, emphasizes the importance of our social lives and the need to strengthen the spiritual bond between believers. Therefore, gatherings and visits between believers, especially between relatives and kin, are some of the greatest deeds in the eyes of God. These gatherings are also highly rewarded if they lead to restoring broken family ties and strengthening them; in forgetting the past and its disputes; and in forgiving and pardoning others. Narrations state that Imam al-Sadiq (p) said, "Maintaining family ties is done through visiting them if they are near, and through writing to them if they are traveling."[188] Therefore, whoever

---

187. The Holy Quran 87:14–15, MS.

188. al-Kulayni, *al-Kafi*, vol. 2, p. 638.

is unable to visit their family in person for any reason, must at least reach out with a message, especially since it has become an easy task with today's technology, social media, and the many ways of communication we have readily available to us. Therefore, we do not have an excuse. However, we must be extremely careful that these gatherings do not turn into a setting where prohibited acts are performed, such as backbiting, mocking others, or mixing and meeting with the opposite gender in an inappropriate and tempting manner. All of these will negate the purpose of legislating the celebration of the day of Eid al-Fitr, which is to enjoy God's blessings and divine rewards after completing the month of Ramadan.

Praise be to Allah,
Lord of the worlds

Glossary

adhan (أَذان). Call to prayer.

akhlaq (أَخْلاق). Good morals.

aql (عَقْل). Sanity.

asr (عَصْر). Afternoon prayer that follows dhuhr prayer (see below).

al-Bayt al-Mamur (البَيْتُ المَعْمُور). The built house.

bida (بِدْعَة). An innovation.

bulugh (بُلُوغ). The age at which a person becomes responsible for performing religious duties such as daily obligatory prayer and fasting during the month of Ramadan. A girl becomes *baligha* (reaches this time) upon completing nine lunar years, and a boy becomes baligh (reaches this time) upon completing fifteen lunar years except for when one of the signs of bulugh, such as the growth of stiff pubic hair or the discharge of semen, appears before that age.

dahwu al-ard (دَحْوُ الأَرْض). The day of the spreading of the earth

dhan (ظَنّ). Assumption.

dhihar (ظِهار). When a husband makes a statement to his wife falsely claiming that she is like his mother in terms of being sexually impermissible to him.

dhimmah (ذِمَّة). Conscience (as in an unspecified act of worship that remains in the conscience of a person).

dhuhr (ظُهْر). Zenith.

dinar (دِينار). Type of money

dananir (دَنانِيْر). Plural of dinar.

fajr (فَجْر) or ***al-fajr al-sadiq*** (الفَجْرُ الصّادِق). Dawn when fajr prayer commences.

al-fajr al-kadhib (الفَجْرُ الكاذِب) false dawn. Dawn.

fidyah (فِدْيَة). 0.75 kg of food for each fast day missed.

ghusl (غُسْل). Major ablution performed by washing (with water only) the whole body—either by washing every body part in stages from the head and neck to the rest of the body (as one would have to do in a shower) or by immersing the whole body in water at once (as one could do in a river).

hadath (حَدَث). The state of impurity.

hadith (حَدِيْث). Tradition, narration.

hadd al-tarrakhuss (حَدُّ التَّرَخُّص). The point outside of a town where its residents, including those who live on its outskirts, cannot see a traveler nor can the traveler see them or where the buildings are no longer visible, which is usually 2 to 3 miles away from the town but also depends on the geographical location.

hajj al-tamattu (حَجُّ التَّمَتُّع). The obligatory pilgrimage to Mecca.

haram (حَرام). Forbidden.

haydh (حَيْض). Menstrual bleeding.

iftar (إفْطار). Food with which one breaks their fast.

ihram (إحْرام). An act of worship among the rituals of pilgrimage that entails wearing the garb of a pilgrim (for men), adhering to temporary prohibition of certain acts and recitation of the *talbiyah*.

imamah (إمَامَة). Leadership.

imsak (إمْسَاك). to abstain from eating and drinking and the rest of the nullifiers of fasting a few minutes before dawn (fajr) as a precautionary measure to ensure a valid fast.

isra (إسْرَاء). Night journey.

istibra (اسْتِبْرَاء). A recommended act performed by men after urinating in order to be confident that no urine is left in the urethra.

istifta (اسْتِفْتَاء). Response to a jurisprudential question.

istihadha (اسْتِحَاضَة). Non-menstrual blood

istikhara (اسْتِخَارَة). Supplicating to God for the best when making a decision in a matter of great concern. This can be performed either through spiritual inspiration by way of prayer or by seeking a definitive indication through the Holy Quran or prayer beads.

istishab (اسْتِصْحَاب). To consider it is still night and therefore continue eating and drinking until they know or are content that dawn has set in.

itikaf (اعْتِكَاف). Spiritual retreat.

janabah (جَنَابَة). The state of ritual impurity that occurs as a result of intercourse (penetration), even without ejaculation, by a man or woman. Such a state requires ghusl of janabah.

kaffarah (كَفَّارَة). The religious penalty to absolve a sin. It can be in the form of food, money, an act of worship, or other things (based on the specific sin someone may have committed).

maghrib (مَغْرِب). The time for prayer after sunset, when the redness of the eastern sky, which persists in the east for some time after sunset, disappears from above one's head when one looks vertically upwards.

mahaq (مَحاق). The stage of the crescent moon when it is just a few hours old.

makruh (مَكْرُوه). Detestable.

makruhat (مَكْرُوهات). Detestable acts.

mandub (مَنْدُوب). Recommended

miraj (مِعْراج). The ascension.

mudd (مُدّ). A measurement equal to approximately 1.65 pounds (e.g., wheat).

mufattirat (مُفَطِّرات). The fast-nullifiers.

mukallaf (مُكَلَّف). A duty-bound person.

mumayyiz (مُمَيَّز). a child who is near the age of a *baligh*. They are capable of rational actions and knowing the difference between *haram* and *halal*. Some of their religious duties are accepted by God, like following a jurist, undertaking something, and buying and selling.

muqim (مُقِيْم). A person residing in a place in which they have newly arrived.

musafir (مُسَافِر). A traveler.

mustahabb (مُسْتَحَب). Recommended.

nafilat al-layl (نَافِلَةُ اللَّيْل). Supererogatory night prayer.

nifas (نِفَاس). Post-natal bleeding.

Polydipsia (*Arabic: dhul-atash* ذُو الْعِطاش). an illness due to which a person feels extreme thirst, which occurs to the point that their thirst is not quenched.

qada (قَضاء). Make-up (as in act of worship).

qadr (قَدْر). Power (as in night of power).

qudsi (قُدْسِي). The words of God Almighty that are not in the Quran. Rather, they were relayed by Prophet Muhammad (pbuh&hp) to the people.

qunut (قُنُوْت). The act of raising one's hands in supplication to God Almighty and placing them in front of the face with palms facing the sky and with both hands kept next to each other.

raja (رَجاءَ الْمَطْلُوبِيَّة). An intention for an act of worship (e.g., fasting, prayer) that the jurist cannot establish with certainty that it is legislated as such by God (wajib); "hope that it is required by Allah."

rutab (رُطَب). Fully ripened dates.

al-rayyan (الرَّيَّان). A gate in heaven.

rayahin (رَيْحَان). The plural of rayhan, which is any plant that has a natural fragrance.

riya (رِيَاء). Showing off.

ruku (رُكُوْع). Bowing down.

sa (صَاع). A unit of weight that is equal to 6.6 pounds (three kilograms).

salat al-layl (صَلاةُ اللَّيْل). The night prayer.

salawat (صَلَوات). To send peace and blessings on Prophet Muhammad (pbuh&hp).

sawm al-wisal (صَوْمُ الْوِصَال). Fasting beyond sunset.

shaf (شَفْع). Two-unit recommended prayer performed in the middle of the night

sharia (شَرِيْعَة). Religious law

shaya (شَيَاع). Common news.

sirat (صِرَاط/سِرَاط). The path

suhur (سُحُوْر). A predawn meal.

tamr (تَمْر). Dates in the process of ripening.

taqiyya (تَقِيَّة). Dissimulation

tashriq (تَشْرِيْق). 11th, 12th and 13th of Dhul Hijjah

tawatur (تَوَاتُر). Widespread news from which one can obtain knowledge or contentment.

tayammum (تَيَمُّم). A substitute for wudu and ghusl when water is unavailable. It is done by striking the hands on the earth and then wiping the forehead and the hands. With the inside of the left hand, wipe the outside of the right hand. Then with the inside of the right hand, wipe the outside of the left hand. For ghusl, strike the ground and wipe in the same way again.

ummah (أُمَّة). The Muslim nation.

umrah (عُمْرَة). The lesser pilgrimage

urf (عُرْف). The common understanding.

wakil (وَكِيل). An agent.

wali (وَلِي). A guardian.

al-watan al-asli (الْوَطَنُ الْأَصْلِي). Hometown of origin.

al-watan al-iqamah (وَطَنُ الْإِقَامَة). Domicile of temporary stay.

al-watan al-itikhadhi (الْوَطَنُ الْإِتِّخَاذِي). A place where a person plans to stay long-term for work, school, summer or spring vacations, or similar purposes, even if they do not own property or a home there.

wilayah (وِلَايَة). Guardianship

witr (وِتْر). One-unit recommended prayer performed in the middle of the night

wudu (وُضُوء). Ritual ablution.

zakat (زَكَاة). Alms tax.

zakat al-fitra (زَكَاةُ الْفِطْرِ). Alms tax which becomes obligatory at the eve of Eid al-Fitr and paid on the day of the Eid.

Other publications from I.M.A.M.
Available online

- ❖ Islamic Laws
  by Grand Ayatullah Sayyid Ali al-Sistani
- ❖ 100 Pearls
  by Grand Ayatullah Sayyid Ali al-Sistani
- ❖ Advice to Youth
  by Grand Ayatullah Sayyid Ali al-Sistani
- ❖ Fasting: A Haven from Hellfire
  by Grand Ayatullah Sayyid Ali al-Sistani
- ❖ Islamic Laws of Expiations
  by Grand Ayatullah Sayyid Ali al-Sistani
- ❖ Islamic Laws of Death and Burial
  by Grand Ayatullah Sayyid Ali al-Sistani
- ❖ The Islamic Laws of the Will
  by Grand Ayatullah Sayyid Ali al-Sistani
- ❖ Islamic Laws of Food and Drink
  by Grand Ayatullah Sayyid Ali al-Sistani
- ❖ Shia Muslims: Our Identity, Our Vision, and
  the Way Forward by Sayyid M. B. Kashmiri
- ❖ Who Is Hussain?
  by Dr. Mehdi Saeed Hazari
- ❖ Who Is Zaynab?
  by Hajjah Chahnaz A.Kbaisi-Hazari
- ❖ God's Emissaries: Adam to Jesus
  by Shaykh Rizwan Arastu
- ❖ Tajwid: A Guide to Qur'anic Recitation
  by Shaykh Rizwan Arastu
- ❖ The Illuminating Lantern: An Exposition of
  Subtleties from the Quran
  by Shaykh Habib al-Kadhimi

Vehicle Dynamics Institute

PROFESSIONAL
DRIVING TECHNIQUES

By Anthony J. Scotti

Special Edition

PhotoGraphics Publishing

Vehicle Dynamics Institute
1162 St. Georges Avenue
Suite 277
Avenel, NJ 07001

732-738-5221

Info@vehicledynamics.net

www.vehicledynamics.net

PhotoGraphics Publishing

23 Cool Water Court, Palm Coast, Florida 32137

www.PhotoGraphicsPublishing.com

ISBN 13: 978-0982973066

Professional Driving Techniques © 2014 Anthony J. Scotti

Shell materials   © Shell Oil Company

Dedicated. . .

In loving memory of my wife Judy,

and to my daughter, Toni-Ann

About the Author

Anthony J. Scotti

For more than 40 years, Tony Scotti has catered to the driver training needs of industry and public service agencies.

He has trained governments, corporations, law enforcement agencies and military organizations to protect themselves while in a vehicle. He has trained more than 300 corporations in 33 countries on five continents.

His educational publications are used in schools and universities worldwide.

Mr. Scotti personally oversees the VDI Instructor Development Program, a comprehensive, ongoing process that serves to distinguish VDI's instructors from all others.

He has been the subject of numerous interviews in the national media, and has been a speaker at conferences throughout the world. He holds a B.S. in Engineering from Northeastern University.

Prologue

In 2003, Joe Autera, his business partner Larry Side and I sat down in Medford, MA, home of *the Scotti School of Defensive Driving*, to discuss a plan for resurrecting the Scotti School's training philosophy and methodology. Having traveled that same path for more than three decades, I expressed my belief that it would be a daunting task. But both Joe and Larry were convinced that it could be done and were ready and willing to make the huge commitment of time, energy and resources it would take to continue the traditions of the original Scotti School. So we sat down and developed a plan that would combine a time tested philosophy and methodology with modern technology to achieve the same goal as the original school – provide world class training in skills that would keep people alive around the world. That meeting was where Tony Scotti's Vehicle Dynamics Institute (TSVDI) got it's start.

Today, more than a decade later, in a typical ten week time span, TSVDI typically conducts 20 to 30 training programs and interacts with 200 to 300 security, law enforcement and military professionals responsible for protecting corporate executives, high net worth individuals, government officials, military officers and their respective family members. VDI will typically deliver those programs in four or five states in the US and three or more foreign countries. While my opinion may be slightly biased, it seems to me that that meeting back in 2003 worked out pretty well.

So, it's my pleasure to introduce Tony Scotti's Vehicle Dynamics Institute and the team that I am confident will carry forward the Scotti School methodology and philosophy for the next thirty years and beyond.

Tony Scotti

Joseph Autera
President and CEO

A former Non-Commissioned Officer in the US Army, Mr. Autera is widely recognized as Tony Scotti's protégé and one of just two Scotti-certified Master Instructors in the world. An active member of the VDI training cadre, his career in the private sector spans over twenty years, during which time Mr. Autera has had the opportunity to plan, direct and participate in protective security operations focusing on detecting and interdicting a broad range of threats in moderate and high risk locales to include South and Central America, Europe, and both the Middle and Far East.

Prior to founding VDI, he held positions as the Director of Security with a multi-national technology concern and Vice President of Global Security Services for one of the world's leading providers of crisis management and risk mitigation services to multi-national corporations as well as non-governmental organizations.

Mr. Autera has authored articles on the subjects of driver training, threat recognition and surveillance detection which have been featured in some of the security industry's most highly regarded publications including *Security Management Magazine*, the *FBI National Academy Associate*, *Intersec* and the *Journal of Counterterrorism and Homeland Security*.

Additionally, he has been invited to speak on these topics at the *2013 New Jersey State Police Executive Protection Training Symposium*, *29th* and *30th Annual Executive Protection International Conference*, the *2007, 2008 & 2011 Protective Security Conference*, the *American Society for Industrial Security (ASIS) 50th Annual Seminar and Exhibition*, and the *International Association of Counterterrorism and Security Professionals (IACSP) Terrorism Trends and Forecasts Symposium*.

Larry Side
VP of Operations & Chief Instructor

Mr. Side retired as a Non Commissioned Officer in the US Army after twenty years of Active, Reserve and National Guard service during which he was responsible, at various times, for developing and implementing a variety of training programs related to vehicle operations, advanced driving techniques and mobile force protection tactics. He is also one of just two Scotti-certified Master Instructors in the world.

His private sector experience includes an eight year tenure as a Performance Test Driver and Lead Test Driver under contract to the US government, during which time he was directly involved in the testing and evaluation of a wide variety of experimental and prototype vehicles. Mr. Side's experience on the test track and various types of driving ranges has contributed extensively to a number of research, development and testing projects conducted by VDI on behalf of various private sector entities, government agencies and industry related publications.

Mr. Side's professional experience extends to the protective security realm as well, where he has participated in planning and conducting close protection, surveillance detection and secure transportation operations in moderate and high risk security locales around the globe, from the Middle East to Latin America. Currently, as VDI's Chief Instructor, he is responsible for overseeing the preparation and conduct of VDI's training courses, ranging from open enrollment driver training and surveillance detection courses conducted at the firm's primary training facilities to client-specific, custom designed driver training, surveillance detection and instructor development programs conducted as mobile training programs throughout the world.

VDI Professional Training Staff

While there are many things that differentiate VDI from every other driver training provider in the world today, the one that stands out the most is the fact that in addition to having real world experience conducting protective security, military and/or law enforcement operations, each and every VDI instructor is fully qualified and certified to provide training using a proprietary methodology that Tony Scotti developed and refined over the course of more than forty years as the leader in specialized driver training.

Achieving and maintaining the highly sought after Scotti certification requires completion of a rigorous and extensive instructor development program overseen by Tony Scotti. A comprehensive train-the-trainer course is just one step in a process that may take the successful candidate more than a year to complete. Once certified, and in order to maintain his or her Scotti Instructor Certification, every VDI instructor is required to participate in in-service training on an ongoing basis, mentor other staff members, and participate in research and development projects related to driver training, adult learning theory and the applied science of vehicle dynamics. It is this exhaustive process which ensures that VDI's students receive the most advanced, highest quality driver training available, regardless of which courses they participate in.

Author's Acknowledgments

I would like to thank the people that made this book possible.

First, there are the instructors of Tony Scotti Associates who did the research and the testing, and who spent many a day in God-forsaken hell-holes proving that all this theory actually works.

Then there is my daughter Toni Ann, who is my biggest critic and best friend, and who continues to prove the theory that the apple does not fall far from the tree. Poor kid.

Then there is Larry Snow. Larry did not actually help with the book, but he is married to my daughter and the kid deserves all the credit in the world.

I don't know what I can say about publisher Joyce Huber. Her persistence, patience, and understanding are what made this book possible. Without her there would be no book. May all those who choose to write have a Joyce Huber.

Special thanks to our editor, Claudia Sammartino; photographer, Jim Spencer; Dan Raber; consultant, Eleanor Eidson; Kathy Chiariello, Mercedes Benz Corporate Communications; Holly Hutchins, Shell Oil Company; Denise Wilkinson, Shell Oil Company; Tina Foley, The National Highway Traffic Safety Administration; Lyndy Lyle Moore, Bike Florida and Florida's Share the Road Campaign; and Bryan T. Sammartino, NJ Level II Fire Instructor.

Over the 30 years I have spent in the driver training/consulting business, I have worked and consulted with many top-notch specialists and drivers of all levels and abilities. Although there are too many to mention here individually, they — and the experiences we shared "in the trenches' — have enriched the pages of this book.

Brief Contents

About the Author iv

Detailed Table of Contents viii

List of Figures, Tables, and Boxes xix

Acknowledgments xxii

Introduction 1

PART I — DRIVING IS A STATE OF MIND — AND BODY— AND VEHICLE 9

Chapter 1 - The Mind/Body Driving Connection . . 11

Chapter 2 - Your Vision and Sense of Space . . . 19

Chapter 3 - Your Reaction Time/Sense of Timing . . 29

Chapter 4 - The Windshield and Mirrors:
Your "Windows" to the Road 35

Chapter 5 - Seat Belts and Child Safety Seats . . . 43

Chapter 6 - Air Bags: How They Work and
Precautions to Take 51

Chapter 7 - Tires, Part I: Type and Quality
Make a Big Difference 63

Chapter 8 - Tires, Part II: Care and Maintenance
Make an Even Bigger Difference . . . 77

Chapter 9 - Smart Car Care: Tips for Keeping Your
Vehicle Safe and on the Road 89

Chapter 10 - Know Your Car:
The Ten-Minute Checklist 95

Chapter 11 - The Glove Compartment and Trunk:
Keep Them Well Stocked for Safety . 101

**PART II — THE SCIENCE AND TECHNIQUES OF
          EVERYDAY DRIVING** .   .   .   **107**

Chapter 12 - Introduction to Vehicle Dynamics: The
              Physical Basis of Car Control   .   .   .   109

Chapter 13 - Maintaining Traction: Tire-to-Road
              Grip and Weight Transfer   113

Chapter 14 - Losing and Regaining Traction:
              How to Handle Braking Skids,
              Power Skids, and Cornering Skids .   .   125

Chapter 15 - Steering and G-Forces:
              Vehicle Dynamics in Action   131

Chapter 16 - Curves and Cornering at Speed:
              How to Handle the Road When
              It's *Not* Straight.   145

Chapter 17 - Speed and Stopping Distances .   .   .   157

Chapter 18 - Braking Control, Part I:
              The Science of How a Car Stops   .   .   171

Chapter 19 - Braking Control, Part II: Non-ABS
              and ABS Techniques   177

Chapter 20 - Turning Left, Turning Right,
              Backing Up, and Turning Around .   .   185

Chapter 21 - Passing and Being Passed   195

PART III — ACCIDENTS **207**

Chapter 22- Accident Stats: Who, What,
              When, and How   209

Chapter 23 - What Causes Accidents?   215

Chapter 24 - Typical Accident Scenarios:
              And How to Deal with Them   .   .   .   225

Chapter 25 - Crash Course: Simple Tips
              that Could Help Save Lives   239

**PART IV — DRIVING IN SPECIAL
               SITUATIONS** **245**

Chapter 26 - Foul Weather Driving 247

Chapter 27 - Driving Safely at Night: There's
               More to It Than Good Headlights . . 261

Chapter 28 - Roadside Breakdown: Roadside
               Emergencies and How to Deal
               with Them 267

Chapter 29 - Road Rage: How to Avoid It,
               How to Deal with It 275

Chapter 30 - Alone Behind the Wheel 279

Chapter 31 - If Trapped in Water 287

PART V — RESOURCES **291**

Website Resources 292

Index **299**

Detailed Contents

About the Author iv

Brief Contents v

List of Figures, Tables, and Boxes xix

Acknowledgments xxii

Introduction 1

"The Good Driver" Myth 1

Basic Rules of the Road (Then and Now) . . . 2

What This Book Is All About 5

PART I — DRIVING IS A STATE OF MIND — AND BODY— AND VEHICLE . . . . .

Chapter 1 - **The Mind/Body Driving Connection** . 11

Physical and Mental Fatigue 12

And Just What Kinds of Problems Does
Driving While Fatigued Create? 13

The Way You Sit in a Car Can Help
You Remain Alert 14

"Avoid Driving While Taking This
Product" 16

Driving While Under the Influence 17

Chapter 2 - **Your Vision and Sense of Space** . . **19**

Protecting Your Vision. 19

Seeing at Night 20

Protecting and Enhancing Your Driving
Vision — Day and Night 21

Car Design and Visibility 23

The Myth of "Tired Eyes" 24

Selective Vision and Your Sense of Space . . . 24

Looking Near, Looking Far 24

Always Leave Yourself an "Out". . . . 26

Sense of Space in Traffic Situations. . . . 26

Chapter 3 - **Your Reaction Time/
Sense of Timing** **29**

What Is Reaction Time? 29

A Hypothetical Example of Reaction Time/
Sense of Timing 30

Many Factors Other Than Age Affect
Reaction Time 30

Decision Making Behind the Wheel 32

Over-dependence on Reaction Time 33

Training *Can* Improve Reaction Time 34

Chapter 4 - **The Windshield and Mirrors: Your
"Windows" to the Road** **35**

The Windshield 35

Windshield Visibility 35

Windshield Wipers 37

Rearview and Sideview Mirrors 39

How Important Are Mirrors? 40

Adjusting the Mirrors 40

"Blind Spots" 42

Chapter 5 - **Seat Belts and Child Safety Seats** . **43**

Seat Belts 43

Why Do We Need Seat Belts? 43

How to Wear a Seat Belt Properly . . . 44

Child Safety Seats 45

For Short Trips, Why Bother with a
Child Safety Seat? 45

An Adult's Lap Is Pretty Safe, Right? . . . 46

When Are Kids Big Enough for a
Regular Seat Belt? 46

There Are So Many Kinds of Safety Seats.
Which One Is Best? 46

Why Does an Infant Seat Have to Face
the Rear? 47

How do I Make Sure the Child Safety Seat
Is Working Properly? 48

Where's the Safest Place for Kids
in the Car? 48

But I'm Not Comfortable with My Child in the
Back. Shouldn't She Be Closer to Me? . . 48

If an Older Child *Must* Be Seated in Front . 49

Chapter 6 - **Air Bags: How They Work and
Precautions to Take 51**

How Air Bags Work 52

Air Bag System Components 52

Rapid Deployment 53

Dust 54

Side and Curtain Air Bags 54

Precautions to Take 56

The Risk Zone 56

Air Bag Fatalities 57

Protecting Yourself and Your Passengers
from Potential Air Bag Injury 58

Tilt and Telescoping Steering Wheels . . . 60

Manual On-Off Switches for Air Bags . . . 60

Chapter 7 - **Tires, Part I: Type and Quality
Make a Big Difference 63**

Tire Tread Design 63

All-Weather Tires 64

Snow Tires 64

Chains and Studded Snow Tires 66

How to Decode a Tire: The Sidewall Story . . 66

Typical Information on the Sidewall of a
Passenger Car Tire 67

Typical Information on the Sidewall of a
Light Truck Tire 71

Replacement Tire Selection 72

Tire Size and Construction 73

Speed Rating 73

Tire Mounting Do's and Don't's 74

Chapter 8 - **Tires, Part II: Care and Maintenance
Make an Even Bigger Difference . . 77**

Proper Tire Inflation Pressure 77

The Correct Air Pressure 77

Keeping Tires at Proper Pressure Is Easy . . 79

The Perils of Improper Inflation 80

Symptoms of "Sick" Tires 82

Proper Tire Rotation 83

Worn Tires 83

Tire Abuse — Yours and Nature's 84

    Wheel Spinning 84

    Driving Speed 85

    Temperature and Temperature Changes . . 86

Chapter 9 - **Smart Car Care: Tips for Keeping Your Vehicle Safe and on the Road . . . 89**

Stick to Your Routine (Maintenance) . . . . .

Keep Your Vehicle a Well-Oiled Machine . . . 89

Go with the Flow: Your Vehicle's Fluids . . . 90

Know the Positives and Negatives of
    Your Battery 90

Check Wipers & Washer Fluid Intermittently . . 92

Light the Way to Safer Driving 92

Help Your Tires Tread Lightly 93

Conserve Fuel 93

Chapter 10 - **Know Your Car: The Ten-Minute Checklist 95**

Air Filter 95

Battery 95

Belts and Hoses. 95

Brake Fluid 96

Brake System 96

Coolant /Antifreeze. 96

Engine Oil 96

Lights 97

Power Steering Fluid 97

Shock Absorbers 97

Tire Pressure 97

Wheel Alignment 98

Tire Rotation 98

Tire Tread 98

Transmission Fluid 99

Washer Fluid 99

Wiper Blades 99

Chapter 11 - **The Glove Compartment and Trunk: Keep Them Well Stocked for Safety   101**

What to Carry in the Glove Compartment
in Case of a Breakdown 103

What to Carry in Your Trunk 103

What to Keep in a First-Aid Kit 106

Cold Weather Gear 106

PART II — THE SCIENCE AND TECHNIQUES OF EVERYDAY DRIVING 107

Chapter 12 - **Introduction to Vehicle Dynamics: The Physical Basis of Car Control   .   109**

Loss of Control — Two Types 109

Wherever the Laws of Physics Take It 110

Chapter 13 - **Maintaining Traction: Tire-to-Road Grip and Weight Transfer 113**

Tire Adhesion — Tire-to-Road Grip 113

Rolling Contact 116

Weight Transfer to the Tire Patch 117

"Car Feel" — Keeping in Touch with the
Control Limits of the Car 120

Chapter 14 - **Losing and Regaining Traction: How to Handle Braking Skids, Power Skids, and Cornering Skids .   125**

Braking Skids 125

Front-Wheel Braking Skid 126

Rear-Wheel Braking Skid 126

Four-Wheel Braking Skid 127

Power (Acceleration) Skids 128

Rear-Wheel Drive Power Skid 128

Front-Wheel Drive Power Skid 128

Cornering Skid 129

Chapter 15 - **Steering and G-Forces: Vehicle Dynamics in Action . . . 131**

Newton's Laws of Motion Applied to Driving —
Simplified 131

Your Vehicle's Control Limits 132

The "Driving Equation" — Figuring Out
   the G-Force 134
Small Changes in Speed/
   Very Big Changes in G-Forces 136
The Tire Adhesion Factor 138
The Phenomenon of Understeer
   and Oversteer 139
   Neutral Steer, Understeer, Oversteer . . . 140
   The Physical Dynamics of Understeer
      and Oversteer 141
   Causes of Understeer and Oversteer . . . 142
   How to Compensate for Understeer
      and Oversteer 143

**Chapter 16 - Curves and Cornering at Speed:
How to Handle the Road When
It's *Not* Straight 145**
The Three Types of Corners (Curves) 146
The Science of Handling the Curves 148
Cornering Techniques 149
   "Straightening Out the Corners" 150
   Outside-Inside-Outside Technique . . . 151
   Speed and Braking while Cornering . . . 153
   Remember, You Cannot Judge the
      Next Curve by the Last One 155

**Chapter 17 - Speed and Stopping Distances:
The Time-Distance Relationship
to Stopping and Turning** **157**
Speed Plays All Kinds of Tricks on Us 157
Miles Per Hour (mph) vs
   Feet Per Second (fps) 158
Time-Distance Driving Scenario 161
Time-Distance-Weight Driving Scenario . . . 162
Time Needed to Cross an Intersection . . . 163
Time Needed to Turn at an Intersection . . . 164
Safe Following Distances and Braking . . . 166
   A Typical Following Distance Scenario . . 166
   How Much Space *Should* You Keep
      in Front of You 168

How Do Your Figure Out How Much
Space You *Have*? 168
Safe Following Distances When Driving
at Night 169
Specific Following Distances for
Certain Vehicles 170

Chapter 18 - **Braking Control, Part I:
The Science of How a Car Stops** . . **171**

Brakes Don't Stop Cars 171
Brake Pedal Pressure and Loss of Control . . 172
The Vehicle Stopping Equation 173

Chapter 19 - **Braking Control, Part II: Non-ABS
and ABS Techniques** **177**

The Difference between Non-ABS and ABS . 177
Non-ABS Braking. 178
"Controlled Braking" in Non-ABS Vehicles . 179
ABS Braking 181
Brake Failure 182
Brake Fade 182
Practice Makes Perfect 183

Chapter 20 - **Turning: How to Turn Left, Turn Right,
Back Up, and Turn Around** 185

Turning Left 185
Turning Right 186
Backing Up 187
Cars Are Designed to Go *Forward* . . . 187
Key Points to Keep in Mind When
Backing Up. 188
Turning Around 189
U-Turns 190
Two-Point Turns 191
Three-Point Turn 193

Chapter 21 - **Passing and Being Passed** . . . **195**

When NOT to Pass 195
When to Pass 196
How to Pass Safely 199
Signaling Your Intent to Pass . . . 199
Safe Passing Distance 199

Safe Passing Speeds 201
Special Passing Situations 203
Passing on Three-Lane Highways 203
Passing on the Right 203
Being Passed 204
Give Way to the Right 204
Maintain a Steady Speed 204

PART III — ACCIDENTS **207**
Chapter 22- **Accident Stats: Who, What, When,
and How** 209
Gender 210
Age 210
Age/Gender Differences 210
Alcohol Involvement 211
Vehicle Types 211
Crash Types 213
Chapter 23 - **What Causes Accidents?** **215**
The Driving System 215
The Driving Problem 217
Types of Accidents 218
Accident-Producing Situations Caused by
Drivers Themselves 221
Accident-Producing Situations Caused by
Defective Vehicles 222
Chapter 24 - **Typical Accident Scenarios:
And How to Deal with Them** . . . **225**
Yield the Right of Way 225
Basic Accident Situations 226
Oncoming Car 227
Entering & Merging 227
Ongoing Cars or Cars Ahead 228
Cars Following Too Closely. 230
Cars Backing Out. 230
Motorcyclists 230
Pedestrians and Bicyclists 230
Other Driving Dangers 234

Someone Runs a Red Light   234
You Have a Blowout.   234
You Start to Skid   235
Your Brakes Fail   235
Your Accelerator Sticks   236
Your Hood Flies Open   236
Your Car Goes into Deep Water   237

Chapter 25 - **Crash Course: Simple Tips
that Could Help Save Lives** **239**

I've Just Seen a Bad Collision.
    What Can I Do to Help?   239
Should I Always Stop?   240
What's My First Step in Treating the Injured?   .   241
I Don't Think She's Breathing. Now What? .   .   241
How Do I Control Severe Bleeding?   .   .   .   242
All This Blood and Breathing.
    Should I Be Worried about AIDS?   .   .   .   242
If I Do Move Someone, How Should I Do It?   .   243
I Think She's in Shock. Now What?   .   .   .   243
How Can I Help Myself If I'm in a Wreck?   .   .   244

PART IV — DRIVING IN SPECIAL SITUATIONS 245

Chapter 26 - **Foul Weather Driving**   247

Driving in Rain   247
    Hydroplaning   248
When Rain Causes a Flood or There Is
    Rushing Water   249
If Your Vehicle Stalls in Water   250
Driving in Snow   250
    Prepare to Get Under Way   250
    Maintaining Traction on Snow   251
    If You Get Stuck in Snow or Ice   .   .   .   252
Blizzard Conditions   253
Driving on Ice   254
    Stopping and Braking on Ice   255
    To Recover from an Ice Slide   255
Winter Driving Scenario — The Dynamics
    in "Action"   256

Fog 257

Extreme Heat 258

What to Do If Your Car Overheats . . . 258

Lightning 259

Chapter 27 - **Driving Safely at Night: There's
More to It Than Good Headlights . 261**

Keep Your Headlights in Good
Working Order 261

Keep Your Windshield and Mirrors Clean . . 262

Adjust Your Speed to the Range of Your
Headlights 262

Keep Your Eyes Moving 263

Protect Your Eyes from Glare 264

Use Your Lights Wisely 264

Make It Easy for Others to See You 265

Avoid Steady Driving at the Hour of Your
Usual Bedtime 265

Chapter 28 - **Roadside Breakdown: How to Deal
with Roadside Emergencies . . . 267**

How Do I Know Something Is Wrong
with My Vehicle? 267

If There's Something Wrong with My Vehicle,
Should I Stop Where I Am or Continue? . . 268

If I Have to Pull Over, How Do I Do It
Safely? 268

How Should I Get Help? 269

Should I Stay in My Car While Waiting
for Help? 269

What If a Stranger Approaches? 270

Are There Any Repairs I Can Make to Get
Myself Moving Again? 271

What If I Get a Flat Tire? 271

How Can I Jumpstart a Battery Safely? . . . 272

What Can I Do to *Prevent* a Breakdown? . . 274

Chapter 29 - **Road Rage: How to Avoid It,
How to Deal with It 275**

What Starts Road Rage? 275

Who Commits Road Rage? 276

Things to Do/Don't Do to Avoid or
   Deal with Road Rage 276
Chapter 30 - **Alone Behind the Wheel** **279**

What Should I Know about Parking Safety? . . 279

Should I Do Anything Special in
   Parking Garages? 280

If I Lock My Car Before I Leave It,
   Is that Enough? 280

I Hear a Lot about Carjackings.
   Is There Any Way to Avoid Them? . . . 281

Got Any Safety "Trip Tips"? 282

Should I Always Have My Doors Locked
   When I'm Driving? 283

What Do I Do If My Car Just Conks Out? . . 283

Is Having a Phone in the Car a Good Idea? . . 284

I Seem to Get More Tired When I Drive Alone.
   What Can I Do about It? 285

What If I Plan and Prepare But Someone
   Confronts Me Anyway? 286

Chapter 31 - **If Trapped in Water** **287**

PART V — RESOURCES **290**

Website Resources 290

Index **299**

List of Figures, Tables, and Boxes

FIGURES

Figure I-1:   The First Four-Wheel Car 3

Figure 1-1:   Drive with Two Hands on the
Steering Wheel in Proper Position . . . 15

Figure 3-1:   Reflexes in Decision Making 31

Figure 3-2:   The Effects of Various Reaction Times on
Total Stopping Distances 32

Figure 4-1:   Keep Your Windshield Clean 37

Figure 4-2   Mirror Zones 41

Figure 6-1:   Front- and Passenger-Side Air Bags —
Deployed 52

Figure 6-2:   Side Air Bags — Deployed 54

Figure 6-3:   Curtain Air Bags — Deployed 55

Figure 7-1:   Sidewall Tire Information 65

Figure 7-2:   Sidewall Tire Information on
Lite Truck Tires 67

Figure 8-1:   How Tires Look with Various Amounts of
Inflation 82

Figure 8-2:   Common Correct Tire Rotation Patterns . 83

Figure 13-1: Tire Adhesion — Four Patches of
Rubber 114

Figure 13-2: Maximum Performance Available
from a Vehicle 115

Figure 13-3: Block Diagram of Weight Transfer . . 118

Figure 15-1: Relationship of Speed to Lateral
Acceleration 137

Figure 15-2: Understeer 140

Figure 15-3: Oversteer 140

Figure 16-1: A Little Bit of Road Utopia 145

Figure 16-2: Increasing, Decreasing, and Constant
Radius Corners 146

Figure 16-3:   Diagram of a Radius 147
Figure 16-4:   Big Radius vs Small Radius Corners . . 150
Figure 17-1:   Time Needed to Cross an Intersection . 163
Figure 17-2:   Time Needed to Make a Right Turn . . 164
Figure 17-3:   Time Needed to Make a Left-hand Turn 165
Figure 17-4:   Night Vision vs Stopping Distances . . 169
Figure 18-1:   Brake Pedal Pressure and
               Loss of Control 172
Figure 20-1:   Car Making a U-Turn 190
Figure 20-2:   Two-Point Turn 192
Figure 20-3:   Three-Point Turn 193
Figure 23-1:   The Driving System 215
Figure 24-1:   Avoiding Car Ahead Stopped
               at Intersection 229
Figure 28-1:   Correct Jumper Cable-to-Battery
               Connections for Jumpstarting a Vehicle. 273
Figure 30-1   Trapped in Water 287l

TABLES

Table 17-1:   How Long Does It Take to Stop a Car? . 158
Table 17-2:   Conversion from Miles Per Hour to
               Feet Per Second 159

BOXES

Box 5-1:   Child Safety Checklist 49
Box 7-1:   New Tire Tread Simulation 65
Box 8-1:   Your Driving Habits and Tire "Health" . 86
Box 8-2:   Checklist to Help Your Tires
            Last Longer 83
Box 9-1:   Recognizing Fluid Leaks 91
Box 11-1:   Fire Extinguishers and Automotive Fires 105
Box 15-1:   G-Force Ratings of Popular Car Models 132
Box 16-1:   The "Early Apex" Phenomenon . . . 152
Box 17-1:   How to Convert from Mph to Fps . . 159
Box 17-2:   The Easier Way to Convert Mph to Fps. 160

Box 22-1:   Passenger Vehicle Fatalities 212

Box 23-1:   The Top 10 Two-Car Crash Situations . 219

Box 30-1:   Your Keychain: Potential Crime
             Prevention in the Palm of Your Hand . 282

**See Index for a full list of
"DRIVING SCENARIOS"
(how to's and examples)**

Introduction

THE "GOOD DRIVER" MYTH

A common misconception about driving is the definition of the "good driver."

Whether you drive for a living, live to drive, or just drive to get yourself around, if you think you're a "good driver" just because you can drive *fast*, you're sadly mistaken. Simply driving fast requires little skill if you're simply driving in a straight line. (Sure, professional drag racing drivers might differ with this evaluation, but that's a highly-specialized form of straight-line driving.)

Or you may think that your "maneuvering" skills are top notch if you routinely:

- Pass other cars when you please, without regard to safety
- Try to beat a yellow light
- Squeal tires every time you accelerate from a dead stop
- Weave through traffic
- Drive with one hand
- Cut people off in order to get ahead of them

People who regularly do this aren't "good" drivers, they're *aggressive and unsafe drivers.* They mistake *prudent caution* for timidity in driving. They mistake using their head before making a move as being timid — and they mistake fear for cowardice.

But, any racing driver will tell you that only *fools* take unnecessary chances on the road. *Caution* is the byword of racing — and it should be for everyday driving as well.

But prudent caution alone is not enough to make you a "good driver." There are several things you have to know and a lot you have to be able to do — and do consistently and intuitively — before you can call yourself a "good driver" — a safe driver.

- You have to know the rules of the road.

- You have to know your own physical and mental driving limitations.

- You have to know how to use, maintain, and control your vehicle properly.

- And you have to know how to handle the hazards and dangers that can crop up in the driving environment at any time.

Learning the basic rules of the road is the first step you should take.

BASIC RULES OF THE ROAD

Then ...

Seventy years ago, when there were few vehicles and roads were narrow, there were two simple traffic rules.

1. One required a driver to turn to the right when meeting a vehicle coming from the opposite direction.

2. The other required him to turn to the left when overtaking and passing a vehicle going in the same direction.

At other times, *a driver could use the center or any other part of the road.*

It is easy to imagine the confusion and wreckage that would result if these were the only rules followed today!

Figure I-1. The First Four-Wheel Car. Courtesy
Mercedes-Benz

And Now ...

Today, rules of the road are standardized throughout the United States to promote highway safety.

Any modifications will be normally indicated by traffic control personnel or by signs or markings.

> **ALWAYS obey directions given by traffic control personnel or signs *regardless* of conflict with the general rules listed here.**

Although there are many rules to cover specific situations (which we won't go into here), there are a few rules that apply generally — and it is your responsibility as a "good" driver to know them.

As you'll see, these rules are not that much different from the rules of yore — but HOW you observe them on *today's* roads with *today's* vehicles makes a big difference in whether you have a safe trip or become a statistic.

So what are today's basic "rules of the road"?

> **The following list is a brief outline, but we'll be looking *in detail* at those listed — and the techniques for following them safely and legally — in the many chapters to come.**

1. **Drive on the Right.** You must operate vehicles on the right of the highway, giving approaching traffic at least one-half of the road unless conditions or directions indicate otherwise.

2. **Signal Your Intentions** — "properly and adequately." You must give clear warning signals that are standard, appropriate to your intentions, and timed to give other drivers reasonable warning.

3. **Pass on the Left.** When overtaking and passing other vehicles, pass to the left and remain on the left until safely clear of the overtaken vehicle.

4. **Pass on the Right ONLY When ...** You may pass on the right when the vehicle you are passing has signaled and is making a left turn. You may also pass on the right if you are on a street or highway designed for two or more lanes of traffic in both directions or on a one-way street with at least two lanes. You may *NOT* pass on the right if you must drive off the pavement or the main portion of the roadway to get around another vehicle.

5. **Change Lanes Sparingly and Cautiously.** When changing lanes to pass another vehicle and return to your lane — or to position yourself for a turn or road exit — keep movement from one lane to another to the minimum. If you must change lanes, signal your intentions; then ensure that such movement can be made safely and does not interfere with the movement of traffic in other lanes.

6. **Turn the "Correct" Way** — To turn right at an intersection, approach the turn at the extreme right of the traveled way and make the turn itself as close to the right as practicable. To turn left, approach the turn to the right

of, and close to, the centerline, leaving the intersection to the right of the centerline of the entered road. A turn to reverse the direction of a vehicle (u-turn, where legal) should not be made unless a vehicle approaching from either direction can see the movement from a distance of 500 feet.

7. **Yield the Right of Way**. Observe the rules of right-of-way with judgment and courtesy. The safe driver gives the right-of-way rather than taking it.

8. **Observe Speed Limits**. Highway speeds to be observed under normal conditions vary somewhat from state to state. These speeds are generally posted on regulatory signs with warnings where reduction in speed is directed. At no time should vehicles be operated in excess of posted limits. Driver judgment should be consciously developed to determine speeds suitable to other conditions.

9. **Assess Your Moves — *Before* You Make Them**. Do *not* start, stop, or turn a vehicle from its course on the highway without ensuring that making such a change is reasonably safe. You must know how to judge the effect of YOUR vehicle's movement upon *another* vehicle's speed or direction.

> **Safe driving requires *constant* adjustment to changing driving conditions.**

WHAT THIS BOOK IS ABOUT

Although the rules of the road and the roads and vehicles themselves have changed over the years, remarkably much has remained the same. Vehicles now — as then — still have the same basic controls for accelerating (gas pedal), steering (steering wheel), and braking (brakes). And the physical principles that create forces on a vehicle as you maneuver it using these controls — friction, momentum, G-forces, centrifugal force — have the same effect now as they did then.

What we're getting at here is that **a "good driver" — a safe driver — is determined by qualities (knowledge and skills) of the driver him/herself.**

> **A "good" driver — a safe driver — knows and practices good, safe driving techniques — *regardless* of the vehicle he's driving, the road she's on, or the environment he's in.**

The book you hold in your hands, *Driving Techniques for the Professional and Non-Professional, 3rd Edition*, shows you how to develop all the knowledge and skills you need to become a "good" driver — a safe driver.

Part I, DRIVING IS A STATE OF MIND — AND BODY — AND VEHICLE.

This Part begins with **a discussion of the driver him/herself.** We explore, for example, the driver's physical and mental state; effects of fatigue; vision and sense of space (two key factors that underlie your ability to interpret and negotiate safely in the driving environment); and reaction time and sense of timing.

Then we look at the vehicle itself, focusing on features that directly affect driving safety and that a driver should know how to use properly and to maintain — the windshield, windshield wipers, mirrors, seat belts and child safety seats, air bags, and tires. These are all designed to help you maintain control of your vehicle, to help you drive safely, and to help you avoid serious injury if you are in a collision.

We then consider **some general maintenance rules for your vehicle** — what to check or have checked, and how often. We even include a convenient Ten Minute Checklist that covers 17 items to check, and when to check them.

This Part concludes with a look at **what should be inside every safe driver's glove compartment and trunk,** along with some cautions and warnings. You may never have cause to use some of the items — but if you ever have an emergency on the road, you'll be more than glad you have them.

Part II, THE SCIENCE AND TECHNIQUES OF EVERYDAY DRIVING

This Part is the meat of *Driving Techniques, 3rd Edition.* Most drivers never think of car control until an emergency occurs. When the emergency does occur, it's often too late to think about it. To control a car as efficiently and effectively as possible, you must understand some of the science — as *well* as the techniques — of driving.

So, this Part looks in detail at **the control maneuvers you can make with a car — accelerating, steering, braking.** It covers the basic science behind these maneuvers and discusses specific techniques you can use to maintain maximum control of your vehicle.

It also points out — perhaps more importantly — **what can happen if you *lose* control by not accelerating, steering, or braking *properly*** — and WHY. And it tells you **how to *regain* control** if you've lost it.

We'll look closely at major topics such as: vehicle dynamics; maintaining traction (tire-to-road grip and weight transfer); losing and regaining traction when the traction/weight transfer equation goes out of balance (how to handle braking skids, power skids, cornering skids); steering at speed and G-forces (how speed and tire adhesion enter into the steering control equation); techniques for safe cornering at speed; speed and stopping distances (time-distance relationship in stopping and turning); safe following distances; braking control (how a car stops; non-ABS and ABS techniques); proper turning techniques (turning left, turning right, backing up, and turning around); and passing and being passed. (when to pass, when NOT to pass, how to pass, and how to yield the right of way.)

Part III, ACCIDENTS

Part III, considers what can happen if either you, or the drivers around you on the road, *don't* maintain control — or you, or they, can't *regain* it.

We begin with a look at **current accident statistics to see the who, what, when, and how of accidents.** Then we explore **what causes accidents** (driver, environment, vehicle). Then we consider **typical accident scenarios and tell you how to avoid or deal with them.** And since you'll likely encounter not only vehicles, but pedestrians and bicyclists on the road as well, we give you tips on **how to safely "share the road."**

And finally we offer a Q&A "Crash Course" that provides some suggestions on **how you can help if you come upon or are involved in an accident yourself.**

Part IV, DRIVING IN SPECIAL SITUATIONS

Part IV looks at strategies and techniques for driving in situations that pose special hazards — **driving in foul weather of all types, driving at night, roadside breakdowns, road rage, and driving alone.**

Part V, RESOURCES

Part V provides list of **websites** where you can find the most up-to-date information on driving-related matters.

> So, how can you become a "good driver" — a safe driver? *READ ON!*

PART I

DRIVING IS A STATE OF MIND — AND BODY — AND VEHICLE

In following chapters we look at the driver him/herself — physical and mental state, vision and sense of space, reaction time and sense of timing.

Then we look at the vehicle itself, focusing on the components that directly affect driving safety and that a driver should know how to use properly and to maintain — the windshield, wipers, mirrors, seat belts and child safety seats, air bags, and tires.

We then consider some general maintenance rules for your vehicle — what to check or have checked, and how often. We even include a convenient *Ten-Minute Checklist* that covers 17 items to check, and when to check them.

The Part concludes with a look at what should be inside every safe driver's glove compartment and trunk. You may never have cause to use some of the items — but if you ever have an emergency on the road, you'll be more than glad you have them.

Chapter 1
The Mind/Body Driving Connection, p. 11

Chapter 2
Your Vision and Sense of Space:
Day and Night, p. 19

Chapter 3
Your Reaction Time/Sense of Timing, p. 29

Chapter 4
The Windshield and Mirrors:
Your "Windows" to the Road, p. 35

Chapter 5
Seat Belts and Child Safety Seats, p. 43

Chapter 6
Air Bags:
How They Work and Precautions to Take, p. 51

Chapter 7
Tires, Part I:
Type and Quality Make a Big Difference, p. 63

Chapter 8
Tires, Part II:
Care and Maintenance Make an
Even Bigger Difference, p. 77

Chapter 9
Smart Car Care:
Tips for Keeping Your Vehicle Safe and on the Road, p. 89

Chapter 10
Know Your Car:
The Ten-Minute Checklist, p. 95

Chapter 11
The Glove Compartment and Trunk:
Keep Them Well Stocked for Safety, p. 101

Chapter 1

The Mind/Body Driving Connection

To drive in a safe and secure manner, you must be in good physical and mental condition. This is the very foundation of safe driving. If your driving ability is impaired by illness or injury, or by fatigue or the effect of medications — to say nothing of alcohol or illegal drugs — you should seriously consider *not* driving a vehicle.

How important is physical condition to safe driving? Consider this scenario:

You have developed **a shoulder injury.** Thanks to your sore shoulder, it now takes you just a little longer to move the steering wheel — say, about one second longer.

You are driving along at 40 mph when suddenly someone ahead of you runs a stop sign. Since you are traveling at 40 mph, you are also traveling at the rate of 58.8 feet per second. And, since it now takes you a second longer to react at the wheel, **you also need an *additional* 60 feet (more or less) to get out of the way.**

Those 60 feet could mean the difference between a wild story to tell at the office, or spending years recovering from injury — or worse.

And don't drive while you are emotionally unstable. Never let your emotions get hold of you while driving. Driving while emotionally upset, especially while unusually angry or sad, can reduce your ability to recognize danger and avoid it.

> **The solution to avoiding possible catastrophe is simple: if *anything* makes you feel like you can't drive, don't. If there is any way you can avoid it, avoid it.**

Physical and Mental Fatigue

A driver can be in excellent condition — and have the eyes of an eagle. But a driver, like all other mammals, has a central nervous system, and can get tired. Most drivers, however, often don't think that their fatigue at any given time is a serious impediment to their driving ability — until the fatigue becomes so serious that they are in real danger.

Physical fatigue can be caused by things you did *before* you even got into your vehicle. Driving into work after an all-night party may be a memorable experience, but if your condition is such that you have a hard time finding the door handle of the vehicle, you can wind up with an experience you'd rather forget. Scmetimes just the realities of day-to-day living — such as an all-night session with a sick child or other personal emergencies — make it impossible to drive bright-eyed and bushy-tailed.

Mental fatigue can cause the same problems as physical fatigue. Worries over personal problems, irritation with someone on or off the job who just gave you a hard time — are some of the things that can cause mental fatigue. And you often don't get an opportunity to take a moment to unwind after a stressful day.

> **Driving tired or hung over can literally be fatal. You don't have to lead a life of sainthood, but your state of fatigue should never be *self-induced*.**

You can resist the effects of fatigue by simply being aware of them, knowing they exist, and being alert to the first warning signs.

The symptoms of fatigue are obvious. After all, everyone has had trouble keeping his or her eyes open at one time or another time. **However, the *early* signs of fatigue are NOT so obvious.** All of us have had the following experience:

> We drive a car down a route we travel every day. Nothing noteworthy happens on the drive, and at some point on the route — at an intersection, a bridge, wherever — we suddenly realize that we don't really recall the drive to that spot. It is as if we suddenly materialized at that intersection or bridge. *This is a strong warning that you are fatigued.*

And, if your eyelids are heavy and your eyes are burning, you're *definitely* fatigued!

And Just What Kinds of Problems Does Driving While Fatigued Create?

- **When driving at night, you may have a hard time concentrating on your driving.** This is no great revelation. When you are tired, you have a hard time concentrating on *anything* you do.

- **When fatigued, you tend to take more risks.** You may do things while fatigued you would *never* think of doing when well rested. Fatigue dulls your mind.

- **When you're tired, you may have a tough time keeping your car in the proper lane.** You may weave side to side and appear drunk, even though you're not. You're just very, very tired. But the results are the same. It's a dangerous, accident-producing situation.

- **When you're fatigued, you often speed up and slow down erratically.** If you often find yourself doing that, be aware of it. *You're fatigued.*

- **If you're fatigued and you ignore these early warning signals and continue to drive — you develop "tunnel vision."** Your vision deteriorates. It gradually becomes very difficult to see. Your attention focuses forward You will begin to miss signals or signs in the peripheral vision area. This accounts, in part, for many of the accidents that occur near the end of a long day at work.

The surest way to recover from fatigue is to stop and rest or take a short nap.

The most successful driving is performed when the driver rests 20-30 minutes for every one-and-a-half to two hours of driving.

The time-honored cure of drinking coffee to stay awake is only a stopgap, temporary measure. Sure, the caffeine can bring you up fast, but as the kidneys eliminate it from the body, it will also bring you down fast.

Even a brief stop and just a leg-stretching short walk can be valuable in fighting fatigue.

The Way You Sit in a Car Can Help You Remain Alert

There is no single clear-cut fool-proof way to beat fatigue — but seating position is often critical.

Many people blame car seats for an uncomfortable ride. Most of the time the seats aren't to blame — it's the way you sit in them. Sitting erect allows you to stay alert longer. Shoulder and arm positions are also important.

- **When you get into your vehicle, place your hand at the top of the steering wheel.** *Your shoulder should be in contact with the seat back.* If your shoulder rises off the seat back, you'll find that when you execute an emergency maneuver, you'll be lifted right off your seat. Instead of using the steering wheel to control the car, you'll be using it to hold yourself in place.

- **Consider the steering wheel as a clock** — with the top as 12 o'clock and the bottom, six. Ideally, your hands should be at the three- and nine-o'clock positions. Both hands should remain on the wheel unless it is necessary to operate another control in the car with either hand.

- **As you sit comfortably, look at your arms.** If they are bent at the elbow more than 90 degrees, the result will be poor circulation and very tired arms in a short time.

Figure 1-1. Drive with Two Hands on the Steering Wheel in Proper Position — Photo © Jim Spencer/SeaNotes

- **One of the most common errors is caused by sitting too close to the steering wheel.** This often indicates a lack of confidence on the part of the driver, or poor eyesight, or both.

- **The opposite extreme, getting too relaxed behind the wheel, can also be a major problem.** A driver with the window rolled down, elbow propped up on the sill, and driving with one hand is probably just a little *too* relaxed and over-confident.

"Avoid Driving While Taking This Product"

All drugs — prescription, over-the-counter, and illegal — have the potential to suppress your brain's ability to process information. And the amount of information processing needed to control a vehicle can become more than an impaired brain can handle.

The warning "*Avoid driving while taking this medication*" appears on the back of many over-the-counter medications and on many prescription bottles. The makers of these medications are trying to tell you something. Even something as mild as a hay fever pill can seriously impair your ability to control a vehicle.

> **Read the label before you take *any* medication and then drive.**

If you're taking prescription medication, ask your doctor about the effects it may have on your driving. If it can have any negative effects, do whatever you can to avoid driving while on the medication.

Driving While under the Influence . . .

All tests examining **the role of alcohol in driving impairment** have indicated the same thing: alcohol reduces the capacity of the mind to process information from both the road and the overall-driving environment.

Similar tests performed using marijuana showed different results. Although reaction times were slowed by marijuana, they were not slowed as much as when test subjects were given alcohol. The conclusion would seem to be that marijuana is less dangerous than alcohol when it comes to driving. Nevertheless, it is still a dangerous, foolhardy, and illegal thing to do.

What happens when **driving under the influence of marijuana** is what has been termed a "perceptual failure" — you simply do not see things in time to react to the them. Put more bluntly, you're so stoned, you don't recognize you're in trouble until it is too late to do anything about it. There is very little good research data on marijuana and driving.

Chapter 2

Your Vision and Sense of Space

When driving, the most important aspect of your physical well-being is the quality of your eyesight. Every action you take behind the wheel is based on eye-hand and/or eye-foot co-ordination. Although you use *all* your senses when driving, over 90 percent of the information you need to control a vehicle comes from what you *see*.

And, equally important, you need to develop your sense of *space* while behind the wheel — where your vehicle is in relation to everything around you. You have to develop a *questioning attitude* that heightens your awareness of both what you can and *cannot* see.

- **You can't avoid an accident if you can't see it coming.**

- **You can't leave yourself an escape route for every maneuver you make** if you aren't aware of the space around you.

- **And you could potentially *cause* an accident yourself** if you cannot see the road and surroundings well.

PROTECTING YOUR VISION

Even if your eyesight is healthy — with or without corrective lenses — **hazards such as glare and the low light conditions of night** can make seeing difficult for anyone. Even some features of **a car's design** can hinder your visibility while behind the wheel.

> **A safe driver knows how to protect his vision in all situations.**

Seeing at Night

The human eye works far better in daylight than in reduced light conditions. Plainly said, it's hard to see at night.

- Your **peripheral vision is decreased.**

- Your normally wide **field of vision is narrowed** to the field of view illuminated by your headlights, the headlights of other vehicles, and fixed road lights.

- When viewed **at night, most objects exhibit relatively low contrast,** which makes their detection, especially against certain backgrounds, extremely difficult.

- **Colors fade at night.**

- And **your eyes simply need time to adjust to low light conditions** before your night vision kicks in — and **the older you get,** the longer this adaptation process takes place.

Night vision

Dusk and dawn are the two most difficult times of the day for good vision. In the changing light of dawn and dusk, the eye is caught in the middle. At dusk, as the light fades and evening comes on, your eyes gradually adapt to the light and you are given the gift of night vision. But, until that happens, there will be a period of time when you cannot see very well.

At night, if you leave your well-lit house or office and go out and jump into your car and start off, it's the same as when you walk into a movie house after the picture has already started. There you are in a darkened theater, probably juggling an armload of popcorn and soda, trying to find a seat you simply cannot see. You blunder into a seat, stepping on a few toes on the way, and after a few minutes, you notice how much more light the theater has. Your eyes have had the time they need to adapt to the new lighting situation.

So, in those first minutes after you jump into your car, **you can blunder just as badly behind the wheel** as you can in a darkened movie theater — and that's one of the reasons that each and every day people run cars into each another in every imaginable way.

So when you get into a car at night, give your eyes a chance to adjust to the changes in light conditions *before* you head out on the road.

Effects of prolonged daylight exposure on night vision

Prolonged exposure to glare from sunlight during the day (or, similarly, from headlights at night) **can temporarily ruin your night vision,** and can also lead to eye strain and drowsiness.

To alleviate the effects of such exposure, wear good sunglasses on bright days and take them off as soon as the sun goes down. Also, rest a while before driving at night after a long session of steady daytime driving.

Protecting and Enhancing Your Driving Vision — Day and Night

Eye "protection" against the affects of glare and low-light conditions is important for driving whether or not you normally wear corrective lenses. And, as we'll see, there are some specifications for lenses that make both sunglasses and regular glasses better for driving than others. But regardless of the lens type, *all* eyewear should provide sufficient lens coverage for peripheral vision, non-obstructive frames and temple pieces, and lightweight, comfortable ear and nose pieces.

Sunglasses

Because the glare of sunlight on bright days can be blinding —
and too much exposure to sunlight can affect your night vision
— you should always wear sunglasses when driving during
daylight hours.

> **Make sure you wear good-quality sunglasses. Buy
> them with consideration toward how well they'll
> treat your eyes — and not toward how good they
> look on you!**

Antireflective coating (AR)

If you wear eyeglasses and want to drive at peak efficiency
day or night, wear glasses with an antireflection (AR) coating on
the lenses.

The AR coating does much the same thing as similar
coatings on binocular and camera lenses — it increases the
lenses' efficiency by allowing them to transmit more light. At
least 8 percent of the light is absorbed within a clear glass lens,
but the same lens with an AR coating transmits 99 percent of
the light.

Tints

- **Gray lenses worn during the day provide the
  right amount of light while properly
  preparing your eyes for the coming darkness.**
  After wearing gray lenses all day, your eyes will make
  the transition to reduced light levels much more
  readily, and what you see will be a much more
  accurate picture of what's really happening after dark.

- **Yellow lenses are recommended for night use**
  because the eye is most sensitive to the yellow portion
  of the spectrum, and because they effectively increase
  the apparent viewing brilliance and alleviate 20 percent
  of usual night-driving fatigue.

- **Yellow lenses also help on cloudy days,** but the effect is usually too brilliant for sunny weather

- **Adding a yellow tint (for cosmetic purposes)** will not reduce the light transmission characteristics of the lenses below 92 percent as long as the lenses are AR coated.

Car Design and Visibility

You can do your part to protect your vision against the glary hazards of day and night driving, but **some features of a car's design** — while providing comfort in one way or another — **can actually make visibility difficult at night.** And there's not much you can do about it. But you should be aware of such features and understand how they can affect your ability to see at night.

- **Tinted glass,** which helps keep the interior temperature low during sunny days, also cuts visibility considerably in the dark of night.

- **Greenish or bluish tint of instrument panel lights** is bad for night vision. These colors are at the end of the spectrum to which the eye is *least* sensitive in low light.

- Many cars, however, come equipped with **red instrument lighting**, a practice that's been common for quite some time in the aircraft industry.

    Red light does not interfere with vision outside of the car, and it makes the instruments much clearer to read. Red panel lighting eliminates the endless squinting down at the panel and the need for the eyes to continually readjust from glances at the instruments, or gazes at the road. This does much to reduce overall eye fatigue and makes long night drives more comfortable.

See Ch. 27, *Driving Safely at Night* for additional tips on how to prepare for and combat the hazards of low-light conditions on the road.

The Myth of "Tired" Eyes

At one time or another all of us have complained of **tired eyes**. But the eyes *themselves* do not tire. The nerves, brain, and body fatigue. The heavy eyelids and burning sensation that most people associate with tired eyes are really the physical reactions of a **tired body.**

If your eyes become "tired" while you're driving, heed the warnings of oncoming fatigue and take the necessary precautions. (See the discussion on Physical and Mental Fatigue, p. 12.) *Don't drive tired!*

SELECTIVE VISION AND YOUR SENSE OF SPACE

A great deal of the success of the various safe driving and emergency maneuvers depends on the driver's alertness and powers of observation. You must know what is going on *at all times* around your vehicle, and you must *anticipate* what can and might happen. You need *space* all around your vehicle, because when things go wrong, space gives you time to think and act. And to have space *available* for when something goes wrong, you need to *manage* space.

Looking Near, Looking Far

Not looking properly is a major cause of accidents. Don't just base your driving performance on what you can *see* directly in front of you. **All drivers look ahead, but many do not look *far enough* ahead.** Stopping or changing lanes can take a lot of distance, so you must know what the traffic is doing on all sides of you. You must look far enough ahead to be sure you have room to move — or stop — safely.

> **Perhaps the most important thing to remember is that you should be able to *stop* your car within the distance you can *SEE*. You'll learn the real importance of this in Ch. 17, *Speed and Safe Stopping Distances*.)**

- **Most good drivers look 12 to 15 seconds ahead.** That means looking ahead the distance you will *travel* in 12 to 15 seconds.

- **At lower speeds**, that is about **one block;** at **highway speeds**, about **a quarter of a mile.**

- **If you do *not look* that far ahead,** you may have to stop too quickly or change lanes quickly.

Looking 12 to 15 seconds ahead does not mean not paying attention to *closer* things. **Good drivers shift their attention back and forth, near and far.**

- Look for **what could be lurking** around **corners,** on the other side of **hills,** and moving through **intersections**.

- Look for **vehicles** coming onto the highway, into your lane, or turning.

- Watch for **brake lights** from **slow moving vehicles.**

- Look for **hills, curves,** or anything **for which you must slow down or change lanes.**

- **Pay attention to traffic signals and signs.** If a light has been green for a long time, it will probably change before you get there. Start slowing down and be ready to stop. Traffic signs may alert you to road conditions where you may have to change speed.

> **By seeing these things far enough ahead, you can change your speed or change lanes if necessary to avoid a problem.**

Always Leave Yourself an "Out"

One of the basic points about avoiding accidents is easy to understand and very fundamental to safe driving: **Leave yourself an out — an escape route for every move you make.**

To do this, you have to **be aware of *what's going on around you* all the time.** Your best tools for doing this are your mirrors, both rearview and sideview. (Too many of us only use our rearview mirrors when we want to pull out into traffic.)

- **Use all your mirrors in order to see the big picture.** You need accurate information about what's going on on your right, left, and rear.

In an emergency situation, such as a collision right in front of you, you need all the information you can get about what's happening around you, and you need it fast. Mirrors are your best way of getting this information. *(See Ch. 4, Windshields and Mirrors* for tips on how to properly adjust and use your vehicle's mirrors.)

Sense of Space in Traffic Situations

It's hard to avoid traffic. *All* of us have to drive in traffic. It's impossible to avoid, so we learn to live with it. It's a fact of life.

In **heavy, stop-and-go traffic,** it's *vital* to pay attention to what's going on around you. That can be tough because, from minute to minute, it may not seem like much *is* happening, especially if the traffic isn't moving very fast.

- Keep your eyes and *mind* **focused on the tasks in front of you.**

- **Maintain a safe distance** from the car in front of you.

- Be watchful for **cars pulling out of parking spots**. Many do so without looking where they are heading.

- Watch out for **the distracted person** — the one with the map or the one trying to read the directions he's been given to the local Moose hall, trying to spot landmarks and otherwise relate his directions to the world around him — all the while not looking where he's going at all.

And there's another kind of traffic — one that's even more deadly — **high-speed traffic.** This is traffic bunched together and moving at high speed. Cars are being driven very fast, very close to one another. There's not much you can do about this. **Try to give all the vehicles around you as much space as you can.**

Chapter 3

Your Reaction Time/Sense of Timing

What Is Reaction Time?

Many factors can affect your reaction time, but before we talk about them, let's find out just what reaction time is.

Reaction time is the sum of the time needed for:

1. **The brain to receive information from the senses.** The senses we're referring to also include sensations of motion and related "seat of the pants" sensations.

2. **Making decisions on what to do next.** Many times, this is a reflexive reaction that carries a potential for danger with it, such as immediately smashing down on the brake pedal when we feel the car begin to skid.

3. **Transmission of the messages from the brain to the muscles needed to react and move the controls.**

4. **The muscles to respond.**

> **The most critical portion of the reaction process is Step #2. After the senses detect the danger, a decision has to be made about what to do with the received information.**

The challenges and dangers faced by racing drivers present a good example of this process

Many racing drivers are surprisingly "old." Their reflexes may not be quite what they were when they were younger, but the *decisions* they make in the course of a race are the right ones.

These decisions are based on their years of experience behind the wheel. Knowledge gained through experience often becomes *intuitive*, so that it becomes part of our reflex reaction. Experienced pilots often gain this sort of reflexive knowledge.

A Hypothetical Example of Reaction Time/Sense of Timing

As an example, let's set up a hypothetical situation with two drivers, one young, and the other much older. Both are driving vehicles equipped with standard (non-ABS) brakes. (See Figure 3-1, p. 31.)

- They are both driving toward the same intersection from opposite directions.

- Ahead of them, a truck runs a stop sign and illegally enters the intersection so as to block the path of both drivers' cars.

- **The younger driver gets his foot on the brake before the older driver,** but smashes the pedal to the floor and locks up both front wheels, enters an uncontrollable skid, and crashes into the truck.

- **The older driver takes more time to react,** but once he does, he brakes carefully, applies the proper amount of brake force and steering control and avoids the collision.

- **The younger driver won the race to the brake pedal, but lost the battle with the truck.**

> **Without intuitive experience, the quickest decision can easily be the *wrong* decision.**

Many Factors Other Than Age Affect Reaction Time

Reaction times can vary a great deal between people of the same age group.

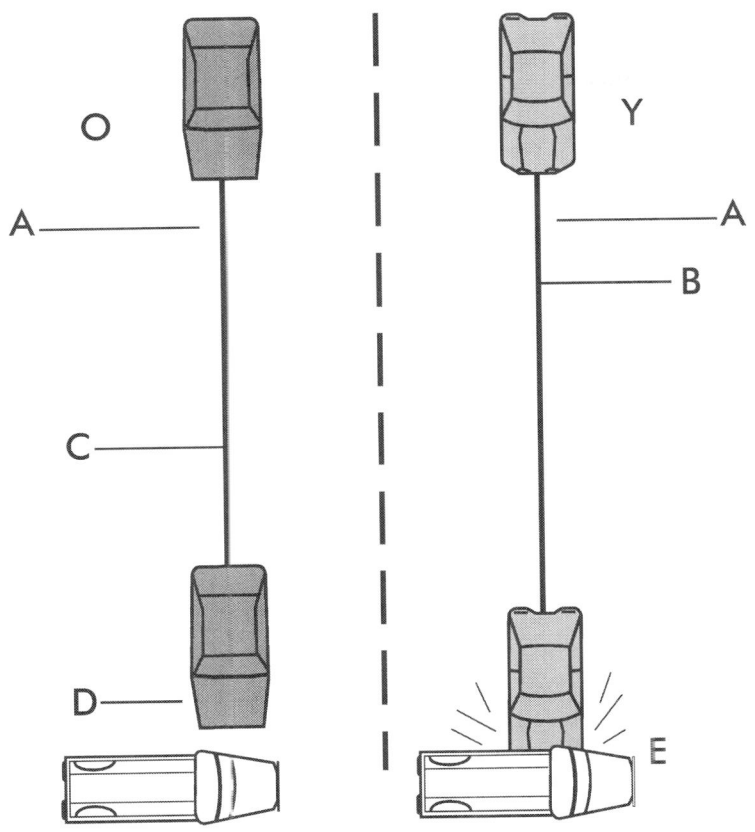

Figure 3-1. Reflexes vs Decision Making.

Car "Y" driven by young man.

Car "O" driven by o der gentleman.

At point A both see emergency.

Car "Y" reaction time to get his foot to the brake is 0.5 sec., which will use up 45 feet. Point B.

Car "O" reaction time to the brake is 1 sec., which will use up 90 feet. Point C.

Car "Y" driver has slammed on the brake, locking up both wheels. The car enters an uncontrollable skid, lasting 1.5 seconds or 135 feet. Car "O" takes 0.5 sec. to make a decision; he travels 45 feet.

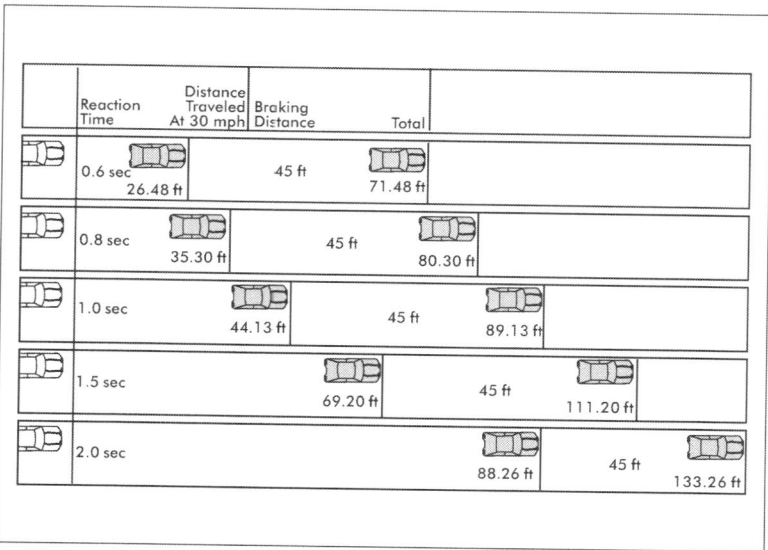

Reaction Time	Distance Traveled At 30 mph	Braking Distance	Total	
0.6 sec	26.48 ft	45 ft	71.48 ft	
0.8 sec	35.30 ft	45 ft	80.30 ft	
1.0 sec	44.13 ft	45 ft	89.13 ft	
1.5 sec	69.20 ft	45 ft	111.20 ft	
2.0 sec		88.26 ft	45 ft	133.26 ft

Figure 3-2. Reaction Time Diagram. The effects of various reaction times on total stopping distances.

Reaction times can vary according to the time of day — as much as four-tenths of a second in the morning to as much as a full second when a driver is fatigued at day's end. Four-tenths of a second may not sound like much, but at 60 mph a car travels 35 ft. in that amount of time. That could make a life and death difference in an accident situation. (See Figure 3-2, p. 32.)

Reaction times among tired or ill drivers can be as long as two full seconds. Again, at 60 mph, that means a driver will cover 123 ft. before reacting to a threat.

> **The standard reaction time for a healthy person is .75 sec.**

Decision Making Behind the Wheel

After an accident, some people might ask, *Why did the driver just drive into the other car when there were so many other options open to him?*

The answer could simply be that the driver could not *reach* a decision before it was too late. **The time required by the brain for a simple decision depends on how complex that decision is.**

- **A simple decision,** such as a reflex action, can be reached in **three-tenths of a second.**

- **If the problem faced by the brain is sufficiently complex** to require some thought, that decision can take as long as **five-tenths to two full seconds**, depending on the available options and the capabilities of the individual.

Over-Dependence on Reaction Time

The most important lesson to be learned about reaction time is that we know *not* to depend on it to get us out of trouble. The classic example of over-dependence on reaction time is encountered in the tailgater.

The Tailgater — The classic example of over-dependence on reaction time

We have all been plagued by this kind of driver — the one that drives too fast and so close you can practically count the fillings in his teeth in the rear-view mirror.

An emergency can easily and quickly develop with no way for someone following you so closely to have adequate time and enough room to react. The tailgater is going to smash into you if you have to stop quickly, that's for sure.

If you were to pull that tailgater over and ask him why he follows you so closely, you might encounter someone who honestly doesn't know what you're talking about, someone that really doesn't consider what he's doing as something dangerous, or, more disturbingly, someone who thinks he is Superman — the super-driver that can react to anything, handle any driving emergency. Both attitudes are idiotic.

Training *Can* Improve Reaction Time

While it cannot make muscles move faster, training can cut the time required in reaching a decision.

Through training, a driver can experience situations simulating driving emergencies. This:

- Helps **build the decision-making process.**

- Encourages the driver to focus attention on **the proper course of action in a given emergency situation.**

- Helps drivers stay aware of **their own limitations and that of their vehicles.**

IN THE NEXT SEVERAL CHAPTERS, we move on to examine the features of the car itself that — if used and maintained properly — are designed to help you maintain control of your vehicle, to help you drive safely, and to help you avoid serious injury if you are in a collision.

Chapter 4

The Windshield and Mirrors:

Your "Windows" to the Road

Vision is a complex sense, affected by a number of variables, many of which you have no control over. Your vision inside the car is not only affected by your own physical limitations, but by factors such as tinted windshields and convex rearview or sideview mirrors that can distort the image you see in the mirror.

THE WINDSHIELD

Perhaps the most important window you look through in your car is the windshield.

Windshield Visibility

Just how much visibility do you have when looking through a windshield? A non-tinted windshield permits 89 percent of the perpendicular light to pass through. Since almost no modern vehicles have perpendicular windshields (the exceptions being Jeeps and other utility vehicles), the real-world windshield value in this area is more like 82 to 84 percent of the light.

What does the National Highway Traffic Safety Administration (NHTSA) have to say about this? Their rule is that the windshield needs to pass only 70 percent of the light to meet safety standards — and that is as measured through a perpendicular windshield.

*The result is that most windshields on commercially available cars today permit about **62 percent of 65 percent** of the light to come through.*

Clear away the fog

NEVER drive with a fogged windshield (or side mirrors). This sounds pretty elementary, I know. Yet we've all seen people driving down the road with a windshield nearly completely fogged. Usually they've managed to clear a little peephole in the windshield, but their side and rear windows are completely fogged or covered with snow. Their cars look like little tanks, with the drivers peering through tiny slits. You cannot *afford* to indulge in such foolishness.

Clear away the grime — inside and out

It's amazing just how much grime and dust can accumulate on the outside and *inside* of a windshield, the windows, and on the mirrors.

Most drivers, if they clean their windshields at all, concentrate on the *outside*. But it's just as important to keep the *inside* clean as well. Clear visibility is important in driving *at all times,* but it takes on a whole new meaning when you're driving at night and in foul weather. (See Chs. 26, *Foul Weather Driving*, and 27, *Driving Safely at Night*.)

If you smoke in your vehicle, the accumulation of grime is even worse! **If you smoke or drive with someone who does,** clean the inside of the windshield *every other day*. It's amazing how fast smoke residue builds up on the inside of a car's windshield.

Do not drive until you have cleared *all* windows and mirrors — *INSIDE* and *OUT*.

REMEMBER: Clear vision is the foundation of safe driving.

Windshield Wipers

Perhaps the most important safety feature of all is right in front of your eyes — yet you tend not to see them or pay much attention to them until they don't work: your inexpensive windshield wipers.

Although many drivers take their wipers for granted, when they're needed, they're needed *now*. It doesn't take long for wiper blades to deteriorate, and if they're not in good working condition when you click on the switch, you can be left virtually blind for crucial moments of driving time. To avoid an accident, you need to see it developing; therefore, the benefits of a clean windshield are obvious — you can see better.

Figure 4-1. Keep Your Windshield Clean.
Dan Raber of Key Largo, Florida, frequently cleans pollen and mosquitoes from his windshield.
Photo ©Jim Spencer/SeaNotes

A clean windshield is vital for driving, whether in day or night. Streaks and smears on windshields can produce extremely disorienting kaleidoscopic effects when lights shine on them at night. Make sure your windshield washers work, that your windshield wiper blades are clean and not old and worn out, and that the windshield wiper fluid container is kept filled.

How do you make wipers work better and last longer? You can add years to the life of your wiper blades—and get a clearer windshield in the bargain—just by taking a few extra seconds to "wipe your wipers."

> "We recommend cleaning your windshield wipers regularly with a clean cloth soaked in windshield washer fluid," says Dick Hazell, Reliability Engineer for Delco Chassis (which designs and manufactures wiper systems and components for General Motors). "We suggest cleaning them every second or third time you wash your car — more often if you notice your wipers streaking."

Wiping your wiper blades with windshield washer fluid removes dirt, oil, bird droppings, and oxidized rubber from the edges and keeps the cleaning edge clean. The safety benefits are obvious: you'll see better in rain and sleet — especially at night — with streak-free wipers.

In dry weather, you should operate the wipers about once a week for a minute or so to prevent heat set. Be sure to keep the windshield well-lubricated with washer fluid or spray from a hose while the wipers are operating — *don't run them on dry glass*. While you're at it, clean the windshield using a good ammonia-based glass cleaner. With care, a set of wiper blades should last for one or two years, depending on the operating environment.

In harsh winter conditions, ice and snow can wreak havoc with a wiper's ability to keep the windshield clear. That's where special-purpose winter blades come in. Anco's winter design covers the wiper assembly and all of the moving parts with a neoprene boot. This protects the arms from the elements and prevents snow and ice from packing into them. Trico offers a similar design for its Winterblade. In addition, the winter wiper's compound is softer to help maintain flexibility when the mercury dips, the profile is a

little larger to help plow snow off the windshield, and it's heavier to provide more strength in its clearing action.

> **(See Ch. 9, *Smart Car Care* for additional tips on keeping your wipers in their best possible condition.)**

REARVIEW AND SIDEVIEW MIRRORS

How many times have you been driving down the road and another driver moving in the same direction drives into your lane. Either the person obviously did not see you in her mirrors, or simply did not look before turning the steering wheel. Many times you blame the latter for the problem, but in reality the driver *did* look, but just did not see you. His/her mirrors where not adjusted properly.

All vehicles must have one to three mirrors — by law. But all vehicles *should* have three mirrors. There is no excuse at all for having cars with only two mirrors (a rearview and left-side mirror). Most people don't understand the importance of a right-side mirror.

- **Having no right-side mirror** assumes no one will ever pass you on the right, or that you will never have to move to the right.

- It is also necessary that **all the mirrors be adjustable from the *driver's* position.** You should not have to reach across the car to adjust the right-side mirror.

How Important Are Mirrors?

Without them, the only way you know what's behind you or coming along side you would be to turn and look. It only takes a second or two to look and that may not seem like much, but at 50 mph a car is traveling at the rate of 75 feet per second. If you look over your shoulder for two seconds, you would cover 150 feet without the knowledge of what's going on in front of you. At 65 mph you would cover almost 200 feet.

   You cannot afford to turn and look while driving on a highway or in slow city driving. Your attention *must* focus on what's in front of you. Reaction time and braking time could all be gone in two seconds.

If you are about to pass another vehicle and use a convex side mirror, remember that it is not to be used as an accurate indication of where the other car is in relation to your vehicle — it just indicates that the other vehicle is *there*.

   You should be cognizant of what is in your mirrors every few seconds, because traffic changes — and so do your escape routes. Properly adjusted mirrors could give you the emergency time you need to avoid an accident.

Adjusting the Mirrors

1. **Start with the right-side mirror.** (See Figure 4-2, p. 41) Adjust it so it gives a clear view of traffic on your right (Zone 1). It must be adjusted so you can see a vehicle, or part of a vehicle, on the right until your peripheral vision picks up the vehicle on the right. Therefore, as the vehicle leaves your vision in Zone 2 (rearview mirror), it must appear in Zone 1 (the right-side

mirror). As the vehicle leaves Zones 1 and 2, it must appear in your peripheral vision.

2. **Now adjust the center mirror (rearview mirror)** (Zone 2). The center mirror will cover everything directly behind you, but it also covers the blind spot on your right that your right-side mirror fails to pick up. It must also cover part of the left side of the vehicle where you will also have a blind spot on the left-side mirror. The rearview mirror must be adjusted so that as a vehicle disappears from it's view, it will appear in one of the side mirrors (Zone 1 or Zone 3).

3. **Now adjust the left-side mirror.** Adjust it so you can see a vehicle coming up on your left side and keep it in view until your peripheral vision picks it up.

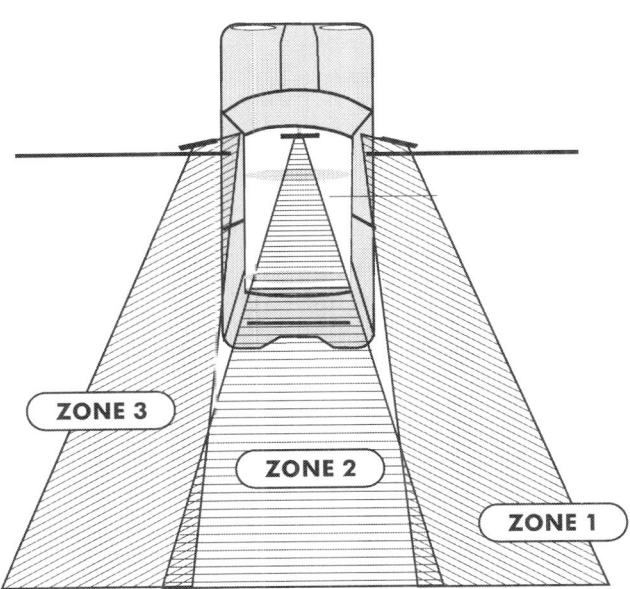

Figure 4-2. Mirror Zones. Rearview and sideview mirrors (left-side and right-side) must be adjusted properly to give you the maximum view of your driving environment. Checking that view every few seconds keeps you aware of changes in traffic, aware of possible escape routes should you need one, and gives you the emergency time you need to avoid an accident.

Why is it so important to know if a car is coming up behind you? When you have to make an evasive action, you need to know what's behind you and what may inhibit a move either left or right. Therefore, when the vehicle leaves the rearview mirror (Zone 2), it must appear in the left-side mirror (Zone 3). When it leaves the left-side mirror it must appear in the driver's peripheral vision.

"Blind Spots"[1]

Virtually all cars have "blind spots," spots where it's difficult to see cars close behind them to the left or right.

1. **To tell if you're driving in someone's blind spot,** just glance at his rearview mirror. If you can't see his face, assume he can't see you.

2. **Move forward or fall back so he can see you.**

3. **If you're behind a car at a *diagonal* angle,** you could be in its blind spot.

3. **There are probably blind spots in *your* car, too.** That's why it's always safer to *quickly* turn to visually check for other vehicles traveling in lanes next to yours before you pull over. [However, don't turn around so long that you compromise your ability to stop quickly should a situation develop in front of you.]

> **The Vampire Rule — Another place to check to see if you're in someone's blind spot is the outside mirror. If you can't see the driver's face, chances are he/she can't see you.**

---

[1] Copyright Shell Oil Company material written by Mike Carpenter, used with permission.

Chapter 5

Seat Belts and Child Safety Seats

SEAT BELTS

The facts are in on seat belts: THEY SAVE LIVES. Plain and simple. People have sometimes questioned the use of seat belts, expressing fears that belts could get in the way of fast exits from the car. But by *not* wearing a seat belt, you could experience a faster — and *deadly* — exit: right through the windshield or a flung-open door.

Even in a minor fender-bender you could be bounced around severely inside the car. And just *think* about what would happen in a **rollover.**

THERE IS NO EXCUSE FOR NOT WEARING A SEAT BELT!

Why Do We Need Seat Belts?

It's amazing that even some driving *professionals* ask that question when the answer is so obvious. Sure, we all know the story of the guy who didn't wear a belt and was tossed free of the car in the accident when the car blew up and became an inferno. That guy must be the most popular man in the world because everybody knows him. Stop and think about this story. Can you imagine what it would be like to be thrown free or jump out of a car that was moving along at 40 mph? It could ruin your whole day. Along with your face, and most of what's attached to it.

Wearing a seat belt is merely a recognition of Sir Isaac Newton's Laws of Motion. Objects at rest tend to stay that way; likewise, moving objects tend to keep moving. A large, stationary object, such as a roadside telephone pole or tree, wants to stay that way. Your car, traveling towards that stationary object, wants to keep moving. When the stationary and the moving meet, something has to give. Generally, those "something's" are you and your car.

When your car hits the pole, it stops. Unfortunately, unless you are secured to the car by a seat belt, *you* don't stop moving. You travel forward to meet — and sometimes go through — the windshield. Seat belts are designed to keep this from happening.

Rollover crashes can be particularly injurious to vehicle occupants because of the unpredictable motion of the vehicle. In a rollover crash, unbelted occupants can be thrown against the interior of the vehicle and strike hard surfaces such as steering wheels, windows and other interior components. They also have a great risk of being ejected, which usually results in very serious injuries. Ejected occupants also can be struck by their own or other vehicles.

How to Wear a Seat Belt Properly

If your seat belt is uncomfortable, you're probably not wearing it properly.

A lot of people complain that seat belts are uncomfortable — and many people don't wear them for that reason. Try wearing a neck brace or spending a few weeks in traction. You'll *really* know what discomfort is.

- **Belts should be worn so there is none of the slack that allows the body to move forward before being stopped by the belt.** In a severe collision, a too-loose belt might produce bruises, but bruises are far better than having your face introduced to the windshield.

- **The lap portion of the belt should be comfortable but tight.**

- **The buckle should never be over your stomach**. It should be at your side, on the hip.

Most cars today have **inertia-reel seat belts** that allow passengers and drivers freedom of movement inside the car, while retaining the ability to lock in place when sudden tension, such as that encountered in a sudden stop or collision, takes place.

> **Where mandatory seat belt laws are in effect, automobile fatalities have gone down. That is not speculation. That is fact.**

If you're going to be a responsible, safe driver, you must take responsibility for the safety of your passengers as well as yourself. Make sure all adults wear their seat belts and that all children are secured in child safety seats.

CHILD SAFETY SEATS[1]

For Short Trips, Why Bother with a Child Safety Seat?

The greatest number of crashes occur on short trips at low speeds. Three-fourths of all crashes happen within 25 miles of home. And 40% of all fatal crashes take place on roads where the speed limit is 45 mph or less.

> **THINK OF A CHILD SAFETY SEAT AS A *LIFE* PRESERVER.**

---

[1] Copyright Shell Oil Company material, used with permission.

An Adult's Lap Is Pretty Safe, Right?

Wrong. **Grown-up arms are no substitute for a safety restraint.** In a 30-mph crash, a child is thrown forward with a force equal to 20 times his or her weight. Plus, **if the adult is not wearing a safety belt,** the child could get crushed between the adult and the windshield or dashboard.

When Are *Kids* Big Enough for a Regular Seat Belt?

In general, **when they're over 80 pounds and approximately eight years of age.** Too many children start using regular belts too soon. Your child has a proper fit when:

- **The lap belt stays low and snug across the hips** without riding up over the stomach.

- The **shoulder belt does not cross the face or front of the neck.**

There Are So Many Kinds of Safety Seats. Which One Is Best?

> **The best child safety seat is the one that fits the child, fits the vehicle, and can be installed and used correctly every time.**

There are **three basic types:**

1. **Rear-facing infant seats** are designed **for babies from birth until at least 20 pounds and one year of age.** Rear-facing infant car seats are small and portable and fit newborns best. Don't confuse them with infant carriers.

2. **Convertible safety seats** "convert" from rear-facing to forward-facing **for toddlers between one and**

four years of age, who weigh between 20 and 40 pounds. Convertible seats are used rear-facing for infants and forward-facing for toddlers.

3. **Booster seats** are used as **a transition to safety belts by older kids who have clearly outgrown their convertible seat but are not quite ready for the vehicle's belt system.** A booster seat raises the child so that the lap and shoulder belts fit properly. If your car only has lap belts, use a shield booster.

> **IN ALL CASES,** check your owner's manual and car seat instructions to see if you need a "locking clip" to help secure the child's seat. It comes with all seats.

Why Does an Infant Seat Have to Face the Rear?

Babies need the extra protection provided by the back of the safety seat, which absorbs and spreads the force of the crash. The infant's neck muscles are weak. If the baby faces forward, the head could snap forward in a crash, risking serious injury to the neck and spinal cord.

> **NEVER PUT A REAR-FACING INFANT SEAT IN THE FRONT WHEN THERE'S A PASSENGER AIR BAG.**
>
> **Air bags inflate at speeds up to 200 mph!**
>
> **A safety seat in the front puts the child too close to the bag when it's inflating and can cause serious injury or death.**

How Do I Make Sure the Child Safety Seat Is Working Properly?

Always read the instructions that come with a child safety seat (keeping them handy at all times), and read all sections in your vehicle owner's manual that discuss safety seat installation.

> **This is especially important because many child safety seats and vehicle belt systems are *not* compatible.**

Children are properly restrained *only* when:

1. **The child fits securely in the safety seat,** AND

2. **The safety seat itself fits securely in the vehicle seat.** If it doesn't, contact the safety seat manufacturer. Don't forget to mail in the registration card that comes with a new seat. Then the manufacture can let you know of any problems or recalls.

Where's the Safest Place for Kids in the Car?

The back seat is the safest place for a child of *any* age. And the safest place in the back seat is in the center — if you have center belts and an appropriate vehicle seat. **The most distance from impact usually means the most protection.** In the back, the child is farther away from the impact of a head-on collision, which can cause the most serious injuries. Just as important, the child is safely removed from the passenger air bag.

But I'm Not Comfortable with My Child in the Back. Shouldn't She Be Closer to Me?

No. The back seat is the safest. It may help to compare your child in the back to when your child is home sleeping. You probably don't feel the need to be right next to your baby all through the night or during a nap. A healthy baby properly secured in a safety seat should not need constant watching.

> **If a child in the back *does* need attention, don't try any one-hand-on-the wheel maneuvers. Just pull over.**

If an Older Child *Must* Be Seated in Front

If an older child must be seated in front, make sure he or she is correctly restrained for age and size — and **always slide the vehicle seat as far back as possible** — to put *maximum* distance between the child and an air bag.

> *See Ch. 6, Air Bags: How They Work and Precautions to Take,* for a detailed discussion of the proper positioning of children in a car to protect them from potential air bag injury.

Box 5-1. Child Safety Checklist

Get in the habit of asking yourself some key questions about your child's safety *before* turning on the ignition:

- ☑ Is my child riding in the back seat properly restrained?
- ☑ Is the safety seat facing the right way?
- ☑ Are belts and harness straps secured tightly?
- ☑ Is my older child wearing the seat belt correctly?

REDUCED
SPEED
35

Chapter 6

Air Bags:

How They Work and Precautions to Take[1]

Standard driver-side and passenger-side air bags are designed to save lives and prevent injuries by cushioning vehicle occupants as they move forward in a moderate-to-severe front-end or near front-end crash. They keep the occupants' head, neck, and chest from hitting the steering wheel or dashboard.

> **Air bags inflate when the crash forces are about equivalent to striking a brick wall head-on at 10-15 miles per hour or a similar-sized vehicle head-on at 20-30 mph.**

Standard driver-side and passenger-side air bags are *not* designed to deploy in side, rear, or rollover crashes. (As we will discuss later, however, special side air bags are available for some vehicles.)

> **Since standard driver-side and passenger-side air bags provide *supplemental* protection only in frontal crashes, safety belts should always be used to provide maximum protection in rollovers and all crashes. (See Ch. 5, *Seat Belts and Child Safety Seats*.)**

---

[1] Material in this chapter was supplied by the National Highway Traffic Safety Administration.

**Figure 6-1 Front and Passenger-Side Air Bags —
Deployed.** Photo courtesy of Mercedes-Benz.

Check your owner's manual to see whether or not your
vehicle is equipped with air bags, and whether or not you have
a passenger-side air bag. Check for a warning label on the sun
visor and/or the front of the right door frame. A passenger-side
air bag is in a compartment in the dash board. The
compartment *may* have a cover labeled SRS (Supplemental
Restraint System) or SIR (Supplemental Inflation Restraint).

Since model year 1998, all new passenger cars have dual air
bags (driver and passenger side). Starting in model year 1999,
all new light trucks have dual air bags. Each vehicle is equipped
with a unique air bag which will deploy with a different force.

HOW AIR BAGS WORK

Air Bag System Components

Most air bag systems consist of three main components:

- An **air bag module**
- One or more **crash sensors**

- A **diagnostic unit**

The **air bag module,** which contains an inflator and a vented, lightweight fabric air bag, sits in the hub of the steering wheel on the driver side ,and, if the vehicle is so equipped, in the instrument panel (dashboard) on the passenger side.

Crash sensor(s), on the front of the vehicle or in the passenger compartment, measure deceleration — the rate at which a vehicle slows down. When these sensors detect rapid decelerations that indicate a crash, they send a signal to the inflator that deploys the bag.

The **diagnostic unit** monitors the readiness of the air bag system whenever the vehicle ignition is turned on and the engine is running. A warning light on the dashboard will alert the driver if the air bag system needs service.

> **Once an air bag is deployed, it cannot be reused. Air bag system parts must be replaced by an authorized service dealer for the system to once again be operational.**

Rapid Deployment

The entire deployment, inflation, and deflation cycle is over in less than one second.

- **The bag inflates within about 1/20th of a second after impact.**

- **At 1/5th of a second following impact, the air bag begins to deflate** and **deflates rapidly** as the gas escapes through vent holes or through the porous air bag fabric.

- **Initial deflation enhances the cushioning effect of the air bag** by maintaining approximately the same internal pressure as the occupant strikes into the bag.

- **Rapid deflation enables the driver to maintain control** if the vehicle is still moving after the crash, and prevents the driver and/or the right-front passenger from being trapped by the inflated air bag.

Dust

Dust particles present during the inflation cycle come from dry powder used to lubricate the tightly-packed air bag to ease rapid unfolding during deployment. Small amounts of particulate produced from combustion within the inflator also are released as gas is vented from the air bag. **These dust particles may produce minor throat and/or eye irritation.**

SIDE AND CURTAIN AIR BAGS

A number of auto manufacturers offer side-mounted and curtain-like side air bags which deploy from the roof and may span the entire side of the passenger compartment.

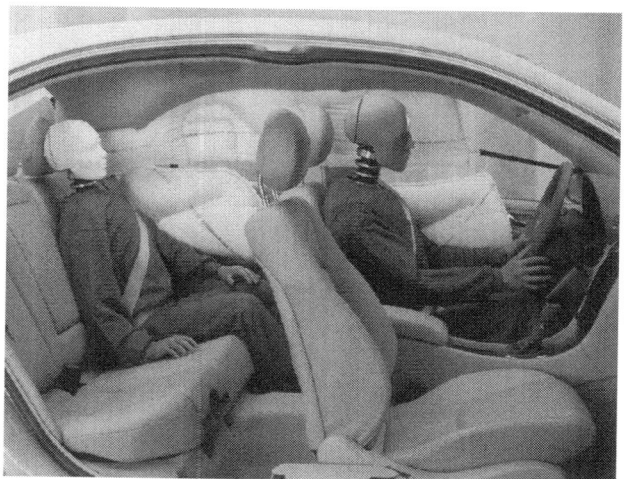

Figure 6-2. Side Air Bags - Deployed.
Photo courtesy of Mercedes-Benz

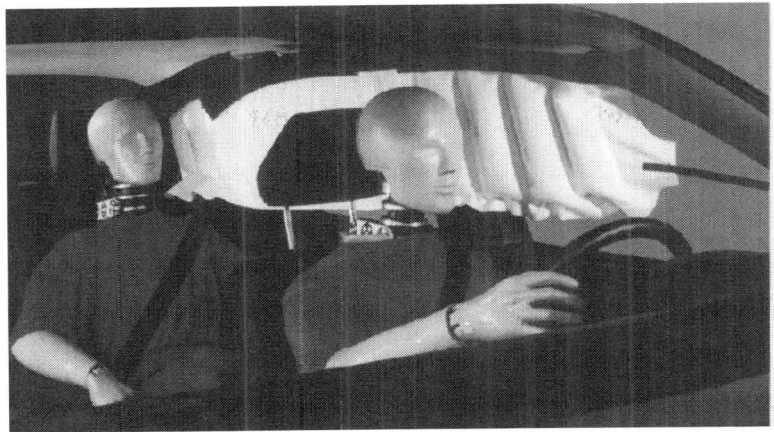

Figure 6-3. Curtain Air Bags - Deployed.
Photo courtesy of Mercedes-Benz.

- **Side air bags** protect drivers and front-seat adult passengers in certain **side-impact collisions.** (A few manufacturers offer side air bags in the rear seat, too.)

    Side impact air bags can provide **significant safety benefits to *adults***; however, as with ALL air bags (as we shall *see*), *children* seated in close proximity to a side air bag may be at risk of serious or fatal injury, especially if the child's head, neck, or chest is in close proximity to the air bag at the time of deployment.

> **Because there are variations in the design and performance of side air bags, you should carefully read your owner's manual to see if it is safe for children to sit next to the side air bags.**

- **Curtain air bags** come down along the window to protect your head and neck. The curtain air bags work in conjunction with side air bags and can prevent both front and rear occupants from hitting their heads on the side windows or roof pillars in a severe side collision.

Plus, the air-filled cushion can block glass splinters or other objects that could cause injuries in a side impact or rollover.

- **Door-mounted air bags** break out of the armrest of the door just above the armrest. These protect your chest.

- **Seat-mounted systems** deploy from the side of the seat-back cushion closest to the door. Some inflate to the size of a small pillow, while others can inflate to the size of a large cushion. The smaller ones shield your chest, while the larger ones protect both your head and chest.

PRECAUTIONS TO TAKE

Whether a deploying air bag is an effective lifesaver or a danger *itself* depends on where and how occupants are seated and restrained in the vehicle.

The Risk Zone

- **The force of a deploying air bag is greatest in the first 2-3 inches** after the air bag bursts through its cover and begins to inflate. Those 2-3 inches are the "risk zone."

- **The force decreases as the air bag inflates further.**

- **Occupants who are very close to, or in contact with, the cover of a stored air bag** when the air bag begins to inflate **can be hit with enough force to suffer serious injury or death.**

- In contrast, **occupants who are properly restrained** and **who sit 10 inches away from the air bag cover** will contact the air bag only after it has completely or almost completely inflated. The air bag then will cushion and protect them from hitting hard surfaces in the vehicle and thus provide a significant safety benefit, particularly in moderate to serious crashes.

The big danger is contact with or close proximity to the air bag module at the *initial* instant of deployment.

Air Bag Fatalities

On the driver side, fatally-injured drivers have been those who are believed to have sat close to their steering wheels either by habit or because they couldn't reach the steering wheel or gas and brake pedals if they sat farther back. Some had grown accustomed to sitting close to their steering wheel as matter of a preference.

On the passenger side, it has been primarily *children* who get too close to the air bag; however, confirmed adult deaths involving passenger-side air bags have also been caused by their proximity to the air bag when it deployed. The most common reason for the adults' proximity was failure to use seat belts.

Most passenger-side air bag fatalities have been infants and young children. Older children killed by frontal air bags were either unbelted or improperly belted and moved too close to the air bag during braking.

Some air bag fatalities have been attributed to the air bag's *design*. As a result, new air bag designs deploy first *radially* and *then* toward the occupant. Advanced air bags adjust deployment force or suppress deployment altogether.

Protecting Yourself and Your Passengers from Potential Air Bag Injury

Children

> All new cars must have labels placed con-
> spicuously on the sun visors, dashboards, and
> child restraints to highlight the *dangers* of placing
> children in the front seat of vehicles with air bags.

- **Rear-facing infant car seats** place infants in great danger in the front seat because the child's head is too close to the dashboard where the air bag is stored.

> Infants in rear-facing car seats in vehicles
> with passenger-side air bags should **NEVER**
> be placed in the front seat. Period.

- **Older children in the front seat** get too close when they are allowed to ride completely unrestrained. During pre-crash braking, these unrestrained children slide forward and are up against or very near the dashboard when the air bag begins to deploy. Because of their proximity, the children can sustain fatal head or neck injuries from the deploying passenger air bag.

- Similarly, some **children who wear seat belts, but who are really too small to be using just a vehicle lap and shoulder belt,** are equally at risk.

So how can you protect children from potential air bag injury?

- To begin with, as discussed at length in Ch. 5, *Seat Belts and Child Safety Seats*, **the best place for children to be seated in a vehicle is in the back seat, preferably in the center** (if proper restraints are available in that position, and the children are properly restrained for their age and size.)

- **Depending on the size of the child,** you should use a booster seat plus a lap/shoulder belt, or a lap/shoulder belt alone (for larger children). (Again, see Ch. 5, *Seat Belts and Child Safety Seats* for specifics.)

- **The vehicle seat needs to be pushed all the way back,** to maximize the distance between the child and the air bag.

- **The child needs to be sitting with his/her back against the seat back,** not wiggling around or leaning forward, **with as little slack as possible in the belt** in order to minimize forward movement in a crash.

Adults

Adults sitting in the **front passenger seat** of a vehicle equipped with a passenger-side air bag should:

- Be **properly restrained in a seat belt** (see Ch. 5, *Seat Belts and Child Safety Seats* for specifics.).

- **Sit at least 10 inches away** from the air bag compartment.

- **Avoid leaning or reaching forward.**

- **Remain seated against the vehicle seat back,** with **as little slack in the belt as possible** to minimize forward movement in a crash.

Short adults

Short adults in the **front passenger seat** of a vehicle equipped with a passenger-side air bag should *additionally*:

- **Move the seat as far *rearward* as possible.**

- **Tilt the seat back slightly** to help maximize the distance between their chest and the instrument panel (to 10 inches or more).

- **Refrain from moving around or sitting on the edge of the seat** — which could move their head too close to the air bag.

Elderly drivers and passengers

Elderly people, like all other drivers and front seat passengers, should be properly restrained and should move the seat as far rearward as possible, being careful to remain seated against the vehicle seat back and keeping the arms away from the area in which the air bag will deploy.

Tilt and Telescoping Steering Wheels

- **A tilt steering wheel should be tilted down** so that the air bag will deploy toward the chest and not the head.

- **Pregnant women should make sure the steering wheel is also tilted toward the chest,** not the abdomen or the head.

- **A telescoping steering wheel should be positioned so that it extends toward the driver as little as possible,** ensuring that the air bag has plenty of room to deploy.

Manual On-Off Switches for Air Bags

The National Highway Traffic Safety Administration **allows passenger air bag cut-off switches to be installed in vehicles with no rear seats or small rear seats.** Manufacturers may also use lower-powered air bags, which permits air bags to be depowered by 20 to 35 percent.

- **For a copy of the government rules** call the AutoSafety HotLine (800-424-9393) or visit the website (http://www.nhtsa.dot.gov).

- **All written comments/questions concerning air bags** should be addressed to the Administrator (NAO-10), NHTSA, 400 Seventh St., SW, Washington, DC 20590.

- Vehicle owners may request **authorization for a dealer to connect the air bag** (driver side, passenger side, or both) **to an on-off switch.**

  Vehicle owners can request an on-off switch by **filling out an agency request form** and submitting the form to the National Highway Traffic Safety Administration. (Website: www.nhtsa.dot.gov). Since the risk groups for *drivers* are different from those for *passengers,* **a separate certification** must be made on an agency request form **for *each air bag*** to be equipped with an on-off switch.

  If NHTSA approves a request, the agency will send the owner a letter authorizing the installation of one or more on-off switches in the owner's vehicle. The owner may **give the authorization letter to any dealer or repair business,** which may then install the switch(s).

NEVER ATTEMPT TO DISABLE THE AIR BAG YOURSELF. An air bag system is highly sophisticated and the air bag deploys with great force. Tampering with an air bag system is very risky. An inadvertent deployment can cause serious injuries.

Chapter 7

Tires, Part I

Type and Quality Make a Big Difference

Tires are one of the most important components of your car. **The quality of control you maintain over your vehicle is only as good as the tires that vehicle rolls on.** A car with outstanding handling qualities can have those qualities ruined by the installation of a poor set of tires.

   So what do you need to know about the type and quality of the tires on your vehicle? Ideally, everything — from the chemical compound of the rubber, to the tire's construction (bias, bias-belted, or radial-ply), to the tread design (snow, all-weather, or conventional type passenger tires) — and more. Depending on your particular driving situation, all these characteristics in combination would either add to, or detract from, the optimum handling qualities of your vehicle.

TIRE TREAD DESIGN

First of all, **the purpose of tires is to create the road friction needed to do the things that can be done with cars, such as go, stop and turn.** And the more rubber in contact with the road, the more traction you have – up to a point. But your driving purpose and road conditions can dictate how much and what kind of traction is necessary. Many emergency vehicles,

such as police cruisers, for example have tires wider than more conventional passenger cars for this reason. And, if we could guarantee that no rain or snow would ever fall, and that roads would never get slippery, then we could use racing slicks (tires with no tread whatsoever) on all cars. (Racing tire rubbers include a compound that produces a maximum amount of friction with the road.) But if it rains, these tires are useless.

> **All tire designs are compromises of some sort, surrendering one advantage in order to gain another.**

All-Weather Tires

When the ground is covered with water, a good tire design swallows that water into the tread pattern and pushes it out to the sides of the tires. All-weather tires do this better than others. (Snow tires are completely different and require a different sort of design. See below.)

All-weather tires won't be as good as snow tires on some types of snow, and won't be better than performance tires in high-performance use, and may not last as long as a long-life passenger car tires — but all-weather tires are still better than all the others in matching the broad variety of driving conditions encountered in everyday driving.

Snow Tires

Snow tires may enable you to deal better with snowy conditions, but the most important drawback to snow tires comes in the area of driving performance — **they simply do not have the cornering performance of conventional tires.** A car equipped with snow tires in the rear and conventional tires up front is much more likely to go out of control in emergency situations. Even worse, **snow tires are not as good at stopping the car as conventional tires.**

Box 7-1. New Tire Tread Simulation

Tire companies such as Bridgestone Corporation, have strengthened winter tire design with computer simulation technology.

- The computer technology analyzes specific tread patterns in powering, stopping, and in turning a vehicle in slippery winter conditions.

- The new technology simulates the action of the various tread patterns as they compact and grip snow.

- Tire designers can thus view a simulated tread pattern in motion on a snowy road.

- These simulations even allow for quantifying the shear forces that arise between the tread grooves and the snow.

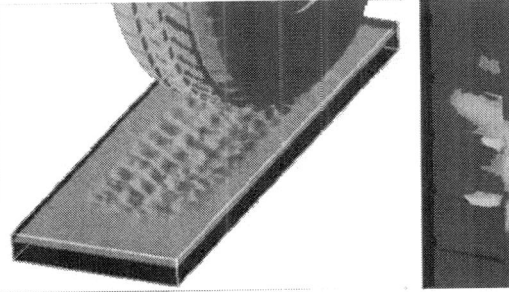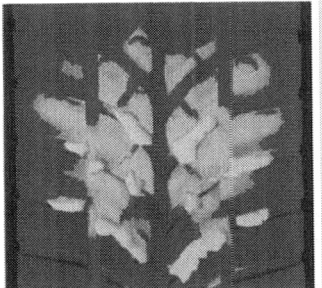

Figure 7-1. Tire Tread Simulation. Simulation of a tire in motion on snow (left) and a computer image of the distribution of the shearing forces that arise between the compacted snow and the tread (right). Photo courtesy of the National Highway Traffic Safety Administration.

> In snowy areas, many cities and counties have "snow emergency" regulations which are invoked during heavy snowfalls. Check with authorities for the rules in your area. Under some rules, motorists are subject to fines if they block traffic and do not have snow tires on their vehicles.

Chains and Studded Snow Tires

In areas where heavy snowfalls are frequent, many drivers carry chains for use in emergencies, or have their tire dealer apply studded snow tires for even greater traction.

- **Most states have time limits on use of studs, or ban them altogether**. Before applying studded tires, check the regulations in your area.

- **If you use chains, make sure they are the proper size and type for your tires.** Otherwise they may damage the tire sidewall and cause tire failure.

HOW TO DECODE A TIRE:
THE SIDEWALL STORY

The US Department of Transportation requires tire manufacturers to provide a wealth of information molded into the sidewall of every tire. Other useful information, not government mandated, may appear there as well.

The following examples will help you decode the tires already on your — or any — vehicle. Understanding the codes will help make you an informed tire purchaser and user, and will enable you to more easily follow the "latest" news in tire reports and testing.

Typical Information on the Sidewall of a Passenger Car Tire

A tire sidewall shows, for example, the name of the tire, its size, whether it is tubeless or tube type, the maximum load and maximum inflation, an important safety warning, and much more information.

The trouble is, most of this information is in code.

For example, on the sidewall of a popular "P-metric" speed-rated auto tire, you'll find several codes:

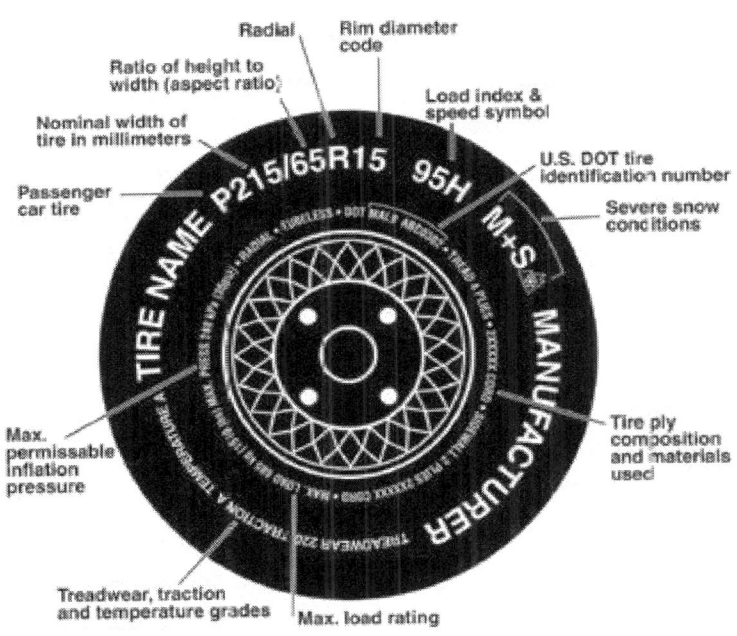

Figure 7-2. Sidewall Tire Information. Federal law requires tire manufacturers to place standardized information on the sidewall of all tires. This information identifies and describes the fundamental characteristics of the tire, and also provides a tire identification number for safety standard certification and in case of a recall. Illustration courtesy of the National Highway Traffic Safety Administration.

Example Code: P185/70R14

- The **"P"** indicates a **passenger-car** tire.

- The **"185"** is the nominal **width of the tire's cross-section in millimeters.**

- The **"70"** is the **aspect ratio** — the ratio of the sidewall's height to the tire's cross-sectional width. The sidewall in this example is 70% as high as the tire is wide.

- The **"R"** stands for **radial.** Virtually all passenger-car tires use radial-ply construction these days. (A **"B"** in place of the "R" means the tire is a **belted bias** construction. A **"D"** in place of the "R" means diagonal **"bias"** construction.)

   Tire longevity depends on the type of material the tire is belted with. In radial tire designs, nylon-belted tires last only half as long as their steel-belted counterparts.

- The **"14"** is the **diameter of the tire, in inches.**

Example Code: 87S

- The **"87"** is a code indicating the **maximum weight the tire can carry at its maximum rated speed** (This is not very useful information to most people.)

- The **"S"** is one of several possible **speed ratings,** or **the maximum speed that the tire is supposed to sustain without failure.** Some common speed ratings are: S, 112 mph; T, 118 mph; H, 130 mph; V, 149 mph; Z, 149 mph or more.

Example Code: Max. Load 730 kg (1609 lbs) 300 kPa (44 psi) Max. Press.

The maximum load is shown in lbs. (pounds) and in kg. (kilograms), and maximum pressure in PSI (pounds-per-square inch) and in kPa (kilopascals). Kilograms and kilopascals are metric units of measurement.

Example Code: Plies: tread 2 steel + 2 polyester + 1 nylon / sidewall: 2 polyester

The type of cord and number of plies is indicated for both the tread and the sidewalls.

Example Code: DOT Y7J6 CCD 053

- The letters **"DOT" certify compliance with all applicable safety standards** established by the U.S. Department of Transportation (DOT).

- The **"Y7J6"** is **an example DOT tire identification or serial number.** This serial number is a code with up to eleven digits that are a combination of numbers and letters.

- The **"CCD"** is **an example letter code indicating which plant made the tire.**

- The **"053"** is **an example three-digit date code** (in a rectangular depression), indicating when the tire was manufactured. The first two numbers are the week of the year. Hence, a date code of 053 would indicate the fifth week of 1993.

Example Code: TREADWEAR 420

The DOT requires tire manufacturers to grade passenger car tires based on three performance factors: Treadwear, Traction, and Temperature Resistance.

Tread-wear index or grade is a gauge of expected tread life, and is a comparative rating based on the wear rate of the tire when tested under controlled conditions on a specified government test track.

- **A tire graded 200** would wear twice as long on the government test course under specified test conditions as the "reference" one graded at 100.

- **A tread-wear rating of 420,** therefore, means that (in theory, at least) the tire should last 4.2 times as long as the reference tire.

- On typical tires, **a tread-wear index of 180 is quite low,** while **an index of 500 is quite high.**

- However, **it is erroneous to link treadwear grades with your projected tire mileage.** The relative performance of tires depends upon the actual conditions of their use, and may vary due to driving habits, type and condition of the vehicle, service practices, differences in road characteristics and climate.

> **Many observers within and without the tire industry have criticized the government-specified tests on several technical bases and because the tests are run by the tire makers themselves, without independent verification. The criticisms may be apt, but, as of now, the tread-wear index is the only game in town.**

Example Code: TRACTION A

The traction grades, from highest (the best) to lowest (the worst), are A, B, and C. They represent the tire's ability to stop on wet pavement as measured under controlled conditions on specified government test surfaces of asphalt and concrete.

- The traction score is an index of **straight-line stopping ability on a wet surface**. It's an undemanding test.

- **About half the passenger-car tires made are rated A.**

Example Code: *TEMPERATURE B*

The temperature grade is an index of a tire's ability to withstand the heat that high speeds, heavy loads, and hard driving generate.

The temperature grades are A (the highest), B and C, and represent the tire's resistance to the generation of heat when tested under controlled conditions on a specified indoor laboratory test wheel.

Typical Information on the Sidewall of a Light Truck Tire

- **"LT"** stands for Light Truck.

- **"LT235/85R16"** is the size designation for a metric light truck tire.

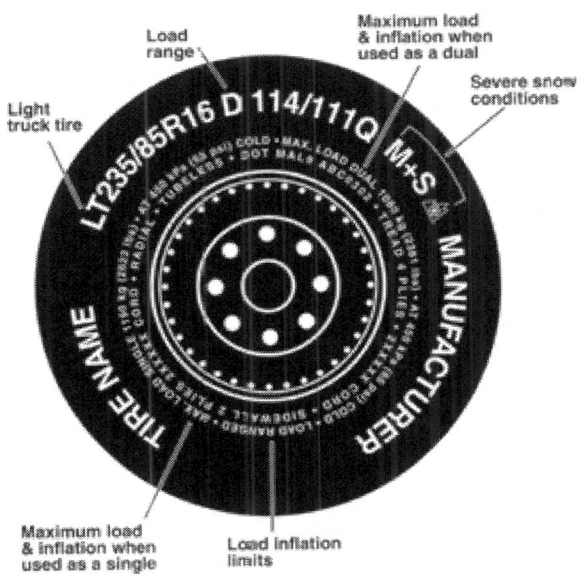

Figure 7-3. Sidewall Tire Information on Lite Truck Tires.
Lite truck tires have additional markings.

Illustration courtesy of the National Highway Traffic Safety Administration

- **"LOAD RANGED"** identifies the load and inflation limits.

- **"RADIAL"** identifies that the tire has a radial construction.

- **"MAX LOAD SINGLE 2623 lbs. AT 65 psi COLD"** indicates the maximum load rating of the tire and corresponding minimum cold inflation pressure for that load when used as a single.

  "MAX LOAD DUAL 2381 lbs. AT 65 psi COLD" would indicate the maximum load rating of the tire and corresponding minimum cold inflation pressure when used in a dual configuration.

  In simpler terms, when you have packed the maximum amount of weight allowed by the vehicle manufacturer, your inflation pressure should be whatever the recommendation marked on the tire suggests.

  > **For normal operation, follow pressure recommendations in your owner's manual or on the vehicle placard.**

- **The other markings on the sidewall have the same meaning as described for the passenger car tire.**

REPLACEMENT TIRE SELECTION

When tires need to be replaced, don't guess what tire is right for your vehicle.

> **Tire types are specific for each type of vehicle.**

As we'll see later, in Ch. 13, *Maintaining Traction*, tires must be able to provide the friction necessary to handle the various maneuvers you put the vehicle through by accelerating, steering, and stopping — all usually at speed. And when you do this, you're transferring a lot of different forces to each tire. **The wrong tires on your vehicle could mean they simply won't be able to hold the road as they were designed to.** And you'd probably find this out in a big hurry in an emergency situation.

To find out what type of tire you need for your vehicle, first look at the tire placard.

> **The tire placard (or sticker) is attached to the vehicle — on the door edge, door post, or glove compartment.**

If your vehicle doesn't have a placard, **check the owner's manual.**

Tire Size and Construction

As you will see, that placard tells you **the size and type of the tires which were on the vehicle as original equipment.**

- Tires should **always be replaced with the same size designation**, or *approved options*, as recommended by the automobile or tire manufacturer.

- **Never choose a smaller size** with less load carrying capacity than the size on the tire placard.

Speed Rating

Some tires are now marked with letters to indicate their speed rating, based on laboratory tests which relate to performance on the road. (See p. 68)

- If the vehicle manual specifies speed-rated tires, **the replacement tires must have the same or**

higher speed rating to maintain vehicle speed capability.

- If tires with different speed ratings are mounted on the same vehicle, **the tire or tires with the lowest rating will limit permissible tire-related vehicle speed.**

When buying new tires, be sure your name, address and tire identification number (**DOT** code) are recorded and returned to the tire manufacturer or his record-keeping designee.

Tire registration enables the manufacturer to notify you in the event of a recall.

TIRE MOUNTING — DO'S AND DONT'S

It is preferred that all four tires be of the same size, speed rating, and construction (radial or non-radial). But in some instances it may be necessary to use **tires that do not match.** Here are some guidelines:

- **Match tire size and construction designations in pairs on an axle** (or four tires in dual application), except for use of a temporary spare tire.

- If **two radial and two non-radial tires** are used on a vehicle, put the radials on the rear.

- If **two radial and two non-radial tires** are used on a vehicle equipped with **dual rear tires**, the radials may be used on either axle.

Never mix radial and non-radial on the same axle except for use of a temporary spare tire.

- **Snow tires** should be applied in pairs (or as duals) to the *drive* axle (whether front or rear) or to all four positions.

- Never put **non-radial snow tires** on the rear if radials are on the front, except when the vehicle has duals on the rear.

- If **studded snow tires** are used on the front axle, studded tires must also be used on the rear axle.

- Match all tire sizes and constructions on **four-wheel drive vehicles.**

> **Only specially trained persons should demount or mount tires. An explosion of a tire and wheel assembly can result from improper or careless mounting procedures.**

Chapter 8

Tires, Part II[1]

Care and Maintenance Make an Even Bigger Difference

Tires must be treated with care, for there are many factors that can affect their life and performance — weather, driving habits, inflation pressure, vehicle alignment and wheel balance, and vehicle loading.

PROPER TIRE INFLATION PRESSURE

One of the most important maintenance procedures is checking your tires — **including the spare** — for proper inflation pressure.

With the right amount of air pressure, your tires wear longer, save fuel, and help prevent accidents. The "right amount" of air is the pressure specified by the vehicle manufacturer for the front and rear tires on your particular model car or light truck.

The Correct Air Pressure

The correct air pressure (cold tire pressure) is shown on the tire placard (or sticker) attached to the vehicle — the door edge, door post, or glove box door. If your vehicle

---

[1] Sections in this chapter marked with * are copyright Shell Oil Company materials, used with permission.

doesn't have a placard, check the owner's manual or consult with the vehicle or tire manufacturer for the proper inflation.

Inflation pressures are determined by the auto maker based on the car's weight and the anticipated load it will carry. However, it is difficult for the car builders to figure out exactly how much weight will be transferred to the front of the car during heavy braking. So, although a *perfect* tire pressure for all conditions is nearly impossible to come up with, the indicated psi is the one you should follow for most driving situations.

> **REMEMBER: The tire pressure number that is molded into the sidewall of a tire is the tire *maximum* — not the *recommended* — inflation pressure. (See pp. 67, 68)**

Freeway or expressway driving and tire inflation

Those who spend a lot of time in prolonged freeway or expressway driving (that is, routinely drive at a sustained speed of 60 mph) should *increase* tire pressure over the manufacturer's recommended pressure — **as long as that pressure doesn't exceed the maximum psi figure printed on the tire sidewall.**

4.0 psi increase in radial tires

5.5 psi increase in bias belted tires

7.0 psi increase in bias tires

Cold/hot weather driving and tire inflation

Many parts of the U.S. have cold weather driving conditions at least part of the year. Here are some things you should know about cold weather driving and its effects on tire inflation:

- **Every time the outside temperature drops 10 degrees Fahrenheit, the air pressure inside your tires goes down about one (1) pound per square inch.** You should check your tire pressures frequently during cold weather and add the necessary air to keep them at recommended levels of inflation at all times.

- Similarly, **pressure may increase when the temperature rises.**

- **Never reduce tire pressures in an attempt to increase traction on snow or ice.** It doesn't work and your tires will be so seriously underinflated that driving will damage them.

The new D-metric tires and tire inflation

If you are driving a car equipped with a set of the new D-metric tires (which will eventually replace the alpha-numeric size tires), you should know that **the D-metric tire pressures can be exceeded by two or three psi over the recommended pressures listed in the owner's manual** or on the tire placard. Not only can these pressures be exceeded by a small amount, D-metric tires are inflated to a higher pressure overall.

Keeping Tires at Proper Pressure Is Easy

It's vitally important to keep track of the amount of air in your tires — including the spare.

How often should you check your tire inflation pressure? Ideally, you should check the pressure:

- At least once a month

- When the temperature changes

- Before, during, and after every long trip

Check your tires when they are COLD — that is, when your vehicle has not been used for at least three hours.

Tire pressure gauges are inexpensive and fit in a pocket. There are many models to choose from. You can pick one up at most service stations and auto parts stores. **Compressed air is available at almost every gas station.**

> **The hardest part to keeping tires properly inflated is simply taking the few moments required to do the job.**

THE PERILS OF IMPROPER INFLATION

If you don't take proper care of your tires, the results can be serious.

- **Under- or overinflation can cause tire failure/explosion of tire/rim assembly.** In fact, most manufacturers now mold a safety warning on the sidewall of the tire. It points out that serious injury may result from tire failure due to underinflation or overloading:

> **WARNING: Serious injury may result from:**
> *** Tire failure due to underinflation/ overloading. Follow owner's manual or tire placard in vehicle.**
> *** Explosion of tire/rim assembly.**

- It is far **easier to go out of control on underinflated tires.**

  Tire pressure affects the tire's ability to corner. The sharper the turn required by a corner, the more effect tire pressure has. This is due to the fact that a sharp turn puts more stress on a tire than a gentle turn, and an underinflated tire accepts less stress before losing its grip on the pavement and going out of control. For example, a tire rated for inflation to 32 psi but only carrying 24 psi loses 10 percent of its handling capability on sharp turns. (See p. 142)

A car is a weight-bearing machine. Every time you move the controls, you are shifting weight throughout the vehicle (see p. 117). These shifts are all eventually felt at the tires — and the tires' ability to bear that weight is dependent on the tire pressures.

- **Underinflation prematurely wears tires.** The rule of thumb is that **a single pound of underinflation takes 500 miles off a tire's life.** Most tires only last 70 percent of their design life, thanks to underinflation.

- **Tire pressures affect fuel consumption.** Properly inflated tires are part of the fuel economy equation. If a tire intended to be inflated to 32 psi is inflated to 24 psi, the result is a 20 percent boost in fuel consumption. This is due to the fact that a properly inflated tire offers less rolling resistance than one that's underinflated, so it requires more energy to roll an underinflated tire than one with the proper amount of air in it, and in an automobile, energy is gasoline. **If the tires on your car aren't properly inflated, you're wasting hundreds of miles' worth of gasoline.**

On the average, cars lose mileage at the rate of about a half a mile per gallon if the tires fall six pounds below a recommended inflation (of 25 pounds per square inch [psi]).

- Underinflated tires also exhibit **less overall durability** and can be **more easily damaged.**

- **Tire type makes a difference.** Radial tires have two-thirds the rolling resistance of a cross- or bias-ply tire. Over 40,000 miles, a properly inflated radial tire pays for itself.

SYMPTOMS OF "SICK" TIRES

When tires get "sick," they show their drivers an abundant number of symptoms in plenty of time for the tires to be "cured." By learning to read the early warning signs, you can prevent situations that both shorten tire life by thousands of miles, and that make those tires unsafe to drive on.

- As we have said, when a tire is **underinflated,** most of its road contact is on the outer tread ribs, causing the outside edge of the tire to wear faster than the middle.

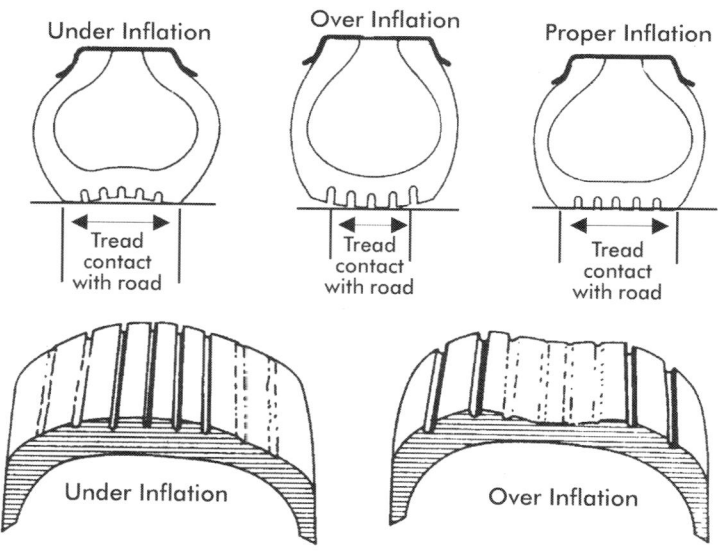

Figure 8-1. How Tires Look with Various Amounts of Inflation.

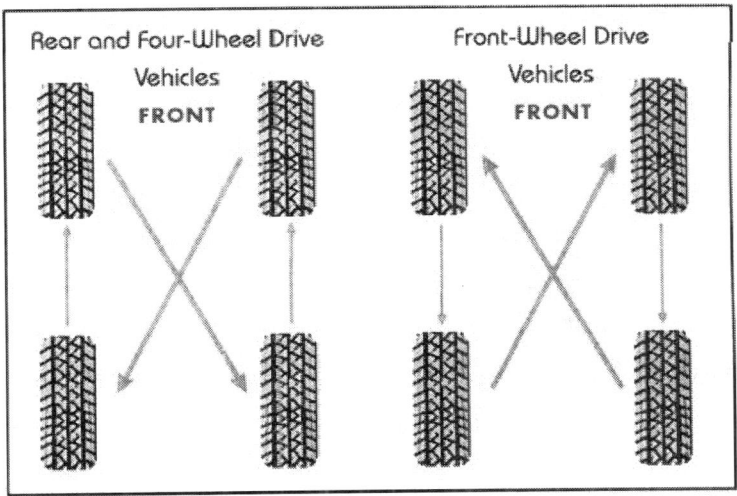

Figure 8-2. Common Correct Tire Rotation Patterns.
Illustration courtesy The Department of Transportation,
National Highway Traffic Safety Administration

- With **overinflation,** the opposite wear pattern appears. The center tread area bulges out slightly, causing it to wear faster than the outer ribs.

PROPER TIRE ROTATION

For maximum mileage and uniform tire wear, **rotate your tires every 5,000-6,000 miles,** and be sure to **follow the correct rotation pattern for your vehicle** as specified in your owner's manual

WORN TIRES

Worn tires are trouble. If you're driving on worn tires, you're **driving without the tread depth that controls stopping, acceleration, and cornering.** When driving on worn tires, you've thrown away some of the control you should have over your vehicle.

- Worn tires are **prone to hydroplaning** (see p. 248), are much **more susceptible to puncture** and could otherwise be hazardous to your health.

    Studies by several auto safety organizations, among them the National Bureau of Standards, showed that **cars riding on tires with less than one-sixteenth of an inch of tread are up to 44 times more likely to experience a blow-out.**

- More than just unsafe, **worn tires are often illegal.** The Tire Industry Safety Council reports that 30 states now have laws on the books requiring that automobile tires have **at least one-sixteenth of an inch of tread** — any less and the driver is issued a summons. (See Box 8-2, p. 87 for quick tips on measuring tread depth.)

TIRE ABUSE — YOURS AND NATURE'S

Wheel Spinning

Picture it: **Your car is stuck in mud or in snow, or on a patch of ice**. If your first reaction is to shove the "pedal to the metal" and spin the tire free, you're only asking for more trouble — some of it quite serious.

A spinning tire creates friction, producing tremendous amounts of heat — and heat is a tire's worst enemy. This heat, combined with the centrifugal forces produced by spinning, could cause the tire to fail.

The worst case scenario for this situation is a catastrophic tire failure, resulting in tire detonation and the possibility of a dangerous shower of hot rubber!

In such a situation, most drivers don't realize just how fast their tires are spinning.

A spinning tire's speed is often *twice* that displayed on the speedometer.

Here's why: if one tire is spinning and the other is in a situation that doesn't allow it to spin, the spinnable tire will receive the engine's total power output because the car's differential will transfer the engine's power to the point of least resistance. So, if the speedometer reads 60 mph, the tire is really spinning at 120 mph!

Do not exceed 35 mph *speedometer* speed — and make sure *no one* stands near the spinning tire.

As if all this tire danger weren't bad enough, **spinning the tires doesn't get the car free.**

- For one thing, **spinning the tires makes the road surface slicker** by melting snow which then refreezes as ice and also creates ruts that can further complicate the process of freeing the car.

- For another, **increased tire speed is not going to create traction.** Peak traction is generated at very low speeds. Once a tire is spinning 15 percent faster than the car is moving, maximum traction has been lost.

To free a trapped car, briefly rock the vehicle, tow it, or apply a traction aid such as sand or kitty litter to the surface under the tire.

Driving Speed

The faster you drive, the faster you'll wear out your tires. As a car is driven, the rear wheels press down on the pavement. At 30 mph, the rear tires exert a 5 horse power (hp) push against the pavement. At 50 mph, some 15 hp are exerted, and by 70 mph, this figure grows to 38 hp.

Box 8-1. Your Driving Habits and Tire "Health"*

Perhaps the easiest factor to control is your driving behavior. Simply following these good driving habits will help extend the life of your tires:

- **Obey posted speed limits.**

- **Avoid fast starts, stops and turns.**

- **Avoid potholes and other objects** on the road.

- **Do not run over curbs or hit your tires against the curb** when parking.

- **Do not overload your vehicle**. Refer to your vehicle's tire information or owner's manual for the maximum recommended load.

Temperature and Temperature Changes

Temperature also has an extreme effect on tires. *Low* temperatures, or *changes* in temperature wear tires out faster.

- Tests have shown that **a change from a winter temperature such as 41 degrees** Fahrenheit **to a hot summer day temperature of 95 degrees** Fahrenheit **increases tire wear 400 percent,** all other conditions being equal.

Box 8-2. Checklist to
Help Your Tires Last Longer*

☑ **PRESSURE** - One-fourth of all cars and one-third of all light trucks have at least one substantially underinflated tire. Underinflated tires can cause blowouts and tire failure, which can lead to serious accidents. And appearances can be deceiving - a tire can lose up to half of its air pressure and not appear to be flat. Overinflation, on the other hand, puts unnecessary stress on tires, which can result in irregular tread wear. Check tire inflation with an accurate gauge. They can be found in any auto parts store and most service stations.

☑ **ALIGNMENT** - Improper alignment of your car's steering mechanisms - including the front and rear tires and the steering wheel - can reduce the lifespan of your tires by thousands of miles. Have a tire dealer check the alignment if you notice:

- Excessive or uneven tire wear
- The steering wheel "pulling" to the right or the left
- A feeling of "looseness" or "wandering"
- Steering wheel vibration
- The steering wheel is not centered when the car is moving straight ahead

☑ **ROTATION** - If you fail to rotate your tires, the front tires may last only 10,000 - 20,000 miles, while the rear tires will last 50,000 - 80,000 miles. Therefore, to achieve more uniform wear experts recommend that you have your tires rotated every 6,000 miles. Refer to your vehicle's owner's manual for correct pattern rotation. Common patterns include straight forward and straight back or crisscrossed.

☑ **TREAD** - Advanced and unusual wear can reduce the ability of tread to grip the road in adverse conditions - especially on wet roads. When checking tires, look for uneven wear, high and low areas, bubbling or excessively smooth areas, as well as cuts or foreign objects in your tires.

- **Tires must be replaced when tread has worn down to 1/16 of an inch. *Quick tip:*** If you don't have a measurement device handy, you can simply use a penny to check tread depth. Insert a penny with the head pointed down into the tread groove. If you can see all of Lincoln's head, your tires need to be replaced.
- **When shopping for new tires, it is usually best to replace all four at the same time** — *if* you have been rotating your tires as recommended. You also should think about the type of driving you do most often and choose tires that are right for you.

IN THE NEXT TWO CHAPTERS, we consider some general maintenance rules for your vehicle — what to check or have checked, and how often. And a convenient **Ten-Minute Checklist** covers 17 items to check, and when to check them.

Chapter 9

Smart Car Care:

Tips for Keeping Your Vehicle Safe and on the Road[1]

Stick to Your Routine (Maintenance)

Next to a home, a vehicle is probably the most expensive purchase people make. That's why it makes good economic sense for owners to take proper care of their vehicles through preventive and routine maintenance. Following the quick and simple procedures outlined in this chapter will not only add years to the life of your vehicle, but will help keep it operating in a safe and cost-efficient manner. Plus, finding and fixing a smaller problem before it turns into a major problem can help save you a bundle.

> **Note: This chapter is intended to provide a general overview of routine maintenance. Because there are so many different makes and models of vehicles and auto parts and accessories, recommended procedures may vary. Please consult your owner's manual or the product manufacturers for recommendations.**

Keep Your Vehicle a Well-Oiled Machine

A regular oil change is the service most likely to prolong the life of your vehicle; yet, recent nationwide vehicle inspections

---

[1] Copyright Shell Oil Company material reproduced with permission. Written with assistance from the National Highway Traffic Safety Administration (NHTSA), the National Institute for Automotive Service Excellence (ASE), the Rubber Manufacturers Association, and the AAA Foundation for Traffic Safety.

found that 22 percent of vehicles have low or dirty engine oil, indicating that many motorists fail to perform this important task. Not changing your oil for lengthy periods of time will cause additives in the oil to break down, leading to increased wear and tear on your engine.

To keep your vehicle running smoothly:

- Check the oil level regularly.

- Change the oil every 3,000 miles or every three months, whichever comes first, unless your manufacturer recommends otherwise. Some newer vehicles need less frequent oil changes.

- Replace the oil filter with every change.

- For an accurate reading of your oil level, shut off the engine, remove the dipstick, wipe it with a clean cloth or paper towel and then reinsert it. Remove the dipstick again to "read" the oil level.

Go with the Flow: Your Vehicle's Fluids

Engine oil is not the only fluid your vehicle needs to run properly. Other vital fluids include brake fluid, power steering fluid, transmission fluid, and coolant. Checking them on a regular basis can prevent breakdowns and costly repairs.

Your owner's manual can show you where fluids are contained, exactly how to check them, the type your vehicle uses and how much should be in each "reservoir." (See Box 9-1, p. 91 and Ch. 10, *Know Your Car: The Ten-Minute Checklist* for suggestions on frequency of fluid checks and how to identify leaks.)

Know the Positives and Negatives of Your Battery

Cars run on three components: fuel, air, and electricity. Many people never think of vehicles as being "electronic," but they are complex machines with many electronic components, ranging from the radio to on-board computers. The battery is

---

Box 9-1. Recognizing Fluid Leaks

If you see drops of fluid under your vehicle, you should be able to identify them by color or consistency. A few small drops are probably not a cause for concern, but you should take note of small puddles.

- If the fluid is **yellow-green, blue, or fluorescent orange**, it could indicate a cooling system leak or an overheating problem.

- If the fluid is **dark brown or black**, it is most likely engine oil. The engine could have a bad seal or gasket or a loose oil filter.

- A **red** oily spot means you probably have a transmission or power steering fluid leak.

- A **puddle of water** is usually normal and is simply condensation from the air conditioning system or the defroster.

---

the primary source of power for these electronic components, so it is important to make sure it is working properly.

Batteries can fail for a number of reasons, including insecure mounting, frequent "deep cycling" (the recharging of a dead battery) and dirty or poor connections.

Here are some ways to help prevent your battery from failing and leaving you stranded:

- **Have the battery checked with every oil change.**

- **Cables should be securely attached and free of corrosion.** You can clean the battery terminals and case with a mixture of baking soda and water.

- **Don't wait until your battery fails before you replace it.** Vehicles that are three years old or older are most likely to experience battery failure.

Check Wipers & Washer Fluid Intermittently

Like other components, windshield wipers also wear out and need to be replaced. Not being able to see clearly while driving is very dangerous. In fact, 90 percent of all driving decisions made are based solely on visual cues. That's why car care experts recommend **wipers be changed once a year for cars that are parked inside and two to three times a year for cars that are parked outside.** A good rule of thumb to follow is: "change your clocks, change your wipers." (See Ch. 4, *Windshields and Mirrors* for additional discussion on wipers.) Here are some other tips:

- **You can tell when a blade is becoming worn** out if it just streaks and smears the water rather than wiping it away.

- **Inspect the wiper blades whenever you clean your windshield.** Do not wait until the rubber is worn or brittle to replace them.

- **Most of the time, only the rubber squeegee,** usually called the "44 refill," **needs to be replaced.**

- **When buying a blade,** take the old rubber squeegee with you to the store so you can compare sizes.

- **When refilling the windshield washer fluid,** use some of the fluid to clean the wiper blades.

Light the Way to Safer Driving

Lights are one of your vehicle's most important safety features. They help you and other drivers make decisions based on visual cues. However, recent statistics indicate that 20 percent of vehicles tested are operating with at least one external light not functioning. Therefore, it is important to check your lights often to make sure they are clean and in good working order. This includes headlights (both low and high beams), parking lights, blinkers, taillights, and brake lights.

- If any of these lights is not in working order, you can be ticketed.

- Typically, if any of these lights is not working, all you will need is an inexpensive bulb or fuse.

Help Your Tires Tread Lightly

(Because there are many factors that affect the life of your tires — and because properly maintained tires are *fundamental* to vehicle control and safety — **an entire chapter is devoted to a discussion of their care and maintenance.** (See Ch. 8, *Tires, Part II: Care and Maintenance Make an Even Bigger Difference.*)

Conserve Fuel

Non-commercial vehicles in the United States consume close to 90 billion gallons of gasoline each year — that's 661 gallons per car. While many of the tips in this chapter will help increase your vehicle's fuel mileage, there is even more you can do to maximize fuel efficiency:

- **Avoid high speeds.** Fuel efficiency decreases significantly at speeds in excess of 55 miles per hour. Reducing your speed from 62 mph to 55 mph reduces fuel consumption by 10 percent.

- **Avoid excessive idling.** If you must warm up the engine, one to three minutes should be sufficient.

- **Don't rev the engine;** it wastes gas and may cause engine damage.

- **Drive smoothly** and **avoid sudden braking and starting.**

- **Minimize drag** by keeping your car clean, driving with windows and sunroofs closed, and removing roof and rear racks. Having a clean car can reduce drag by as much as 12 percent.

- **Be sure to replace the gas cap tightly** to prevent gasoline from evaporating.

- **During the summer, fuel your car early in the morning or late in the evening.** Heat expands gasoline, so you'll spend more money for less gasoline if you refuel during the afternoon.

> **While the tips in this chapter will help lengthen the life of your vehicle and enhance the safety of its occupants, they are not a substitute for the recommendations of a qualified auto technician or your vehicle's owner's manual.**

Though preventive maintenance will minimize the chance for breakdowns, it is important to be prepared by traveling with an appropriately-stocked "emergency kit," and by knowing what to do to get help and stay safe if your car breaks down on the road.

For a full discussion of these topics, see Ch. 11, *Your Glove Compartment and Trunk: Keep Them Well Stocked,* and Ch. 28, *Roadside Breakdown: How to Deal with Roadside Emergencies.*

Chapter 10

Know Your Car:
The Ten-Minute Checklist[1]

Air Filter

- Check every two to three months.
- A dirty air filter reduces gas mileage and the lifespan of your motor.
- Replace it when it is dirty or during your annual engine performance check.
- If you drive in very dusty conditions, you may need to check your air filter more frequently.

Battery

- Have the battery checked with every oil change and periodically check cables for corrosion.
- Use of felt rings (positioned around the battery post under the clamp) — available at any auto parts store — will reduce corrosion.
- Consider replacing your battery if it is three years old or older.

Belts and Hoses

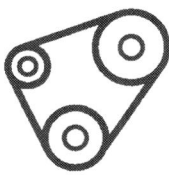

- Check monthly.
- If your belts or hoses look or feel hard, spongy, cracked or shiny, they should be replaced right away.
- It's best to leave the replacement to an expert.
- Also, be on the lookout for loose, cracked or missing clamps.

---

1 Copyright Shell Oil Company material, reproduced with permission.

Brake Fluid

- Check monthly.
- First, wipe any dirt from the master brake cylinder cover. Then remove the cover.
- If you need fluid, add the proper type (refer to your owner's manual) and check for possible leaks. Don't overfill.

Brake System

- Experts recommend having your brake system thoroughly inspected once a year or every 12,000 miles, whichever comes first.

Coolant/ Antifreeze

- Check frequently.
- You should be able to see the level of coolant in the reservoir.
- Follow the manufacturer's instructions to determine if the level is low.
- If necessary, add coolant to the reservoir — NOT the radiator — and fill to the proper level.

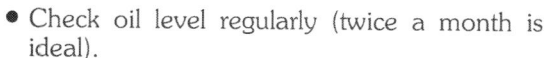

Engine Oil

- Check oil level regularly (twice a month is ideal).
- Have the oil (and oil filter) changed every three months or every 3,000 miles, whichever comes first, unless your vehicle's manufacturer specifies otherwise.

Lights

- Check regularly to ensure they are clean and in good working order.
- Remember to check:
- Headlights
- Taillights
- Brake lights
- Turn signals

**Power
Steering Fluid**

- Check monthly using the reservoir dipstick.
- If low, add the proper type of fluid (refer to your owner's manual).
- Inspect the pump and hoses for leaks.

**Shock
Absorbers**

- Test once every two to three months by bouncing your car up and down; when you step away, the car should stop bouncing.
- Always replace shock absorbers in pairs.

Tire Pressure

- Check monthly when tires are cold — that is, when they have not been used for at least three hours — using a tire gauge.
- For proper tire inflation, refer to your owner's manual or the label on the driver's side door edge or in the glove compartment of your vehicle.
- The number molded into the sidewall of your tires is the maximum, not the recommended, tire pressure.

Wheel Alignment

- Have the alignment checked immediately if the vehicle feels "loose," "pulls" to one side or if there is uneven tire wear.

Tire Rotation

- Have your tires rotated approximately every 6,000 miles or with every other oil change.

Tire Tread

- Look for uneven wear, separation or excessive smoothness.
- Replace tires immediately if the tread has worn down to 1/16 of an inch or less.
- Use a measuring device or the "penny test": Insert a penny with the head pointed down into the tread groove. If you can see all of Lincoln's head, your tires need to be replaced.

Transmission Fluid

- **Automatic**:
  - ✓ Check your owner's manual for the exact procedure.
  - ✓ Most vehicles should be running at normal operating temperature with the parking brake firmly set.
  - ✓ Then shift the transmission into park or neutral (refer to the owner's manual or look on the dipstick), remove the dipstick, wipe it clean, fully reinsert it and remove it again.
  - ✓ Read the fluid level and add fluid of the recommended type as needed.

- **Manual:**
  - ✓ Checking the fluid on a manual transmission is better left to a service professional, as the car must often be raised.

Washer Fluid

- Check the washer fluid reservoir regularly and add fluid as needed.

Wiper Blades

- Check at least twice each year for signs of wear.
- Replace if wipers streak or smear.
- Don't wait until the rubber is brittle or worn.

IN THE NEXT CHAPTER, we look at what should be inside every safe driver's glove compartment and trunk. You may never have cause to use some of the items — but if you ever have an emergency on the road, you'll be more than glad you have them.

Chapter 11

The Glove Compartment and Trunk:
Keep Them Well Stocked for Safety

Our vehicle's glove compartment and trunk are often like our closets at home.

- **Some of us have them stocked to the gills with everything imaginable** — a lot of it often just "stuff" and "junk" we don't even know we have, much less need.

- **These days, some of us carry our "offices," "tool shops," or our complete collection of gym and sports items in our trunks — or even the overflow from our closets or garages.** (A friend's neighbor keeps her *vacuum cleaner* in her trunk — no room for it in her small apartment!)

- **Others have hardly *anything* in their glove compartments or trunks.** You know, those who like to be extra neat or who don't think there's anything they'll ever need in their car besides themselves and their passengers, or who think it's senseless to carry things they don't know how to use — and never would.

- And many drivers **mistakenly think that if they have a valid motor club "road service" card, that *that's* all they'll ever need in an emergency.**

- And some even **think they'll NEVER be involved in a road side emergency,** however minor.

But all of these practices and attitudes are very short-sighted. Emergencies – large and small – happen on the road every day (as we'll see in Chs. 22-30). You never know if you'll be faced with, or involved in, a breakdown, an accident, or bad weather. And, you may be stuck in a situation or location where "road service" can't help.

Safe drivers make sure they are prepared for emergency situation by equipping their vehicles with an "emergency supply kit" and at least one indispensable tool that can be easily reached from the driver's seat. This kit should be stocked with the tools, safety, and first-aid items that you – or someone else – can use to help you with a roadside emergency.

The following lists suggest articles you should have in your vehicle at all times -- some in the glove compartment, some in the trunk – wherever you can readily get your hands on them if, and when, you need them.

When putting together your kit, consider the area of the country in which you drive and ADD ITEMS ACCORDINGLY.

Always carry a CELL PHONE while on the road.
Emergency and communication systems offered by On-star®   for GMC vehicles, Sync® for Ford and Personal Assistant® for Infiniti® offer varied remote assistance for lockouts, navigation and phone services.

These lists were compiled from Shell Oil Company materials (used with permission, and originally written in cooperation with the American Red Cross, the Federal Highway Administration, the National Crime Prevention Council, and the National Institute for Automotive Service.

WHAT TO CARRY IN THE GLOVE COMPARTMENT
in Case of a Breakdown

- ☑ The vehicles User's Manual
- ☑ Call Police sign (often found on the back of store-bought sunshades)
- ☑ Bright handkerchief or cloth
- ☑ Numbers of who to call in an emergency
- ☑ Pen or marker and message pad
- ☑ Flashlight and extra batteries
- ☑ Automobile registration
- ☑ Insurance documents
- ☑ Copy of Health insurance card
- ☑ Emergency medical alert information, if applicable.
- ☑ Resqme® tool. (see page 287).

What to Carry in Your Trunk
in Case of a Breakdown

☑ SPARE FUEL®

Surprisingly, the second leading cause of roadside breakdowns is running out of fuel. Nearly 3,000 people die each year in accidents that occur while being stranded on the shoulder or median of a road, often due to simple breakdowns that force one's vehicle off the road.

For those of us in the security driving profession, this is a scenario we don't take lightly and take appropriate measures to ensure it does not happen. However, that is not necessarily the case for our families and friends, or the families and friends of those that we protect.

Fortunately, we have discovered an amazing product called **Spare Fuel**®, which addresses the "what if…" of running out of gas. As we have experienced in our own testing, Spare Fuel® will start any car that has run out of gas and, based on today's average MPG ratings, provide enough range to get you to the nearest gas station. Spare Fuel® is non-flammable and can be kept in a vehicle's trunk for years-- liquid insurance against being stranded. Or, in the event you are stranded due to weather (i.e. snow and ice), this innovative product will allow you to run the car's engine intermittently to maintain heat…even after you have "run out of gas."

What to Carry in Your Trunk continued

Also, see "Roadside Breakdown: How to deal with Roadside Emergencies," Chapter 28.

To find out more about Spare Fuel®, and to watch a video of it working with one of the VDI vehicles, visit the official VDI website or go to www.sparefuel.net.

In addition to carrying Spare Fuel in your trunk, we also recommend:

- ☑ Flares or reflective devices (flares burn hot, do not put them close to brush, grass or debris that can catch on fire).
- ☑ Jack and lug wrench (practice using at home as per your owner's manual)
- ☑ Spare tire, properly inflated (check often).
- ☑ Tool kit (adjustable wrench, insulated pliers, two insulated screwdrivers; one Phillips head, one standard); duct tape; fuse puller).
- ☑ Jumper cables.

Warning: Jumper cables can be dangerous if used improperly. See Ch. 25, Roadside Breakdown, p. 272, for instructions and cautions.

Fire Extinguisher – unexpired and securely stored with the correct charge (make sure it's the right type and that you know when and how to use it properly. See page 105, box 11-1 for warnings and precautions before using a fire extinguisher).

- ☑ Extra light fuses (check size in *Owner's Manual*).
- ☑ Tire repair canister (sealant-inflator).
- ☑ Strong rope or tow chain.
- ☑ All-purpose wire (to lash down a sprung trunk, door, whatever)
- ☑ Flashlight/spotlight and extra batteries (check batteries often to be sure they work).
- ☑ Swiss Army-style knife.
- ☑ At least one quart of oil (check type in *Owner's Manual*).
- ☑ First aid kit — (see list on p. 106 for contents).
- ☑ Blankets –regular and solar.
- ☑ Empty, approved gas container.
- ☑ Siphon
- ☑ Umbrella, poncho or raincoat.
- ☑ Gloves.
- ☑ Bottled drinking water — at least a gallon (replace every three months).
- ☑ Non-perishable, easy-open food items (i.e. Protein snack bars).

Box 11-1. Fire Extinguishers and Automotive Fires*

A fire extinguisher is a handy device to have in your trunk — but it is essential that you have the right type and that you know not only how to use it safely, but when and when *NOT* to use it.

☑ **The best all-around fire extinguisher for automobiles** would be an **"ABC Dry Chemical" with a UL rating of 3A:40B:C.** This extinguisher usually contains 5 lbs. of extinguishing agent. It is rated to put out Class A fires (ordinary combustibles), Class B fires (flammable liquids), and Class C fires (fires in electrical equipment).

☑ The extinguisher should be **securely mounted in its bracket** and **kept accessible for immediate use.** It should be **checked every six months** to ensure that it has proper pressure and is not damaged.

☑ Be sure to **carefully read and understand the operating instructions. ONLY IF YOU FEEL CONFIDENT ABOUT THE USE OF FIRE EXTINGUISHERS AND *WHEN* TO USE ONE SHOULD YOU ATTEMPT TO USE ONE ON AN AUTOMOBILE FIRE.**

☑ Consider that **aside from the fuel in the vehicle, all of the plastics used in modern automobiles are also highly flammable.** Keep in mind that the **smoke from a burning automobile is *extremely toxic*** and breathing the smoke could have serious consequences.

☑ **A fire that appears small can rapidly grow out of control.** In any event, **NOTIFY THE LOCAL FIRE DEPARTMENT AS SOON AS POSSIBLE** so that they can begin their response. The longer you wait to notify them, the longer the fire has to get out of control.

☑ **Fires near or involving the gas tank are especially dangerous** and should be left to the fire department to handle.

☑ **If the fire is in the engine compartment,** it will be necessary to open the hood to effect extinguishment. However, opening the hood can be *very* dangerous as fresh air will be introduced and may make the fire flare up and burn you.

☑ **If the fire is producing large volumes of smoke, and/or flames are shooting out of the engine compartment,** it is best to leave the hood closed and await the arrival of the fire department.

☑ **Special note regarding newer alternate-fueled and hybrid automobiles.** Fires in these types of automobiles can be *especially* hazardous and should be left to the fire department to extinguish.

*Information provided by Bryan T. Sammartino, NJ Level II Fire Instructor

resqme, an indispensable tool

*Car entrapment is a present danger with cars today equipped with electronic components, electrical windows, central locking systems and anti-theft systems.

*About 10% of all drownings occur in vehicles in North America. 39% of flood fatalities are found in vehicles submerged annually. 400 North Americans lose their lives submerged in their vehicles annually.

*Car fires killed an average of 4 people each week in the U.S.

*43 children left in cars died from heatstroke in the US in 2013.

The resqme tool allows you to get out – or get in, to assist someone – in record time, "when seconds count..."

resqme is the original 2-in-1 car escape tool, which uses patented technology, was originally developed for first responders, and provides an effective solution against vehicle entrapment; it is a must-have for every driver.

Keep it at all times with you on your key chain, sun visor or attached to your rear view mirror.

What to Keep in a First Aid Kit

Sterile adhesive bandages	Scissors	Plastic bags
2" and 4" sterile gauze pads	Tweezers	Flashlight, flares and reflectors
Gauze rolls	Mouth barrier	Activated charcoal
Hypoallergenic adhesive tape	Antiseptic	Syrup of Ipecac
Hypoallergenic surgical gloves	Thermometer	Sting relief pad
Cold pack	Tongue depressor	Alcohol swabs
Triangular bandages	Petroleum jelly	An up-to-date first-aid instruction card (or manual)
2" & 3" sterile bandages	Hand cleansing agent	
	Safety pins	
	Sunscreen	
	Aspirin and no-aspirin pain reliever	

Cold Weather Gear

And to be prepared for a cold weather emergency:

• Stock your vehicle with extra gloves, hats, blankets, a windshield scraper and thermal packs.

• Carry sand, salt or calcium chloride.

• If you don't have snow tires, carry chains. (Practice putting on the tire chains so you know how to use them.)

PART II

THE SCIENCE AND TECHNIQUES OF EVERYDAY DRIVING

Most drivers never think of car control until an emergency occurs. When the emergency does occur, it's too late to think about it. To control a car as efficiently and effectively as possible, you must understand some of the science — *as well as* the techniques — of driving.

This Part looks in detail at the control maneuvers you can make with a car — accelerating, steering, braking. It covers the basic science behind these maneuvers and discusses specific techniques you can use to maintain maximum control of your vehicle.

It also points out — perhaps more importantly — what can happen if you *lose* control by not accelerating, steering, or braking *properly* — and WHY. And it tells you how to *regain* control if you lose it.

108

Chapter 12
Introduction to Vehicle Dynamics:
The Physical Basis of Car Control, p. 109

Chapter 13
Maintaining Traction:
Tire-to-Road Grip and Weight Transfer, p. 113

Chapter 14
Losing and Regaining Traction:
How to Handle Braking Skids, Power Skids,
and Cornering Skids, p. 125

Chapter 15
Steering at Speed and G-Forces:
Vehicle Dynamics in Action, p. 131

Chapter16
Curves and Cornering at Speed:
How to Handle the Road when It's Not Straight, p. 145

Chapter 17
Speed and Stopping Distances:
The Time-Distance Relationship in Stopping and Turning,
p. 157

Chapter 18
Braking Control, Part I:
The Science of How a Car Stops, p. 171

Chapter 19
Braking Control, Part II:
Non-ABS and ABS Techniques, p. 177

Chapter 20
Turning:
Turning Left, Turning Right, Turning Around, Backing Up,
p. 185

Chapter 21
Passing and Being Passed, p. 195

Chapter 12

Introduction to Vehicle Dynamics:
The Physical Basis of Car Control

When you are driving a vehicle, you can do just two things: change speed and change direction. And you do these through the car's controls — the gas pedal, the brake pedal, and the steering wheel. But you don't just use these "controls" — in essence, you have to "control the controls" as the vehicle encounters various and ever-changing conditions in the driving environment.

Cars don't lose control all by themselves — except in the rare occurrence of an outright mechanical failure. It is vastly more likely for the *driver* to lose control of the car.

> **Cars can be compared to computers. A computer is an inanimate object until someone programs it. In the same way, a car is an inanimate object until someone drives it. We frequently talk about cars and computers in much the same way. We say "the computer said such-and-such..." or "the computer made a mistake." Which is nonsense. Computers don't make mistakes; they either work or they don't. The "mistake" is made by the computer's operator. Claiming that a car "lost control" is like saying the computer made a mistake.**

Loss of Control — Two Types

There are two basic kinds of loss of car control.

- The first isn't so much a control loss as it is just plain **sloppy driving habits.** All of us are guilty of sloppy driving from time to time. Remember the time you were trying to pull out of a driveway and ran over the curb? Or that time you didn't see the car that was pulling out of the parking spot and nearly hit it?

This type of loss of control really means that, although you were sitting behind the wheel, you were basically along for the ride. Loss of concentration and not paying attention resulted in the fact that you weren't a driver — **you were a passenger who just happened to be sitting behind the wheel.** This is a very dangerous place for a passenger to sit!

- **The second type of control loss is a perfect expression of the term "loss of control."** Only it is not so much the *car* that is out of control as the *driver is* out of control. In this sense, "out of control" means everything you would imagine it to be: heart pounding, eyes bulging, palms and forehead sweating, mouth going dry, stomach in a knot, and one central thought — *"Oh my God, I'm going to die!"* — occupying center stage in your mind. At this point **you have absolutely no control of either yourself or the car,** and the vehicle is going wherever the laws of physics take it. This is truly "out of control."

Wherever the Laws of Physics Take It ...

Anyone who spends time behind the wheel of a car needs to understand what is takes for a car to go *out* of control. To do this, you must have a basic understanding of vehicle dynamics.

Don't let the term "vehicle dynamics" scare you off. It's nothing more than a term for the physical forces acting on the vehicle — physical forces that affect the driver's ability to change a car's speed and/or direction.

- **Each vehicle is designed with (force) "control limits"** *specific* **to the vehicle** — a Hummer, for example, handles forces differently than a VW Beetle.

- **If the driver takes action** (through the car's accelerating, braking, or steering controls) **that exceed these limits,** the driver will be unable to control the vehicle.

In other words, you have to understand **the capabilities of your vehicle,** and exactly what happens when **you move the vehicle's controls.** It's very simple.

And to understand *this,* it is vital that you understand the various physical forces that act on the vehicle.

These forces include:

- **Friction** created between the tires and the road.

- **Momentum** built up in the vehicle while underway.

- **Centrifugal forces** placed on the car when its path is altered while underway.

In the next several chapters we will explain how these forces are created as you:

- **Go** (change speed)

- **Stop** (change speed)

- **Turn** (change direction)

by controlling a car's four modes of operation:

1. **Forward travel at a steady speed** (mode)
2. **Accelerating** (mode)
3. **Turning** (mode)
4. **Braking** (mode)

And, you'll see that **you rarely operate a vehicle in one mode in isolation.**

- You may travel forward at a steady speed, but you'll probably turn a corner or curve, or change lanes at least sometime while doing so.

- Or you may accelerate while cornering.

- And you may have to slow down while you're traveling or turning, so you'll be braking some, too.

IN THE NEXT SEVERAL CHAPTERS, you'll not only see **how all these forces are interconnected as you drive,** you'll learn **specific techniques for controlling your vehicle in each mode.**

Chapter 13

Maintaining Traction:

Tire-to-Road Grip and Weight Transfer

The most important concept to understand in vehicle dynamics is that for a car to perform the four modes of operation (forward travel at a steady speed, accelerating, turning, braking), it must rely on **adhesion between the tire and the roadway.**

Tire Adhesion — Tire-to-Road Grip

Automobiles are supported by a cushion of air contained in four flexible rubber tires. If you could place a car on a glass floor and look at it from below, you would see *four patches of rubber, each a little smaller than a hand,* touching the glass. These are **the only points of contact between your vehicle and the road.** (See Figure 13-1, p. 114.) Each of these four small patches of rubber is known as a "contact patch" and these four tire patches create the traction that makes the car go, stop, and turn. (They are also the sources of the control feedback you receive from the car. See "Car Feel," p. 120)

The "limit of adhesion"

The maximum control capacity of the tire patches is called the "limit of adhesion." This limit is the maximum performance available from a *particular vehicle and tire design.* The "limit of adhesion" is determined by the **grip of the tires to the road**, which in turn is determined by:

1. The vertical force placed on the tire.
2. Tire design.
3. Condition and type of road surface.
4. Vehicle speed
5. Amount of turning force.

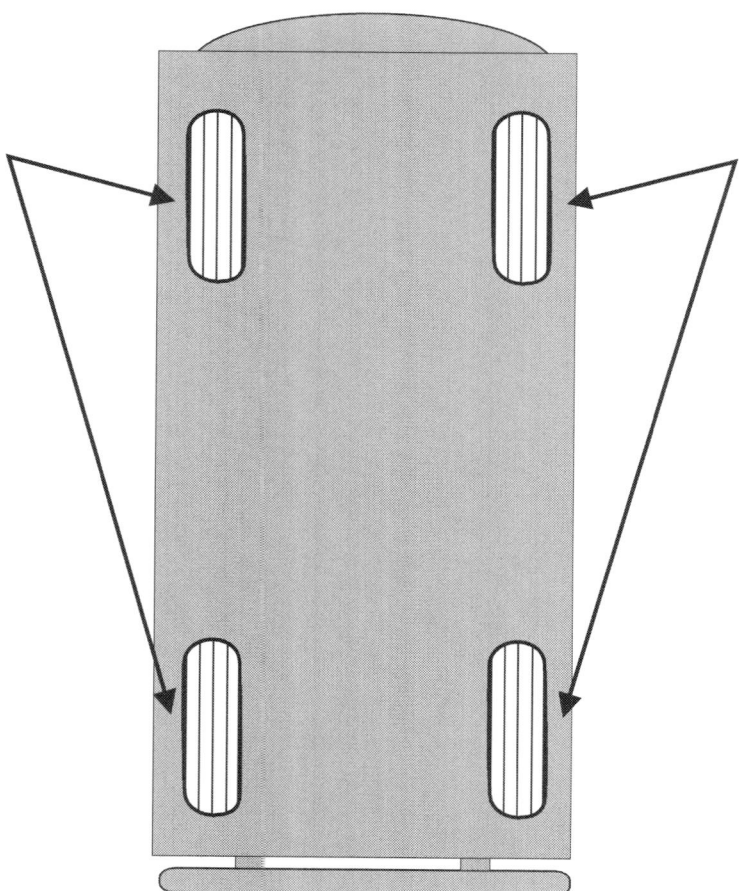

Figure 13-1. Tire Adhesion: Four Patches of Rubber. Each patch is a little smaller than a hand. The tire patches are the only points of control between your vehicle and the road.

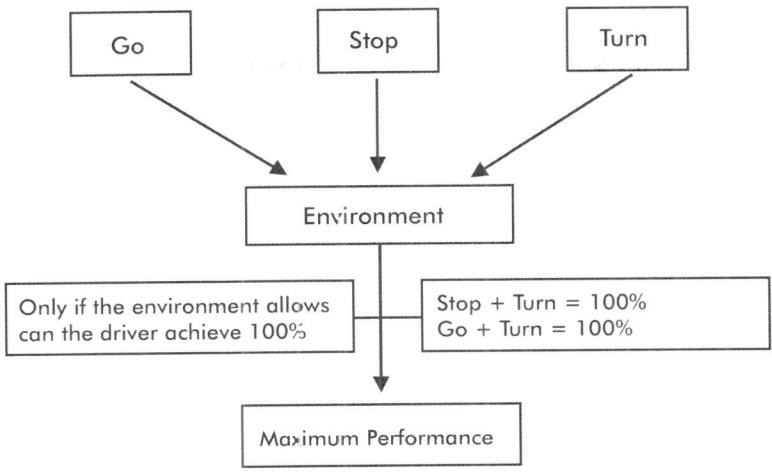

Figure 13-2. Maximum Performance Available from a Vehicle

> **The maximum amount of acceleration, braking, and cornering (steering) forces possible with a given set of tires are all determined by this tire-to-road grip.**

Although there is a limit to what a car and its given set of tires can do, we sometimes force a car to *exceed* those limits — by over accelerating, over-steering, over-braking. And, if you *do* try to force a car to go beyond those limits — especially beyond the "limit of adhesion" — you will go out of control.

Maximum tire patch capability for performing a given action

The four tire patches enable the car to go, or stop, or turn. In motion, tire patches have a given amount of capability for performing a given action, such as stopping. If that capability is used up in a given action, then the patch cannot do anything else. (See Figure 13-2, p. 115)

- There can only be 100% performance from the vehicle if the environment allows it.

- If the driver uses 100% to stop, the car will not turn.

- If the driver uses 100% to turn, the car will not stop.

- If the driver uses 60% to stop, he can use 40% to turn.

- If the driver tries to use more than 100% by applying too much braking and too much steering, the driver will lose control of the vehicle.

- This all assumes that the environment allows the driver to use 100%. If the environment only allows 50%, then the driver will be able to use only 50% of the vehicle's capability.

Rolling Contact

To control a car, *rolling* contact between tires and the road surface must be maintained. If, for example, while you're driving along, something happens or something you do (accelerate, brake, turn) causes the tires to stop *rolling* and start *spinning without traction* or *sliding outright*, life gets exciting in a hurry.

If, for example, the tire patches on the two front tires (which are used to steer the car) stop rolling for any reason, you lose the ability to steer the car. Therefore, we are correct when we say:

- **The steering wheel does not steer or turn the car**; it merely **aims the front wheels.**

- **Rolling tires stop the car and turn the car.** Front tires must be rolling in order for the car to turn.

- To put it in simpler terms, **rolling friction is greater than sliding friction.**

- **Once the tires have stopped rolling** — and started sliding — **it is not possible to steer the car.**

> Although it is important to understand what makes tires develop traction, it's far more important to understand what causes cars to *lose* traction and go out of control.

Weight Transfer to the Tire Patches

Weight transfer problems develop when a driver applies too much steering and braking force, or too much power and too much steering. The result in both cases is *excessive weight transfer to the tires*, which, in turn, puts too much pressure on the tire patches. **Too much weight on the tire patches causes the driver to lose control.**

- **Anytime you move a vehicle control** (gas pedal, brake pedal, or steering wheel), **you are transferring weight through the car's suspension system to the tire patches.**

- **If these forces produce stresses on the *tires* greater than they can accept,** those tires reach their limit of adhesion and let go. Again, the vehicle is out of control.

Referring to Figure 13-3, p. 118, you can easily see how weight transfers to the rear, front, left, or right depending on a driver's actions — and how excessive weight transfer can cause loss of control.

Weight transfer to the rear

The driver (Square 1) presses down on the gas pedal (Square 2). If we could put scales under the front and back wheels of the car when the gas pedal is depressed, we would see that the

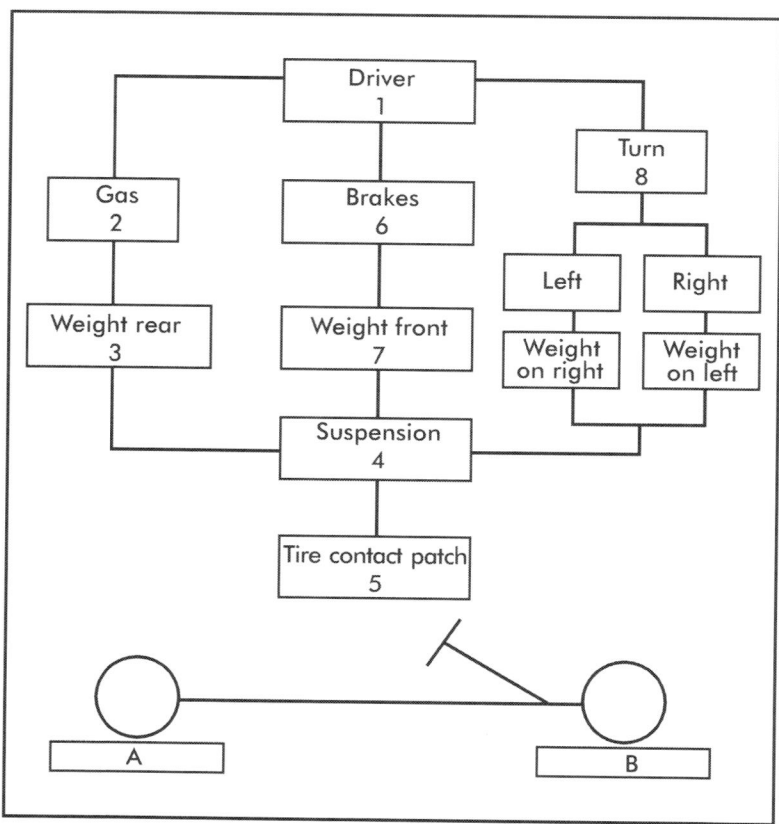

Figure 13-3. Block Diagram of Weight Transfer.

weight on the rear scale (A) increases and the weight on the front scale (B) decreases. In acceleration, weight was transferred from the front to the rear of the car (Square 3). This additional weight in the rear presses down on the car's suspension, affecting tire contact in the rear. If too much weight is applied, the rear tires will spin.

Weight transfer to the front

Once more, the car is on our imaginary scales. The driver (Square 1) applies the brake (Square 6), shifting weight onto the front end of the car (Square 7). This time, the front-end weight increases and the rear-end weight decreases. In this case, if too much weight is shifted forward, the front tires will lock up and steering control will be lost.

Weight transfer to the left or right

With the car under way, the driver turns the steering wheel (Square 8). If the wheel is moved to the right, weight is transferred to the left — once more, by way of the suspension and onto the tire contact patch.

Driving scenario — weight transfer in action

- You're driving your car, exiting a major highway, and **entering the off ramp at a speed of 25 mph.**

- Your car has **tires with a 1,500-lb adhesion limit.**

- **By turning onto the off ramp, you have placed 1,400 lbs. of force on your tires.** This is fine, the tires can handle this — unless, you have to apply the brakes or increase the angle of your turn. By doing either — or both — you will create more force on the tires, exceed their adhesion limits, and lose control of the car.

Remember: If your vehicle has tires capable of accepting 1,500 lbs. of vertical load, it can accept that load from braking, accelerating, or turning. It can take 1,500 lbs. and no more.

If you use all 1,500 lbs. accelerating, then try to turn or brake, you will reach the tires' adhesion limit and the tires will let go their grip on the pavement and you will lose control.

> **It is vital to understand the interrelationships among acceleration, braking, and cornering (steering) forces. The ways in which they *interact* is one of the most important concepts in driving.**

- **The amount you can move the steering wheel before losing adhesion** is determined by how hard you have applied the **brakes** at the time.

- The opposite is also true; **the amount of brakes you can apply** is determined by how much **steering force** has been applied.

> In later chapters we will discuss how to drive yourself out of trouble, concentrating on the fact that the foundation of trouble-free driving is the relationship between the forces of stopping, accelerating, and turning as represented by the brake and gas pedals and the steering wheel.

"Car Feel" — Keeping in Touch with the Control Limits of the Car

The characteristics of weight transfer onto the suspension and how those transfers affect the limit of adhesion is a major determining factor in just how the car *feels* to the driver. And it's not only possible but *desirable* to feel the control limits of a car long before those limits are exceeded.

> Feeling the limits is mandatory because they permit careful drivers more control and give them a better idea of what is happening in the vehicle around them.

But, **today many people feel that driving a car should feel like sitting on their living room sofa.** Operating their car's controls should not disturb their comfort in any way.

The people who feel this way buy the vast majority of the cars built every year in this country, so automobile manufacturers go to great lengths to abolish car "feel." **The end product is a car for people who are missing nearly all of the experience of driving.**

Most of us tend to be irrationally attached to certain makes of cars. Some of us come from families in which everyone owns and drives Chevrolets, others were raised in families where Ford may be the "officially sanctioned" car. We feel that some makes of cars are *intrinsically* better than others. But if we take a moment to think about these preferences from a rational point of view, the fact emerges that a car is simply a piece of machinery and nothing more. **And how that machinery communicates to you in terms of control — not just in comfort or aesthetics — should be taken into consideration.**

Cars communicate to their drivers in two basic ways: ride and handling. These are two very distinct sensations that are often confused with each other.

Ride

Ride is the vertical motion of the wheels and tires as they rise and fall over irregularities in the road surface. Auto design engineers try to dampen this motion as much as possible, isolating it from the car's frame through the use of shock absorbers and other attenuating devices.

Ride is a comfort factor, one that can be hard or soft. A soft riding car smooths out the bumps on the road. A passenger could be drinking a cup of coffee as the car drove over a railroad crossing and not spill a drop. If a lot of the motion is felt in the car's body and passenger compartment, the result is a hard-riding and frequently uncomfortable car. In a hard-riding car, that same passenger would end up wearing that cup of coffee.

Many people mistakenly confuse ride with comfort — but, as we've said, ride is just one factor of comfort. A car that smooths out all the bumps of the road may be very *comfortable*, but may not necessarily be a good car for all *drivers*.

Handling

What is *handling*? Handling is the car's ability to remain in control when cornering or being driven through evasive maneuvers — that is, **it's ability to handle various weight transfers.**

It is also a complicated quality involving the entire driving system. **Handling depends on the machine and the environment, centering on the fact that a car is, at all times, a compromise between many factors.** While it is hard to define handling precisely, it is easy to make qualitative judgments as to what is good handling and what is bad.

In a study conducted by West German automaker Daimler Benz, researchers evaluated the current state of automotive handling technology. They came up with a compromise judgment as to **just what can be regarded as satisfactory handling qualities.**

- First, **the vehicle should respond quickly, but not skittishly or in a nervous way to control inputs.** Small movements of the wheel should not produce disproportionately large movements of the car. This response should be largely independent of vehicle speed.

- Secondly, **the vehicle should follow normal steering inputs correctly and without need of further correction.** Additionally, it should be possible for large lateral(sideways) movements of the car to be corrected with uncomplicated steering motions.

- Thirdly, **alternating quick releases of throttle and subsequent braking should produce no unexpected and/or dangerous side movements of the car.**

- Finally, **under varying road irregularities between the left and right sides of the car,** and in crosswind conditions, the driver **must be able to maintain a straight course easily.**

IN THE NEXT CHAPTER, we discuss what happens when the traction/weight transfer equation goes out of balance — and what you can do to regain control of your vehicle.

Chapter 14

Losing and Regaining Traction:

How to Handle Braking Skids, Power Skids, and Cornering Skids

As you have learned in the previous chapter, loss of tire adhesion (skids) is caused when a driver applies more input to the car than the design can take. Of course, the amount of input a given design can handle is affected by the weather, road conditions, and other environmental factors, but essentially, it is the driver who goofs by applying **too much input on the brakes, the accelerator, or steering wheel.**

> **When you lose control of the car, you have entered a skid situation — and *not all skids are created equal*. Skids have their own characteristics.**

Braking Skids

Fortunately, braking skids are less of a problem as more and more passenger cars come off the assembly line equipped with anti-lock (ABS) brakes and/or traction control mechanisms. (Most commercial vehicles have no ABS or traction control.)

> **Even if your own vehicle is equipped with all the bells and whistles the auto manufacturers offer, there is always the possibility of rentals being ill-equipped — so you should know how to handle braking skids with both ABS and non-ABS. (See Ch. 19, *Braking Control, Part II: Non-ABS and ABS Techniques*.)**

Front-wheel braking skid

In a front wheel braking skid severe enough to stop the forward wheels (usually caused by a hard brake application), the driver may suddenly find that steering the car has become impossible. No matter how much the steering wheel is turned, the car continues in a straight line ahead.

All the available friction capability of the front tires is being used by trying to stop. No turning, or "cornering" force, as it's known, can develop at the front wheels. If all the tire patches' friction capability is used trying to stop, then it becomes impossible to steer the car. The reason the car continues in a roughly straight line is due, in part, to simple physics (moving objects tend to take a straight path unless another force is exerted on them), and also the fact that the rear wheels, which continue to roll even though the front wheels are locked up, act as a sort of "rudder," keeping the car traveling forward.

Paradoxically, a front-wheel braking skid almost always creates the situation that drivers try hardest to avoid. Drivers slam on their brakes to stop, only to find themselves skidding right into what they were trying to avoid.

How do you control such a skid in a non-ABS car?

- **Get off the brakes,** which allows the front tires to start rolling again, and, above all, **keep the front wheels pointed straight.**

- **If you have moved the steering wheel sharply to the left** while skidding, and *then* release the brakes; *the car will turn sharply and violently in that direction.*

Rear-Wheel Braking Skid

What happens if the rear wheels stop rolling and lock up? **With rear wheels locked, the car reacts violently to the slightest movement of the steering wheel,** producing the maneuver known as **"spinning out."**

How do you avoid this?

- **Stay off both the accelerator and the brake** while regaining control by means of a technique known as "countersteering," or **turning the wheel in the same direction the rear end of the car swings.**

- Since the rear end may tend to "fish-tail," or swing back and forth, **it may be necessary to change the direction of the wheel several times before regaining control.**

- Throughout this procedure, keep in mind that **the general idea is to keep the nose in front of the skidding wheels at all times.**

Four-wheel braking skid

This is the type of skid that results when the driver tries to shove the brake pedal through the floorboards.

Unless you have Anti-Lock (ABS) brakes (see p. 181), this unusually hard application of the brakes locks up those wheels, which cease to rotate. In such a skid, the path of the car will not be predictable. There's just no way of predicting where the car is going.

Unfortunately, many drivers in a four-wheel braking skid don't immediately think they're in this kind of skid because they don't feel they hit the brakes hard enough to produce a skid.

There's only one solution to this problem: You must get those wheels rolling again. (See Ch. 19, *Braking Control, Part II: Non-ABS and ABS Braking Techniques* for in-depth discussion.)

- **If you *do not* have anti-lock brakes,** take your foot off the brake pedal — *now!*

Once the front tires are rolling, control is returned to the driver, who may then be able to steer out of trouble.

- **If you *have* anti-lock brakes,** maintain pressure and continue steering in the direction you want to go.

- **If the present danger requires some
  additional braking,** this must be done *gently,* with
  less pressure than before, or this whole dangerous
  chain of events will repeat itself.

Power (Acceleration) Skids

**Excessive acceleration causes what is known as a
power skid.** Most power skids happen when roads are
slippery.

Rear-wheel drive power skid

Power skids occur almost exclusively on rear-wheel drive cars.
They're caused by too much power going to the rear wheels.
The tire/road combination cannot accept that much power and
the tire begins to spin. In a rear-wheel drive power skid, the
back end of the car will swing out — in some instances spinning
the car in a complete 360-degree spin.

This maneuver is probably familiar to anyone who has ever
driven on ice.

- The solution to the rear-wheel power skid is to **ease
  your foot off the accelerator until the wheels
  stop spinning.**

- Then, and only then, **make any necessary
  steering corrections.**

Front-wheel drive power skid

Since front-wheel drive means the front wheels are the pair
accepting power from the engine, in a front-wheel drive power
skid, those are the wheels that are spinning. And, once again,
this type of skid generally takes place on slippery surfaces.

- The best way out of a front-wheel drive power skid is
  to **take your foot off the gas** and **try to steer out
  of the skid without using the brakes.**

- If needed, **apply the brakes *very sparingly.***

Cornering Skid

A cornering skid takes place when a driver enters a turn too fast and too sharply. This causes the rear end of the car to swing out.

- The best thing to do in this situation is **ease off the gas** and **avoid braking.**

- When you ease off, you'll find **the car's rear end will begin to track in its original position again.**

> **See Ch. 26, *Foul Weather Driving* for discussions on skidding and various weather/road conditions.**

IN THE NEXT CHAPTER, we discuss the science behind steering maneuvers — and how speed and tire adhesion enter into the steering control equation.

Chapter 15

Steering and G-Forces:

Vehicle Dynamics in Action

Newton's Laws of Motion Applied to Driving — Simplified

Sir Isaac Newton formulated several Laws of Motion that we can apply to driving. Basically the laws say that:

- **An object at rest tends to remain at rest** — *unless* you apply a force to it.

- **An object in motion tends to continue moving in a straight line at constant speed** — *unless* you apply force to it — which will either change its speed or direction, or both.

Applied to driving, we could say that if you step on the gas pedal (and your steering wheel is straight), you apply the force that will get the car moving — moving in a straight line.

And, if, while the car is in motion, you move the steering wheel to maneuver around a corner, or to avoid an obstacle, the car *tries* to follow a path dictated by the direction of the front wheels.

However, by turning the steering wheel while the car is moving, you also create *another* force that pushes on the car sideways, forcing it *away* from the desired direction of travel. The amount of this force depends on how *fast* you are going, how *sharp* you turn the steering wheel, and how *much* your vehicle weighs.

And, in order for the car *not* to be pushed sideways, the four tire patches on your car that are gripping the road must be able to "push back" with a force *equal* to the force generated by making the turn.

Your Vehicle's Control Limits

The forces we are talking about are called G (gravitational) forces and centrifugal forces — and **each vehicle is designed to withstand — or absorb — only so much of these forces before it becomes unstable.**

Box 15-1. G-Force Ratings of Popular Car Models

Various cars are designed to absorb a certain amount of G force. The amount of G force exerted on a car is a function of both the degree of sharpness of the turn and the speed at which the car is traveling during the turn. If this G force limit is exceeded, the result is loss of control.

If you're interested in how many Gs various car designs can take, pick up some of the automotive magazines available on any news stand. In them, you'll find reviews of various cars that include road tests and the G-force ratings that resulted from those tests.

Here are a few of the maximum G-force ratings of some of the cars we know and love:

Chevrolet Corvette	0.892 Gs
BMW 745i	0.87Gs
Cadillac Escalade	0.73Gs

Remember: A car is merely a machine; if we try to use that machine in such a way that its design limits are exceeded, then this machine, like any other, will not work.

So it is important for you to not only understand how the various *combinations* of your vehicle's speed and weight and the sharpness of your turns of the steering wheel can develop forces that affect your ability to control your car in any given situation, you must also understand **the control *limits* that are designed into your particular vehicle.**

To do this, you have to follow a two-step process:

- First you have to **figure out the G-force that is created by your handling of the vehicle —** how much you step on the gas pedal and how sharply you turn the steering wheel.

- Then you have to **compare the amount of Gs generated with the amount of Gs your vehicle was designed to absorb** (it's G rating) before it would become unstable — and you'd lose control.

Understanding these forces and control limits should give you an *intuitive* understanding of how you can better handle your vehicle.

In the next section, we introduce the Driving Equation and show you step-by-step how to use it to figure out the G forces created in a given situation — and how to interpret them in terms of control.

A WORD ABOUT EQUATIONS. Equations are engineers' ways of confusing us mortals. They are also a useful shorthand way of expressing complicated concepts. It's not as important for you to profoundly understand the equation as it is for you to intuitively know its consequences — that is, understand what you can do as a driver to overcome the effects of these forces and stay in control of your vehicle.

THE "DRIVING EQUATION" — FIGURING OUT THE G-FORCE

To figure out the G-force we use the following equation (the "Driving Equation")

$$LA = V^2 / R32.2$$

First, let's review the equation:

LA - This is lateral acceleration; the amount of G force exerted on the car. This is what we're trying to figure out.

V - This is how fast the car is traveling in feet per second. (To change mph to fps, multiply the speed (mph) by 1.47.)

R - This is the radius of the turn, roughly equivalent to the degree of sharpness of the turn, or the amount the steering wheel is turned.

32.2 - This is the force of gravity (this is a constant).

WHAT THIS EQUATION IS SAYING is that the amount of force imparted to the car is determined by how fast we're driving and how sharp we'd like to turn, which is another way of saying how much we move the wheel.

Let's take an example and plug the figures into the equation:

Let's make a turn at an average street corner which has a 55-ft radius. We'll take that corner at a speed no one would think unreasonable, say, 20 mph. So for our equation:

V = 20 mph or 29.4 ft/sec

R = 55 ft

The driving equation **LA = V^2 / R32.2** in this scenario thus becomes:

$$LA = \frac{(29.4)^2}{(55)\,(32.2)} = \frac{864.36}{1771} = .49$$

So, LA — or the G-Force = **.49Gs**

If you compare this G force (.49) with the G-Force rating of your vehicle (let's say it's 0.8Gs), you'd be in fat city going around that corner with no control problems. If you exceed your vehicle's G-rating, however, you'd be in trouble.

You can further see this if you take the car's weight into consideration. If you multiply the weight of the car by the Gs in the scenario, you can figure out how many pounds of force are pushing the car sideways away from its desired path.

Let's follow the same example, figuring in the car's weight.

If the car, let's say, was a sedan that weighed 4,000 lbs., you'd multiply the G-force from our scenario (.49Gs) times the weight of the car (4,000 lbs.).

.49Gs x 4,000 lbs. = 1,960 lbs.

So 1,960 lbs. of sideways G-force on a 4,000 lbs. car would not throw it out of control.

How many pounds of sideways G-force *could* your 4,000-lb car with a G-rating of 0.8G absorb before becoming unstable? Simple. Multiply the weight of the vehicle times the G-rating:

4,000 lbs. x 0.8G = 3,200 lbs.

Your vehicle could absorb 3,200 lbs — and no more.

> **Remember: The lateral G-forces created in a turn is based upon both the vehicle's weight and the degree, or sharpness, of the turn.**

- If we turned our 4,000 lb car in such a way that .7G was created, then we would have created 2,800 lb of force or 4,000 X .7 = 2,800 lb.

- If the car weighed *3,000* lbs. and was turned the same way, the equation would read 3,000 X .7 = 2,100, and so forth.

- And, if 4,000 lbs. of force are exerted on a 5,000-lb car, that's no big deal. But if you take a corner in such a way that 4,000 lbs. are being exerted on a 2,000-lb car, you're in big trouble.

So, what does all this mean in terms of what you as a driver have to do to maximize control while steering at speed? It means that you have to somehow control the Gs that your maneuvers create.

As we'll see in the next section, **a small change in G-force can make a very big difference in the way a vehicle handles.** And, if you study the Driving Equation, you can see that for the same scenario — same car (means same weight), and same corner (means same radius), **the only thing that can change the G-force results is your SPEED.**

Small Changes in Speed/Very Big Changes in G-Forces

Let's stick with our same example and run some different speeds through the equation.

If we double the speed to 40 mph, will there be twice as much force exerted on the car? Plugging those numbers into the equation gives us:

V = 40 mph or 58.8 ft/sec

R = 55 ft

$$LA = V^2/R32.2 \ = \ \frac{(58.8)^2}{(55)(32.2)} \ = \ \frac{3457}{1771} = 1.95Gs$$

If we multiply the weight of the car by the Gs we get:

4,000 lbs. x 1.95Gs = **7,808 lbs. of force**

In other words, with the same 4,000-lb car going around the same 55ft corner, we have increased the amount of lateral force to 7,808lbs. — or approximately **four times the force encountered at 20 mph!**

It doesn't require a Ph.D. in mathematics to figure out that if you exert 7,808 lbs. of force on a 4,000 lb car, that force is more than sufficient to push that car into the *Twilight Zone*, or at least off the road.

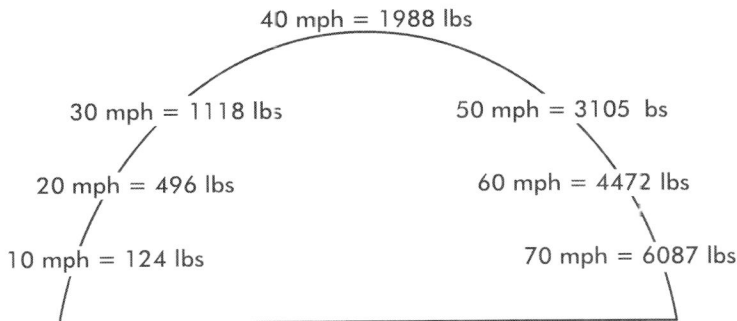

Figure 15-1. Relationship of Speed to Lateral Acceleration. A 4,000-lb car turns the same corner at varying speeds. At 10 mph there is 124 lb of force on the car; at 40 mph there is 1,988 lb of force on the car.

This should be a startling observation! **Doubling the speed of a car doesn't double the force exerted on the car, it quadruples it** — because the force increases according to the *square* of the speed — the speed times itself. So, in the equation, when you go from 20 mph to 40 mph it's really like going from 20 mph to 400 mph!

In other words, if a driver increased his speed by a factor of *two*, the amount of force exerted on the car goes up by a factor of *four*. Therefore, under the correct condition, **a small change in speed can easily produce far more force than the car was designed to accept** (see Figure 15-1, p. 137).

So what's the solution to maintaining control? (Drivers are always looking for magic answers to this one.) Guess what? *Don't drive too fast!*

> **According to the National Safety Council, 33.5 percent of fatal accidents are caused by excessive speed.**

THE TIRE ADHESION FACTOR

The Driving Equation has shown us how speed affects the maneuverability of a car when turning/steering — how speed, the sharpness of a turn, and the weight of the vehicle determine whether or not you might suffer an accident. **But there is another factor that comes into play, here, too** — the all-important **tire adhesion principle.**

- We have seen that when a driver moves the steering wheel to drive around a curve/corner, he creates a side force (lateral acceleration), pushing on the car's center of gravity.

- Let's say that in turning, the driver creates 3,000 lbs. of force pushing on the car.

- There must be a force of 3,000 lbs. pushing *back* on the car or the car will slide off the road.

- The resisting force is created by the tire contact patches. (See p. 113)

If, for example the turn produced 3,000 lbs. of force pushing on the center of gravity of the car, the tires at the front and rear of the vehicle *altogether* would have to push *back* with 3,000 lbs. of force. In this case, the car would be balanced and *wouldn't* slide off the road.

The scenarios in our Driving Equation examples indicate the effects of vehicle dynamics on cars whose tires are in optimum condition — that is, they can perform (grip the road) to the vehicle's intended performance standards.

But what happens if your tires are NOT in their best condition — they're not properly inflated and/or don't have at least the minimum tread depth — or you have mixed tire types on your vehicle (radials and bias-ply)? Even though you may be maneuvering your vehicle within the limits of its G-rating, and your speed is controlled, you may experience the phenomenon of understeer or oversteer when you attempt to control your vehicle through steering.

THE PHENOMENA OF
UNDERSTEER AND OVERSTEER

Sometimes you'll be driving along and your car starts "talking" to you. Not like one of the modern, computerized cars that tell you to fasten your safety belt or that your windshield washer fluid level is low, but in the *seat of the pants* way with which pilots are familiar. **The car simply doesn't respond the way it should when you're steering. It seems to oversteer or understeer.**

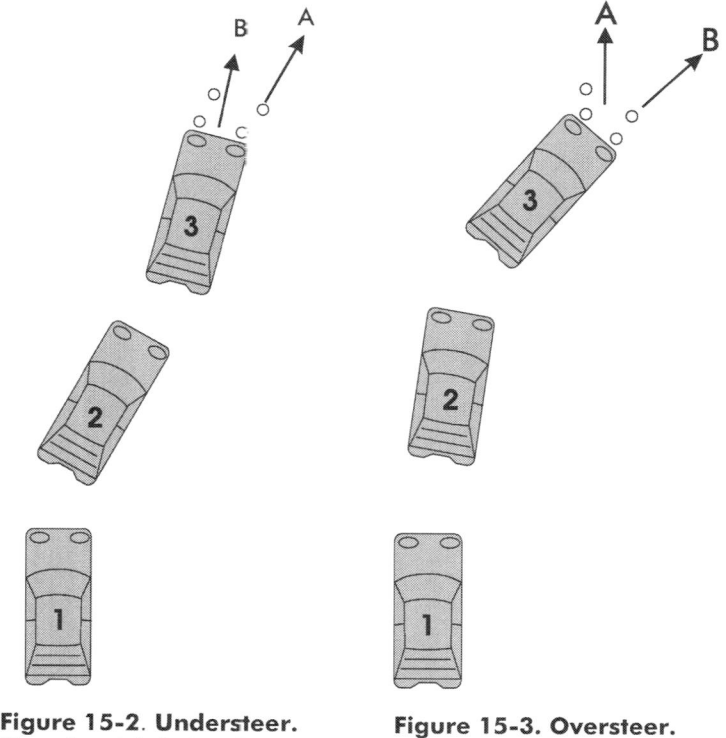

Figure 15-2. Understeer.
You aim at A, but arrive at
B

Figure 15-3. Oversteer.
You aim at A, but arrive at
B.

Neutral Steer, Understeer, Oversteer

In **neutral steer,** when the driver moves the steering wheel to negotiate a corner, he aims at a point and the car arrives at that point.

In **understeer** and **oversteer**, the driver moves the wheel to allow the car to enter the corner. He aims the car at Point A. But instead of arriving at Point A, the car goes to Point B — too far to the left in understeer (see Figure 15-2, above) and too far to the right in oversteer (see Figure 15-3, above). In both cases the car *fish-tails* in a see-saw motion.

The Physical Dynamics of Understeer and Oversteer

In a nutshell, understeer and oversteer are the interrelationship of the front and rear ends of the car. Let's take the same scenario we looked at in discussing tire adhesion a moment ago:

- The driver steered around a curve and created 3,000 lbs. of force pushing on the center of gravity of the car.

- To keep the car from sliding off the road, there must be a force of 3,000 lbs. of resisting force generated by the tire contact patches pushing back.

- Ideally the tires at front and rear of the vehicle would be pushing back with 1,500 lbs. from the front set and 1,500 lbs from the back set. The resisting force would be balanced.

In understeer, the *front* wheels have *less* traction than the rear. If, for some reason, the front tires can only provide 1,200 lbs. worth of resisting force (traction) and the rear tires provide 1,500 lbs., the result will be a sensation that suggests the front end of the car is going too far to the *left* from where the driver would like it to go.

In oversteer, it's the *rear* tires that are providing the lighter amount of traction, and the front tires that are loaded so that they adhere to the pavement better. The result is that the rear end of the car loses traction first, so that the rear begins to move toward the *outside* of the turn. This fish-tail effect may be encountered during a sudden application or withdrawal of *power* during a turn, or by a sudden movement of the *steering wheel* during a turn.

(The above is a bit of an over-simplification of what actually takes place, but only because it's rather complicated to explain the specifics of the vehicle dynamics involved.)

Causes of Understeer and Oversteer

The causes of understeer and oversteer are related to the condition and type of the tires on the vehicle — and the vehicle design.

Tire condition and type

- **Low tire pressure**

    Low *front* tire pressure (understeer)

    Low *rear* tire pressure (oversteer)

- **Uneven tire pressure**

    Uneven *front* tire pressure (understeer)

    Uneven *rear* tire pressure (oversteer)

- Sometimes a car will **understeer or oversteer in one direction and not in another.** This is due to the fact that **one tire has lower pressure than the other.**

    On the *front* (understeer)

    On the *back* (oversteer)

- **Bald tires**

    In the *front* (understeer)

    In the *back* (oversteer)

- **Mismatched tires.** In understeer this involves radials in the back and bias-ply tires on the front. The front of the car will push out, that is, resist the turn.

CAUTION: A quick shift from understeer to oversteer is very dangerous. If a car does this, check for tire inter-mix, the mismatching of bias-ply tires and radials in the same car. Cars must have one or the other type of tire *on all four wheels.*

Vehicle design and understeer

It is interesting to note that most automobiles built in the U.S. are designed to *produce* understeer.

In a study conducted by the Society of Automotive Engineers, results indicated that as the tendency for an automobile design to understeer increases, the accident rate decreases.

A reason for this may be that a car with a high value of initial understeer will tend to wander when traveling down a straight road and be relatively insensitive to minor steering inputs. This handling quality could be important in situations in which the driver's attention is momentarily distracted from the road. So American engineers feel it's safer for a car to have a degree of understeer built in.

How to Compensate for Understeer and Oversteer

To overcome understeer:

- Your objective should be to **get some of the vehicle's weight onto the front tires.** This will make the front tires grab the pavement more securely and start turning the vehicle.

- **Sometimes, just taking your foot off the gas** will transfer enough weight forward to do the job.

- In some cases, **it may be necessary to apply the brakes** in order to increase the weight transfer to the front wheels. If this is done, great care must be taken not to over-control the car and throw the vehicle into a state of *oversteer*.

To overcome oversteer:

- **Turn the front wheels to the outside of the turn.** That is, turn them in the direction the rear wheels are attempting to move.

- **Use the accelerator to apply power** so that power is applied to the rear wheels, which will force the car toward the inside of the turn and regain control. Applying power at this moment is tricky; too much power can spir. the vehicle in the opposite direction.

IN THE NEXT CHAPTER, we discuss the science and techniques for steering safety and effectively around curves and corners at speed.

Chapter 16

Curves and Cornering at Speed:

How to Handle the Road when It's <u>Not</u> Straight

In automobile Utopia, all the roads are the same width, all corners the same angle. The road surfaces are all the same, all uniformly wonderful and smooth as silk. There are no steep hills, no deep valleys, and drivers seldom have to even move the steering wheel because the roads are so incredibly straight.

Unfortunately, this automotive paradise rarely exists and we do need to do things like move steering wheels, and brake and accelerate. And, we have to drive around curves and corners — whether we're driving just around town or around the country.

Figure 16-1. A Little Stretch of Road Utopia.
Scenic Route, New York State © Jon Huber 2003

THE THREE TYPES OF CORNERS (CURVES)

As far as drivers are concerned, there are three types of corners: constant radius, decreasing radius and increasing radius corners. (See Figure 16-2, below.)

- A **constant radius corner** has a radius or "distance from a center line or point to an axis of rotation" (as the dictionary puts it) that is constant.

  A constant radius corner would become a circle if permitted to continue a full 360 degrees around.

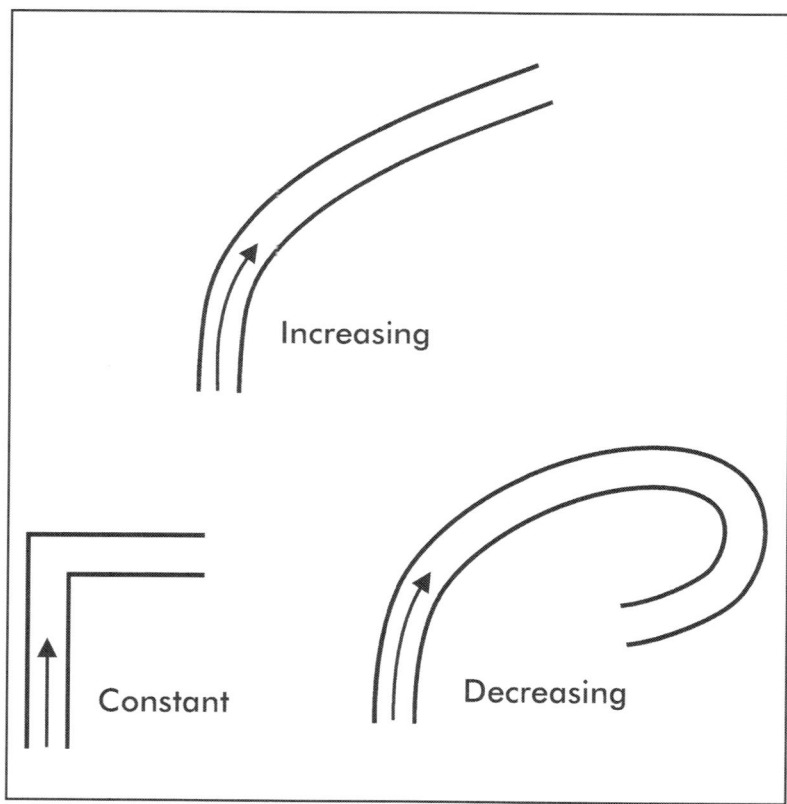

Figure 16-2. Increasing, Decreasing, and Constant Radius Corners.

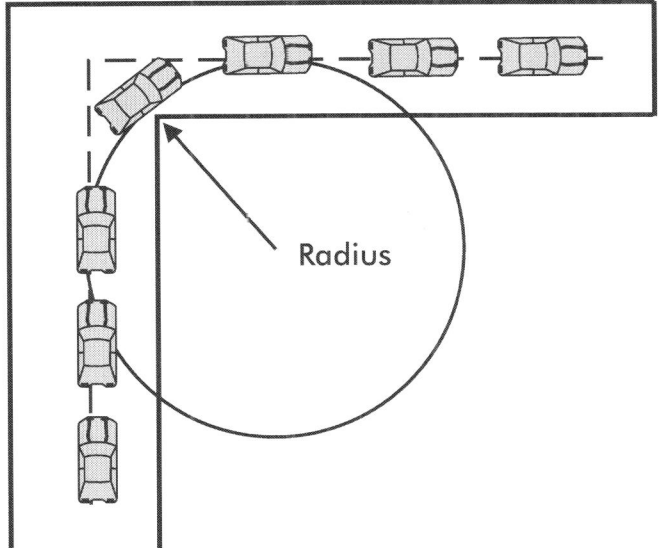

Figure 16-3. Diagram of a Radius.

- A ***decreasing radius* corner** is a curve in which the turn angle becomes sharper as you drive around it. (See Figure 16-2, p. 146)

   A good example of a decreasing radius corner can be found on highway underpasses, in which an exit ramp curves around and under the highway.

- An ***increasing radius* corner** requires a sharp turning angle at first, and then gradually straightens. (See Figure 16-2, p. 146)

   Some freeway access ramps are like this, beginning with a sharp turn required to get off the surface street and onto the freeway, then gradually straightening to allow traffic to speed up and enter the freeway traffic flow smoothly.

Knowing the various corner/curve types is very important, because they all require different types of driving.

THE SCIENCE OF HANDLING THE CURVES

Thousands of people are killed each year in collisions between vehicles, but more are killed in one-vehicle accidents. A driver loses control of her vehicle, skids off the road and careens into a telephone pole, or his vehicle turns over and over as it rolls down an embankment into a ditch. A curve is a likely place for this kind of accident.

As we covered in the previous chapter, there are two rules of physics about moving bodies that pertain to steering:

1. **Moving bodies tend to remain in motion.**

2. **Moving bodies tend to follow a straight path.**

To make a moving body follow a curved path, you have to use force to overcome its natural tendency to follow a straight one. A vehicle on a curve is a moving body with a natural tendency to go straight ahead. At each point on the curve the driver must use force — through steering — to keep the vehicle turning. The natural tendency to go straight ahead increases much more rapidly than the speed.

At 60 mph, there is *nine* times as much force on the vehicle than at 20 mph.

And as we covered in earlier chapters:

- **Effective steering depends on the traction between the road and the tires.** (Remember, traction refers to the tendency of the rubber of the tire to stick to the road instead of slipping and sliding over it.) (See Ch. 13, *Maintaining Traction*).

- **The part of a tire in contact with the road at any one time is about the size of the sole of a shoe.**

- **Four small patches of rubber are the only connection between the road and the vehicle.**

- **Anyone who has ever been in a skid knows that traction can be broken.** Whenever the tendency of the vehicle to travel in a straight line becomes too powerful for the traction holding the vehicle on the curve, the tires slide on the road and the vehicle starts to skid. (See Ch. 14, *Losing and Regaining Traction.*).

- **The force represented by the natural tendency of the vehicle to follow a straight line is opposed by the force you place on the car when you move the steering wheel.** These opposing forces can cause you to lose control of the vehicle.

So control of the car while cornering is vital. As driver, your job is to drive as efficiently as possible, and to do this, you must overcome the tendency of the car to move to the *outside* of the turn.

CORNERING TECHNIQUES

Knowing how to maneuver around corners/curves is important for *all* drivers — whether you're an everyday motorist hoping for a smooth ride to work or uneventful Sunday afternoon spin, or an emergency worker who must drive through corners as quickly as possible.

   The term used in driving schools for this move is "fast through the corner." But this doesn't mean how fast you are driving when you *enter* the corner/curve. Anyone can approach and enter a corner going fast — even too fast. "Fast through the corner" means to safely drive through a corner as quickly and efficiently as possible with skill and precision. In

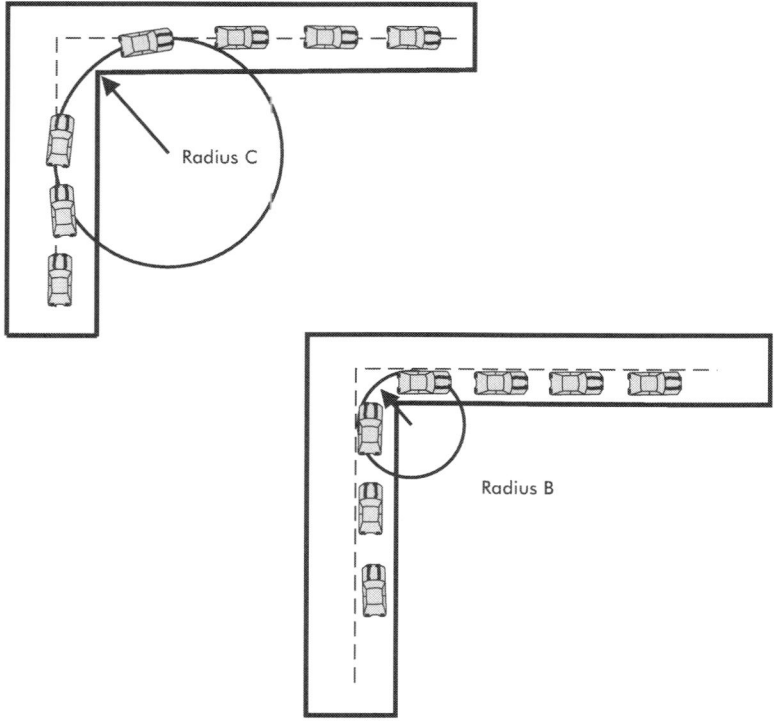

Figure 16-4. Big Radius vs Small Radius Corners. A car can be driven faster around radius C than it can around radius B.

order to do this, drivers need only put as little steering force as possible on the car. And to do *this,* you "straighten out the corners."

"Straightening Out the Corners"

To drive a corner quickly and efficiently, you'll have to "straighten out the corner" or, in other words, make the path of the car through the corner the biggest radius possible. (See Figure 16-4 above.)

Remember (see Ch. 15, Steering and G-Forces) that in the Driving Equation (LA = V^2/R32.2), the letter R represents the radius of the corner. If the value for *R* is big, it means the corner had a larger radius.

A corner with the "biggest radius possible" means a corner not with a sharp turn, but with a gentle, gradual turn — one in which very little steering force is imparted on the car. Since the steering required is slight, the ride through the corner will be a comfortable one. What's more, the larger the corner's radius, the faster it can be driven through.

A corner's apex

There is an imaginary point on a corner or curve in the road called the "apex." This is the point at which the road begins to turn — which, depending on the dimensions of the curve itself, will be at some point on the curve's *inside* path.

Outside-Inside-Outside Technique

In racing, this is called "taking a line." The line referred to is the path your car takes as it passes through the corner. Every corner in the world has a line and apex that allows a careful driver to maneuver through it as quickly and efficiently as possible.

The proper procedure for taking a corner at speed is to drive from the outside edge of the road as you enter the corner, then move to the inside to intersect the apex, and then back to the outside to exit the corner — all *without* driving into the other lane of traffic.

1. **As you enter a corner, your car should be on the *outside* of the curve**, still in your assigned lane (see Figure 16-4, p. 150), of course, but to the *outside* of that lane.

> **Never drive in the oncoming lane, or a lane that rightfully belongs to another car — but do make good use of the entire road available to you.**

2. **Entering the corner, gradually steer your car to the *inside* of the corner.** Your inside tire (the tire on the side of the car in the direction you are turning) should ride over the "apex" — which, as we've said, depending on the dimensions of the curve itself, will be at some point on the curve's inside path. (See Box 16-1 below.)

Box 16-1. The "Early Apex" Phenomenon

Accurately locating the apex of a curve is vital.

- **If you pass over what you thought was the correct apex point too early into the turn,** you won't have enough road to complete your turn through the corner — at least not at your present speed. As you exit the corner, **you'll either drive off the road or enter another lane.**

- **This "early apex" phenomenon is caused by *turning the wheel* too soon into the turn.** This usually happens when a driver starts the turn as soon as he *sees* it. While it's a natural reaction, it's better to wait a little longer and turn the steering wheel a little later.

The next time you're cruising your favorite freeway, check out the exit ramps to your right. See the frequent tire tracks, all those skid marks? Those marks were made by drivers who entered the exit ramp too fast, turned the wheel too soon, drove through an early apex, and ran out of road by hitting the curb on the outside. Their problem? Picking an early apex.

3. **Once safely past the apex, the car will return to the outside of the road** pretty much all by itself.

Outside-inside-outside scenario

Let's take your **average run-of-the-mill 90-degree street corner, with the street 33 feet wide.** We'll drive through it two different ways and get some interesting results.

- **If we take the corner by hugging the inside of road,** we make a 50-ft. radius.

- But, **if we take the ideal line through this corner,** entering on the outside, covering the inside apex, and exiting on the outside, we have driven the largest radius possible: 138 ft.

If you wish, you can work out the mathematics of this maneuver with the equation

$$LA = V^2/R32.2$$

If you don't, it should be obvious that it is far easier and quicker to drive a corner with a 138-ft. radius, than a 50-ft. radius.

Speed and Braking While Cornering

You can take the best possible "line" through a corner, but if you take it with too much speed, you could still wind up off the road or into another lane — and suffer the consequences.

Approaching a corner very fast, only to have to slam on the brakes and crawl around the corner is inefficient, dangerous, and accomplishes nothing.

As you approach a corner, judge the speed at which you feel you can *safely* enter that corner.

- **Often corner and ramp speeds are posted** on highways.

- **Pick a speed a little lower than you feel the turn requires.** You are not a racing driver, trying to blow through the corner while setting a new world's record in the process. *Leave room for error.*

- **As you approach a curve, slow down enough** so that after you are in the curve, you can keep your engine pulling, maintain your speed, and then accelerate to leave the curve faster.

- **Do not wait until you are in the curve to apply your brakes.**

- **If you *must* apply your brakes in a curve,** be careful. Use a gentle pumping motion until you are sure it is safe to keep continuous pressure on the pedal.

> **Never enter a corner as fast as you can and hope that your brakes can slow you down sufficiently for you to survive this experience. If you've already used up your tires' capacity for stopping and then try to use them for control, you're in for a big, nasty, tire-screeching, fender-bending surprise.**

- **Start turning your wheels** just *before* you reach the point at which the road begins to turn (the apex).

- **Once in a curve, stay on your own side of the road and stay as far over as you reasonably can.**

> **Do not try to make a curve easier by cutting across the lane of oncoming traffic.**

- **Maintain a moderate speed** and the curve will be easy enough to handle on your side of the road.

A cornering skid

Remember from our discussion on *Losing and Regaining Traction* (Ch. 15), a cornering skid takes place when a driver enters a turn too fast and too sharply. This causes the rear end of the car to swing out.

- The best thing to do in this situation is **ease off the gas and avoid braking.**

- When you ease off, you'll find the car's rear end will begin to track in its original position again.

Remember, You Cannot Judge the Next Curve By the Last One

Roads with uniformly sharp or gentle curves are probably safer than roads with curves of varying degrees. But on most roads, curves vary a good deal. Assume that unfamiliar curves are *sharp.* You can always speed up if you are wrong, but you may not always be able to slow down.

IN THE NEXT CHAPTER, we look at how your speed affects the distance you need to stop safely — and how to determine and maintain safe following distances to give yourself an "out" should you have to brake suddenly in an emergency.

Chapter 17

Speed and Safe Stopping Distances:

The Time-Distance Relationship
in Stopping and Turning

There are many occasions where we have to drive fast. **But how fast is fast enough, and how slow is too slow?**

Most of us would agree that 100 mph is fast and 20 mph is slow. But these are both relative values dependent on conditions. For anyone who has ever tried to drive on an icy road down an icy hill toward a busy intersection, 20 mph is downright *exciting*.

Speed Plays All Kinds of Tricks On Us

Among the most deadly lurk in the relationship of speeds to stopping distances. Table 17-1, p. 158 for example, shows that it takes 55 feet to stop a car on dry pavement at 30 mph.

If we double that speed, do we double the stopping distance? Sadly, no. In fact, the stopping distance increases by a factor of *four*. That's a good rule of thumb to remember.

> **For every doubling of the car's speed, it takes *four* times as much distance to bring the vehicle to a halt.**

Similarly, **if you drive from a dry surface onto a wet surface, the time needed for safe stops increases dramatically.** Why? Drivers will usually answer, "Because the road is slippery." But just what does that mean? It means the coefficient of friction between the road and tire is less than that needed for good, safe traction. (See Ch. 13, *Maintaining Traction*.)

mph	Dry(ft.)	Wet(ft.)	Snow(ft.)	Ice (ft.)
20	25	70	105	160
30	55	110	170	275
40	105	170	275	
50	188	250	410	
60	300	350		
70	455			

Table 17-1. How Long Does It Take to Stop a Car?

You must be aware of the effects of speed on braking distances. The faster you go, the longer it takes. Learn this intuitively, so you won't have to think about it — you'll just know it. Misjudging or disregarding speed can be a killer.

According to the National Safety Council, excessive speed is the single largest cause of accidents. This doesn't mean just driving over the speed limit. This means going too fast for the traffic situation developing around you, plain and simple.

Take a closer look at Table 17-1 above. Unless it's a real emergency, driving fast merely for the sake of driving fast is not too bright.

Miles Per Hour (mph) vs Feet Per Second (fps)

As a car is in motion down a road, the driver of that car is managing time and space (distance). As we drive, we measure time and space by using the car's speedometer. However, the speedometer is not the *best* reference possible for measuring time and space (or distance).

Speedometers indicate speed by measuring it in terms of *miles per hour* (mph) — a natural unit of reference that everyone is familiar with in driving discussions. But in terms of controlling a vehicle in split-second scenarios, mph is not a very useful unit of measure.

Consider: Accidents do not take *hours* to happen; they occur in *seconds*, even tenths of seconds. And they happen in very small physical areas, measurable in *feet* and sometimes inches, and certainly not in *miles*.

So, we need to rethink our frame of reference when we talk about controlling a car about how accidents happen. The frame of reference we'll find most valuable for this is feet per second (fps).

Table 17-2. Conversion from Miles Per Hour to Feet Per Second

Speed (mph)	Distance (ft./sec.)
20	29.4
30	44.1
40	58.8
50	73.5
60	88.2

Box 17-1. How to Convert from Mph to Fps

- **To change mph to fps, multiply the speed (mph) by 1.47.**

  Where does the 1.47 come from?

  5280 ft in a mile divided by 3600 seconds in an hour = 1.47.

Box 17-2. The *Easier* Way to Convert Mph to Fps

If you don't mind being off a bit in your calculations, or you're a driving instructor and would like to explain this concept to your students, but don't feel like multiplying by 1.47 every time you want to convert mph to fps, there is an easier way of doing all this.

- **First, round off 1.47 to 1.5.** That's a mathematically legal maneuver. The math cops won't write you a citation for doing that.

- **Now to change mph to fps, multiply by 1.5 instead of 1.47.**

- **You can do this easily by *adding*.**

> **Take *half* of the original mph and add it to the original mph.**

Say you're going 20 mph and want to know how much that is in fps.

> **Take *half* of 20 (which is 10) and *add* it to 20 (which will give you 30).**
> **(Half of 20 = 10, and 20 + 10 = 30).**

So if you were going 20 mph you would be moving at the rate of approximately 30 fps.

- **You can easily apply this to any mph conversion:**

Half of 20 mph is 10 — 20 + 10 = 30 ft/sec

Half of 30 mph is 15 — 30 + 15 = 45 ft/sec

Half of 40 mph is 20 — 40 + 20 = 60 ft/sec

Using feet per second as a measurement makes a big difference when discussing accident causes.

Time-Distance Driving Scenario

You're driving along at 40 mph (or 58.8 fps) . . .

- Something causes you to look away from the road for three seconds.

- At the same moment, another driver starts to cross an intersection 300 feet (the length of a football field) in front of you.

- Since your attention was diverted for three seconds and you were traveling at 58.8 fps, you drove a total 176.4 feet without looking where you were going (58.8 x 3 seconds = 176.4 ft).

- This puts you 123.6 feet from the intersection and its conflicting traffic.

- At this point, you look forward again, see the other traffic and realize you've got to do something.

- Can you avoid hitting that other car? Can you manage the remaining time and distance?

Let's examine this situation a little more closely.

- You're now 124 feet in front of the conflicting traffic, and closing with that traffic at 58.8 fps.

- If you can get your foot on the brake in a half of a second, you're very fast. Traveling at your speed, that half of a second represents about 30 feet. So at the point you start applying your brakes, you are about 92 feet from the traffic, still doing 40 mph (58.8 fps). Can you stop in time? Can you manage the distance?

- At this point, avoiding a collision would depend more on luck than skill. The problem here is excessive speed.

Time-distance-weight driving scenario

If you remember from Ch. 13 on the effects of weight transfer and tire traction (adhesion), you know that there is another factor that must be considered here as well. Let's see what happens when we factor weight into the situation when you have to make a sudden stop in a potential accident scenario.

- Your hypothetical car is equipped with tires capable of absorbing 1500 lbs. of vertical force. At this point, they will lose adhesion.

- Your speed is 30 mph, which multiplied by the conversion factor of 1.47, works out to 44 ft/sec.

- Your hypothetical day is a clear, sunny one, road conditions are excellent, our tires have a good grip on the road.

- Suddenly, a child on a bicycle appears 90 ft in front of you. It takes you half a second to get your foot to the brake pedal — meaning you have consumed 22 ft just getting your foot in position to apply the brakes. You now have 68 ft left before your car will strike the child.

- You panic and smash down hard on the brake.

- By doing so, you have transferred excess weight from the back end to the front end of the car. The weight transferred is more than the 1,500 lbs. the tires are designed to accept.

- This causes the front tires to slide, because they have passed their limit of adhesion. And since you use the front tires to steer, you've also lost directional control of the car.

- Therefore, sadly, you cannot steer away from the child.

Sadly, this mathematical scenario ends in hypothetical tragedy.

Time Needed to Cross an Intersection

According to an accident fact book prepared by the National Safety Council, 27.9 percent of all fatal urban traffic accidents occur at intersections. Another study, funded by the Federal government, indicates a higher incidence of intersection accidents — some 37 percent.

It's easy to misjudge the amount of time needed to cross an intersection. It takes about 4 seconds to cross a two-lane road safely.

If another car is approaching the intersection at 40 mph, and that car is 180 feet away (which translates to about three seconds away from you), and you choose that moment to cross the road, you're probably going to have an accident. Two objects cannot occupy the same space at the same time, at least not in this universe.

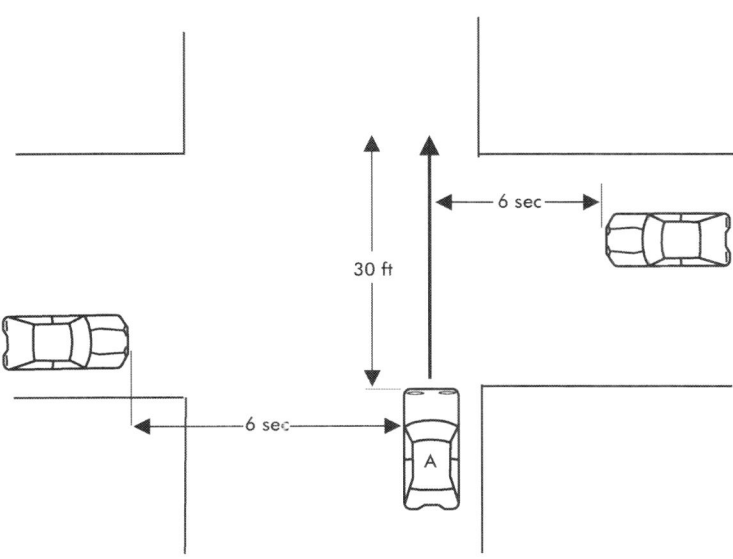

Figure 17-1. Time Needed to Cross an Intersection

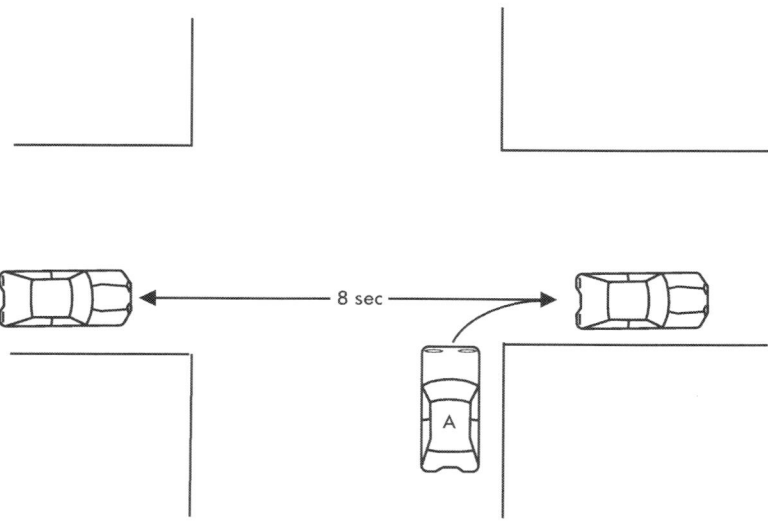

Figure 17-2. Time Needed to Make a Right Turn. From a stop, it takes six seconds to turn right and accelerate to 30mph. You should have at least eight seconds lead time before turning to the right.

Time Needed to Turn at an Intersection

Turns are also potential causes for disaster in intersections.

 If you want to turn right (see Figure 17-2 above):

- From a stop, it takes six seconds to turn right and accelerate to 30mph.

- Beginning such a turn, make sure that any vehicles approaching from the left are at least seven or eight (or even more) seconds away.

 If you want to make a left turn (See Figure 17-3, p. 165):

- You'll need seven seconds to make the turn, attaining a top speed of 30 mph in that time.

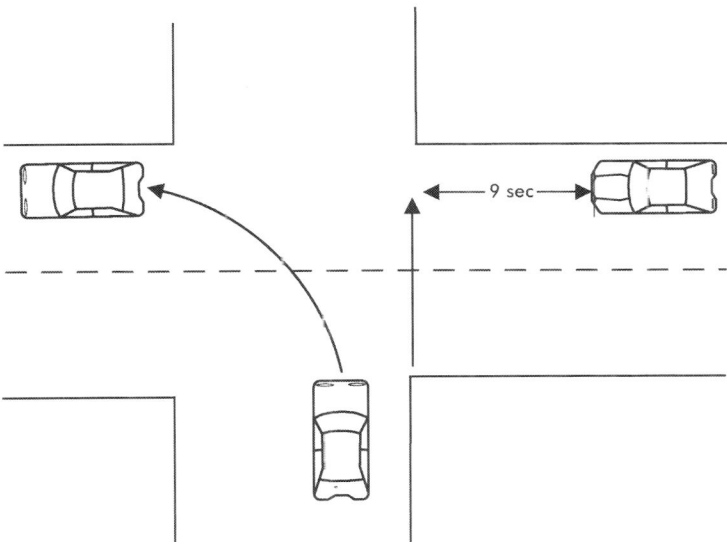

Figure17-3. Time Needed to Make a Left-Hand Turn. From a stop it takes seven seconds to turn left and accelerate to 30 mph. You should have at least nine seconds lead time before turning to the left.

- You should have at least nine seconds lead time before turning to the left.

  For example, if a car is approaching the intersection at 40 mph, and is 300 feet away, it will be at the intersection in about five seconds. For you, making a seven-second left-hand turn, this scenario spells collision.

> *Remember:* **The left-hand turn requires *more* time because you are crossing one or more traffic lanes. The left-hand turn is more dangerous because in many situations it will put you into a conflicting path with oncoming cars — twice.**

SAFE FOLLOWING DISTANCES AND BRAKING

A great deal of the success of the various emergency-braking maneuvers depends on the driver's alertness and powers of observation. **To be a safe driver, you need space all around your vehicle.** When things go wrong, space gives you time to think and act. To have space available when something goes wrong, you need to *manage* space.

Of all the space around your vehicle, **the area ahead of the vehicle — the space you are driving *into* — is most important.** You need space ahead in case you must suddenly stop.

When driving, you should be looking ahead; indeed, **you should mentally be ahead of your car by at least six seconds.** At 30 mph, a six-second-eye lead means your eyes should be focused at least 285 ft in front of the car.

Sadly, **when driving in traffic, most untrained drivers are focused so closely they only react to the brake lights of the car in front of them.** When the driver in front of them hits the brakes, so do they. Sometimes they're too late. If you ask these brake-light followers why they persist in this strange habit, they'll invariable tell you, "I can't see around the car in front of me, so I have to react to that car's brake lights." These people don't realize that the reason they cannot see around the car in front of them is because they are following them *too closely.* If the vehicle they are following is a large one, such as a tractor-trailer, it only makes matters worse.

A Typical Following-Distance Scenario

Let's look at a scenario that happens every day.

- A motorist is driving at 30 mph and you are following him at the same speed, some 30 ft behind.

- Both cars approach an intersection and the light changes yellow. The motorist hits the brakes.

- It's a beautiful day in the neighborhood, so you are not as alert as you should be and you allow a whopping full second to pass before starting to react to the situation.

- Once the motorist applies the brakes, it will require about 55 ft to stop that 30 mph car.

- So now, a stopped car is 85 ft in front of you. If you are doing 30 mph, you are moving at 44ft/sec. Assuming a normal reaction time of .75 seconds, and adding the fact that your attention was diverted for one second, that means you will not get a foot to the brake pedal before having traveled 77 ft.

- If the front of the motorist's stopped car is 85 ft from you, and the car is 15 ft long, then its rear end is just 70 ft away from the your front end.

- Since it's going to take 77 ft before you get your foot to the brake, everyone involved is in for whole lot of hurting.

If the same example is re-examined and that one second of diverted attention is eliminated, an accident is *still* the outcome — even if you applied the brakes the instant you saw the motorist's brake lights come on. The rear end of that car is still 70 ft from your car's front end. How long does it take to stop at 30 mph? It takes 88 ft to come to a complete stop. That isn't enough and an accident is the result. The problem? You where following too closely.

ABS or non-ABS braking, throwing out an anchor, dragging your feet, all the fancy braking techniques in the world won't help if you follow other traffic too closely.

So, our objective when it comes to following is simple: Keep a safe distance between you and the car ahead.

How Much Space *Should* You Keep in Front of You?

* One good rule is to keep **at least one second for each 10 feet of vehicle length at speeds *below* 40 mph.** For the average 20-foot car, this means if you're driving below 40 mph, you'd leave 2 seconds of space between you and the car ahead.

* **At greater speeds,** for safety, you must **add one second for every additional 10 mph.**

This becomes particularly important if you are driving a long vehicle — an RV or a truck, for example.

---

* **If you are driving a 40-foot vehicle at a speed below 40 mph,** you should leave 4 seconds between you and the vehicle ahead.

  In **a 60-foot vehicle,** leave 6 seconds.

* **If you are driving that 40-foot vehicle faster than 40 mph,** you should leave 5 seconds between you and the vehicle ahead.

  In the **60-foot vehicle,** leave 7 seconds.

How Do You Figure Out How Much Space You Have?

1. **Pick a fixed object on the road** (a shadow on the road, a pavement marking, or some other clear landmark).

2. **When the car ahead of you passes the marking, count off the seconds** — one thousand and one, one thousand and two, and so on — **until you reach the same spot.**

3. **Compare your count with the rule of one second for every 10 feet of length.**

4. **If you pass it before the time is up,** you're driving too closely.

Safe Following Distances When Driving at Night

Remember that your vision is affected by the availability of light (see p. 20, *Seeing at Night*). Quite simply, you don't see as well at night as during the day — and this affects safe driving distances.

- At night, **you can only see safely as far as your headlights illuminate the road ahead** — 200 feet for low beams, 300 feet for high beams.

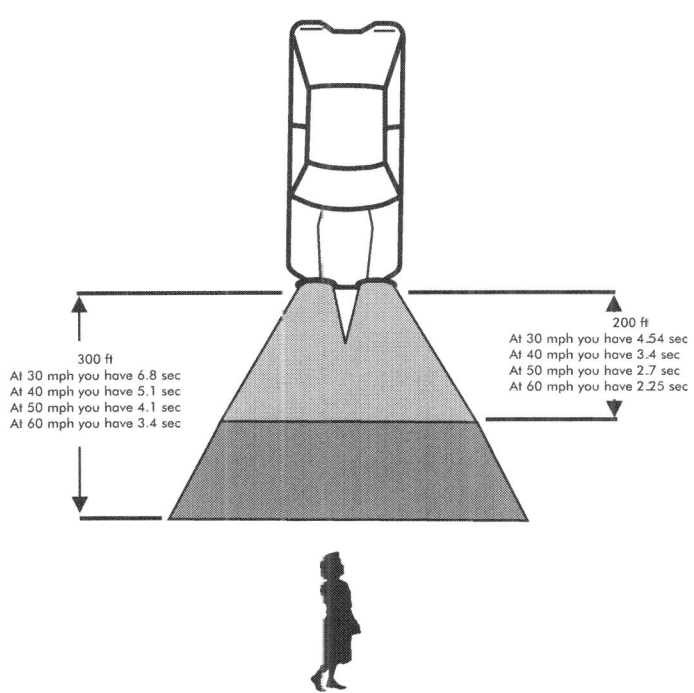

300 ft
At 30 mph you have 6.8 sec
At 40 mph you have 5.1 sec
At 50 mph you have 4.1 sec
At 60 mph you have 3.4 sec

200 ft
At 30 mph you have 4.54 sec
At 40 mph you have 3.4 sec
At 50 mph you have 2.7 sec
At 60 mph you have 2.25 sec

Figure 17-4. Night Vision vs Stopping Distances. Low beams illuminate the road ahead 200 feet. High beams 300 feet.

- Therefore, at night, when driving the average 20-foot car, make sure to **adjust the two-second rule for traffic ahead** of you to a **three-second rule.** When driving a longer vehicle, adjust accordingly (*see* p. 168. Don't overdrive your headlights. (See also Chapter 27, *Driving Safely at Night.*)

Specific Following Distances for Certain Vehicles

The rules for safe following distances differ for some vehicles — for example, **buses, trucks and fire engines.** You should know these rules — whether you are driving such a vehicle or just following behind it.

- When driving outside of cities and towns, a **bus or truck** should not travel closer than 200 feet behind another bus or truck.

- If you are behind **a fire engine when it is answering an alarm,** the minimum safe following distance is 500 feet. **Violators can be prosecuted.**

> **After a little practice, you will know how far back you should drive. Also remember that when the road is slippery, you need *more* space to stop.**

IN THE NEXT CHAPTER, we discuss the science of HOW a car stops when you step on the brake pedal.

Chapter 18

Braking Control, Part I

The Science of How a Car Stops

Brakes are by far the most important, most sensitive automobile control. Brakes are also the most challenging control to operate. And today they come in two flavors — ABS (Anti-locking Brake System) and non-ABS. While the techniques of braking differ between the two during *emergency* braking situations (see Ch. 19, *Braking Control, Part II: Non-ABS and ABS Braking Techniques*), the *science of braking in general* — the laws of physics — is the same for both.

Brakes Don't Stop Cars

Few drivers realize that brakes don't stop *cars*. Brakes stop *wheels* from rolling.

- **The friction of the tires against the road surface stops the car.** If brakes alone stopped cars, then cars would never skid.

- And the **maximum amount of friction** between tire and road **occurs just before the tire stops rolling.**

  The engineering explanation for this is that **rolling friction is greater than sliding friction**, or that a tire rolling across pavement has more stopping capability than a tire sliding across pavement.

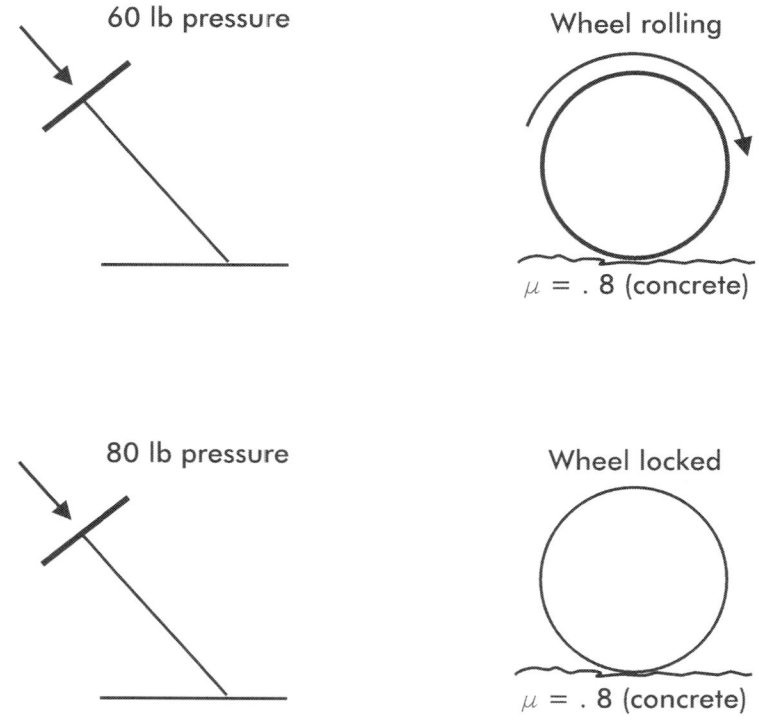

Figure 18-1. Brake Pedal Pressure and Loss of Control.

Brake Pedal Pressure and Loss of Control

Although the concept of tire friction stopping a car is central to the whole dynamic of the moving vehicle, most of us who were taught to drive were taught that to stop the car, all we had to do was step on the brakes. **What most us weren't taught was that after a given point, pressing harder on the brake doesn't stop the car any quicker.** In fact, in a *non-ABS* vehicle, pressing too hard on the brake could get you into big trouble. Consider:

- The average male can step on the brake with 140 to 185 lbs of pressure. The average female can hit the brakes with between 70 to 100 lbs of pressure.

- In an emergency situation, if a driver applies 80 lbs of pressure to the brake pedal, and in so doing locks the wheels and stops the tires from rolling, that driver has actually created less friction between tire and road.

- If the brakes were applied with 60 lbs pressure. enough to slow the car but still allow the wheels to roll, the effect is to create *more* friction between tire and road.

- A locked-up, skidding wheel is experiencing a lower level of friction than a slowing, but still rotating, tire.

- With less friction, more time and distance are required to stop the car.

- The really bad thing that happens is that with the tires locked (not rolling), the driver has lost the ability to steer the car, and that can hurt.

At this point, in a non-ABS vehicle, applying more brake pressure will do nothing but make the situation worse.

Here is where the confusion starts.

- **With an ABS vehicle, however**, you could press as hard as your foot can press and *good* things would happen. You'd still be able to steer the car — and if there is truck in front of you, that is a good thing.

The Vehicle Stopping Equation

When a vehicle is stopping or slowing down, it has to overcome the momentum that has been built up in the moving car. The following equation shows what's involved. You don't have to memorize the equation, but a quick examination of it can do much to help you understand why stopping a car in each circumstance is a completely unique situation. The equation is:

$$S = V^2/2\,\mu g$$

S = Stopping

V = Velocity

μ = Coefficient of friction (pronounced MU)

G = Acceleration of gravity (32.2)

It's the combination of speed(s) and that little μ that can get us in a lot of trouble. From the equation, we can see that the *faster* we go the more distance is required for us to stop, and that the lower the value assigned to μ, the more distance required for us to stop.

> **What's especially disturbing is the fact that as speed is *doubled,* the distance required to safely stop is *quadrupled.***

For instance, if a car traveling at 20 mph is accelerated to 40 mph; its stopping distance does not increase by a factor of two, but by a factor of *four.*

Look what happens when we change the value for μ in the equation.

- **The value μ changes as the environment changes,** and when μ changes, the driving environment can get exciting in a hurry.

- For instance, if you are driving at 50 mph on a surface with a coefficient of friction (μ) of .8 (that of a dry concrete surface), it will require 104 ft to stop the car, not counting driver reaction time.

- If the same car is at 50 mph when it encounters a surface with a coefficient of friction (μ) of .05, the stopping distance increases to 1,888 ft., or a little more than a third of a mile.

Consider this equation a basic fact of life when it comes to stopping a car.

- **The faster the car is traveling, the more distance it needs to stop.**

- Like centrifugal force, **speed and stopping distance are not linear.** Small changes in speed mean *big* changes in the distances required to safely stop.

- **If road conditions are slippery,** the coefficient of friction (or value μ of the equation above) decreases, and the required distance for a safe stop will increase *dramatically.*

- **Those who drive fast on a slippery road** will spend a great deal of time in the hospital and/or in court.

IN THE NEXT CHAPTER, we explain differences between Anti-Lock Brake System (ABS) and non-ABS — and detail the specific techniques for using both effectively and safely.

Chapter 19

Braking Control, Part II
Non-ABS and ABS Techniques

There are almost as many ways of braking a car to a stop as there are reasons for stopping. There is the gentle stop at a traffic light, and there is the *"Oh, my God!"* sort of life-and-death stop that nearly stops your heart as well as your car. Obviously, this latter type is most likely encountered in the emergency situation and is the one we're going to discuss here. And it is here where there is a huge difference between non-ABS and ABS-equipped vehicles.

Braking, you'll see, is not as easy or as simple as "press hard on the brake pedal."

The Difference Between Non-ABS and ABS

ABS is an abbreviation for Anti-lock Braking System, and was developed to reduce skidding and maintain steering control in an *emergency* situation. During normal, non-emergency braking, ABS works the same as non-ABS. But when you have to brake *hard* in an emergency situation, ABS and non-ABS work differently, and each requires a different braking technique on the part of the driver. (The techniques for ABS and non-ABS braking will be covered separately later in the chapter.)

ABS is basically a conventional braking system that is helped by computer technology. During *hard* braking, sensors in each wheel let the computer know if all the wheels are turning at the same speed — or if one or more wheels is trying to stop rolling. If a wheel tries to stop rolling, a series of hydraulic valves limits or reduces the braking on that wheel. The computer in the vehicle essentially pumps the brakes for you in a special way — stopping the car as quickly as possible while preventing skidding and allowing you to have steering control. (Aren't computers great)? If you take your foot off the brake, however, it's like shutting off the computer — and that's not good.

Under normal conditions, the anti-lock system will *not* be activated. However, should the braking force exceed the available adhesion between the tires and the road surface, the system will *automatically* activate.

The bottom line with ABS brakes is that **under most conditions ABS brakes do not help you stop *quicker.*** Their life-saving ability is in helping you **maintain steering control** during braking so you can avoid what ever is in front of you.

> **The ABS is not a miracle worker, cannot repeal the laws of physics, and cannot make you immune to bad road conditions, or worse yet, bad judgment. It is still your responsibility to drive at reasonable speeds for weather and traffic conditions, and to always leave a margin of safety.**

NON-ABS BRAKING

An analysis of what happens in a non-ABS vehicle in emergency crash situations shows a very high likelihood of one or more of the vehicles being completely out of control. "Out of control" here means that just before the accident occurred, the vehicle was either spinning or skidding. In many of these situations, excessive braking was identified as the main culprit.

This news that improper braking can easily throw a car out of control comes as a revelation to most drivers, who associate loss of control with harsh or abrupt movements of the steering wheel.

Bear in mind just what loss of control really is. No control means that the driver is not, and cannot, predict the path the car will follow. The car moves as if it had a mind of its own, spinning, skidding, and sliding. Actually, the car is responding to the laws of physics and those of motion, but those responses can look pretty random to the innocent bystander.

Loss of control *frequently* occurs in emergency situations.

- We will assume, for purposes of discussion, that the driver's reaction to this control loss will be **hard, excessive braking.** In a non-ABS car, hard braking means the application of 50 to 100 lbs of pressure.

- **How hard *should* the brakes be applied in an emergency?** It's not easy to provide an answer that's correct for all situations, due to the many variables involved. The same amount of brake pressure that brings you to a safe and comfortable stop on a sunny, dry-pavement day probably won't work on a rain-soaked evening.

"Controlled Braking" in Non-ABS Vehicles

The braking method preferred by professional driving instructors is known as "controlled braking." This technique calls for pressure to be applied on the brake pedal almost up to the point of lock-up. All the while, the driver must be aware that the more brake pressure applied, the less steering leeway she'll have.

Let's take a step-by-step look, however, at a real-life scenario of the "controlled" braking process for a non-ABS vehicle:

1. The steering wheel is pointing the car's front wheels straight ahead.

2. The driver applies 50 lbs of pedal pressure.

3. The front wheels reach their point of optimal road friction — the point just before they lock and cease rolling.

4. Unfortunately, by this time there isn't enough room between the car and the obstacle that the driver is trying to avoid hitting. The driver sees a collision is quickly becoming unavoidable.

5. In a further effort to avoid the collision, the driver turns the wheel.

6. While the steering wheel is movable, a slight movement of that wheel will cause the front wheels to lock up, rendering steering completely ineffective.

So, while "controlled braking" works well in theory, we see that the theory has a way of being disproved in the real world. When driving, always bear in mind that a brain-boggling, panic-inducing *"Oh, my God!"* sort of situation can happen any time.

In this scenario, you find yourself doing a not-so-hot job of "controlled braking." In fact, you've really messed it up, locking up the front wheels, while turning the steering wheel and making the front-end swerve.

Think of all this as a religious experience. At this point, your only salvation is to get that foot *off* the brakes. Once you have locked up your front wheels and subsequently decided that moving the car you are in out of the path of the oncoming obstacle is suddenly your major goal in life, you must take your foot *off* the brakes in order to get back the *steering control* you need to make that goal a reality.

ABS BRAKING

Here's the bad news: A study conducted in the US indicates that cars with anti-lock brakes are up to 65% more likely to be in fatal crashes than cars without them.

> **But it's not the ABS that's the problem. It's poor driving habits and *lack of driver awareness on how the brakes operate.***

Let's take a step-by-step look at the braking process for an ABS vehicle *during emergency braking:*

- In an emergency situation, **apply your brakes hard and stay on them.** (Unlike in a non-ABS vehicle, pressing harder won't cause problems.)

- You **should not pump the brake pedal at any time on an ABS system.** Pumping could interrupt operation and actually increase stopping distance.

- **Hard application of ABS brakes will cause the brake pedal to vibrate or pulsate.** That's a good thing; don't let the vibration bother you. The pedal is *supposed* to vibrate. It lets you know the system is working.

- Along with the vibration, **you will hear a strange groaning noise** — don't let that bother you, either — it's *supposed* to make that noise.

- A **periodic decrease in brake pedal pressure** may occur.

> **The best thing you can do is read the "Owner's Manual" and get familiar with what will happen when you really need the ABS.**

BRAKE FAILURE

Probably the most frightening thing that can happen to you as a driver is to lose braking control *completely*. Your brakes just fail to do *anything* — they don't help you stop and they don't lock up.

Imagine it: You push down on the pedal and nothing, absolutely nothing, happens. **ABS or non-ABS — if you have no brakes, it does not matter *what* type of braking system you have.** The car just keeps on going.

This situation calls for quick decision making, especially if you are in a busy traffic environment, such as a crowded street, surrounded by plenty of large objects to collide with.

- Your best option is to **steer to avoid obstacles**, use **low gear** to slow the vehicle, and **seek a path of escape.**

- **Using the parking brake is an option,** but the parking brake only stops the *rear* wheels. If you *do* opt to use the parking brake, apply it slowly, keeping the front wheels pointed straight ahead. Any movement of the wheel while applying the parking brake will spin the car around 180 degrees.

BRAKE FADE

Brake fade occurs when brakes are overused and overheat. Hot brakes quickly lose their effectiveness and fail to stop the car in time. Brake fade comes and goes. Brakes take time to overheat and will often provide warning that they are about to fade. Effectiveness decreases slowly.

No matter the circumstances, brake fade makes it advisable to slow down. Brake fade goes away as the brakes cool. This often confuses drivers who experience brake fade. Sometimes they lose their brakes due to fade and run their cars off the road and into the under brush. Shaken but unscathed, they later return to their cars with a repair crew, only to find their brakes in mysteriously good working order. This is typical of brake fade.

PRACTICE MAKES PERFECT

If all this braking technique sounds like something you should practice, it is. The questions are: where and when?

The time to experiment with your car's braking characteristics is *not* while approaching a tractor-trailer truck stalled in your lane while you're traveling at 75 mph.

- **If you happen to live in an area that gets ice and snow in the winter,** find a big, empty parking lot, such as those at shopping malls or large supermarkets, and practice.

- **In a non-ABS vehicle,** see how hard you can press on the brake pedal *without* locking up the wheels.

- **In an ABS vehicle,** get the feel for the sensations of braking with an ABS. (See p. 181)

- **Watch out for light stanchions and parked cars** (we said find an *empty* lot), but **otherwise take it easy and carefully play with your car.** Discover its — and your own — limitations and abilities.

IN THE NEXT CHAPTER, we explore the proper way to make turns and to turn around with your vehicle.

Chapter 20

Turning:

How to Turn Left, Turn Right, Back Up and Turn Around

In Ch. 16 we covered the techniques for turning curves and corners *at speed* — on the open highway, at exit and entrance ramps, or in emergency driving situations. In this chapter, we focus on the simpler rules for turning in general — turning left, turning right, turning around, and backing up.

> **A proper signal of *intention* to turn right or left will be given *continuously* during not less than the last 100 feet traveled by the vehicle *before* turning.**

TURNING LEFT

Sometimes when you are making a left turn at an intersection, a passenger sitting beside you on the front seat will obstruct your vision of traffic coming from the right. If your vehicle is equipped with individual bucket seats, adjusting the passenger seat several inches backward of the driver's seat will give you a better view to the right. If the vehicle has a standard seat, you may have to lean forward to see around your passenger. If necessary, ask him to lean back to give you a better view.

When turning left:

- Be sure there is enough space to turn left.

- Signal your intent to turn and slow down.

- If there are two left turn lanes, take the right-hand turn lane.

- Be sure you are in the center of the intersection. Start to turn only *after* you are sure your vehicle's rear will clear the centerline.

- Be sure there is an adequate gap to turn in front of traffic.

- Watch your vehicle's progress in the side mirrors.

- Steer the vehicle wide of the lane, if necessary.

- When the vehicle's wheels are into the lane, steer left to put the vehicle in the lane and straighten up.

- If applicable, watch for oncoming traffic.

TURNING RIGHT

When making a right turn:

- Be sure there is enough space to turn right.

- Signal your intent to turn at least 100 feet ahead of the intersection, and slow down *gradually* as you approach the turn.

- Be sure to let oncoming traffic clear before you make your turn.

- Stay as close as possible to the right edge of the road or street.

- Never swerve to the left before turning right.

- Position your vehicle in the right-hand lane. Keep your vehicle's rear close to the curb.

- Do not turn wide to the left as you start the turn; the driver behind you might think you are turning left.

- Pull forward into the intersection past the right corner. You must do this so the vehicle's rear wheels can clear the curb. Turn the steering wheel hard to the right.

- Check your vehicle's progress using the right side mirrors.

- Watch oncoming cars if swinging wide into the left or oncoming lane.

- If the speed is right, the turn should be easily made without swerving.

- **If your tires squeal when you turn,** it is likely that you are trying to take the turn too fast, or tire pressures are too low.

BACKING UP

Far too many accidents happen while the car is in reverse. More often than not, these result in fender benders, not dramatic accidents, but nonetheless annoying and expensive. (We're going to cover backing up before turning around, because all the techniques for turning around — except the U-turn — involve backing up at some point.)

Cars Are Designed to Go *Forward*

Automobile suspensions possess a quality known as "caster" — the force that helps to straighten out the front wheels after turning a corner. Caster also gives the car stability while traveling forward.

Unfortunately, this stabilizing forward force *de-stabilizes* the car while it's in reverse. In other words, while driving in reverse, the steering wheel will not center automatically if you loosen your grip on it, as it will when in forward motion. Another little quirk of caster is that **the car becomes *unstable* while traveling backwards** — when small changes in steering wheel movement cause *big* changes in the way the car reacts to your inputs. Of course, the faster you go in reverse, the more difficult control becomes.

Key Points to Keep in Mind When Backing Up

- **No matter how short the distance you wish to travel in reverse, look where you're going and drive slowly.** Most cars feature a blind spot or spots to the rear large enough to hide a small child. Blow your horn. But whatever you do, **be absolutely sure there is no one behind you when you back up.**

- **Before you put the car in reverse, make sure the area in *front* of the car is clear.** Some cars have long hoods and broad front ends. As you maneuver backwards and turn, the noses of **many large cars swing out to the side dramatically** and you could hit something — or someone. Many cars in American today have badly dented fenders because drivers neglected to perform this check.

- **Try not to back into an intersection that contains a lot of traffic**.

- **Make sure you are able to reach all your car's controls.** It's a little foolish to hike yourself up in the seat for good visibility, put the car into reverse, and then discover you can't reach the brake pedal!

- **If you are backing up to the right, look over your right shoulder.** For comfort, you may put your right arm up on the back of the seat.

- **Short people have a hard time backing up** because they have a hard time seeing over the back of the front seat and out the rear window. If you are short, position yourself as best as you can, making certain that you can see out the rear window and access all the car's controls.

- While this may sound a bit foolish, **make sure the car has come to a complete halt before you put it in reverse.** Dropping an expensive transmission out of a car by slamming it into reverse can ruin your whole day.

- **Keep a foot on the brake while putting the car in reverse.** There's nothing like shooting out of a parking space and into the path of an oncoming car to add a little spice to daily life.

- **Another problem with backing up is knowing what to do with the steering wheel.** The correct direction in which to move the wheel while in reverse can be very confusing.

  Actually, the problem is mainly perceptual. **The correct way to move the wheel is really quite simple:** Move the top of the steering wheel in the direction you wish the car to move. It's actually no different from what you do while driving forward; it just feels different in reverse.

- **Never combine a great deal of steering wheel movement with a heavy foot on the gas pedal.** You will surely lose control of the car.

- **Use smooth applications of the brake, steering wheel, and accelerator.**

TURNING AROUND

We're going to look at three ways of turning around or changing direction. No matter what method is used, it must be done carefully. Know the legalities in your area concerning direction changes. Perform these turns in a "safe area" — that is, one having good visibility.

Before attempting the turn, make sure you have a clear view of the road(s) and traffic around you. Obviously you should avoid making turns on hills, curves, and near blind intersections. The three ways to reverse direction are:

- U-turns
- Two-point turns
- Three-point turns

U-Turns

The U-turn is the safest of the three turns. Keep in mind that the U-turn *should* be legal, but *isn't* universally. Although the U-turn is an easy turn to execute, you still need a lot of road and good visibility.

- **The average passenger vehicle needs about 40 feet in which to turn**, so you're going to need at least that much room.

- You should *nct* make a U-turn unless **a vehicle approaching from either direction can see the movement from a distance of 500 feet.**

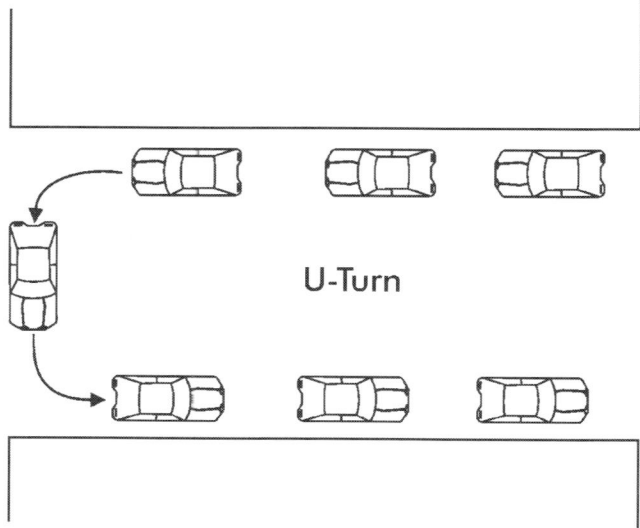

Figure 20-1. Car Making a U-Turn.

To make a proper U-turn:

- First **stop as close to the right side of the road as possible.** This gives you more room in which to execute the turn.

- **Look both ways** before you even begin to turn the steering wheel and start the turn.

- **Let everyone around you know what you're going to do.** Use your left-turn signal to indicate what you're planning.

- When you're *sure* everyone has been notified, **turn the wheel as quickly as possible and as sharply as necessary,** and complete the turn.

- Before pulling out and heading off in the other direction, make sure to **look over your shoulder and check for oncoming traffic.**

Two-Point Turns

A two-point turn means backing into a driveway, side road, or alley in order to make a 180-degree turn when the highway is too narrow, or there isn't enough visibility to make a U-turn, or a U-turn is illegal.

There are two basic ways of driving through a two-point turn: The right-hand road turn and its left-hand brother. The left-hand turn is much more dangerous than the right-hand turn.

The right road turn

The right road turn requires you to stop the car, back it into a road or driveway on the right side of the highway on which you are traveling, and then drive out onto the highway and make your turn.

- **Signal your intention to stop the car.**

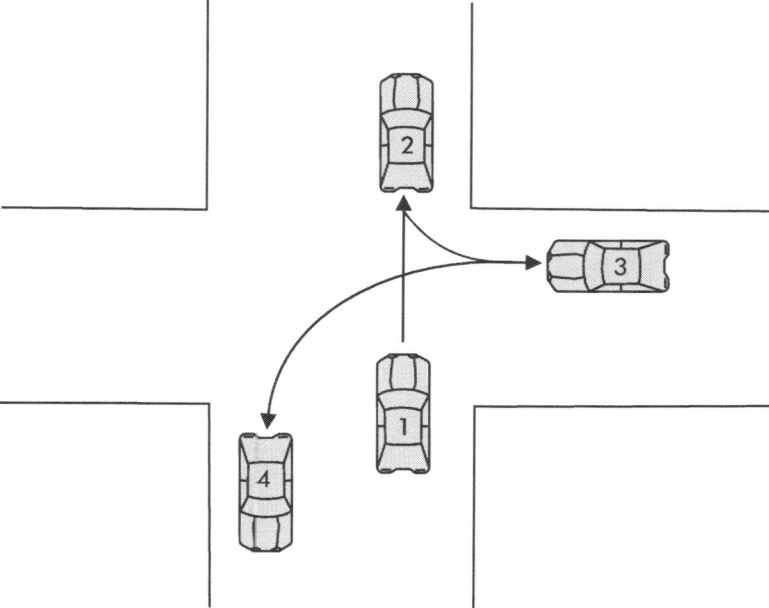

Figure 20-2. Two-Point Turn. These turns are made when the road is too narrow, or restricted visibility does not permit a U-turn, or a U-turn is illegal.

- Before you move backwards, **check to make sure that the path behind you is clear.**

- Be especially watchful for pedestrians.

- Then **back up slowly.** Remember: It is very easy to lose control of the car while traveling in reverse.

- **Before re-entering the traffic again,** make sure you can do so safely.

The left road turn

The left-hand variant of this turn requires the driver to drive nose-first into a road or driveway on the left side of the road, then back onto the highway, straighten out, and drive off.

- **Signal your intention to stop,** as well as **your intention to make a left-hand turn** onto the side road or driveway.

- **The most dangerous moment in this turn is when you are backing into oncoming traffic.** Watch out for this oncoming flow, and make sure all is clear in front of you before moving out into the traffic. Exercise due caution.

Three-Point Turn

The *three-point turn* should be made only where there is no other choice. Use this turn when the road is too narrow for a U-turn and there are no side roads or driveways that allow a two-point turn.

To perform a three-point turn:

- First **pull over and get as close to the right side of the road as possible**, just as if you were doing a U-turn.

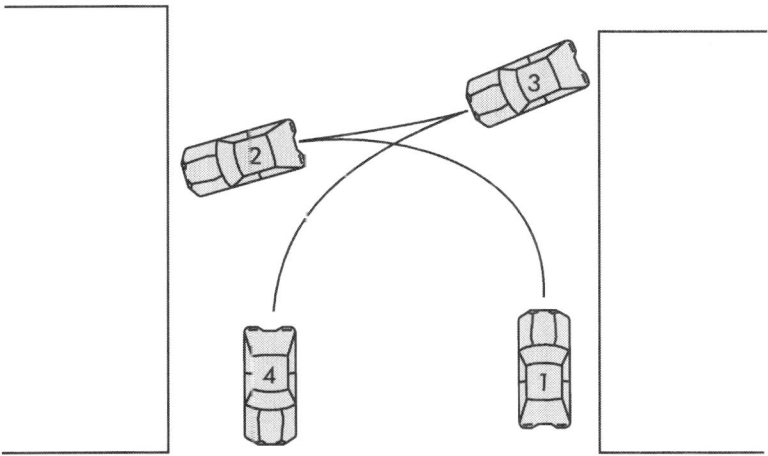

Figure 20-3. Three-Point Turn. Very dangerous turn-around; should not be used unless there is no other way of changing direction.

- **Turn your car as though you were going to do a U-turn** and follow all the standard U-turn precautions described above.

- **Just before the front wheels of your car reach the far side of the road,** turn the steering wheel to the right, check ahead and behind for oncoming traffic, put the car in reverse, and back up across both lanes.

> *Remember:* **Whenever the car is moving backwards, you should be looking the same way.**

- **Just prior to reaching the other side of the road, turn the wheel to the left.**

- **Drive forward.**

You have performed a three-point turn. It's a dangerous way of reversing direction because you are vulnerable to conflicting traffic for far too long a time. Unfortunately, sometimes there's no other way.

IN THE NEXT CHAPTER, we discuss the techniques for passing and being passed safely — when to pass, when NOT to pass, how to pass, and how to yield the right of way.

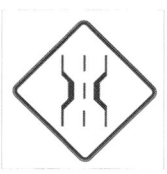

Chapter 21

Passing and Being Passed

You must decide whether to pass or not to pass again and again every time you drive. Do not take chances. Do not move out into the left-hand lane as soon as you see any possibility of getting by the vehicle ahead. On the other hand, do not let opportunities for safe passing go by while irritably following a slow-moving vehicle for mile after mile.

Safe passing depends mainly on your knowing three things:

- When to pass

- When *not* to pass

- How to pass safely

WHEN *NOT* TO PASS

When it comes to passing, there are some NEVERS — situations where passing is *always* dangerous or *unlawful:*

- *Never* pass when you cannot see that the left side of the road is free of oncoming traffic far enough ahead to pass safely.

- *Never* pass on any curve or hill where you cannot see at least 500 feet.

- Never pass at night when you can't see far ahead.

- *Never* pass unless you have sufficient distance to pass and return to the right without coming within 100 feet of an approaching vehicle.

- *Never* pass at an intersection.

- *Never* pass at a railway crossing.

- *Never* pass when there is a single or double solid line between lanes or when your lane's side of a double line is solid.

- *Never* pass at crosswalks where a vehicle has stopped to allow a pedestrian to cross.

- *Never* pass when a stopped school bus has its warning flashers on.

WHEN TO PASS

The question of whether or not to pass is never an easy one. Before you decide to pass someone, always think *before* you make your move — because if you recklessly pass someone, you (and perhaps others) will suffer the consequences. And always be especially wary of passing in traffic.

Here are some questions to ask yourself before making a move to pass:

1. **Is this pass really necessary?** Why do I want to pass this car? Is the maneuver absolutely necessary?

   If you want to pass someone who is slowing you down by driving slowly themselves, then passing is justified.

   If you need to pass the car ahead of you because there is an actual emergency, and you have to get where you're going in a hurry, then passing is justified.

> *But if you want to pass because your ego just can't stand to have anyone ahead of you,* then passing is NOT justified.

2. **Is this pass legal?** Although no responsible driver would or should pass illegally on purpose, there may be an emergency situation where you *must* pass someone — especially if you're an emergency worker or working in an emergency capacity. If you *must* pass illegally in such circumstance, make especially sure you have enough time and space to make it. **If you are involved in an accident while making an illegal pass, you're in *BIG* trouble.**

3. **Is the car you are about to pass aware of your presence?** *Don't* assume this car is aware of your presence. *Don't* assume that the driver is in any condition to react rationally.

4. **Are there side roads ahead that may hide a car about to turn into your path?** Even if you can't see them, *assume* they're there. Use Murphy's Law and proceed, but with caution.

5. **Does the road have many intersections that can often conceal surprises,** such as other cars making turns or proceeding through the intersection? Watch out.

6. **Have you checked the traffic situation all around you in your mirrors?** Someone may be trying to pass *you.* Moreover, it's just good sense to check your mirrors before you make *any* move with your car.

7. **If there is an oncoming car, how far away is it?** Do you *really* have enough time and space?

8. **Are you sure your vehicle has the mechanical ability to make this pass safely?** Some cars aren't as powerful as they should be. Sometimes the luck of the draw gives you one that might be in need of a tune-up or have some other small mechanical problem that could

inhibit performance. ***Know you have the
accelerating power before you need it.***

9. **How long is all this going to take**? Do you have
   enough time to pass and get back in your lane?

   Of course, it's impossible to get out a yardstick and
   measure the distances involved. Estimating whether or
   not the pass is safe requires quick thinking. You haven't
   got much time. Your best friend here is your own good
   sense and your experience as a good driver. But if you
   have to make a mistake, make it on the side of too much
   caution, instead of not enough.

   (See the section on *Safe Passing Distances*, p. 199.)

10. **Can your vehicle stop quickly and safely if you
    have to make an emergency stop?** (See Ch. 17,
    Speed and Safe Stopping Distances.)

**Head-on collisions represent a substantial
number of accidents.**

**If you *MUST* pass someone, realize and remember
that, depending on the highway situation, you and
your car are going to be spending a good deal of
time in the *wrong lane*.**

**If you are traveling at 50 mph, passing someone
going 40 mph, you will need about 10 seconds and
736 feet to safely complete the pass. If the crest of
a hill is just 300 feet away, and there's a car just
out of sight on the other side of that hill, you're
going to have some problems on your hands —
soon!**

HOW TO PASS SAFELY

Signaling Your Intent to Pass

First of all, when passing, do not just pull out and start around the car you're trying to pass. Look ahead and behind to be sure it is safe to pass.

Signaling the driver AHEAD of you

Let the driver of the vehicle ahead know what you intend to do. She may be getting ready to pass the vehicle ahead of her or to turn left.

- **Blow your horn as a signal to her.** The horn signal is required by *law* in most localities, and it puts the driver of the vehicle being passed under *a legal obligation to help you pass.*

- **At night, give the driver ahead an *additional* signal by flashing your headlights from low to high beam and back to low.** However, do not use the light signal as a substitute for the horn signal.

Signaling the driver BEHIND you

The driver of the vehicle *behind* you also needs to know what you are going to do. He may be pulling out to pass *you.*

- Give a **left-turn signal** to let him know that you are about to pull out to pass.

Safe Passing Distance

You cannot pass safely unless you can see far enough ahead to be sure that you can get back in line before you meet any traffic coming from the opposite direction. You must also be able to get back into line before meeting any traffic crossing or turning onto the road on which you are driving.

But how far ahead is far enough? Give yourself and the driver of the vehicle you are passing *plenty of room.* This distance depends on you own speed, on the speed of the vehicle you are passing, and on the lengths of the vehicles involved.

- **Start to pass from a safe following distance.** If the vehicle you want to pass is traveling at 30 mph, start from at least 60 feet behind it.

> **Do *not* speed up directly behind a vehicle and then turn out suddenly just before you get to it.**

Remember: A driver who tailgates does not give himself enough time or distance to handle emergency situations.

Tailgating interferes with your view of the road ahead. The other driver may slow down or stop, and he can do so much more quickly than you can because his speed is lower. If he does, you will almost certainly be unable to slow down or stop in time. If you try to avoid a collision by turning sharply aside, you may skid off the road, turn over, or smash into another vehicle.

- **Drift over to the left and speed up quickly.**

- As you go by another vehicle, **be sure there is plenty of distance between the right side of your vehicle and the left side of the other vehicle.**

> **The law in most localities requires a *minimum clearance of two feet.***

- You have not finished passing until you **get back onto your own side of the road or in the lane where you belong,** leaving the vehicle you have just passed at **a safe following distance *behind* you.**

For example, if the vehicle you are passing is traveling at 30 mph, leave 60 feet clear before returning to your own side of the road (20 feet for every 10 mph of speed).

> **If you force the driver of the vehicle you have just passed to slow down as you get back into line, you have *not* passed safely.**

- Of course, **it is difficult to see the vehicle you have just passed and estimate the distance.**

> **A good rule of thumb is that you can usually be sure it is safe to return to the right side of the road when you can see the vehicle you have passed in your rearview mirror.**

- As a general rule, **do not attempt to pass more than one vehicle at a time.**

    Passing several vehicles increases the danger because it increases the time you spend and the distance you cover while out of your *own* lane.

- **If you come up behind a long line of vehicles,** you can almost be sure that every driver except the first one is waiting for an opportunity to pass. The safe and courteous thing to do is to *wait your turn.*

- On the other hand, **if you are next in line behind a slow-moving vehicle,** it is *discourteous* to the drivers behind you *not* to pass when you have the opportunity.

Safe Passing Speeds

And just how fast should you pass someone? Neither too fast, nor too slow. But how fast is too fast? And how slow is too slow?

For example: Suppose that you want to pass a vehicle that is traveling at 30 mph. You would have to travel whatever distance *it* travels while you are passing, plus an *additional* distance besides. Since the other vehicle's speed is 30 mph, the *additional* distance in this case would be about 160 feet.

- It is generally a good idea to **pass at a speed at least 10 to 15 mph faster than the speed of the vehicle being passed.**

- **If your speed is only 5 mph faster,** it will take you twice the time and almost twice the distance to completely pass the other vehicle.

- On the other hand, **there is no point in passing at too fast a speed.** In passing at 20 mph faster instead of 15 mph faster than the speed of the vehicle being passed, the advantage amounts to only 1 or 2 seconds gained. It is usually offset by the danger of increased speed.

- **If too much increased speed is *required* to pass and return to your lane,** the wise decision is not to pass.

- Similarly, **when the driver ahead of you is traveling just *under* the speed limit,** the safest thing to do is forget about passing.

    For example: Suppose that you want to pass a vehicle traveling at 50 mph when the speed limit is 55 mph. In this case, driving your vehicle 10 to 15 mph faster would be unlawful because passing is no excuse for exceeding the speed limit. Yet if you pass at 55 mph, you will need 2,640 feet or exactly half a mile to pass the other vehicle.

    So, the best thing to do is settle down behind him at a safe following distance. You may reach your destination a few minutes later than if you had attempted to pass, but at least you will not have broken the law.

SPECIAL PASSING SITUATIONS

Passing on Three-Lane Highways

Passing on a three-lane highway demands extra caution.

- **Do not pass except in the center lane, and then only when the center lane is marked for passing in *your* direction.** In some cases, the center lane may be so marked that it is open for passing in *both* directions.

- Before passing, **make sure that none of the vehicles coming from the *opposite* direction are moving out to pass.**

- **Never use the center lane to pass if your view of the road ahead is obstructed** by a hill or curve.

- The one exception to using only the center lane for passing is that **you may pass in the right lane if the vehicle in the center lane is making a left turn.**

Passing on the Right

Passing on the right, except as noted above, is usually dangerous and unlawful. It puts you on the other driver's blind side. He may be intending to make a right turn or to pull over to the right side of the road. In either case, an accident is almost certain.

There are, however, three situations in which passing on the right is usually permissible and reasonably safe:

1. If the highway has at least two lanes going in each direction.

2. If all lanes of traffic move in the same direction (one-way street).

3. If the vehicle you are passing is in a left-turn lane.

BEING PASSED

When you are being passed, *the law requires you to help the other driver get by.*

Give Way to the Right

- When the driver of the passing vehicle blows his horn, you must do one thing — **give way to the right.**

  Even if you are already on your own side of the road, move over as close as safety will permit to the right-hand edge of the road.

Maintain a Steady Speed

- **When you are being passed, it is usually safest to maintain a steady speed.** By doing this, you allow the passing driver to judge passing distance with greater accuracy. If you *slow down*, you may mislead the passing driver into overestimating his speed.

- **The law does not permit you to *increase* your speed when you're being passed.** Speeding up forces the passing driver to cover more distance and take more time to get by you. **It exposes both of you to unnecessary danger.**

- **If an attempt to pass you becomes dangerous,** you may be able to **make it safer for everyone by *slowing* down** and allowing the passing vehicle to get back into the proper lane in less time and distance.

- If, however, you see that **a driver is trying to get back into line behind you, rather than ahead**

of you, do *not* slow down. In this case, it is much safer to speed up a little to give him more room.

When danger develops in passing, do not stand on your rights. Use all driving skills to avoid an accident.

PART III

ACCIDENTS

In the first two Parts, we've covered in detail what you need to know and be able to do to keep yourself and your vehicle under control while on the road. We've also shown you how, in some cases, to regain control if you lose it. But accidents *do* happen — either we, or the drivers around us on the road, don't maintain control — or we, or they, can't regain it.

So in this Part, we look at current accident statistics to see the who, what, when, and how of accidents. Then we explore what causes accidents (driver, environment, vehicle). Then we consider typical accident scenarios and tell you how to deal with them. And finally we offer a "Crash Course" that provides some suggestions on how you can help if you come upon or are involved in an accident yourself.

Chapter 22
Accident Stats:
Who, What, When, and How, p. 209

Chapter 23
What Causes Accidents?, p. 215

Chapter 24
Typical Accident Scenarios:
And How to Deal With Them, p. 225

Chapter 25
Crash Course:
Simple Tips that Could Help Save Lives, p. 239

Chapter 22

Accident Stats:

Who, What, When, and How

In 1975, the US Department of Transportation started **an annual census of motor vehicle deaths,** recording information on crash type, vehicle type, road type, driver characteristics, and a variety of other factors. Institute researchers analyze these data each year to quantify the public health problem of motor vehicle deaths.

Based on analysis of **data from the U.S. Department of Transportation's Fatality Analysis Reporting System (FRS):**

- A total of 42,815 people lost their lives in motor vehicle crashes in 2002. Another 3.0 million people were injured.

- Motor vehicle crashes are the leading cause of death among Americans 1-34 years old.

- The total societal cost of crashes exceeds $150 billion annually.

- Contributing to the death toll are alcohol, speed, and various other driver behaviors, plus the kinds of vehicles people drive and the roads on which they travel.

- The majority of persons killed or injured in traffic crashes were drivers (65%) followed by passengers (30%), pedestrians (3%) and pedalcyclists (2%).

Gender

- **More men than women die each year in motor vehicle crashes.** Men typically drive more miles than women and engage more often in risky driving practices, including not using a safety belt, driving while impaired by alcohol, and speeding.

- However, **deaths of female drivers have increased during the past 20 years while male driver deaths have declined.** More women now are licensed than in the past. They drive more miles and are more likely to be driving at night.

- **One-third of all motor vehicle deaths in 1998 were females.** They accounted for 31 percent of driver deaths, 50 percent of passenger deaths, 32 percent of pedestrian deaths, 13 percent of bicyclist deaths, and 9 percent of motorcyclist deaths.

Age

- The motor vehicle death rate per 100,000 people is especially **high among 16-24 year-olds** and **people 80 years and older.**

- The difference is **least among people younger than 13** and **greatest among people 85 years and older.**

- The difference is **greatest among people age 85 and older,** followed closely by **people age 20-24.**

Age/Gender Differences

- **At all ages, males have much higher motor vehicle death rates** per 100,000 people compared with females.

- The **highest motor vehicle death rate is among males 80 years and older,** followed closely by **males age 16-24.**

- The death rate is **highest among males age 85 and older,** and it is **lowest among males and females younger than 16.**

- **At almost all ages, males have higher passenger vehicle death rates than females.**

- There is **no gender difference among people younger than 16.**

Alcohol Involvement

- Among passenger vehicle drivers in 2002, the proportion of fatally injured males with **blood alcohol concentrations (BACs) at or above 0.10** percent was higher than females at all ages.

- **Alcohol was most common among males age 21-30** and **females 31-40,** when half of male deaths and about one-third of female deaths involved high BACs.

- Since 1980, **proportions of fatally injured drivers with BACs at or above 0.10 percent** have **declined 36 percent among men and 56 percent among women.**

- Since 1985, **the percentage of male driver deaths with high BACs has been about twice that of females.**

Vehicle Types

- **Fifty percent of motor vehicle deaths** in 2002 were **car occupants.**

- **Fourteen percent were occupants of other kinds of passenger vehicles** including pickups, utility vehicles, and cargo/large vans.

Box 22-1. Passenger Vehicle Fatalities

By far the largest number of motor vehicle deaths are occupants of passenger vehicles, including cars, the popular passenger vans (often referred to as minivans), pickups, utility vehicles, and cargo/large passenger vans.

> **NOTE: If the wheelbase of a car fits one size group, but the overall length fits another size group, the vehicle is grouped in the larger category. Passenger versions of vans often referred to as minivans are classified as cars.**

The likelihood of crash death varies markedly among these vehicle types according to size.

- **Small/light vehicles** have less structure and size to absorb crash energy, so more injurious forces can reach their occupants in crashes.

- People in **lighter vehicles** are at a disadvantage in collisions with heavier vehicles.

- **Pickups and utility vehicles** are proportionally more likely than cars to be in fatal single-vehicle crashes, especially rollovers.

- However, **pickups and utility vehicles** generally are heavier than cars, so occupant deaths are less likely to occur in multiple-vehicle crashes.

- **Deaths in pickups and utility vehicles have more than doubled** since 1975.

- Since 2001, **deaths per registered vehicle have declined in all kinds of passenger vehicles.**

- **Forty six percent of passenger vehicle occupant deaths** in 2002 were **car occupants.**

- However, **the proportion of deaths involving pickup and utility vehicle occupants is growing** as the popularity of these vehicles increases.

- Sixty percent of **car occupant deaths** in 2002 occurred in **single-vehicle crashes,** 40 percent in **multiple-vehicle crashes.**

- In contrast, percentages for **pickups and utility vehicles** combined were 59 and 41 percent.

Crash Types

- **Frontal impacts** accounted for 50 percent of passenger vehicle occupant deaths in 2002.

- **Side impacts** accounted for 30 percent (14 percent right side, 16 percent left).

- **Crashes in which a vehicle rolled over** accounted for 31 percent of passenger vehicle occupant deaths in 2002 (54 percent of single-vehicle crash deaths and 11 percent of multiple-vehicle crash deaths).

- **Frontal impacts** accounted for 65 occupant deaths per million registered passenger vehicles in 2002 compared with 45 deaths per million in side impacts and 7 deaths per million in rear impacts.

- **Multiple-vehicle crashes** accounted for 73 occupant deaths per million registered passenger vehicles in 2002 compared with 70 deaths per million in single-vehicle crashes.

- **In single-vehicle crashes,** two-wheel-drive utility vehicles had the highest number of deaths per registered vehicle (127 per million) in 2002.

- **In multiple-vehicle crashes,** cars had a higher number of deaths per registered vehicle (80 per million) than pickups and utility vehicles.

- **Single-vehicle crashes involving rollover** accounted for 41 occupant deaths per million registered passenger vehicles in 2002 compared with 11 deaths per million in **multiple-vehicle crashes.**

- **Single-vehicle rollover crashes** accounted for 50 percent of occupant deaths in utility vehicles in 2002 compared with 31 percent of deaths in pickups and 19 percent of deaths in cars.

- **Lighter utility vehicles are disproportionately involved in fatal rollover crashes.** The single-vehicle rollover death rate in these vehicles in 2002 was more than 5 times as high as the rate in the largest cars (110 deaths per million registered vehicles compared with 22).

IN THE NEXT CHAPTER, we explore the "Driving System" — the driver, machine, and environment combination — and consider how accidents can be caused by a breakdown in any one part of the "system."

Chapter 23

What Causes Accidents?

The Driving System

Your ability to avoid accidents does not depend solely on your ability to control the car. When driving a car, you're at the mercy of the environment around you and at the mercy of the vehicle you are driving. Like Mother Nature, driving is a balance, and that balance is called the "driving system." The driving system is made up of three components:

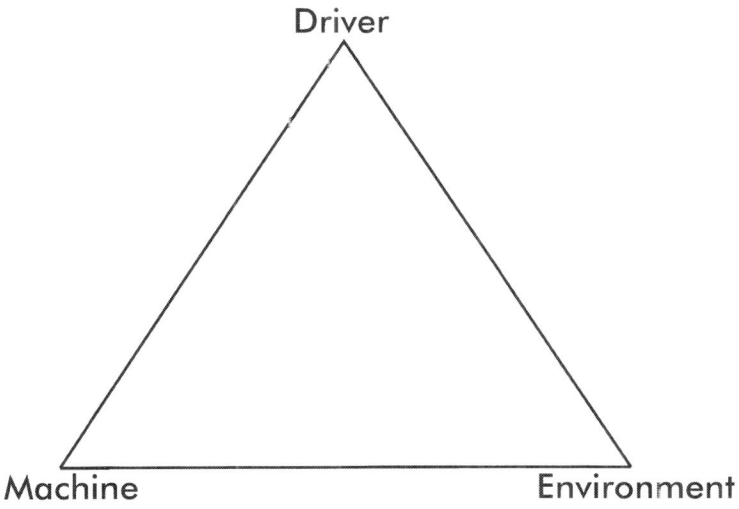

Figure 23-1. The Driving System

THE DRIVER, THE MACHINE, and THE ENVIRONMENT. When an automotive accident occurs, it is caused by a failure of the driving system. Either the driver, the vehicle, or the environment failed.

The Driver

The driver is the only truly flexible, adaptable factor of the driving system triangle. The driver is responsible for the successful implementation of the DRIVER/MACHINE relationship. If the driving system fails, only the driver suffers.

The proof lies in the numbers. **Some 89 percent of all vehicular accidents are caused by driver error** (this number is clouded by the fact that 48 percent of that 89 percent figure is directly attributable to accidents caused by drinking). But the remaining 41 percent were clear-headed drivers who somehow got into trouble.

The Machine

A little-known fact about cars is that **most of them are good handling vehicles.** However, no matter how well a vehicle handles, it is only a machine, and like all machines, **has its limitations.**

These limitations are aggravated when maintenance is poor or insufficient, but accidents caused by outright mechanical failure are relatively rare.

Accidents due to impaired vehicle performance due to poor or relaxed maintenance standards are difficult, if not impossible, to compute.

The Environment

The United States has the best-designed and constructed highway system in the world. Nevertheless, these **roads are not immune to the effects of weather and use.** If the road surface has been modified by nature, then the driver and machine portion of the driving system must cope with these changes.

In some rare instances the road conditions have deteriorated to the point that the driver/machine combination cannot compensate.

It is the environmental portion of the driving system that puts drivers at a distinct disadvantage. People drive in all sorts of weather conditions, when they do they are at the mercy of the environment. (See Ch. 26, *Foul Weather Driving.*)

The Driving Problem

Auto accidents are the fourth leading cause of death in the U.S. This figure gives us an idea of the size of the problem we are dealing with here. The biggest problem with driving is that we don't know *what* the problem is. From the numbers alone, it's obvious we're doing something wrong.

Yet, most people find it difficult to acknowledge their driving deficiencies. In fact, you'd be hard-pressed to find anyone who is willing to admit they have anything to learn about driving at all. Most of us went to some sort of high school driver education program, and then were tested by the local authorities. **After passing our written and road tests and receiving our license to drive, all of us assumed we had become instant *experts*.**

We were wrong. The simple fact is that **we all learn to drive through *experience*.** We become good or bad drivers through the types of driving experiences we have had. If we manage to survive these experiences, there is usually no problem.

The old "there's an infamous intersection near here where all the accidents happen" experience

It's an experience all drivers go through. We all have one intersection nearby that's known far and wide as a dangerous place to drive — the sort of intersection you're just plain lucky to survive. You probably have to drive through that intersection on your way to work, and when you do cross it, you do so with caution. Why? Because *experience* and local legend have taught you that this intersection is dangerous and deserves caution.

Types of Accidents

Accidents are not always accidental. They are an unexpected events that happens by chance — and are caused by **breakdowns in the driving system.** Through research it is possible to determine the cause of an accident. **Drivers must accept that most are caused by driver error.** Most drivers, unfortunately, are extremely unwilling to do this. People disassociate themselves from accidents. Drivers involved in accidents talk about them as though they weren't anywhere near the car when it crashed.

Consider the person who says, "*My car was hit by another car that went through a stop sign.*" To listen to this person, you'd think that no one was in either car at the time of the accident! **Cars don't drive past stop signs all by themselves.** Once we accept the fact that we can actually get *ourselves* into an accident, and that in most cases it will either be you or the other driver who is the cause of the accident, then the next important concept to understand is the type of accident we are likely to become involved *in.*

> **JUST HOW DO ACCIDENTS HAPPEN? If we know the types of driving conditions that produce the greatest number of accidents, then we can be more alert during these conditions.**

Two-car collisions

Ninety-six percent of all two-car collisions (excepting two-car fatal collisions) can be described as taking place under three separate conditions:

1. **The most frequent type of two-car collision is the side collision.** Out of all two-car collisions, 44.6 percent are side collisions. The most common type of two-car crash occurs when both cars are traveling in

parallel courses and one crosses the path and hits the side of the other.

2. **The second most frequent type of accident is the rear-end collision.** Some 27.7 percent of the accidents discussed here fall into this category. This usually happens when one vehicle is stopped and the second car, overtaking from the rear in a straight line, hits the stopped car. The second most common rear-end crash involves the striking vehicle hitting a *parked* car.

Box 23-1. **The Top 10 Two-Car Crash Situations**

1. Two cars traveling straight; one hits the side of the other (13.5 percent)

2. The striking vehicle traveling straight; it hits another vehicle making a left-hand turn (10.3 percent)

3. Vehicle proceeding in a straight line rear-ends a stopped vehicle (8.2 percent)

4. Vehicle traveling in a straight line hits the side of a vehicle that's just started to move(4.3 percent)

5. Hitting a parked car (4.2 percent)

6. Car out of control hits the rear of a stopped car (3.7 percent)

7. The striking vehicle, making a left turn, hits a vehicle head on (3.2 percent)

8. Two vehicles traveling straight and in opposite direction hit each other head on (3.1 percent)

9. Out of control vehicle hits the side of a vehicle making a lefthand turn (2.8 percent)

10. A car traveling in a straight line rear-ends a vehicle that is slowing down (2.6 percent)

3. **The third most common two-car accident type is a bit unusual.** Amounting to 13.6 percent of the two-car, non-fatal accidents, this is the kind of **head-on collision in which the two vehicles are not traveling straight toward each other.** In this category, the most common accident scenario involves a striking vehicle making a left-hand turn and impacting a car coming the other way head on.

The second most frequent type of head-on crash *does* involve both cars traveling in straight lines, directly at each other.

Single-car accidents

The statistics for single-car accidents are very different than those for two-car collisions. According to the figures, in some 50 percent of all single-car accident, the car was out of control *before* it hit anything or went off the road. This means that something happened to cause the driver to lose control.

Amazingly, **in 40 percent of the single-car mishaps, the car was traveling in a straight line before leaving the road.** For some reason, the drivers simply did not understand the problem or sense of the crisis in time to do anything about it, and just drove off the road. **In these straight-crash conditions, the drivers had various options of action, but instead did nothing.** Meaning, more than likely, that the driver didn't have a clue as to either what was happening, or how to get out of danger.

Obviously **some conditions are more conducive to single-car crashes.** Most happen:

- On slippery roads

- On curves

- On 55 mph roads

Statistics reveal that slippery conditions cause 45.8 percent of all single-car accidents — meaning that 54.2 percent of all single-car accidents take place on dry roads. Interestingly, 78.7 percent of *all* accidents happen on dry roads.

Just what causes a no-control situation? Many complex factors affect loss of control of a vehicle. Generally, however, the no-control situation is induced by the driver.

Quite simply, the vehicle does not act in the manner to which the driver is accustomed. Usually, this happens when the driver *over* controls the car. **Over control can take several forms,** among them:

- Turning the steering wheel too much

- Applying the brakes too hard

- Stepping on the gas pedal too hard causing the rear wheels to spin resulting in loss of control

- A combination of the above

In any of these actions, the driver has put a demand on the vehicle that it cannot accept. If the vehicle cannot accept the demands, the vehicle goes out of control. (See all of Part II, *The Science and Techniques of Everyday Driving.*)

Accident-Producing Situations Caused by Drivers Themselves

Here are some examples of accident-producing situations that drivers get themselves into *through their own fault:*

1. **Tailgating.** Driving to close to the vehicle in front of you. When you do this, you won't have time to react if the other driver brakes, or if there is some other type of emergency.

2. **Making a sudden lane change, or a sudden change in speed.** All lane changing should be done as slowly as possible and by giving everyone around you plenty of warning that you are about to make a move.

   Admit it. You're often annoyed by drivers who zip from lane to lane, maneuvering about the highway as if they're the only ones on the road. *So don't do the same thing yourself!* Train yourself to never make a move with your car without first looking to see if someone is in the space you want to be in. And signal in plenty of time before you make that move.

3. **Failure to recognize when you are in trouble.** This is one of the toughest problems you'll face. There's not much you can do to train for this situation, because by the time you know you're in it, you may not be able to get out of it. The best thing for you to do is understand the different situations that can get you into trouble and be able to recognize them before they're inescapable.

4. **Not paying attention to the driving task.** Many times this is not because the driver is lazy, but occurs due to drowsiness, stress, and just daydreaming behind the wheel.

5. **Driving while emotionally unstable.** Never let your emotions get hold of you while driving. Driving while emotionally upset, especially while unusually angry or sad can reduce your ability to recognize danger and avoid it.

Accident-Producing Situations Caused by Defective Vehicles

Vehicle defects

Very few accidents are caused by a defective vehicle. In modern cars, this sort of catastrophic mechanical failure is practically nonexistent. Unfortunately, while a car may be constructed quite adequately for regular civilian, day-to-day driving, it might not be adequate for emergency drivers.

Almost all vehicle defects give the driver some advance warning that a failure is imminent. **Most people ignore the warning signs and keep on driving until there is a dramatic failure of the component or systems.** Luckily for these people, when the component or system does finally fail, the worst thing that generally happens is that the car stops and they have to wait for a tow-truck.

Tire defects

Tires are better than ever. Today's tires are state-of-the-art. But like any mechanical device, a tire will fail if not well treated. Suffice it to say that it's foolish to drive on badly worn tires. (See Ch. 8, *Tires, Part II* for tips on good tire care.)

Brakes defects

Don't wait until you have to toss out an anchor to stop the car, or until you can hear a metal-to-metal scraping when you hit the brakes. At the first sign of something unusual, have the brakes checked.

Vision restrictions

It is truly amazing to see the number of people that drive around with their windshields and rear windows completely covered with dirt. In order to drive, you have to see where you're going. Take the time to clean all your windows, and make sure the windshield wipers are in good working order. (See Ch. 4, *Windshields and Mirrors*, for tips on keeping your windshield and windshield wipers at their best.)

IN THE NEXT CHAPTER, we explore the basic accident situations you're like y to encounter on the road — as well as some specific dangers that you should watch out for and be prepared to handle. And, since you'll likely encounter not only vehicles, but pedestrians and bicyclists as well, we give you tips on how to safely "share the road."

Chapter 24

Typical Accident Scenarios:

And How to Deal with Them[1]

It's impossible to cover *all* the dangerous situations you can find yourself in when you're driving a car. But **a level-headed, quick-reacting defensive driver can do many things to avoid collisions and respond safely:**

- Many times you can avoid a collision merely by **slowing down.**

- Even after it is too late to stop or slow down, you may often avoid a collision by **swerving to one side.**

- It is normally **safer to swerve to the right than to the left.**

- It is **better to run off the road to the right than to collide head on.**

- However, **a speeding vehicle cannot be turned sharply without the risk of turning over.** The faster a vehicle is going, the more distance it takes to turn safely from a straight path.

- And a lot of dangerous situations can be avoided by simply **being more alert.**

Yield the Right of Way

A lot of accidents can be avoided if all drivers followed the rules of yielding the right of way. Always observe the rules of

---

[1] Sections in this chapter marked with * are copyright Shell Oil Company material and are reproduced with permission. Material was written by Mike Carpenter and in cooperation with the National Safety Council.

right-of-way with judgment and courtesy. Safe drivers give the right-of-way rather than taking it — even if the right of way is legally theirs.

- In general, **when two vehicles enter an intersection at about the same time,** the vehicle on the left yields the right-of-way to the vehicle on the right.

- **Always yield right-of-way to the first vehicle arriving at an intersection.**

- **When entering a through highway from a secondary road,** give the right-of-way to traffic on the main thoroughfare.

- **Fire, police, and emergency vehicles** have the right-of-way over all other vehicles.

BASIC ACCIDENT SITUATIONS

One of the basic points about avoiding accidents is easy to understand and very fundamental to safe driving: **Leave yourself an out — an escape route to every move you make.**

To do this, you have to **be aware of what's going on around you all the time.** Your best tools for doing this are your mirrors, both rearview and sideview. (Too many of us only use our rearview mirrors when we want to pull out into traffic.) Use all your mirrors in order to see the big picture — accurate information about what's going on on your right, left, and rear. In an emergency situation, such as a collision right in front of you, you need all the information you can get about what's happening around you, and you need it fast. Mirrors are your best way of getting this information.

Oncoming Car

Oncoming cars may cross the centerline and into your intended line of travel. They can move into your line of travel while making a left turn or while passing another vehicle. Even on freeways, where most drivers consider themselves safe from oncoming hazards, cars can cross medians or even jump guardrails. The results are head-on crashes.

- If you see a car coming at you in what looks like will be a head-on situation, **your two options are to change speed and/or change direction.**

- The best alternative is to **slow down and turn to the right.** It is far better to go off the road than to hit another vehicle head on. While you're moving to the right, **blow your horn.**

- Of course, **you must be aware of what you're turning into.** If the right side of the road is occupied by kids getting off a school bus, you really don't have much choice — your only alternative is to hit the car.

- **If you _must_ move to the left,** remember that there's the chance that the oncoming driver might correct at the last minute and turn back _into_ the direction you've just gone.

- **If you _can't_ avoid a collision, brake firmly and steadily.** Every mile per hour you slow down will reduce the impact.

Entering & Merging

In these situations, cars can squeeze in on your path of travel at a slight angle from either side. Such vehicles are usually accelerating from either a standing or moving position. They may be changing lanes, or starting out from a parked position along the roadside.

Entering and merging is a common freeway occurrence, where cars merge from ramps and acceleration lanes.

- The major problem with the merging car is when it comes equipped with a driver that acts without looking. In this, as in all driving problems, there is no simple solution to the driver who acts and *then* looks.

- The only solution to this in the entering and merging scenario is to make sure the other driver sees *you*.

Be especially wary of drivers who pull away from parking spaces without looking.

- The best way to avoid this on a multi-lane street is to try to **stay in the middle or left lane.**

- Otherwise, **keep an eye peeled for parked cars with their front wheels canted in toward the street, and that have their brake lights on.** They're probably getting ready to pull out and may be in such a hurry they don't bother to look before they move.

Ongoing or Cars Ahead

Ongoing cars (that is, cars traveling in the same direction and at roughly the same speed you are) cause problems in two basic ways.

- The driver of the car ahead of you may **suddenly stop or swerve out of the lane** to avoid hitting another vehicle or object in the roadway. Either move on the other car's part can produce a collision.

- **Give the car ahead of you enough room to maneuver.** Do not tailgate.

When you're stopped in line at an intersection

Two special situations arise when you are stopped at an intersection.

You are the first car stopped at an intersection (with or without a stop sign).

You're waiting to make a left turn. Keep your front wheels pointed straight until it's time to make that turn. Why? Simple. If your wheels are turned left, and you're hit from the rear, your car will be pushed to the left because of the direction the front wheels are pointed. This move would put you directly in the path of oncoming traffic, with the potential of more collisions even more dangerous than the first.

You're the *second* car in line stopped at an intersection that has a stop sign.

The car in front of you pulls out. You look left and right for opposing traffic. It looks OK and you start to pull out, only to

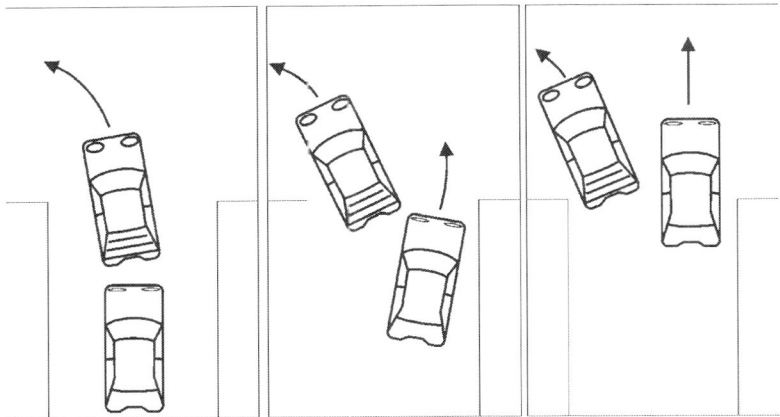

Figure 24-1. Avoiding a Car Stopped at an Intersection. The car ahead is stopped to make a left turn onto the main road. After pulling ahead somewhat, the car ahead slams on the brakes. Stop quickly if you can. If not steer to the car's right. Do not try to pass the other car; it may lead you into the path of oncoming cars that you cannot see.
   Drawing and caption adapted from Medical Economics, by permission of the Medical Economics Company, Inc.

find that the driver in front of you has developed cold feet and stopped. You hit him from the rear.

- In this situation, patience is the key.

- Let the first car pull out and clear the intersection, then look both ways to see if it's safe for you to proceed. (See Figure 24-1, p. 229)

Car Following Too Closely

A car following you too closely, or closing in on you from behind at a high rate of speed, can crash into your vehicle's rear end should you need to stop suddenly. Tailgaters are always a serious problem, a problem made even worse at night. Fortunately, the solution to a tailgater is not too difficult — pull over and let the idiot go by.

Cars Backing Out

In an urban environment, people are prone to backing out of parking spaces without looking to see what's there. If they are heading toward you, a gentle toot on your horn will inform them that you are there and you'd greatly appreciate it if they would not back into you.

Motorcyclists*

Any time you see or hear a motorcyclist near you, be especially cautious. Motorcyclists are difficult to see because they're smaller than most vehicles. Statistics show that motorcyclists are about 16 times as likely as automobile occupants to die in a traffic crash.

Pedestrians and Bicyclists

Vehicles aren't your only problem. Pedestrians and bicyclists are potential challenges to your driving skills as well.

Intersecting pedestrian or bicyclist and vehicular traffic is a source of serious problems, despite the many control devices used to regulate their interaction. Intersections are the sites for a very high percentage of *all* collisions — including vehicles, pedestrians, and bicyclists. Moreover, pedestrians and bicyclists can come into your line of travel at almost *any* time. In general:

- **When you pull up to an intersection,** always look for conflicting traffic entering — vehicular, pedestrian, and bicyclist.

- **Even if you have the legal right of way,** it doesn't protect you from the physical reality of getting hit by a car whose driver just didn't see it your way, or your hitting a pedestrian who decided to cross the street without looking.

- In such situations you will probably not have **enough room or time to stop your car.** Therefore, you will need to know how to swerve out of harm's way and stop as quickly as possible.

Although many *bicyclists* have experience riding in traffic and know how to watch out for cars and trucks, many *motorists* are NOT generally accustomed to bicyclists (and often pedestrians) on the road.

Motorists should therefore learn how pedestrians and bicyclists are *required* to use the road and how to *share* the road with them courteously and safely.

The following tips for motorists on how to share the road with bicyclists and pedestrians are provided courtesy of Bike Florida and Florida's Share the Road Campaign, Lyndy Lyle Moore, www.bikeflorida.org.

Rules/regulations that bicyclists *and* pedestrians *must/should follow*

- **Bicyclists *must* obey the same traffic rules and regulations as motor vehicle drivers.** This means **they ride *with* traffic** (not facing it), and signal, make turns, and stop as any motor vehicle must.

- A bicyclist may ride on a sidewalk unless *forbidden* by local laws — this means than **in many areas bicyclists MUST use the same road as motorists.**

- **Between sunset and sunrise bicyclists** are *supposed* to have a white light on the front and a red reflector and a red light on the rear.

- Unlike bicyclists, **pedestrians should walk *facing* traffic at the edge of the road when there is no sidewalk present.**

- **Pedestrians *should* be visible at night** by wearing bright reflective clothing and carrying a flashlight.

- **Pedestrians *should* look in all directions** before stepping into the road, even at signalized crosswalks.

- **Pedestrians *should* be predictable and cross directly from curb to curb,** staying within the marked area or a straight pathway.

> **Because not all pedestrians and bicyclists (or drivers) follow the rules and regulations perfectly all the time, motorists must ALWAYS be prepared for the unexpected. People don't always do what you expect them to do!**

Sharing the road with bicyclists and pedestrians

- Slow down in **school zones, parks, and residential areas** (areas very likely to have pedestrians and/or bicyclists in the roadway).

- Use extra caution during **peak morning and afternoon riding hours.**

- **When turning at an intersection,** with or without a signal, look for pedestrians and bicyclists crossing from all directions.

- **Yield to bicyclists and pedestrians at both marked and unmarked crosswalks** — especially when turning right on red.

- **Stop behind the stop bar at intersections,** not in the crosswalk, so pedestrians can cross the street safely.

- **Even though a bicyclist's pace may pose a momentary delay in your schedule,** it is important to respect the bicyclist's safety and *legal* right to the roadways.

- **Bicyclists' skills vary.** When possible, assess the rider's capabilities. A safe (experienced) rider holds a steady line.

- **Yield the right of way to a bicyclist** as you would a car.

- **Keep cool and lay off the horn and flashing headlights.** It's *sometimes* OK for a short "toot" to warn bicyclists, but do not BLAST your horn when approaching them — you could startle them and cause them to swerve or fall.

- **When passing a bicyclist,** reduce speed and allow three to five feet of passing space between your vehicle and the bicycle. Add one foot for every 10 mph over 50 mph.

- **A moving vehicle creates wind turbulence that can seriously affect a bicyclist's control.** When meeting or passing cyclists, slow down and give the widest berth possible. Crosswinds compound the problem for bicyclists.

- **Bicyclists worry about road defects you'd never feel in your car.** Allow them plenty of room in case they swerve to miss a pothole, storm drain, debris, or other obstacles.

- Bicyclists require extra courtesy while negotiating **railroad tracks and narrow bridges.**

- **On a two-lane road,** don't pass a bicyclist if oncoming traffic is near.

> **One Road, Many Users — Be Courteous and Share the Road.**

OTHER DRIVING DANGERS*

Someone Runs a Red Light

Never assume a green light means all okay. There's little consolation in knowing an accident isn't your fault just because you had the right of way. Your car is still damaged, and someone may be hurt. Even though you were in the right, perhaps you could have actually avoided the collision simply by looking before you leaped.

- **If your light is green,** make sure other drivers, at or near the intersection, aren't trying to beat the yellow, or red.

- **If you're at an intersection *without* a light,** look left, right, and left again before moving out.

You Have a Blowout

If you slam on the brakes you could lose control completely.

- **If a front tire blows,** the car will pull hard to the side of the blowout. The steering wheel vibrates like crazy.

  1. **Hang on tight with your hands at the 9 o'clock and 3 o'clock positions** on the steering wheel.
  2. **Take your foot off the gas** and concentrate on staying in your lane.
  3. Then **slow down gradually and pull off the road** to a safe location.

- **If a rear tire blows,** the back of the car will weave back and forth and vibrate. But you should **handle it the same way as you would if a front tire blows.**

You Start to Skid

A lot of people hit the brakes hard when their car starts to skid. That generally makes things worse. (See Ch. 14, *Losing and Regaining Traction* for a thorough discussion of the different kinds of skids and how to handle them.) In general:

- Just **take your foot off the gas and turn your steering wheel in the direction you want the front of the car to go.** This helps straighten out the car and often regains traction.

- **Frequently it takes more than one turn of the steering wheel** to correct a skid.

Your Brakes Fail

You must think and act quickly. Remember this word-sequence: pump pedal, parking brake, shift down, safe place. (See Ch. 19, *Braking Control, Part II,* for a thorough discussion of braking techniques. See also p. 182)

1. **Pump the brake pedal.** Sometimes the pressure comes back. (Unless you have an ABS brake system. Never pump the brake pedal on ABS brakes.)

2. **Slowly try the parking brake.** But don't jam it on hard if you're in a curve. That could cause a spin.

3. **Shift into a lower gear** (or lower range on automatic transmissions). The drag on the engine will help slow you down. Do all three of these as quickly and steadily as you can. And keep your eyes on the road.

4. **Look for a safe place to guide your vehicle** onto the shoulder of the road or some other safe location. In an emergency, the quicker you think and act, the safer you'll be.

Your Accelerator Sticks

1. **Try pulling it up with the toe of your shoe.** If a passenger is with you, have him reach down and pull it up. **You should not take your eyes off the road to reach down yourself.**

2. **If your car has a manual transmission,** press down on the clutch. The engine will continue to race, but you can then pull safely off the road.

3. **If it's an automatic transmission,** put it in neutral. It's not a good idea to turn off the key. Some cars will lose power steering or even lock the steering wheel.

Your Hood Flies Open

You need to stop, but if you slam on your brakes, you could be hit from behind.

1. In some cars, from behind the wheel you can actually see ahead by **peeking through the opening between the dashboard and the hood.**

2. If not, then **lean out the window to see what's ahead of you.**

3. In either case, you need to **slow down smoothly and pull off the road.**

Your Car Goes Into Deep Water

While this doesn't happen often, it happens enough that you should know what to do.

1. If you do go in the water, **release your safety belt immediately.** (But don't release it before you go in. The safety belt will help protect you during impact with the water.)

2. Then the best thing to do is to **try to get out quickly through the window,** because power windows can short-circuit in the water.

3. **If you can't get out through the window, try the door.** At first, the water pressure will probably hold it closed. But don't panic. As the water rises, it will equalize the pressure and the door should open.

IN THE NEXT CHAPTER, we provide a Q&A on what you can do if you come upon an accident or if you are in one yourself.

Chapter 25

Crash Course:

Simple Tips that Could Help Save Lives[1]

I've just seen a bad collision. What can I do to help?

First and foremost, **don't make things worse.**

1. **Pass well beyond the wreck before signaling and pulling off of the road, out of harm's way.** This keeps you from blocking the view of the collision to oncoming traffic, and it gives emergency crews room to work.

2. **Turn on your emergency flashers and raise your hood** to call attention to yourself.

3. Then **carefully approach the wreck, avoiding dangerous situations** like wires, fires or hazardous materials.

4. Next, **turn off the ignitions of all vehicles to reduce the risk of fire.** This simple step could keep a bad collision from becoming much worse. Remember, check for spilled gasoline or downed power lines before getting too close. And don't move an injured driver to get to his keys.

---

[1] Copyright Shell Oil Company material reproduced with permission. Written in cooperation with the National Safety Council and the American Trauma Society.

NOTE: Contains general recommendations that we believe will be helpful in many emergencies. Since every emergency is different, the individual driver must decide what to do in any particular case.

6. Now **call for help if possible.** Be sure to stay on the line until the emergency dispatcher hangs up. If you're needed to administer first aid, assign the call to someone else and be specific: "You in the red jacket call 9-1-1!"

7. **Consider carrying a cellular phone in your car**. Many of today's models have emergency numbers programmed into them.

8. **Check for injuries.** Are victims awake and responsive? If so, encourage them not to move. If they don't respond, verify that they are breathing. Then attend to those with severe bleeding (wear latex gloves if possible).

> **Remember: NEVER MOVE A VICTIM UNLESS THERE IS AN IMMEDIATE, LIFE-THREATENING DANGER SUCH AS FIRE, LEAKING FUEL, OR RISING WATER.**

Should I always stop?

Whatever the situation, your intervention might help save a life.

- **Wouldn't *you* want to be helped** if you were the one trapped or injured?

- Also, **if you were involved in the collision, you *must* stop.** All states impose severe penalties on drivers who don't stop in such cases. **Remember, you can be "involved" in a collision without actually hitting anything.** If you contribute to a crash in any way, you're *obligated* to stop.

- If the fear of making a mistake keeps you from stopping, **be aware that most states have "Good Samaritan" laws to protect individuals from liability** if they stop and, in good faith, administer first aid. The scope of protection varies, so check your state's laws.

🚑IF EMERGENCY CREWS ARE RACING TO A CRASH AHEAD OF YOU, pull over to let them safely pass. And don't assume the first ambulance or police car you see will be the only one. Watch for other emergency vehicles following closely behind the first. The last thing you want to do is pull out and cause another collision.

What's my first step in treating the injured?

- Before beginning any first aid, **check to see if any victims are awake and responsive**. This may help you assess the level of care each victim needs.

- **A conscious victim's responses will often help you evaluate the extent of his injuries.** "What hurts?" may reveal broken bones, bleeding or internal injuries. "Can you wiggle your fingers or toes?" could help you assess potential spinal damage. And no response at all might mean a victim isn't breathing.

I don't think she's breathing! Now what?

1. First, **make sure breathing has stopped.** Is the victim completely non-responsive? Is her chest rising and failing? Can you feel breathing? Hear it? If the victim is not breathing, open her airway. Gently move the head into its normal, "eyes front" position and lower the jaw.

2. **Listen for gurgling or gagging.** Both are signs of a blocked airway. If you hear either after opening the mouth, gently clear it of any obstructions.

3. **If the victim is still not breathing, begin artificial respiration.** Pinch the victim's nose shut. Open your mouth wide, take a deep breath, and put your mouth tightly over the victim's (you may wish to carry a pocket mask or mouth barrier for such emergencies). Blow a full breath, then watch for the

victim's chest to rise and fall. If she doesn't start breathing on her own, blow one full breath every five seconds. Do this for at least one minute. Be sure to breathe yourself — you don't want to hyperventilate!

How do I control severe bleeding.

1. **Press firmly against any wounds with some sort of bandage,** preferably a thick pad of clean cloth. This will absorb the blood and allow it to clot. (If possible, place a barrier — several layers of cloth, latex gloves, a plastic bag — between you and the victim's blood.)

2. **If blood soaks through the dressing, don't remove it.** That could open the wound further make bleeding worse. Instead, **add more layers of cloth and apply pressure even more firmly.** If possible, get someone else at the scene to help you tie the bandage in place.

3. **If the bleeding still won't stop' make sure you're pressing on the right spot.** It's *not* a good idea to use your belt as a tourniquet. That might completely cut off the flow of blood, and could potentially lead to the loss of the limb.

All this blood and breathing. Should I be worried about AIDS?

It's a common question, with a comforting answer.

- According to the American Medical Association, **it is "extremely unlikely" that you will contract AIDS from a bleeding collision victim, or from mouth-to-mouth contact during artificial respiration.**

- **The HIV virus,** which causes AIDS, **is transmitted through sexual contact, infected blood, infected needles or childbirth,** and not through casual contact.

- Still, for added peace of mind, **you may want to keep several pairs of latex gloves in your first aid kit** (freezer bags are a good substitute).

If I have to move someone, how should I do it?

Remember, you should only move a crash victim when there is an immediate danger, such as fire or rising water.

- **If you must move a victim, gently align his neck and spine.** Then, if you are alone, carefully drag him backward by the clothes or armpits. **Do not pull a victim sideways,** as this will only aggravate spinal damage.

- **If you have help available,** have one person support the head from underneath, keeping it in line with the spine. The others can then lift the body from the sides, evenly supporting it from underneath.

I think she's in shock. Now what?

Shock occurs when a victim's circulatory system doesn't provide enough blood to his body and brain.

- **A person doesn't have to appear injured to suffer from shock** — in fact, shock victims often walk, talk and at first seem merely "shaken up." **Shock can kill, so know how to recognize it.**

- **Telltale signs** include pale, moist, clammy skin; dilated pupils; a weak and rapid pulse; shivering; thirst; nausea and vomiting; shallow breathing; weakness; a vacant expression and a detached attitude.

- **If you suspect an apparently uninjured victim is in shock, have her lie down and raise her feet slightly.**

- It's generally best to **place blankets and coats under her and around her to conserve heat.**

- **If the victim is nauseated,** have her lie on her side and slightly elevate her head.

- **Then begin any additional first aid, talking to the victim as you work.** A little kindness and understanding go a long way toward treating shock

How can I help myself if I'm in a wreck?

- **If it's a minor collision with no injuries,** you can best help yourself by staying calm and moving out of traffic. The key here is safety first, insurance later. Keep a pad and pencil handy, and use them, along with insurance forms, to exchange information once you've cleared the scene.

- **If you're in a major collision,** you'll have to be the judge of whether or not you are injured and how quickly traffic is moving around you. Often, your best bet is to wait for help from a safe place — which just might be your car. If you're uninjured and traffic permits, you may want to begin first aid on those around you. But don't put yourself at more risk doing so. You'll be no help to anyone if you lapse into shock or get struck by a passing motorist.

See Ch. 11, *The Glove Compartment and Trunk: Keep Them Well Stocked for Safety* for tips and some warnings and cautionary notes on what to have on hand for roadside emergencies.

REDUCED
SPEED
35

PART IV

DRIVING IN SPECIAL SITUATIONS

In this Part, we look at strategies and techniques for driving in situations that pose special hazards — driving in foul weather of all types, driving at night, roadside breakdowns, road rage, and driving alone.

Chapter 26
Foul Weather Driving, p. 247

Chapter 27
Driving Safely at Night:
There's More to It than Good Headlights, p. 261

Chapter 28
Roadside Breakdown:
How to Deal with Roadside Emergencies, p. 267

Chapter 29
Road Rage:
How to Avoid It, How to Deal with It, p. 275

Chapter 30
Alone Behind the Wheel, p. 279

Chapter 26

Foul Weather Driving[1]

Along with coping with the variables of road design, drivers must also cope with weather-related road conditions. Whether it's light rain or heavy snow, high winds or extreme heat, knowing how to adjust your driving and what car safety gear to have with you can mean the difference between being safe or becoming a statistic.

DRIVING IN RAIN

While driving in rain isn't quite as traumatic as driving in snow or ice, it has terrors of its own. Wet weather of any kind demands a gentle touch with vehicle controls. Rain lowers visibility, and creates the need for longer stopping distance, and increases the risks of losing control, especially after radical control movements.

When it rains can be as important as how much it rains. If rains fall after a long dry spell, the road will be far more slippery than if it has been raining regularly for several days. In Florida and other southern states, they refer to this road condition as **"black ice."** The initial rainfall floats off all

[1] Sections in this chapter marked with * are copyright Shell Oil Company materials, used with permission.

the surface oil the road has collected from cars, forming a very slippery suspension that eventually washes away as the rain continues, especially if it rains long or hard enough. (But then all that water itself becomes a problem.) **A merely wet surface can be tricky; an oily wet surface can be deadly.**

When driving in rain, **here are some simple rules to follow:**

- **Drive slower than usual.** Bear in mind that you do not have the vehicular control you usually do.

- **Turn on your headlights** if it is raining. This allows other drivers to see you and is the law in some states.

- Of course, you must **turn on you windshield wipers**. Make sure they're always in good working order. Don't wait for the next cloudburst to find out your wipers don't work, or that the blades are worn to point of uselessness. (See tips on routine wiper care, p. 37)

- **Make sure your outside mirrors and rear window are clear.** If they are covered with water beads, your view can be distorted, or it can be just plain difficult to see.

- **Don't change speed or direction quickly, and don't brake suddenly.** This is a sure way of encountering a potentially disastrous skid.

- **On a multi-lane highway, stay in the middle lanes.** Water usually collects in the outside lanes.

- **Never drive through large pools of water.** They may be deeper than you think.

Hydroplaning*

Hydroplaning occurs when a thin layer of water causes your tires to lose contact with the road. It can happen even at relatively low speeds and, in the blink of an eye, you can lose control of your car. It's frightening, but don't panic.

- **Keep both hands on the steering wheel.**
- **Ease foot off the accelerator.**
- *Don't* **slam on the brakes.**
- *Without* **anti-lock brakes (ABS)**, if wheels lock-up and you begin to skid, simply release the brake pedal then gently re-apply pressure. Steer gently in the direction you want the car to go. (Check your owner's manual to see if you have ABS.)

To avoid hydroplaning:

- Slow down in wet weather.
- Be sure your tires have plenty of tread, and proper inflation. Consider getting "all weather" tires that are specially designed for bad conditions.

When Rain Causes a Flood or There Is Rushing Water*

Always take flood warnings seriously.

Do not drive through standing water and *never* drive through rushing water.

- Water may be very deep in a flooded area and **undercurrents can sweep away even the heaviest vehicles.**
- Watch fences, trees and buildings on the side of the road. **If they appear unnaturally low, slow down immediately.** The road is probably dangerously flooded.

- **Driving into floodwater at high speed is like hitting a wall.**

If Your Vehicle Stalls in Water*

If your vehicle stalls, **abandon it and immediately seek higher ground.**

> **Six inches of rapidly moving floodwater can sweep you off your feet, and two feet of water can carry away the average car.**

DRIVING IN SNOW

Driving in snow can be a white knuckle experience for even the most experienced drivers. The best advice for driving in snow is DON'T. Unless, of course, you drive in an emergency capacity and your job demands it. If you must go out in snow, however, there *are* some things you can do to make life a little easier and safer.  And, if possible, wait until the roads have been plowed before heading out.

Prepare to Get Under Way

- First, **make sure you can see.** Clean all snow from all car windows and mirrors. Don't play *Tank Commander* and just clear a little slit for you to look through.

- *Remember:* **using wipers on an icy windshield can cut wipers to shreds.**

- **Don't drive wearing boots so big they interfere with pedal operation** — a boot so wide that it depresses the brake pedal when you think your foot is only on the gas. This may sound like a ludicrous recommendation but it's surprising how many folks do this.

- Once you've got proper boots on, **make sure to keep them clear of clumps of ice or snow that could interfere with pedal use.** Snow or ice on the soles of boots can cause them to slide off pedals at critical times.

Maintaining Traction on Snow*

To help maintain traction as you are getting underway:

- **Automatic transmission:** Put your car in "D2" and accelerate gently. Shift to "D" once you're moving.

- **Standard transmission:** Use the highest gear, such as 2nd or 3rd, with which you can move the car without stalling.

- Accelerate gently.

As you are driving in snow:

- Slow down.

- Avoid sudden maneuvers.

- Try to keep moving and keep your wheels from spinning, no matter how slow you must go to do so. Use tire chains where allowed by law.

- When driving downhill, use a low gear and let the engine help you keep the car in control.

If you begin to slide:

- Don't slam on the brakes.

- Simply ease off the accelerator, then gently apply brake pressure and steer in the direction you want the car to go.

- Be ready to correct for a slide in the opposite direction.

> **Remember that overpasses and bridges freeze before other pavement. Even if it seems warm enough for ice to melt, it still can be hazardous.**

If You Get Stuck in Snow or Ice

- **Apply a traction aid such as sand or kitty litter to the surface under the tire.**

- **Briefly rock the vehicle.**

- **Avoid spinning the wheels.**

    Spinning the tires doesn't get the car free. Spinning the tires only makes the road surface slicker by melting snow which then refreezes as ice, and also creates ruts that can further complicate the process of freeing the car.

    The increased tire speed is not going to create traction. Peak traction is generated at very low speeds. Once a tire is spinning 15 percent faster than the car is moving, maximum traction has been lost.

> **As you accelerate to get unstuck, do not exceed 35 mph *speedometer* speed — and make sure *no one* stands near the spinning tire.**

- When all else fails, **have the vehicle towed**.

BLIZZARD CONDITIONS*

If you become trapped during a blizzard, DO NOT leave the car unless help is visible within 100 yards.

- It is easy to become **disoriented and lost** in blowing, drifting snow and white-out conditions.

- If you live in an area where heavy snow is a problem, **always carry a cell phone and call for help** as soon as you become stuck.

- **Tie a bright-colored cloth to your antenna; raise the hood.**

- Start the engine, turn on the interior light and heater for about **10 minutes each hour.**

- **Beware of carbon monoxide poisoning.** Keep the exhaust pipe clear. Slightly open a downwind window as a vent.

- **Watch for signs of frostbite and hypothermia.** Clap your hands and move your legs to stimulate circulation.

- Use maps, newspaper or car mats for more **insulation.**

Driving in snow and ice is a serious matter, and winter storms can strand drivers for hours before help can arrive. Being prepared could save your life.

- Stock your vehicle with **extra gloves, hats, blankets, a windshield scraper and thermal packs.**

- Also carry **sand, salt or calcium chloride.**

- If you don't have **snow tires**, carry **tire chains.** Practice putting on the tire chains so you know how to use them.

DRIVING ON ICE

One of the most frightening experiences in driving is suddenly going from a dry road surface to one that's covered with ice. The experience is analogous to running at full speed and then abruptly discovering you are running on ice. You look like something out of a children's cartoon — your feet are windmilling like mad while your body stays put. Eventually, your feet will shoot out from under you and down you'll come.

All this pretty much holds true for a car on an icy surface. Under dry conditions, your *feet* are like little car tires. *Real* car tires grab the surface and propel the car forward. Imagine a car on a dry surface approaching ice. The rear wheels are propelling the car, while the front wheels are steering the vehicle (obviously, on front-wheel drive vehicles, the front wheels are performing both these vital functions). **Suddenly, the car encounters ice and none of the tires have any adhesion whatsoever;** absolutely no propulsive or directional control.

And, as if this weren't bad enough, **it all happens instantly.** A rapid transition from dry pavement to ice can cause a driver to over-react, or react roughly with the car's controls, throwing the vehicle completely out of control.

The first and most obvious solution to ice driving is to slow down. But **the steering or braking you are now contemplating will have to be done as *delicately* as possible,** because nearly any control input on ice will result in the vehicle going wildly, completely, utterly out of control.

Stopping and Braking on Ice

When encountering ice or icy conditions and you need to stop, or you find you have to brake and turn:

- **With non-ABS brakes,** first apply brakes as lightly as possible. Then release the brakes and steer, again, gently.

- **With ABS (anti-lock brakes)**, maintain light pressure and steer in the direction you wish to go.

- **Do not try to stop the car by shifting into a lower gear.** When you shift into low gear, the rear wheels can spin and the car will begin to travel sideways. And one of the reasons you are in trouble on ice in the first place is because your wheels are spinning and not creating any traction on a slippery surface. If you put the car in a lower gear, the rear tires spin faster, making the situation worse, not better.

REMEMBER: Stopping on snow and ice may require up to 10 times the distance as stopping in normal conditions. Keep plenty of distance between you and the vehicle in front of you.

To Recover from an Ice Slide

If you do hit the ice and begin to slide:

- Put the car in **neutral.**

- **Then press *gently* on the brake pedal.** *You must be gentle.* Do not brake abruptly — over-applying the brakes will only increase the trouble you're already in.

- **Steer in the direction you want the car to go**. You MUST use a light touch on the controls here. Be careful how much you turn the steering wheel. If you turn it too much and over correct, the car will begin to fishtail.

- **Once you have straightened out, apply a very slight amount of gas.**

WINTER DRIVING SCENARIO — THE DYNAMICS IN "ACTION"

The following is a scenario familiar to those that have had the chance to drive on ice:

You cruise around the corner of Main and Elm. **It's winter, but today is nice and sunny, but cold.** You approach the corner at 40 mph, slowing to 20 mph and turn the wheel approximately 45 degrees. You round the corner successfully and five seconds later, you've forgotten the entire, routine maneuver.

The next day, the temperature has dropped twenty degrees and it's snowing heavily. The road is very slippery. You approach the same corner at 40 mph, and attempt to slow to 20 mph. The first sign of trouble comes when you try to slow. Not much happens when you apply the brakes. The car is still traveling forward, a little slower than before, but still traveling. Because of the slippery surface, there is no friction to stop the car.

You turn the steering wheel to the same 45 degrees that worked just fine yesterday. Only this time nothing happens. The car continues traveling in a straight line.

What are the dynamics of what worked yesterday and what isn't working today? On yesterday's dry pavement, the tires had sufficient adhesion to propel, control, and stop the car. Today, on a slick surface, they don't.

So the *techniques* for vehicle control are different as well. Today you must lower the forces involved. How is that done? Remove the source of the force; the vehicle's speed, and the angle of the turn. Now, we'll be the first to admit that it is rather difficult to drive around a corner without turning the wheel. So that leaves us with but a single answer: SLOW

DOWN! That's it. It's so simple. If the weather has altered the road conditions: SLOW DOWN.

Wet roads are at their slipperiest when the temperature is near freezing. Solidly frozen ice is the most dangerous. Snow provides better traction than ice if it is not too packed and there's no ice under it.

If you are an emergency worker, slowing down is tough to do when you're trying to get to people in trouble. But those people you're trying to reach in such a hurry are depending on your help, and you can't give them that help if you crack up your valuable rescue vehicle and yourself on the way to them.

FOG*

When it comes to inclement weather, fog is one of the most visually limiting conditions. If you get caught in heavy fog, the best thing to do is to stop well off the road until visibility is better. **If there is no safe place to stop:**

- Take all fog-related warning signs seriously.

- **Slow down.** Fog makes it very difficult to judge speed. Do not believe your eyes — **glance at your speedometer to make sure you have slowed down.**

- **Turn on wipers, defroster and low-beam headlights.** Using high beams can actually decrease your visibility.

- Moisture from fog can make roads slick, so **brake smoothly.**

- **Crack your window and turn off the radio.** Watch for slower moving cars and listen for engine sounds or car horns.

- **If the fog is too dense to continue,** pull completely off the road and try to position your vehicle in a protected area from other traffic. **Turn on your emergency flashers.**

- Consider installing **"fog lights"** if you often drive in fog.

EXTREME HEAT*

Sunscreen and insect repellent are important in the summer, but so is a quick vehicle inspection before heading out to a favorite recreation spot. **During hotter months, it's a good idea to keep extra coolant, at least one gallon of water, jumper cables and a flashlight in your vehicle.** Also:

- Check the battery, belts and hoses.

- Check oil often.

- Have your air-conditioning system checked and serviced by a qualified technician.

- Inspect your coolant and water level and ratio to be sure it is at the proper 50/50 level when the car is cool.

- Never leave children or pets unattended in a car even for a short time. The temperature inside a closed vehicle — even with windows down — can reach dangerous levels very quickly.

- Cover metal and plastic parts on child seats and safety belts to prevent burns.

What to Do If Your Car Overheats

- **Let engine cool and call for service.**

- If your engine overheated because of **lack of coolant,** further operation may damage the vehicle.

LIGHTNING*

With or without accompanying rain, lightning can be dangerous.

- **If you're in your car during a lightning storm,** DO NOT attempt to leave the vehicle and run for cover. The car's metal cage will conduct a charge into the ground and protect you.

- If you're in an open vehicle, such as a convertible, golf cart, tractor, motorcycle or bicycle, find safe shelter.

- **Do not stand under trees or in small, isolated buildings** because lightning will usually strike the tallest object around. Instead, **crouch down on the balls of your feet.**

Chapter 27

Driving Safely at Night:

There's More to It Than Good Headlights

Most drivers think the only difference between day and night driving is that one requires headlights. True, most of the light we have available for our use at night comes from our car's headlights — but **headlights are a poor substitute for daylight.**

Compound this with the fact that even during daylight, safe driving depends not only on **as far as you can see,** but on **how much you can see,** and **how fast you can see it and react to it.** And we know that after the sun goes down, all these factors change *dramatically.*

So, what can you do **to *minimize* the hazards of driving at night.** Here are some tips.

Keep Your Headlights in Good Working Order

Good night visibility is more than just *having* headlights; you must keep them in optimum condition.

- **Make sure your headlights are aligned properly.** You can have the best headlight system in the world, but if those lights point off in crazy directions, they're not going to do much good, except to make your vehicle a kind of traveling light show. Tests can be performed to see if the lights on your car are aligned properly.

- **Keep headlights clean**. As much as half of a headlight's total illumination can be absorbed by dirt on the surface of the glass beam. Keeping headlights clean is especially important in winter when they are frequently covered with road dirt and encrusted with salt.

Keep Your Windshield and Mirrors Clean

The glare through a dirty windshield can make visibility almost nonexistent. The same for mirrors. Keep both the outside and inside of your windshield as clean as possible. And make sure your windshield wipers are in good condition. There's nothing like a smear of bug juice, bird droppings, and road oils on your windshield spread around by worn out wipers to make your night driving an experience to remember. (See p. 37 for tips on how to keep your windshield and wipers in optimum condition.)

Adjust Your Speed to the Range of Your Headlights

Contrary to common sense, **many drivers do not slow down significantly when driving at night** — despite their reduced visibility and the added dangers of inclement weather.

We've all seen this type of driver. *You're* tooling along at a reduced speed at night in a driving rainstorm. The windshield wipers are slapping back and forth at their highest setting when suddenly a pair of headlights appear in your rear-view mirror. These headlights grow bigger and brighter at an alarming rate, and before we know it — zoom! — a car goes flashing past us, apparently oblivious to the darkness, the weather, and the fact that it's hard to see 50 feet ahead of the car on a night like this. This driver is overdriving his headlights and may be headed for disaster!

- **Don't overdrive your headlights.** Never drive so fast that you cannot stop within the distance you can see ahead with your lights.

  High-beam headlights in good working order illuminate the road for about 330 feet ahead; low beams illuminate for about 200 feet ahead.

  If, for example, you're driving with your low beams on and your speed is 40 mph (approximately 60 ft/sec) you have three seconds' worth of vision ahead of you — assuming that your headlights are clean and working at maximum efficiency. (See Figure 17-4, p. 169

- **Establish a safe following distance.** For daylight driving in the average car traveling 40mph or less, the rule of thumb is to keep two-seconds between you and the traffic ahead. For night driving make it a three-second rule. (See p. 168 for tips on figuring out exactly how much space is necessary, especially at higher speeds and for longer vehicles).

Keep Your Eyes Moving

Don't just focus on the middle of the lighted area in front of you. Headlights only illuminate so much and they cannot see around corners.

- **Search the edges of the lighted area.** Look for other patches of light that could be cars. Look for them at hilltops, on curves, or at intersections.

- Where there are many **distracting neon signs or brightly-lit buildings,** try to concentrate on street-level activities.

- **When you turn corners at night,** don't just follow the headlights around the corner. As you turn your car, scan the areas to the side and beyond the headlights.

- **When backing up**, remember that only your backup lights are available; on most makes of cars, they aren't much.

Protect Your Eyes from Glare

Prolonged exposure to glare from sunlight during the day or headlights at night can temporarily ruin your night vision, while also leading to eye strain and drowsiness.

- **Wear good sunglasses on bright days** and take them off as soon as the sun goes down.

- **Rest a while before driving at night after a long session of steady daytime driving.**

- **If the high beams of an oncoming car are not dimmed, avoid looking directly at the bright lights.** When your eyes are hit by a bright beam of light from an oncoming car, you can't see! Drivers can be affected by the oncoming glare of headlights as far as 3,000 feet away. You can be completely blinded for a full one or two seconds, which means that at 40 mph you will drive somewhere from 60 to 120 feet without being able to see anything clearly.

- **Glance toward the right side of the road; then quickly look ahead to determine the other vehicle's position.** Keep doing this until you have passed each other.

- Avoid driving long distances without taking breaks. Continual glare of lights outside and from your dashboard increase the chance of highway hypnosis.

Use Your Lights Wisely

- **Use low beams when driving in cities and towns,** except on streets where there is no other lighting.

- **Use low beams whenever you are following a vehicle.**

- **Use high-beam headlights on highways only when it is safe and legal to do so**, such as when no other vehicle is coming toward you. Switch to low beams when following another car or encountering on-coming cars to avoid blinding the other driver.

Make It Easy for Others to See You

- **Turn on your low beams (not your parking lights) at dusk or dawn.** Used at this time of day, they won't help you see, but they'll help other drivers and pedestrians see you.

- **Some states require you to use headlights from sunset to sunrise.** Most late model cars have automatic "running lights" for daytime driving. If your car doesn't, use your low beams.

- **If you have to pull off the road and stop, for whatever reason, put on your emergency flashers.** It's not a bad idea to turn on the car's interior or dome lights. If the car's electrical system fails, have a combination of flares, a flashlight, and some reflective materials handy.

- **Bright color and high contrast make objects visible at night.** That's why it's a good idea to have some reflecting tape on the outside of your vehicle, especially if the vehicle is a dark color.

Avoid Steady Driving at the Hour of Your Usual Bedtime

- **A person's alertness level decreases around the time one routinely retires for the night.** If you must drive past your usual bedtime, stop every hour or so and walk around. Stretch your legs. Get some air.

And ALWAYS drive *defensively* at night.

Chapter 28

Roadside Breakdown:

How to Deal with Roadside Emergencies[1]

Each year, nearly 3,000 people die in car accidents on the shoulder or median of the road. Sometimes, these fatal scenarios begin with a simple breakdown that forces the vehicle off the roadway. **Learning how to prevent breakdowns and how to protect yourself and your passengers if a breakdown occurs can save your life.**

How do I know something is wrong with my vehicle?

- **Watch the instrument panel.** Your instrument panel gauges indicate engine temperature, fuel and oil levels and other important information. Read your owner's manual to familiarize yourself with all the gauges. Your manual will also indicate what gauge readings are considered "normal" and which signal an emergency situation.

- **However, your instrument panel can't tell you everything.** For example, if your car suddenly pulls to one side, or if you feel a rumbling or vibration,

---

[1] Copyright Shell Oil Company material reproduced with permission. Written in cooperation with the American Red Cross, the Federal Highway Administration, the National Crime Prevention Council, and the National Institute for Automotive Servence Excellence.

NOTE: Contains general recommendations that we believe may be helpful in the event of a breakdown. Because every situation is different, the individual driver must decide what to do in each particular scenario.

safely pull off the roadway. You may have a flat or low tire.

- ***Keep alert*. Your sense of smell, touch, sight or hearing may be the first hint that there's a problem.** Pay attention to your car while driving. An odd odor, an unusual vibration, the sight of smoke or an unexpected sound can signal trouble.

If there's something wrong with my vehicle, should I stop where I am or continue?

It really depends on the nature of your problem.

- As a safe rule of thumb, **any change in your vehicles's steering, braking or acceleration should receive immediate attention.** Pull safely to the side of the road onto a smooth, flat shoulder as far off the roadway as possible.

- On the other hand, with **less urgent problems, such as an underinflated tire, a slight shift in a gauge's reading, or a blown fuse,** it's usually okay to continue cautiously to the closest service station.

If I have to pull over, how do I do it safely?

- **Reduce distractions inside your vehicle** by turning off the stereo and asking passengers, especially children, to remain still and quiet.

- **Gradually reduce speed** and **visually check off-road conditions** before choosing where to pull over.

- **Use your turn signal and not your emergency flashers so other drivers will know you need**

to get over. When your emergency flashers are on, your blinkers don't work.

- Check for traffic and, **when it's clear, move smoothly one lane at a time from the roadway to the shoulder.**

- **Avoid soft shoulders, curbs, uneven areas and curves that will prevent other drivers from seeing you.**

- **Don't jerk the wheel or swerve.** That could cause your tires to "catch" on the side of the road.

- **Even though you are off the roadway, remain extra cautious.** Vehicles on the shoulder or median are still at risk for collisions. After you've stopped, turn on your emergency flashers.

How should I get help?

- Once you're safely off the road, **turn on your emergency flashers.**

- **If you don't have a cellular phone or CB radio, place a sign in the window that says "Call Police."** If you don't have a "Call Police" sign, carry a marker and piece of paper so you can make your own. Many store-bought sunshades have a "Call Police" sign on one side.

- In addition, **use a handkerchief or bright piece of clothing to signal for help.** Attach it to the outside of your car where it can be easily seen, like on an antenna or door handle. If this requires you to exit your vehicle, use the door furthest from the road.

Should I stay in my car while waiting for help?

- Yes. **It's best to stay in your car with the windows up and doors locked** — *unless* there is smoke, the threat of an engine or electrical fire or the possibility of ventilation problems. (See Box 11-1, p. 105 for important cautions and warnings about fire or smoke associated with a vehicle.)

- **Be patient**. Help will arrive.

- **Keep your seat belt fastened while waiting,** in case you're struck by another vehicle.

- **If you experience a breakdown in extreme heat**, keep your windows cracked and drink plenty of water. Always carry emergency drinking water in hot weather.

- **Some repairs may require passengers to exit the vehicle.** For example, no one should be in a vehicle when a tire is being changed.

What if a stranger approaches?

- **Be on guard.** DON'T open the doors or windows to communicate. If the person behaves suspiciously, tell them the police are on their way.

- **If you're offered the use of a cellular phone or CB radio, don't accept.** Instead, write down the number you need to call and show it to the person through the window. (Always keep a message pad and pen in your glove compartment.)

- **If it's absolutely necessary or you feel confident, lower your window just enough to speak through it.** Ask them to call or send for help.

Are there any repairs I can make to get myself moving again?

> **There's so much technology in today's vehicles, many repairs can only be made by certified technicians with the proper diagnostic equipment and tools.**

But there are some minor repairs you may be able to make if you have the right tools and materials.

- For example, **you may be able to change a tire, add oil or coolant, replace a fuse or pour water into the radiator.** (Remember to let your engine cool before removing the radiator cap. The hot water in your radiator is under extreme pressure and can cause severe burns. Be patient, it may take more than an hour to cool.)

What if I get a flat tire?

- *Don't panic.* **Firmly grip the wheel and slowly pull off the road as far as possible.** If you're in an unsafe area or on a busy roadway, don't try to change the tire. Drive slowly to a safer place. This may cause damage to your rim, but isn't it better to risk your rim than risk your life?

How to change a tire the right way

1. After pulling off the road and stopping in a safe place, put the car in park and apply the parking (emergency) brake. If your car has a standard transmission, place the gear shift in reverse or first gear. Park on solid, level ground if possible.

2. Retrieve the spare tire, jack and lug wrench. Remove any hub cap with the lug wrench.

3. Before lifting the car with the jack, first loosen each lug nut one turn counterclockwise while the car is still on the ground. The weight of the car will make this easier.

4. Place the jack under the reinforced section of the car's body. The location of these sections is listed in your owner's manual.

5. Jack up the car until the flat tire is several inches off the ground. WARNING: Never place your hands or feet under the vehicle or tire once it has been raised.

6. Remove the lug nuts and remove the wheel.

7. Place the spare tire on the axle and align the holes. Replace the lug nuts and tighten each lightly.

8. Lower the car, and remove the jack. Then use the wrench to firmly tighten each lug nut.

9. Have the flat tire repaired or replaced and reinstalled right away.

How can I jumpstart a battery safely?

To ensure a safe jump, follow these guidelines and review your owner's manual:

A. Position vehicles so jumper cables can reach, but vehicles ARE NOT TOUCHING.

WHEN HOLDING JUMPER CABLES MAKE SURE THE ENDS NEVER TOUCH.

B. Connect one end of the RED cable to the POSITIVE terminal of the dead battery (1). Connect the other end of the RED cable to the POSITIVE terminal of the good battery (2).

C. Connect one end of the BLACK cable to the NEGATIVE terminal of the good battery (3). Connect the other end of the BLACK cable to an engine bolt head or other piece of non-moving metal (4).

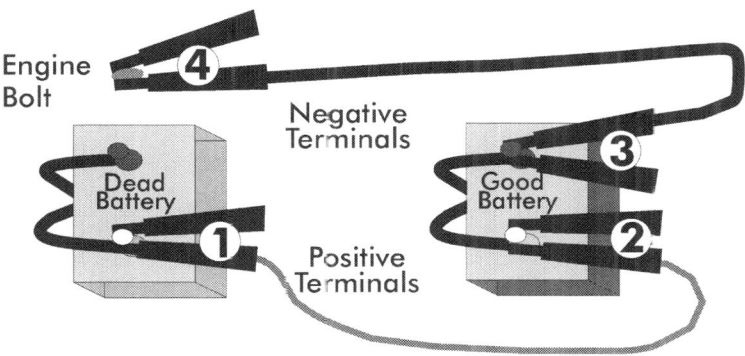

Figure 28-1. Correct Jumper Cable-to-Battery Connections for Jumpstarting a Vehicle.

> **WARNING: ATTACHING THE BLACK CABLE TO THE NEGATIVE TERMINAL OF THE DEAD BATTERY INSTEAD OF AN ENGINE BOLT MAY RESULT IN AN EXPLOSION.**

D. Make sure the jumper cables are away from moving engine parts.

E. Start the engine with the good battery. Run it at moderate speed.

F. Start the engine of the vehicle with the dead battery according to your owner's manual. Once it starts, reduce engine speed to idle.

G. Remove the jumper cables in REVERSE order. First remove the BLACK cable from the engine bolt head or metal connection on the car you jumpstarted.

H. The engine needs to run for at least 30 minutes to start recharging the battery. This can include driving time.

> **Once the car has been jumpstarted, you should have a certified technician test the battery and charging system.**

What can I do to *prevent* a breakdown?

Every time you drive your vehicle, check the following:

- ☑ Tires for proper inflation.
- ☑ Windshield, headlights and taillights should be clean.
- ☑ Survey gauges and warning lights after you have started your car.

As part of *routine maintenance* you should:

- ☑ Check oil level once a week; change the oil every 3,000 miles or as recommended by your owner's manual.
- ☑ Check for oil leaks.
- ☑ Check tires for cuts, nails, stones and proper inflation.
- ☑ Help prevent uneven tire wear; rotate tires every 5,000 to 6,000 miles. Research shows 90% of tire problems occur in the last 10% of a tire's life.
- ☑ Make sure the battery and its terminal are clean and corrosion free.
- ☑ Check the air filter; replace if it's dirty.
- ☑ Check fluid levels for brakes, steering, windshield washer, radiator coolant and automatic transmission.
- ☑ Make sure the exhaust system has no visible leaks or cracks and the tail pipe is not obstructed.
- ☑ Carry only securely stored, non-flammable liquids in the trunk — never gasoline.
- ☑ Before trips, check fluid levels, belts, hoses, and clamps. Refill or replace if necessary.

All procedures should be done in accordance with your owner's manual.

See also: Ch. 9, *Smart Car Care: Tips for Keeping Your Vehicle Safe and on the Road;* Ch. 10, *Know Your Car: The Ten-Minute Check List;* Ch. 11, *The Glove Compartment and Trunk: Keep Them Well Stocked for Safety*

Chapter 29

Road Rage:

How to Avoid It, How to Deal with It

Not like there isn't enough to worry about when we are driving, we now have to cope with **another potentially deadly problem — "Road Rage."**

Anyone who drives on the road these days knows the problem. As you are driving, someone makes an obscene gesture at you, calls you names that are not flattering, questions your parenthood. He may even start tailgating you for long distances, or deliberately cutting you off, or trying to force you off the road. His emotions have gotten the best of him, his anger has boiled over, and he's turned downright aggressive — and ready to risk your life and his. And for what?

What Starts Road Rage?

The American Automobile Association (AAA) indicates that road rage is often started over trivial things — you honked your horn too much, or at all; you took (or wanted to take) a parking space someone else had their eye on. Or maybe you committed the "mortal sin" of slowing someone down, or inadvertently did something that wasn't in the best interest of automotive safety — cut someone off, zigzagged in and out of traffic, or tailgated because *you* were in a hurry — or just not paying attention.

Road Rage often begins with some small gesture

On the other hand, maybe the other driver got behind the wheel *already* enraged by something, and you were just unlucky enough to be on the same road with her at the same time.

> **Whatever the reason, road rage situations can lead to collisions, disputes, even death.**

Who Commits Road Rage?

If you decide to engage a "road rager" in conversation — or worse, decide to play road warrior with him — please understand whom you may be dealing with.

According to the American Automobile Association, **"road ragers" are mostly poorly educated males between the ages of 18 to 26 with criminal records.** They have histories of violence, drug abuse, or alcohol problems, and many have suffered an emotional or professional setback.

Many impatient drivers set themselves up to be victims of road rage. They take risks on the road, which can lead to discourteous driving, which can lead to disputes, which can escalate into road rage.

You may become enraged yourself — "sick and tired" of dealing with aggressive drivers who are "jerks," "idiots," "who don't have all their wagons in a circle," "who have the intelligence quotient of a Styrofoam cup." They can all get you heated up and make you lose your patience, make you do things and take risks you normally wouldn't. They can drag you into their road rage game if you let them. Don't. It can be a *deadly* game.

Things to Do/Don't Do to Avoid or Deal with Road Rage

The general rule is to avoid all conflicts. If another driver wants to get by, let him pass. If she wants a parking space, let her have it. Consider it a contribution to you favorite charity. If another driver challenges you, don't challenge back. Let him go.

Here are some suggestions from the AAA — and then some — on how to avoid and deal with road rage.

- ☑ **DON'T take *traffic problems* personally.** Believe it or not, traffic is not an organized conspiracy to prevent you from being on time.

- ☑ **DO give *yourself* enough time to get where you are going.**

- ☑ **DON'T automatically assume other drivers' *mistakes* are purposely aimed at you.**

- ☑ **If a driver has done something stupid to you — or simply made a mistake, DON'T return the favor.** In other words, don't have a contest to see who is the dumbest — you may just win.

- ☑ **AVOID eye contact with aggressive drivers;** it only encourages them.

- ☑ **If an aggressive driver makes an obscene gesture, DON'T make one or two back at him.** Although it may be incredibly gratifying, it brings you to his level, and can escalate the situation.

- ☑ **If an aggressive driver pursues you, DO find the nearest police station.**

- ☑ **BE CAREFUL about using your horn as a method of communicating** — even a friendly honk can be misinterpreted. **DON'T honk excessively.**

- ☑ **DON'T use high-beam headlights unnecessarily.**

- ☑ **If you drive *slowly*, DO pull over** and let people pass you.

☑ **DON'T block the passing lane** — no matter how fast you are going, there will always be someone who wants to go faster.

☑ **DON'T switch lanes without signaling first.**

☑ **AVOID blocking the right hand turn lane**.

☑ **DON'T tailgate**.

☑ **DON'T take up more than one parking place.**

☑ **DON'T allow your door to hit the car next to you when exiting your car in a parking lot.**

☑ **DON'T inflict your loud music on nearby cars.**

REMEMBER: Always be polite and courteous on the road, even if another driver is acting like an idiot.

Chapter 30

Alone Behind the Wheel[1]

Two violent crimes are committed in the U.S. every minute of every day. Drivers traveling alone can be particularly vulnerable. There are a number of things you can do, however, to keep yourself safe. Both inside your car and out. Read about those things here, then pass the information along to anyone who might be alone behind the wheel.

What should I know about parking safety?

Lots. **Where and how you choose to park can go a long way toward keeping you safer.**

- **When possible, *back into* a parking space.** Should you need to, you'll be able to drive out with less chance of someone trapping you.

- **Try to park close to the building entrance**. This will reduce the time you're alone outside your car.

- **If you know you're going to be working late,** move your car to a well-lighted area closer to the exit. Such a precaution may reduce your risk at night.

---

[1] Copyright Shell Oil Company material reproduced with permission. Written in cooperation with the National Crime Prevention Council and the National Safety Council.

NOTE: Contains general recommendations that we believe to be helpful; however, every emergency is different. The individual driver must decide what to do in any particular case.

- **If you're in a parking lot,** always choose a spot that will be well-lighted and away from shrubs and bushes so you can see under and around your car as you approach it.

Should I do anything special in parking garages?

Yes.

- **Park in a well-lighted spot, ground level if available,** close to the parking attendant station.

- If you can't do that, try to **park close to the elevators or stairwell near the building entrance.**

- **Spend as little time as possible going to and from your car.**

- Try to **stay where you can be seen by others** because there's safety in numbers.

- **If you have any concerns at all,** call the building's security service and have someone accompany you to your car.

If I lock my car before I leave it, is that enough?

No. You should take **additional precautions.**

- **If you have a two-door car,** flip your passenger seat forward when you're leaving your vehicle.

- **If it's a four-door car,** move the driver seat forward.

- **Upon your return,** if you see that it has been returned to its original position, go back to the building you came from immediately and notify security of the police. Someone could be hiding on the back floorboard.

- **As you approach your car,** don't just look around it; look *under* it as well. Criminals sometimes hide there.

I hear a lot about carjackings. Is there any way to avoid them?

The FBI estimates that **approximately 25,000 carjackings occur in the U.S. each year.** There are **defensive techniques** you can use that might keep you from becoming a carjacking victim.

- **Always keep your doors locked.**

- **Always scan ahead and behind as you drive.** Look for individuals who may be loitering near an intersection.

- **If it looks as if you may be driving into a potentially dangerous situation at an upcoming intersection,** slow down and, if you can do so safely, time the light to avoid stopping. Be sure there is no cross traffic that could cause a collision.

- **Try to keep escape routes open.** Stop far enough behind the car in front of you so that you can see its back tires touching the pavement. That way, if you have to pull out quickly, you won't have to back up first. Also, stay in the left-hand land when approaching an intersection.

- **What's that "bump and run" carjacking thing?** It's a technique carjackers often employ. People in one car pull up behind an unsuspecting driver and bump that driver's car. When the driver gets out to inspect the damage, the carjackers forcibly take control of the car and the driver. If you believe that you've been intentionally bumped, don't stop and get out of the car. Drive to a safe, public place close by to check the damage. You'll be a lot less vulnerable.

Got any safety "trip tips"?

- **DO plan your trip before you leave.** Mark your route (how you're going and where you plan to stop) on a map. Give a copy of that plan (with appropriate phone numbers where you can be reached and an estimated time of arrival) to a family member, friend, or business associate.

- **DON'T take maps or other obvious travel aids into rest stops or restaurants.** You don't want to call attention to the fact that you have a long way to travel.

Box 30-1. Your Keychain: Potential Crime Prevention in the Palm of Your Hand

- **Have your keys ready as you approach your vehicle.** Fumbling to find them and unlocking your car takes time and makes you more vulnerable.

- **A small flashlight on your keychain** lets you see your door locks and ignition easier at night. Quicker starts. Quicker getaway.

- **Pepper spray or mace can be attached to your keychain** so you don't have to fumble for it if you ever need it. But be aware that depending on wind direction, spray could blow back in your face. It also could be taken and used against you.

- Sometimes you have to give your keys to others, such as when you valet park. **Keychains that let you easily separate your car keys from your home keys** keep individuals from gaining access to your home.

- **DO check your car out completely before you get on the road.** Many breakdowns are avoidable, especially those involving fuel, oil, cooling or electrical problems.

- **DON'T think just because you have a cellular phone that you won't need to use a public one.** Carry change just in case.

- **DO use valet parking at hotels and restaurants.** It's safer than spending too much time in the parking lots.

- **DON'T try to fix a flat if you think you are in an unsafe area.** Drive slowly to a service station or police station.

Should I always have my door locked when I'm driving?

Yes. All your doors. And you should always have your windows rolled up. If it's hot and you don't have air conditioning, roll your windows down just enough to allow air to flow in, but not enough to allow someone to get his hand in the car.

What do I do if my car just conks out?

- **If your car comes to a stop slowly,** try to pull safely off the road, out of the way of traffic.

- **Stay in your car.**

- **If you have a cell phone, call for help and give them your location.** If you don't have a roadside assistance service, call the police.

- **If you don't have a cell phone, stick a white handkerchief or scarf part way out your**

window. This will alert passers-by that you need assistance.

- **If someone does stop to help you,** stay inside your car with all the doors locked and the windows rolled up high enough so no one can get a hand inside the car. Tell them what kind of help you need. If their concern is genuine, they'll make a call for you or alert someone who can help you at their next stop.

- **Don't get out and raise the hood of your car.** This blocks your view of oncoming traffic (one of whom may be a policeman), and it signals the potential criminal that your car is immobile.

- **You should always carry a "Call Police" window sign in your glove compartment** (or have paper and marker to make one). That way many drivers will see that you need help, and if someone does stop that you are suspicious of, you can tell him that someone saw your sign and has already contacted the police, who are currently en route.

Is Having a phone in the car a good idea?

Yes. But it can be dangerous if not used properly. People using a phone while driving run a 34% higher risk of having a collision.

> **NOTE: Several cities and areas have adopted a "no cell phone use while driving" ordinance.**

- If you must dial, **pull safely off the road, stop, then dial.**

- **Headset or speaker phone units** that allow you to talk and listen without holding a receiver are better, but they can still be dangerous if they pull your attention away from the road.

- If you **preprogram your phone to activate 9-1-1 or other emergency numbers,** you'll be able to react much more quickly in an emergency.

- It's best to **use the phone in the car only as an emergency aid or to let people at your destination know in advance if you are going to be late.** That's better than trying to drive too fast to get there on time.

I seem to get more tired when I drive alone. What can I do about it?

Driver fatigue can be a killer. It's especially dangerous when you are alone. Here are some things you can do to help stay awake:

- **Don't start a trip late in the day**. Get plenty of sleep before you drive.

- **Avoid long drives at night.** The glare of lights outside and from your dashboard increases the chance of highway hypnosis.

- **Adust your car's environment to help you stay awake.** Keep the temperature cool. Don't use cruise control. Keep your body involved in the drive.

- **Use good posture.** Keep your head up, shoulders back, buttocks tucked against the seat back, legs *not* fully extended.

- **Take frequent breaks.** Stop at well-lighted rest areas or service stations, and get out of the car to stretch or have a snack.

- **Avoid alcohol entirely.**

- **Don't allow your eyes to become fatigued.** Wear sunglasses to fight glare during the day.

- **Break the monotony.** Vary your speed levels. Chew gum. Talk to yourself.

- **If you absolutely cannot keep your eyes open,** the best remedy is to **stop and get some sleep.** Staying at a motel for the night is usually the safest bet. If you cannot find a motel, it is still better to be off the road than to fall asleep while driving. If you do pull off the road to take a quick nap, be sure you are *safely* off the road, preferably at a well-lighted, secure rest area, service plaza or truck stop, with all doors locked. If a security guard is present, ask him or her to keep an eye on your car while you're napping.

What if I plan and prepare but someone confronts me anyway?

Your foremost concern should be your personal safety.

- **If you are confronted by a robber or a carjacker, don't resist.** Give up your purse, your wallet and your keys quickly. Do not attempt to reason with a robber. Try to remember what the individual looks like. Remember, possessions can be replaced. Your life can't be.

Chapter 31

If Trapped in Water

The four lifesaving steps described in this chapter are taken from an article, "*Vehicle submersion: A review of the problem, associated risks and survival information,*" which appeared in the scientific publication:. *Aviation, Space, and Environmental Medicine (2013: 84:498.)*

Fact:

- 10% Of all drownings occur in vehicles.
- 400 North Americans will drown in their vehicles this year
- 3 Minutes – The time that a vehicle may float on the surface. But 1 Minute is all the time you really have to exit safely.
- 1minute and the resqme tool can save your life.

Don't Panic. Don't touch your cell phone.
FOLLOW THESE 4 STEPS

1 SEATBELTS: Off or cut

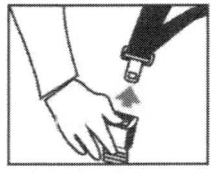
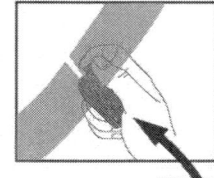

2 WINDOWS:
Open or break

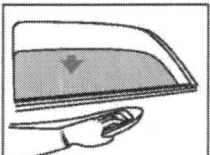

3
CHILDREN:
Undo their
restraints.
Oldest to
youngest.

4 OUT:
Through the window. Children first.

Tips to Avoid Becoming Trapped by Water

- As little as 6 inches of moving water can knock you off your feet or cause you to lose control of your car and just two feet of water can cause a car to be swept off a road or bridge.
- When cars are swept downstream into fast moving water, often the people inside of them drown.
- If you come to a flooded road follow this simple rule: Turn Around, Don't Drown.
- Do not camp or park your vehicles along rivers, streams, or washes, particularly during threatening conditions.
- If flooding occurs, get to higher ground.
- Avoid areas already flooded, especially if the water is flowing fast. Never try to cross a flowing stream.
- Never let your children play near flooded streams, storm drains, roads, rivers or creeks.
- Be especially cautious at night when it is harder to recognize flood dangers.
- Always remember, if you're in doubt, *Turn Around, Don't Drown.*

Special thanks to Dr. Gordon Giesbrecht (University of Manitoba, Canada), Laurent Colasse and Steve Padden.

PART V

RESOURCES

This Part provides an annotated list of selected driving-related websites — some focused exclusively on special driving topics, others broader in focus, but with special-interest forums or sections related to driving or motor vehicles.

You'll find sites with a wealth of driving tips for *everyone* (including new drivers, teenage drivers, older drivers), sites on motor vehicle safety and vehicle crashworthiness, on car maintenance, on buying and selling a car, on RVs, SUVs, even on road safety overseas and driving abroad.

Although far from comprehensive, the list is designed to give you a feel for the broad range of driving-related information available on the Web. Check out the sites, follow their links, type "driver education," "driving techniques," or some specific driving/vehicle-related topic into a search engine or two — and discover the vast resources that await to fill your every driving-information need.

Website Resources

Author's Website

🚗 **Tony Scotti** Offers a wealth of information about both the security industry and driver education. **Website:** SecurityDriver.com

Driving Information Websites

🚗 **Drivers.com** "The world's leading site on drivers and driving." PDE Publications Inc. specializes in driving, driver behavior, and traffic safety, and its website is an information resource for both traffic safety professionals and the general public, with a *wealth* of information on driver training, education, and licensing. Includes special sections for new drivers and older drivers. **Website:** www.drivers.com

🚗 **Seniordrivers.org** (a site of the AAA Foundation for Traffic Safety) Offers tips to help seniors (or any drivers) keep their driving skills sharp. Includes video clips covering some of the trickiest situations drivers might encounter. Also offers information on transportation alternatives for seniors. **Website:** www.seniordrivers.org

🚗 **American Association of Retired Persons (AARP)** Search under "driving" for a *host* of articles on driving-related information and issues and a description of the AARP Driver Safety Program. Many automobile insurers offer discounts to drivers over age 50 who complete the AARP Driver Safety program. The course is the nation's first and largest classroom driver refresher course specially designed for motorists age 50 and older. It is intended to help older drivers improve their skills while teaching them to avoid accidents and traffic violations. The site also offers many safety tips. **Website:** www.aarp.org

🚌 **ABS Educational Alliance** Focuses specifically on anti-lock brakes and driving concerns. Offers a number of educational resources, including online and print brochures on tips for driving with ABS and do's and don't's; driving with intelligent stability and handling systems; ABS videos (viewable online); and ABS curriculum materials for instructors. **Website**: www.abs-education.org

🚌 **U.S. Department of State** Features a section on *Road Safety Overseas* with articles and related links. Covers road safety, road security, international driving permits, tips on driving abroad, auto insurance, treaties on roads and transport, etc. **Website:** travel.state.gov/road_safety.html

🚌 **Enjoy the Drive** "Customize your vehicle for the way you live." This educational consumer website from SEMA (Specialty Equipment Market Association) is about improving vehicles after they have left the factory. For example, custom auto products can help parents make their family vehicle safer; they can help outdoor enthusiasts stow or tow their gear more safely and easily; can help commuters reduce stress and stay more comfortable while on the road, etc. Features a searchable database of accessories, and offers links to the companies that manufacture, sell, and install them. Offers a host of other driving-related features as well. A search for "driving" produces a wealth of driving tips. "Whether you want to learn how to choose the correct tires for your driving purposes, how to tow safely, or how to throw the ultimate tailgate party," this site has the info you need. **Website:** www.enjoythedrive com

🚌 **RV Alliance America (RVAA)** "The RV Insurance Specialist" is committed to seeing safe RVers on the road. Features a wealth of information pertaining to driving an RV (but also applicable to driving in general), including RV driving safety, RV insurance issues, fire and life safety, medical emergencies while traveling, accidents (includes a Medical Information Worksheet for travelers), the unique needs of bus conversion owners (including one woman's perspective on driving a coach), how to share the road with truckers, and much more. **Website:** www.rvaa.com

Vehicle/Highway Safety Websites

Crashes and crashtesting

🚗 **Crashtest.com** Provides international crash-test results, insurance ratings, and auto safety information. **Website:** www.crashtest.com

🚗 **National Crash Analysis Center** is a federally-funded research center concentrating on vehicle crashworthiness research. **Website:** www.ncac.gwu.edu

🚗 **Insurance Institute for Highway Safety (IIHS) and Highway Loss Data Institute (HDLI)** A non-profit research and communications organization funded by auto insurers. A leader on finding out what works and doesn't work to prevent motor vehicle crashes in the first place and reducing injuries in the crashes that still occur. Research focuses on countermeasures aimed at all three factors in motor vehicle crashes (human, vehicular, and environmental), and on interventions that can occur before, during, and after crashes to reduce losses. Find data on crashworthy evaluations, air bags, fatalities and other motor vehicle safety topics. Includes vehicle ratings, educational videos, tips for young and older drivers, and FAQs. **Website:** www.carsafety.org

Vehicle, highway, and traffic safety

🚗 **National Highway Traffic Safety Administration (NHTSA)** NHTSA is responsible for reducing deaths, injuries, and economic losses from motor vehicle crashes. This detailed site offers data on its task of setting and enforcing motor-vehicle safety performance standards, and features an exceptionally broad range of special topic articles focusing on vehicle and equipment information and on traffic safety/occupant issues. (Click on the site's Table of

Contents for the complete list.) **Website:** www.nhtsa.dot.gov

AAA Foundation for Traffic Safety This highly regarded foundation sponsors research that identifies critical traffic safety problems, searches for underlying causes, and advocates possible solutions. The results are posted here. **Website:** www.aaafoundation.org

Advocates for Highway & Auto Safety An alliance of consumer, health, and safety groups, and insurance companies and agents working together to make America's roads safer. Encourages adoption of federal and state laws, policies, and programs that save lives and reduce injuries. Covers safety issues, federal programs, polls and reports, and state-specific issues/programs. **Website:** www.saferoads.org

Department of Transportation, U.S.A. The agency's mandate is broad and its areas of concern are many, but it is a major initiator of highway safety research and a vast repository of data on that topic. **Website:** www.dot.gov

National Safety Council (NSC) The NSC is the nation's leading advocate for safety and health. This non-governmental organization serves as an objective and impartial intermediary by bringing safety and health professionals representing industry and labor together with government, association, and public-interest representatives to form national coalitions on key safety, health, and environmental issues. The NSC library is one of the most complete safety and health information sources anywhere. The site's Driver Safety section features a host of articles and related links. Search "NSC by Topic" - driving. **Website:** www.nsc.org

Federal Highway Administration Provides expertise, resources, and information to continually improve the quality of our nation's highway system and its intermodal connections. Includes news on FHWA programs, highway-related legislation and regulations, and a host of articles on current highway issues. **Website:** www.fhwa.dot.gov

Vehicle-related Websites

Car magazines

Car and Driver Features research tools for automotive buyers and sellers, road tests, photo galleries, and multimedia and radio presentations. **Website:** www.caranddriver.com

Edmunds "Where smart car buyers start" Provides True Market Value (TMV®) pricing, unbiased car reviews, ratings, and expert advice to help you get a fair deal (on new and used cars). Also features online videos, auto loan calculators, ownership/maintenance articles, and much more. **Website:** www.edmund.com

Motor Trend "The World's #1 Automotive Authority" Includes buyer's guide, road tests, special topics, and a host of car care, driving, and equipment checklists, tips, and articles. **Website:** www.motortrend.com

Road & Track Comprehensive automotive reviews, road test and racing news. Includes technical reports, buyer's guide, forums. **Website:** www.roadandtrack.com

Vehicle maintenance

National Institute for Automotive Service Excellence "Certifying the Automotive Professional."The consumer portion of this site is designed to educate consumers about automotive repair. Describes the ASE Blue Seal of Excellence Program and offers a variety of Tips for Motorists (from how to communicate for better automotive service, to choosing the right repair shop or body shop, keeping your vehicle in tune with the environment, preparing your car for the various seasons, etc.). Features a ASE Blue Seal Shop locator, a women's corner, and more. **Website:** www.asecert.org

Tires

🚗 **Tiresafety.com (Bridgestone/Firestone)** Provides information on tire construction, size, and classification, replacement, maintenance, technology, tire terms, safety, and driving tips. You can even sign up for monthly e-mail reminders to check your tire air pressure. **Website:** www.tiresafety.com

🚗 **Rubber Manufacturers Association (RMA)** The national trade association for the rubber products industry. Features a downloadable section on tire maintenance and safety **Website:** www.rma.org

SUVs

🚗 **The SUV Info Link** Launched by Friends of the Earth "so people looking to buy a new vehicle will have all the facts about SUVs." Their interests lie in making SUVs safer and cleaner, in ensuring that perspective vehicle purchasers are educated in their choices, and in encouraging them to make the most environmentally sound decision. Includes descriptions of SUVs, comparisons with passenger cars, environmental concerns, aspects of costs, safety concerns, and other resources. **Website:** www.suv.org

Driver Safety and Security

🚗 **The resqme life-saving tool** allows drivers to safely and effectively evacuate themselves from their vehicle in an emergency. **Website:** www.resqme.com.

🚗 **Sportsfood Technologies Rapid Electrolyte Replacement Strips**, the most effective way for a driver to rehydrate and fight fatigue without consuming fluids. **Website:** www.sportsfood.com.

Index

A

ABS
See anti-lock (ABS) braking system
acceleration
accelerator, stuck, 236
backing up and, 189
breakdown in, 268
cornering and, 154
during ice slide, 256
effects on weight transfer to the tire
        contact patches, 117
G-forces and, 133
handling and, 122
lateral acceleration, 134, 137
maintaining traction in snow and, 251
mode of operation, 111, 113
over-accelerating, 115
oversteer and, 144
passing, 200
power skids and, 128
skids and, 125
tire-to-road grip and, 115
turning at intersections and, 164 - 165
when freeing a car from snow or ice,
        252
worn tires and, 83
accident situations, 225
See also first aid and rescue
accelerator stuck, 236
avoiding, techniques for, 226
blowouts, 234
brake failure, 235
car backing out, 230
car following too closely, 230
car goes into deep water, 237
cars stopped at intersection, 229
entering and merging, 227
hood flies open, 236
motorcyclists, 230
obligation to stop, 240
oncoming car, 227
ongoing or cars ahead, 228
pedestrians and bicyclists, 230
right of way, yielding, 225
skids, 235
someone runs a red light, 234
accidents
See accident situations; accidents,
        motor vehicle
accidents, motor vehicle
See also accident situations; first aid
        and rescue
ABS and, 181
age and, 210

age/gender differences and, 210
alcohol involvement, 211
bicyclists and, 209
causes of, 215
    brake defects, 223
    driver behavior, 221
    tire defects, 223
    vehicle defects, 222
    vision restrictions, 223
cost of, 209
crash types, 213, 218
drivers and, 209
Driving Problem and, 217
Driving System and, 215
excessive speed and, 158
gender and, 210
head-on collisions, 220
miles per hour (mph) vs feet per
        second (fps), 159
obligation to stop, 240
one-vehicle accidents, 148, 220
passenger vehicles , 212
passengers and, 209
pedestrians and, 209
pickups and utility vehicles, 212
prevalence in US, 209
rear-end collisions, 219
side collisions, 218
statistics, 209
two-car collisions, 218
understeer and, 143
vehicle types involved, 211
air bags
curtain air bags, 54
    deployed, 55
    function of, 55
deployment, description of, 53
door-mounted, 56
dust, release of during deployment,
        and irritation, 54
fatalities and, 57
front and passenger-side
    deployed, 52
    location of, 52
function of, 51
manual on-off switches
    obtaining authorization for, 61
    when allowed, 60
precautions to take, 56
    adults, 59
    children, 58
    elderly drivers and passengers, 60
    short adults, 59
rear-facing infant seats and, 58
risk zone, 56
rollovers and, 51

seat-mounted, 56
side air bags, 54
    children and, 55
    deployed, 54
    function of, 55
SIR (Supplemental Inflation Restraint),
    52
SRS (Supplemental Restraint System),
    52
system components, 52
tilt and telescoping steering wheels
    and, 60
air filter, maintenance of, 95
alcohol
accidents, motor vehicle and, 211
effects on driving, 17
alertness
See also fatigue
night driving and, 265
selective vision, sense of space and,
    24
all-weather tires, 64
**American Automobile Association
    (AAA), on road rage, 275 -
    277**
Anco, winter wiper blades, 38
See also windshield wipers
anti-lock (ABS) braking system
brake failure and, 182, 235
brake pedal pressure and, 173
braking on ice, 255
braking skids and, 125
differences from non-ABS, 177
fatal crashes and, 181
four-wheel braking skids and, 127
four-wheel drive braking skids and,
    127
practice braking, tips for, 183
speed and safe stopping distances
    and, 167
anti-reflective coating
See eyewear
apex
description of, 151
early apex phenomenon, 152
aspect ratio, tires
See tires
attention
See alertness
automotive fires, 105

B

backing up, 187
night driving and, 264
techniques for, 188
battery
failure, 91
jumpstarting, procedures for, 272
maintenance of, 95
being passed
give way to right, 204

maintaining steady speed, rules for,
    204
**belts and hoses, maintenance of,
    95**
bicyclists
accident situations and, 230
rules and regulations regarding, 231
sharing the road with, techniques for,
    232
**Bike Florida and Florida's Share the
    Road Campaign, 231**
"black ice", 247
blind spots, 42
blizzard conditions, 253
carbon monoxide poisoning,
    preventing, 253
frostbite and hypothermia, preventing,
    253
blowouts
how to handle, 234
worn tires and, 84
BMW 745i, G-force rating, 132
brake fade
description of, 182
how to deal with, 182
brake failure, 182, 235
description of, 182
how to handle, 182, 235
non-ABS and ABS, 182, 236
brake fluid
maintenance of, 96
brake pedal pressure, 172, 179
brake system, maintenance of, 96
brakes
See also braking; anti-lock (ABS)
    braking system; non-ABS
    braking system
defects, and accidents, 223
function of, 171
maintenance of, 96
braking
See also stopping
ABS braking techniques, 181
backing up and, 189
brake fade, 182
brake failure, 236
brake pedal pressure, 179
    loss of control and, 172
braking distance, 158
braking skids
    four-wheel braking skid, 127
    front-wheel braking skid, 126
    rear-wheel braking skid, 126
breakdowns in, 268
cornering and, 153
cornering skid and, 129
effects on weight transfer to the tire
    contact patches, 118
following distances and, 166
following-distance driving scenario,
    166
fuel economy and, 94
handling and, 122

ice slide and, 255
in front-wheel drive power skids, 128
mode of operation, 111, 113
non-ABS, 178
   "controlled braking" driving
     scenario, 179
   "controlled braking" technique, 179
   hard, excessive braking and, 179
non-ABS vs ABS, 177
on ice, ABS and non-ABS, 255
over-braking, 115
oversteer and, 143
parking brake used in brake failure
   emergency, 182 236
practicing non-ABS and ABS, tips for,
   183
rain and, 248
reaction time and, 29 - 31
science of, 171
skids and, 125

stopping equation, 173
tire-to-road grip and, 115
breakdowns, 267
acceleration problems, 268
brake failure, 182, 268
"car feel" warnings, 267
car overheats, 258
flat tire, changing, 271
getting help, 269
instrument panel warnings, 267
jumpstarting battery, 272
minor repairs, 271
personal safety, 283
   precautions, 269 - 270
preventing, a checklist for, 274
pulling over safely, 268
steering problems, 268
underinflated tire, 268
warning signs, 268
Bridgestone Corporation, and
   winter tire design simulation,
   65

C

Cadillac Escalade, G-force rating,
   132
car ahead
avoiding collision with, 228
following distances, safe, 168
   at night, 169
passing distance, safe, 200
car design
caster and, 187
control limits and, 110
instrument panel lighting and visibility,
   23
tinted glass and visibility, 23
understeer and, 143
visibility and, 23
"car feel"
See also ride; handling

control limits and, 120
warning of problems, 267
car seats
See child safety seats
carbon monoxide poisoning,
   preventing, 253
carjackings, 281
caster
backing up and, 187
turning and, 187
cell phone
for emergencies, 102
use of while driving, 284
centrifugal force, 111, 132
chains, tire, 251
changing lanes
rules for, 4
Chevrolet Corvette, G-force rating,
   132
child safety seats, 45
air bag dangers and, 47
proper installation and fit in car, 48
rear-facing infant seats, cautions, 47
short trips and, 45
types of, 46
   booster seats, 47
   convertible safety seats, 46
   rear-facing infant seats, 46
children in car
child safety checklist, 49
safest place for, 46
   See also child safety seats; seat
     belts
older child, 49
coefficient of friction, in stopping
   equation, 174
cold weather driving
additional emergency supplies for,
   106
tire inflation pressures and, 78
collisions
See accidents, motor vehicle
constant radius corner, 146
   See also corners
control limits
See vehicle control limits
control, loss of
definition, 179
overcontrol and, 221
controlled braking
See braking
coolant
identifying leak, 91
maintenance of, 96
cornering, 145
apex, 152, 154
   "early apex" phenomenon, 152
cornering skid, 129, 155
effects of tire inflation pressure on, 80
front-wheel braking skids and, 126
night driving and, 263
snow tires and, 64
speed and braking and, 153

techniques, 149
  "fast through the corner", 149
  "straightening out the corners", 150
  outside-inside-outside ("taking a
    line"), 151
  outside-inside-outside driving
    scenario, 153
  tire-to-road grip and, 115
cornering skid, 129
corners
  See also cornering; turning
  apex, 151
  big radius vs small radius, diagram,
    150
  science of handling, 148
  types of, 146
    constant radius corner, 146
    decreasing radius corner, 147
    increasing radius corner, 147
crashes
  See accidents, motor vehicle
curves
  See corners; cornering

D

Daimler Benz, 122
decision making
  reaction time and, 32
decreasing radius corner, 147
  See also corners
D-metric tires, 79
  inflation pressure and, 79
driver
  aggressive and unsafe, behaviors of, 1
  Driving System and, 216
  emotional condition, 11
  good driver, definition of, 2
  physical condition, 11
driving at night
  See night driving
Driving Equations
  for figuring out G-force, 133-134
  stopping equation, 173
driving on right, rules for, 4
Driving Problem, 217
driving scenarios
  accelerator stuck, 236
  backing up, 188
  being passed, 204
  bicyclists and pedestrians, 230, 232
  "black ice", 247
  blowouts, 234
  brake failure, 182, 235
  car following too closely, 230
  car goes into deep water, 237
  carjackings, 281
  changing a flat tire, 271
  controlled braking in non-ABS, 179
  cornering skid, 129
  crash scene/first aid Q&As, 239-244
  driving alone Q&As, 279-286
  driving at night, 261

driving in extreme heat, 258
driving in floods/rushing water, 249
driving in fog, 257
driving in lightning, 259
driving in rain, 247
driving in snow, 250
driving on ice, 254
effect of shoulder injury on reaction
  time, 11
emergency ABS braking techniques,
  181
entering and merging, 227
following-distance driving scenario,
  166
four-wheel braking skid, 127
front-wheel braking skid, 126
front-wheel drive power skid, 128
G-forces generated by various driving
  scenarios, 134
hood flies open, 236
hydroplaning, 249
ice slides, 255
jumpstarting a battery, 272
oncoming car, 227
ongoing or cars ahead, 228
outside-inside-outside (cornering)
  technique, 151, 153
overdriving your headlights, 263
oversteer, 140 - 141
passing on the right, 203
passing on three-lane highways, 203
pedestrians and bicyclists, 230, 232
pulling over/breakdown, 268
reaction time/sense of timing, 30
rear-wheel braking skid, 125
rear-wheel drive power skid, 128
road rage, 275
roadside breakdowns Q&As, 267-274
safe passing, 199
safe passing distance, 199
safe passing speeds, 201
signs of fatigue while driving, 13
speed and braking while cornering,
  153
stopping and braking on ice, 255
stuck in snow or ice, 252
three-point turn, 193
time needed to cross an intersection,
  163
time needed to turn at an intersection,
  164
time-distance driving scenario, 161
time-distance-weight driving scenario,
  162
trapped in blizzard conditions, 253
turning left, 185
turning right, 186
two-point left road turn, 192
two-point right road turn, 191
understeer, 140 - 141
u-turns, 190
weight transfer in action, 119
weight transfer to the front, 118

weight transfer to the left or right, 119
weight transfer to the rear 117
wheel spinning in mud, snow, ice, 84
winter driving scenario, 256
yielding the right of way, 225
Driving System, 215
driver, 216
environment, 216
machine (vehicle), 216
drugs
effects on driving, 16
marijuana, 17

E

emergencies
See breakdowns
emergency flashers, 265
signaling for help with, 269
emergency supply kit
additional items for heavy snow areas,
253
cold weather gear, 106
first aid supplies, 106
glove compartment, items to stock
with, 103
trunk, items to stock with, 103
emotional condition of driver
importance of, 11
engine oil
identifying leak, 91
maintenance of, 96
entering and merging, 227
environment, driving
See weather conditions
**escape route, leaving yourself an
"out", 26**
extreme heat, driving in, 258
eyeglasses
See eyewear
eyes
See eyesight
eyesight
See also vision; eyewear
protecting, 19
protecting from glare, 264
eyewear
anti-reflective coating , 22
specifications for driving, general, 21
sunglasses, 22
tints, 22

F

fast through the corner, 149
fatalities
See also accidents, motor vehicle
ABS and, 181
air bag, 57
on road shoulder and median, 267
passenger vehicles and, 212
fatigue
alleviating, 14

driving problems created by, 13
mental, causes of, 12
physical, causes of, 12
reaction time and, 32
seating position and, 14
symptoms of, 13
tunnel vision and, 14
while driving alone, avoiding, 285
**feet per second (fps) vs miles per
hour (mph)**
See miles per hour (mph) vs feet per
second (fps)
field of vision, and night driving, 20
fire extinguishers, 105
automotive fires, cautions in using for,
105
fires, automotive, 105
first aid and rescue, 239
breathing and artificial respiration,
241
concerns about AIDS, 242
evaluating the injured, 241
Good Samaritan laws, 240
if you're in an accident yourself, 244
initial response, 239
moving the injured, 243
severe bleeding, 242
shock, 243
**first aid supplies, to carry for
emergencies , 106**
fish-tailing, 140 - 141
flares, cautions in using, 103
flashers
See emergency flashers
flooding, rushing water, 249
stalls in, 250
fluids
See vehicle fluids
fog, driving in, 257
windshield and, 36
following distances, 166
driving scenario, 166
how to determine how much space
you have, 168
how to determine safe (vehicle/speed
ratio length), 168
night driving and, 169, 263
passing and, 200
specific, for certain vehicles, 170
four-wheel braking skid, 127
four-wheel drive vehicles
braking skids and, 127
freeways
tire inflation pressures for, 78
friction, 111, 171
coefficient of, in stopping equation,
174
rolling, 116, 171
tires, creation of, 63
wheel spinning and, 84
front wheels
locked, 126
oversteer and, 143

understeer and, 141
front-wheel braking skid, 126
front-wheel drive, 254
   power skids and, 128
front-wheel drive power skid, 128
fuel efficiency, 93
   braking and, 94
   drag and, 94
   gasoline evaporation and, 94
   idling and, 93
   speed and, 93
   time of day and, 94
   tire inflation pressure and, 81

G

gas mileage
   See fuel efficiency
gas pedal
   See acceleration
gear-shifting
   during brake failure, 182, 236
   on ice, 255
   when driving on snow, 251
G-force
   car's weight and, 135
   Driving Equation and, 134
   ratings of popular model cars, 132
   sideways G-force, 135
   speed, effects on, 136
G-force ratings, of popular model
     cars, 132
glare
   highway hypnosis and, 285
   protecting eyes from, 264
glove compartment, 101
   what to carry in for emergencies, 103
Good Diver Myth, 1

H

handling
   See vehicle handling
headlights
   See also lights
   bicyclists, and flashing, 233
   flashing, to signal intent to pass at
     night, 199
   fog lights, 258
   high beams
     glare from oncoming cars, avoiding,
      264
     illumination in feet, 169
     road rage and, 277
     use of, 265
   in rain, 248
   low beams
     illumination in feet, 169
     use of at dawn and dusk, 265
     use of in cities and towns, 264
     use of in fog, 257
   maintenance of, 261
   night driving and, 261

running lights, 265
heat set, and windshield wipers, 38
highway hypnosis, 285
horn, use of
   bicyclists and, 233
   road rage and, 277
   to alert oncoming car, 227
   to signal intent to pass, 199
hoses and belts, maintenance of,
     95
hot weather driving
   extreme heat, 258
   tire inflation pressure and, 78
hydroplaning
   all-weather tires and, 249
   defined, 248
   how to avoid, 249
   how to handle, 249
   tire condition and, 249
   worn tread depth and, 84

I

ice
   driving on, 254
   driving scenario, 256
   freeing a car stuck on, 85, 252
   sliding on, recovery from, 255
   stopping distances on, 158
   tire inflation pressure and, 79
ice slide, 255
idling, and fuel efficiency, 93
increasing radius corner, 147
   See also corners
inflation pressure
   See tires, inflation pressure
instrument panel, 267
   glare from, and highway hypnosis,
     285
   lighting and visibility, 23
intersections
   accident situations, 231
   backing up and, 188
   bicyclists and pedestrians in, 233
   car stopped at, avoiding collision with,
     229
   dangerous situation and personal
     safety, 281
   passing and, 196
   time needed to cross, 163
   time needed to turn at, 164
   turning at, rules for, 4
   with and without traffic lights,
     precautions, 234

J

jumper cables
   cautions in using, 104
jumpstarting a battery, 272

L

lateral acceleration
Driving Equation and, 134
speed and, 137
left-side mirror, adjusting, 41
lightning, driving in, 259
lights
See also emergency flashers;
headlights
maintenance of, 97
locked wheels
front, 126
front and rear, 127
rear, 126
low gear
for emergency braking during brake
failure, 182, 236
for emergency braking in snow, 251
to stop on ice, cautions against, 255

M

mace, pepper spray, 282
marijuana
"perceptual failure" and, 17
reaction time and, 17
medications
effects on driving, 16
mental fatigue
See fatigue
**miles per hour (mph) vs feet per
second (fps), 158**
easy conversion method, 160
formula for converting, 159
speed (mph)-distance (fps) table, 159
mind/body driving connection, 11
mirrors, 39
adjusting, 40
importance of, 40
rain and, 248
right-side, 39
sense of space and, 26
side mirrors
using when turning left, 186 - 187
using to avoid accidents, 226
modes of operation, 111
momentum, 111
motor vehicle accidents
See accidents, motor vehicle
mud, freeing a car stuck in, 85
myths
Good Driver, 1
Tired Eyes, 24

N

National Bureau of Standards, 84
**National Highway Traffic Safety
Administration (NHTSA)**
passenger air bag cut-off switches and,
60

windshield visibility standards and, 35
National Safety Council, 158
neutral steer, 140
**Newton's Laws of Motion, applied
to driving, 131, 148**
night driving, 261
alertness and, 265
field of vision and, 20
following distances and, 169, 263
headlights and, 261
overdriving your headlights, 263
peripheral vision and, 20
protecting eyes from glare, 264
speed, adjusting for, 262
windshield and mirrors and, 262
windshield condition and, 38
your vehicle's visibility and, 265
night vision
adapting to, 20
prolonged exposure to glare and, 21
stopping distances and, 169
non-ABS braking system
See also braking
brake pedal pressure, 173
braking on ice, 255
four-wheel braking skid and, 127

O

oncoming car
avoiding head-on collision with, 227
headlight glare from, dealing with,
264
passing and, 197 - 198
**outside-inside-outside cornering
technique, 151**
driving scenario, 153
overheating engine, 258
oversteer, 139
causes of, 142
description of, 140
diagram of, 140
overcoming, 143
physical dynamics of, 141
over-the-counter medications
See medications

P

parking
personal safety and, 279 - 280
road rage and, 278
**parking brake, used in emergency
braking situations, 182, 236**
passing, 195
See also being passed
bicyclists, 233 - 234
distances, safe, 199
following distance, 200
how to pass safely, 199
on left, rules for, 4
on right, rules for, 4, 203
on three-lane highways, 203

passing speeds, safe, 201
   techniques for, 199
   when not to pass, 195
   when to pass, 196
pedestrians
   accident situations and, 230
   rules and regulations regarding, 231
   sharing the road with, techniques for,
     232
pepper spray, mace, 282
**perceptual failure, and marijuana.
   17**
**peripheral vision, and night driving,
   20**
personal safety, 279
   carjackings and, 281
   cell phone and, 283 - 284
   confrontations and, 286
   fatigue and, 285
   keychain add-ons for safety, 282
   locking doors, 280, 283
   parking garages and, 280
   parking lots and, 279
   trip tips for, 282
   vehicle breakdowns and, 283
physical condition of driver
   importance of, 11
physical fatigue
   See fatigue
power (acceleration) skids, 128
power steering fluid
   identifying leak, 91
   maintenance of, 97
prescription medication
   See medications

R

radius, 134, 147, 150
rage
   See road rage
rain
   "black ice" and, 247
   driving in, 247
   hydroplaning and, 248
   rushing water and flooding, 249
   stopping distances in, 158
   See also wet roads
reaction time
   decision making and, 32
   definition of, 29
   driving experience and, 29
   example of, 30
   factors that affect, 30
   fatigue and, 32
   illness and, 32
   improvement through training. 34
   marijuana and, 17
   normal, 32
   over-dependence on, 33
   reflexes and decision making, 31
   stopping distances and, 32
   time of day and, 32

rear wheels
   as rudder, 126
   locked, 126
   oversteer and, 141, 144
rearview mirror
   See also mirrors
   adjusting, 41
rear-wheel braking skid, 126
rear-wheel drive power skid, 128
**reflecting tape, for visibility at
   night, 265**
resqme tool, 287
ride
   See vehicle ride
right of way
   accident situations, 231
   yielding, 5, 225
     to bicyclists, 233
right-side mirror, adjusting, 40
road conditions
   See also snow; rain; ice; wet roads;
     slippery roads
   "black ice", 247
   differences in, dangers of, 257
   slippery, and stopping equation, 175

   stopping distances and, 158
road rage, 275
   causes of, 275
   characteristics of "road rager", 276
road, rules of, 2
rolling contact
   See tire adhesion, rolling contact
rolling friction, 171
rollovers
   accident statistics, 213
   air bags and, 51
   curtain air bags and, 56
   seat belts and, 44
   statistics, 214
rules of the road, 2
   early, 2
   modern, 3

S

seat belts
   See also child safety seats
   children, when appropriate for, 46
   if you're waiting in car at roadside,
     270
   if car goes into deep water, procedure,
     237
   importance of, 43
   proper way to wear, 44
   rollovers and, 44
seating position, proper, 14
   arm position, 15
   distance from steering wheel, 16
   hand placement, 15
   shoulders, 14
selective vision
   See also vision

looking far enough ahead, 24
what to look for, 25
sense of space
See space, sense of
shock absorbers, maintenance of, 97
side air bags
See air bags
side-impact collisions
curtain air bags and, 56
side air bags and, 55
sideview mirrors
See also mirrors
adjusting, left-side, 41
adjusting, right-side, 40
convex, and distortion, 40
right-side, 39
sidewall codes, tire
See tires
signaling, 4
turning, rules for, 185
when making a two-point turn, left road turn, 193
when making a U-turn, 191
when passing, 199
when pulling over, breakdown, 268
when turning right, 186
single-car accidents, 220
SIR (Supplemental Inflation Restraint)
See air bags
skids
braking skids, 125
ABS brakes and, 125
four-wheel braking skid, 127
front-wheel braking skid, 126
rear-wheel braking skid, 126
cornering skid, 129, 155
power (acceleration) skids, 128
front-wheel drive power skid, 128
rear-wheel drive power skid, 128
slippery roads, 257
smoking, effects on windshield, 36
snow
blizzard conditions, dealing with, 253
boots and pedal operation, 250
clearing from windows and mirrors, 250
cold weather gear supplies, 106
driving in, 250
driving scenario, 256
freeing a car stuck in, 85, 252
maintaining traction on, 251
snow emergency regulations, 66
snow tires, 75
stopping distances in, 158
tire inflation pressure and, 79
snow emergency regulations, 66
Society of Automotive Engineers, 143
space, sense of, 19, 24
following distances and, 166
night driving and, 263

traffic situations and, 26, 166
spare tire, 74, 77, 103
speed
cornering and, 153
effects on G-force, 136
fuel efficiency and, 93
lateral acceleration and, 137
miles per hour vs feet per second, 158
night driving, adjusting for, 262
rain and, 248
safe passing, 201
safe stopping distances and, 157
stopping equation and, 174
tire wear and, 85
varying to avoid fatigue, 286
speed limits, observing, 5
speedometer, limitations of
driving in fog and, 257
mph vs fps, 159
wheel spinning speed and, 85
SRS (Supplemental Restraint System)
See air bags
steering
See also neutral steer; understeer; oversteer
at speed, and G-force, 136
backing up and, 189
breakdowns in, 268
cornering and, 148
front-wheel braking skids and, 126
G-force and, 131, 133
handling and, 122
ice slide and, 255
over-steering, 115
skids and, 125
tire-to-road grip and, 115
turning and weight transfer to the tire contact patches, 119
steering wheel
See also steering; turning; turns
function of, 116
hand position on, 15
seating position, distance from, 16
tilt and telescoping, and air bags, 60
stopping
See also braking; stopping distances; stopping time; stopping equation
on ice, 255
time-distance relationship and, 157
stopping distances
on ice and snow, 255
reaction time and, 32
speed and, 157
time needed to cross an intersection, 163
time needed to make a right-hand turn at an intersection, 164
time-distance driving scenario, 161
stopping equation, 173
stopping time
See also braking; following distances; stopping distances; stopping

dry vs wet surfaces, 157
effects of road condition and speed
    (table), 158
speed and, 157
time needed to cross an intersection,
    163
time needed to make a right-hand
    turn at an intersection, 164
time-distance driving scenario, 161
time-distance-weight driving scenario,
    162
"straightening out the corners', 150
stuck accelerator, 236
sunglasses
    See eyewear

T

tailgating
    cause of accidents, 221
    over-dependence on reaction time
        and, 33
    safe passing distances and, 200
"taking a line," cornering technique,
    151
three-point turn, 193
    See also turning
tilt and telescoping steering wheels,
    and air bags, 60
time needed
    to cross an intersection, 163
    to stop
        See stopping distances
    to turn at an intersection, 164
time of day, reaction time and, 32,
    261
time-distance driving scenario, 161
time-distance relationship in
    stopping and turning, 157
    See also speed; stopping; stopping
        distances
time-distance-weight driving
    scenario, 162
tinted glass, windshield and
    windows, 23
tints, eyewear, 22
tire adhesion
    balanced G-force and, 141
    function of, 171
    G-force and, 138
    interrelationship between accelerating,
        steering, and braking, 120
    limit of adhesion, 113, 119
    oversteer and, 141
    rolling contact and, 116
    tire contact patches and, 113 - 114
        maximum capability to perform a
            given action, 115
    understeer and, 141
    weight transfer and
        diagram of, 118
        driving scenario, 119
        effects of acceleration on, 117

effects of braking on, 118
effects of turning on, 119
tire contact patches and, 117
to the front, 118
to the left or right, 119
to the rear, 117
tire chains, 66, 251
tire contact patches, 139
    See also tire adhesion
    front-wheel braking skids and, 126
    G-force and, 141
    tire adhesion (tire-to-road grip), 113
Tire Industry Safety Council, 84
tire inflation pressure
    checking, 79
    cold/hot weather driving and, 78
    determined by auto maker, 78
    D-metric tires, 79
    effects on car's ability to bear weight
        transfer, 81
    effects on cornering, 80
    effects on fuel consumption, 81
    effects on tire/rim assembly, 80
    effects on wear and longevity, 81
    freeway or expressway driving and, 78
    maintenance checklist, 87
    maintenance of, 97
    maximum, 68
    overinflation, signs of, 83
    perils of improper, 80
    tire durability and, 81
    tire pressure gauges, 80
    underinflation, signs of, 82
        See also underinflated tire
    understeer and oversteer and, 142
Tired Eyes Myth, 24
tires
    abuse of, 84
        driving habits and, 86
        driving speed and, 85
        temperature and temperature
            changes and, 86
        wheel spinning and, 84
    all-weather, 64, 249
    aspect ratio, 68
    blowouts, 234
    chains, 66, 251
    construction type, 68
    flat tire, procedures for changing, 271
    four-wheel drive vehicles and, 75
    freeing a car stuck in mud, snow, or
        ice, 85
    hydroplaning and, 249
    identification or serial number, 69, 74
    inflation pressure, 77
        See also tire inflation pressure
    load, maximum, 68
    longevity, and type, 68
    maintenance checklist, 87
    manufacturing date, code for, 69
    manufacturing plant, code for, 69
    matching, mismatched, 74
        understeer and oversteer and, 142

mounting, do's and don't's, 74
placard, location of, 77
purpose of, 63
radials, 68, 74, 81
replacement selection, 72
   size and construction, 73
   speed rating, 73
rotation of, 83, 98
   maintenance checklist, 87
sidewall codes, 66 - 67
   lite truck tire, 71
   passenger car tire, 67
snow tires, 64, 75
   cornering and, 64
   studded, 66, 75
spare tire, 74, 77, 103
speed rating, 68, 73
temperature grades, 71
tire contact patches, 139
tire failure, 84
traction grades, 70
tread
   depth, 83 - 84
   design, 63
   design simulation, 65
   maintenance checklist, 87, 98
   treadwear index, 69
US DOT safety compliance
   certification, 69
wheel alignment, maintenance
   checklist, 87
wheel spinning
   effects of and tire failure, 84
   reasons for staying stuck, 85
   speedometer speed and, 85
worn, 83 - 84
   understeer and oversteer and, 142
tire-to-road grip
   See tire adhesion
traction
   maintaining on snow, 251
   See also tire adhesion; skids
traffic situations
   sense of space and, 26
transmission fluid
   identifying leak, 91
   maintenance checklist, 99
trapped in water, 287
treadwear index, 69
Trico, Winterblades, 39
   See also windshield wipers
trunk, what to carry in for
   emergencies, 103
tunnel vision, and fatigue, 14
turning
   See also turns; corners; cornering
   around, 189
      three-point turn, 193
      two-point turns, 191
         left road turn, 192
         right road turn, 191
      U-turns, 190

at intersections, procedures for, 4
G-forces and, 133
mode of operation, 111, 113
night driving and, 263
skids and, 125
techniques for
   turning left, 185
   turning right, 186
time needed
   to make a left-hand turn, 165
   to make a right-hand turn, 164
turns
   See turning
two-car collisions, 218
two-point turns, 191
   See also turning

U

underinflated tire, 79-82, 87, 268
   See also tire inflation pressure
understeer, 139
   accident rates and, 143
   causes of, 142 - 143
   description of, 140
   diagram of, 140
   overcoming, 143
   physical dynamics of, 141
US Department of Transportation
   (DOT)
   accident statistics, motor vehicle, 209
   Fatality Analysis Reporting System
      (FRS), 209
   tire identification or serial number
      and, 69
   tire safety compliance certification
      and, 69
   tire sidewall information and, 66
U-turns, 190
   See also turning
   two-point turns, as alternative for, 191

V

vehicle control
   loss of, types, 109
vehicle control limits, 110
   "car feel" and, 120
   G-force and, 132
vehicle defects, and accidents, 222
vehicle design
   See car design
vehicle dynamics
   introduction to, 109
   Newton's Laws applied to, 131
   steering and G-force, 131
   winter driving scenario, 256
vehicle fluids, 90 - 91
   brake fluid, 96
   coolant, 91, 96
   engine oil, 91
   power steering fluid, 91

transmission fluid, 91, 99
washer fluid, 92, 99
vehicle handling qualities, 122
vehicle maintenance
    air filter, 95
    battery, 95
    belts and hoses, 95
    brake fluid, 96
    brake system, 96
    breakdown prevention checklist, 274
    coolant/antifreeze, 96
    engine oil, 96
    fluid leaks, identifying types of, 91
    lights, 97
    power steering fluid, 97
    shock absorbers, 97
    tire pressure, 97
    tire rotation, 98
    tire tread, 98
    transmission fluid, 99
    washer fluid, 99
    wheel alignment, 98
    wiper blades, 99
**vehicle performance, maximum
    available, 115**
vehicle ride
    definition of, 121
    hard vs soft, 121
visibility
    car design and, 23
    fog and, 257
    instrument panel lights and, 23
    of *your* vehicle at night, 265
    tinted glass and, 23
    windshield and, 35
    windshield condition and, 38
vision
    See also eyesight; selective vision
    eyewear specifications for driving, 21
    night driving, eye movement, 263
    night vision, 20
    prolonged exposure to glare and, 21
    protecting and enhancing, 19, 21
    restrictions, and accidents, 223
    seeing at night, 20

W

weather conditions, driving in, 247
    blizzards, 253
    extreme heat, 258
    fog, 257
    ice, 254
    lightning, 259
    rain, 247
    snow, 250
    wet roads, 257
weight of car, and G-force, 135
weight transfer
    See also tire adhesion; weight transfer
    tire inflation pressure and, 81
wet roads
    See weather conditions, driving in

**wheel alignment, maintenance of,
    98**
wheel spinning
    avoiding, in snow, 251
    reasons for staying stuck, 85, 252
    speedometer speed and, 85
    tire abuse and, 84
windshield
    fog and grime, 36
    NHTSA and visibility standards for, 35
    night driving and, 38
    smoking and, 36
    visibility and, 35
windshield wipers, 37
    heat set and, 38
    maintaining, procedures for, 38
    maintenance checklist, 99
    winter blades, 38
winter driving scenario, 256
wipers
    See windshield wipers
worn tires
    blowouts and, 84
    hydroplaning due to, 84
    illegal, 84
    susceptible to puncture, 84

Y

yielding right of way
    See right of way

16259320R00190

Made in the USA
Middletown, DE
11 December 2014

ROCK ART ALONG THE WAY

ROCK ART
ALONG THE WAY

JANET WEBB FARNSWORTH

Photographs by **BERNADETTE HEATH**

RIO NUEVO PUBLISHERS
TUCSON, ARIZONA

Rio Nuevo Publishers®
P.O. Box 5250, Tucson, Arizona 85703-0250
520-623-9558, www.rionuevo.com

Library of Congress Cataloging-in-Publication Data

Farnsworth, Janet Webb.
Rock art along the way / Janet Webb Farnsworth ; photography by Bernadette Heath.
    p. cm.
Includes bibliographical references and index.
ISBN-13: 978-1-887896-79-5 (pbk.)
ISBN-10: 1-887896-79-1 (pbk.)
1. Indians of North America—Southwest, New—Antiquities—Guidebooks. 2. Cave
paintings—Southwest, New—Guidebooks. 3. Rock paintings—Southwest, New—
Guidebooks. 4. Petroglyphs—Southwest, New—Guidebooks. 5. Southwest, New—
Antiquities—Guidebooks. I. Title.
E78.S7.F36 2005
709.01'130979—dc22
                              2005028148

Design: Karen Schober, Seattle, Washington

Pictured on front cover, Sears Point, AZ (main photo); back cover, Valley of Fire State Park,
NV (top), and Baby Jesus Ridge, AZ, Puerco Pueblo, AZ, and Little Petroglyph Canyon, CA
(bottom, left to right); p. 1, Ayers Rock , CA; pp. 2-3, Temple Mountain Wash, UT; p. 6,
Cañon Pintado National Historic District, CO; p. 7, Petroglyph National Monument, NM,
and El Morro National Monument, NM.

Printed in Korea.

10 9 8 7 6 5 4 3 2 1

ACKNOWLEDGMENTS

A big thank-you goes to my wonderful husband, Richard. Living with
a writer is not an easy task, and he has endured it with ultimate patience. Thank you
to my six children, the inspiration for this book. To preserve our sanity and make sure you did
no bodily harm to each other, your father and I stopped often to let you roam and explore. I
love you. My appreciation goes to museums, guides, travel departments, BLM officials, and all
those who aided in the research that helped make this book possible. My deep appreciation go
to Lisa Cooper and the rest of the staff of Rio Nuevo Publishers who questioned,
edited, and suggested until my thoughts and words merged into something
readable. My last thanks go to photographer Bernadette Heath.
Her beautiful photos bring rock art to life. Her friendship
and humor made the effort fun.

—JWF

Not being a native of the Southwest, I am truly grateful to
my friend and neighbor Mina Brooks, who sparked my interest 25 years ago in the
Hohokam Indians. Thanks to photographer Jonathan Kerry of London, England, who knows
more about our Southwest rock art than most, for his research and interest in this project.
To my husband, Bill, who always managed to "find the ruin/monument/rock art"—I thank
you from the bottom of my heart. When our three children were teens, our family vacations
were spent visiting every known ruin in the Four Corners states—and now they grant
me the privilege of taking my grandchildren. And to all the people who willingly
and enthusiastically helped Janet and me so we wouldn't
get lost "along the way," thank you.

—BH

CONTENTS

Introduction 9

Arizona Rock Art Sites 15

Painted Cave • Kanab Creek Wilderness Area • Keyhole Sink • Rock Art Ranch • Palatki • Honanki • V-Bar-V Ranch Petroglyph Site • Puerco Pueblo • Homolovi Ruins State Park • Lyman Lake State Park • Polimana • K5 High Country Adventures • Sipe White Mountain Wildlife Area • Blue River • Hieroglyphic Point • Hieroglyphic Canyon • Deer Valley Rock Art Center • White Tank Mountain Regional Park • Painted Rocks Petroglyph Site • Bouse Fisherman (*also known as Fisherman Intaglio*) • Antelope Hill • Sears Point • Baby Jesus Ridge • Signal Hill

California Rock Art Sites (Southeastern California) 61

Bishop Petroglyph Loop • Ayers Rock • Little Petroglyph Canyon • Sheep Springs • Steam Wells Petroglyph Site • Blythe Intaglios

Colorado Rock Art Sites (Western Colorado) 75

Cañon Pintado National Historic District • Dragon Road Sites • Deer Creek • McDonald Creek Cultural Resource Area • Ute Mountain Tribal Park

Nevada Rock Art Sites (Southern Nevada) 87

Red Rock Canyon National Conservation Area • Valley of Fire State Park • Grapevine Canyon • Topock Gorge

New Mexico Rock Art Sites 95

Waterflow • Crow Canyon • Bandelier National Monument • Tsankawi Loop Trail • La Cieneguilla • Petroglyph National Monument • Tomé Hill • El Morro National Monument • Three Rivers Petroglyph Site • Gila Cliff Dwellings National Monument

Utah Rock Art Sites 115

Nine Mile Canyon • Sego Canyon (*also known as Thompson Wash Site*) • Temple Mountain Wash • Great Gallery, Horseshoe Canyon • Moab Rock Art Tour Golf Course Site • Kane Creek Boulevard Sites • Courthouse Wash Site • Potash Road Sites • Wolfe Ranch, Arches National Park • Cave Spring • Newspaper Rock State Historical Monument • Parowan Gap • Rochester Rock Art Panel (*also known as Rochester Creek Site*) • Fremont Indian State Park • Sand Island Recreation Area • Wolfman Site

Other Sites to Visit 146

Glossary 149

Suggested Reading 151

Index 152

Grapevine Canyon, Nevada

INTRODUCTION

I've been intrigued by rock art for as long as I can remember. As a girl, I climbed to petroglyphs near my home in Snowflake, Arizona, and wondered who made them, how old they were, and perhaps the greatest mystery of all, what they might mean.

I assumed that archaeologists must surely know these answers, but as I grew older I learned that, although they can sometimes tell the culture and estimate a date, the meaning of rock art is a mystery to them, too. Looking at these figures carefully made on stone is like cloud-watching. Each individual viewing them imagines something different. Present-day tribal members have attempted to associate the glyphs with their cultural stories, and this is probably as close as we come to actual meanings. In large part, though, your guess is as good as the next person's, so put your imagination to work and let your thoughts fly free.

This book is not a scientific explanation of rock art or its meaning. It is designed for people, especially those with small children, who want to stop along the way, enjoy rock art, and make their own interpretations. All places listed are open to the public, although some require going with a guide or group. A variety of sites are presented, from wheelchair-accessible to real "adventures" that require prior arrangements. From traveling with my own six children, I've learned that kids like to search for certain images on a panel. I've posed many "Can you find?" or "Do you see?" questions that will have even adults searching the glyphs. Since rock art meanings are so varied, I have taken liberties in describing the figures in a way that children can identify the motifs. I mean no disrespect by my descriptions, but encourage everyone to enjoy the mystery and beauty of these sites, to make their own interpretations, and, above all, not to damage them.

Different Cultures

Over thousands of years, different tribes and peoples have occupied the Southwest. They left proof of their inhabitation and clues to their cultures in rock art. Some cultures had subcultures, and cultures often overlapped, so a site might contain rock art images from different dates and different cultures. Experts disagree on the exact time periods for the cultures, so these dates are approximate.

Ancestral Puebloan These ancient people inhabited the Four Corners region of Arizona, New Mexico, Utah, and Colorado, along with a few sites in southeastern Nevada, from approximately 400 B.C. to A.D. 1300. Other sources give dates of A.D. 1 to 1450. Navajo guides for early archaeologists and anthropologists called this culture the "Anasazi"—a word that translates to "ancient ones" or "enemies of our ancestors." Present-day Hopis object to the name Anasazi and prefer "Hisat'sinom," meaning "long-ago people." Most Pueblo peoples and anthropologists now use the term Ancestral Puebloan to describe this culture.

Why the Ancestral Puebloans began leaving the Southwest around A.D. 1250 is a mystery. Abandoning their pueblos, they left behind many of their belongings. The most popular theory is that a severe drought made food scarce. Other suppositions include overuse of natural resources, overpopulation, religious differences, and warfare.

Another mystery is where the Ancestral Puebloans went. Some experts think they simply died out from lack of food or were killed off. The Hopi people strongly believe they are the direct descendants of the Ancestral Puebloans. Ceramic and art styles suggest the early peoples consolidated into villages near the Hopi and Zuni pueblos as well as along the upper Little Colorado River and the Rio Grande valley.

Archaic The people of this desert culture lived throughout the Southwest from 5500 B.C. to A.D. 100. A hunting and gathering society.

Fremont This group occupied the top three-quarters of Utah and a small portion of western Colorado. Exact occupational dates are controversial, but most experts estimate A.D. 500 to 1300. The Fremont Culture began to disappear about the same time (A.D. 1250) as the Ancestral Puebloans. It is not clear who are their descendants.

Hohokam These ancient farmers lived along the river valleys and the deserts of south-central Arizona between 300 B.C. and A.D. 1450. Their artifacts, ball courts, and architectural styles suggest they migrated north from Mesoamerica. Many Hohokam villages developed extensive irrigation systems. It is not known what happened to the Hohokam people, but it is possible that some tribes of southern Arizona are their descendants.

Mogollon Living in southern New Mexico, southeastern Arizona, western Texas, and northern Mexico, the complex and diverse Mogollon (pronounced "muggy-OWN") culture fell into two groups: the Mountain Mogollon and the Desert Mogollon. Occupation dates vary by location, covering approximately A.D. 1 to 1500. Rock art styles include Mogollon Red, Jornada, Great Basin Abstract, and Reserve Petroglyph style.

Navajo Their arrival date in the Four Corners area is uncertain, but it was certainly before A.D. 1500. Navajo rock art discussed in this book covers the period from 1640 to 1868.

Paleo-Indian This cultural group dated from about 10,000 to 5500 B.C. The few rock art images remaining from this period are particularly difficult to date.

Ute Ute people still live in their traditional lands of Utah, Colorado, and far northern portions of Arizona and New Mexico. Historic Ute period rock art dates from A.D. 1600 to 1880.

*Wolfman Site, Utah
(petroglyph)*

Types of Rock Art

Rock art falls into four basic categories, based on how they are made. Petroglyphs are by far the most common, with pictographs second. Geoglyphs are mostly found in desert areas, but the rarest type is pictoglyphs. There are only nine known pictoglyphs in all of Utah, seven of them in Fremont Indian State Park.

Petroglyphs Images carved, pecked, and/or abraded into rock.

Pictographs Designs or images painted onto rock.

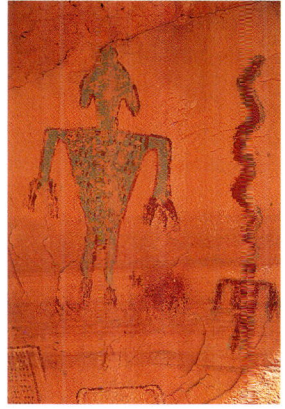

*Painted Cave, Arizona
(pictograph)*

Fremont Indian State Park, Utah (pictoglyph)

Pictoglyphs Figures or designs on rocks that incorporate both carving and painting techniques.

Geoglyphs Also called *intaglios* or *earth glyphs*. Images, usually very large, made by scraping away surface material on the desert floor. Most of these designs are so large they must be viewed from the air.

Bouse Fisherman, Arizona (geoglyph)

Methods of Dating

Rock art is extremely hard to date. It is hoped that a future method will allow researchers to pinpoint more exact dates of creation, but at the present, the following methods are used.

Repatination Once the natural patina of the rock surface, also called desert varnish, is chipped away, a new patina starts to slowly form again over the glyph. In a panel of petroglyphs, in general the fresher-looking glyphs are the youngest, while the darker the glyph, the older it is. This can be misleading, though. Occasionally, some glyphs appear younger and brighter because they are better protected from weathering.

Association with datable habitation sites If a nearby village can be dated by radiocarbon dating, tree-ring analysis of wooden beams, or by pottery style, it is possible some of the nearby rock art is from that time period, too.

Patterns If the rock art image is similar to a motif on pottery or textiles, it may be from the same time period. Also, rock art from different cultures had distinct designs, and this helps define not only the culture, but also the age.

Known dates By knowing the date that a culture first used bows and arrows or that horses were re-introduced in the Southwest, glyphs showing these features are easily dated.

Superimposition Newer glyphs are carved on top of older glyphs.

Rock Art Manners

Although rock art may have endured for thousands of years, it is still fragile. Nature's natural weathering is destroying these images fast enough. We do not need to add to the damage.

Do not:

- Touch (oil from hands can damage glyphs.)
- Walk on or slide down rocks that have rock art.
- Build fires within a quarter mile.
- Move the rocks or disturb the site in any way.
- Add your own graffiti.
- Visit sites on private land without permission.
- Shoot at glyphs.
- Make latex molds.
- Outline the designs in chalk.
- Put yourself in danger by climbing high cliffs.
- Pick up pottery or other artifacts. This is against the law, and strict penalties and fines apply.

Do:

- Check to make sure public access is allowed on government land. Some sites are so fragile, they are completely off limits.
- Stay on trails.
- Be prepared for back-country travel.
- Respect "no trespassing" signs.
- Report vandalism.

Back Roads Manners

In the back country of the Southwest, the rule is leave the gate the way you found it. If the gate was shut before you went through it, close it again behind you. If it was open, then leave it open. This rule comes from cattlemen. Shutting the gate keeps cattle from roaming, but if you shut a gate that was purposely left open, you might prevent cattle from reaching a waterhole.

Saguaro National Park, Arizona

ARIZONA ROCK ART SITES

PAINTED CAVE

location: *far northeast Arizona (Navajo Nation)*
reservations required
directions: *Contact Will Tsosie, Coyote Pass Hospitality Bed and Breakfast (in Tsaile), 928-724-3383 or 928-787-2295. E-mail: coyotepass@excite.com, www.navajocentral.com. Tsosie's tours include visiting silversmiths, rug weavers, archaeology sites, and other Navajo cultural tours. You can even sleep in a hogan.*

Painted Cave is on the Navajo Nation, so you can't visit it without a Navajo guide. Will Tsosie, owner of the Coyote Pass Hospitality Bed and Breakfast, drives us on a sandy dirt road to a red cliff north of Canyon de Chelly. The hike up the talus slope is quite steep, but the climb is worth it. Near the top, a sandstone overhang shelters the remnants of an Ancestral Puebloan (Anasazi) site. The ruin is interesting, but the real treasure is the hundreds of pictographs painted on the back wall of the cave.

Painted Cave contains one of the greatest concentrations of picto–graphs on the Navajo Nation. Our attention is drawn first to the handprints—hundreds of them—painted in turquoise-green, yellow, red, white, and black, all still amazingly colorful. All the handprints are vertical and one pair of hands has six fingers.

The images extend for hundreds of feet and include large figures of long-forgotten religious significance. Multicolored, the human-like figures stand up

to 5 feet tall. Many are painted turquoise, then outlined in red. One figure is white with a red outline and wears a horned headdress. Most of the figures are square-shouldered. Painted among the handprints and human forms are animals and geometric forms.

Tsosie shows us that the painted designs extend under the walls of the ruin. He believes this proves the pictographs were there before the pueblo was built, and he estimates the images to be about 2,000 years old. A kiva from the pueblo period has a protruding beam. Tree ring analysis shows the tree was cut in A.D. 1247, so the rock art is probably at least that old. Some of the plaster and paint still remain inside the kiva.

Sidelight

Dendrochronology, the science of tree-ring analysis, dates events through the study of tree ring growth. A. E. Douglass of the University of Arizona in Tucson discovered the method. Each year a tree grows a new layer, so when viewing a cross section of the tree you can see the rings. In years with plenty of moisture, the tree ring is wide, while it is narrow during droughts. Douglass collected samples from various trees and cut beams to make a chart of the climatic changes. Today, scientists bore a small hole into a log or beam and, by comparing the tree rings to Douglass's chart, are able to determine the year and the season the tree was cut down.

KANAB CREEK WILDERNESS AREA

location: *North Rim of the Grand Canyon*
reservations required
directions: *Mel Heaton of Honeymoon Trail Western Outfitters offers his 7-day Grand Canyon Winter Pastures horseback ride only three times a year. It is too hot in this region for summer trips. This ride is for experienced horseback riders only and starts from the North Rim of the Grand Canyon and travels through the Kanab Creek Wilderness area bordering Grand Canyon National Park. Honeymoon Trail Western Outfitters, 928-643-7292, www.honeymoontrail.com.*

This trip is not for whiners, but it is an unforgettable journey. You will ride horseback for six days, sleeping on the ground and eating delicious Dutch-oven cooking. The Kanab Creek drainage leads to the Esplanade level of the Grand Canyon, where early ranchers wintered their cattle safe from frigid northern Arizona temperatures.

The second day of the trip, you'll wake to the beauty of a Grand Canyon sunrise and the smell of campfire coffee. A short walk from camp leads to a small rock overhang where pictographs cover the walls and low ceiling. You must crawl into this small cave and lie on your back to see the array of paintings. The pictographs left here by ancient peoples have such a sense of mystery and power, the spot might have been a shrine.

One human figure with two tall horns stands among motifs of deer, turtle, and geometric designs, the white symbols still bright against the sandstone.

Another man-figure has a very large head. Sun and rain signs, bighorn sheep and deer figures intermingle with strings of dots, slashes, and crosses. No one knows why the ancient ones came here or what their paintings mean, but they've left their mark in one of the most magnificent canyons on earth.

Sidelight

The sparsely populated Arizona Strip stretches from the North Rim of the Grand Canyon to the Utah border. Although it is part of Arizona, it is geographically attached to Utah. For

residents of the western Arizona Strip to reach their county seat in Kingman, they must travel through Arizona, Utah, and Nevada, across Hoover Dam, and back into Arizona.

Side Trip

Pipe Spring National Monument near Fredonia, Arizona, a two-story rock fort, was originally built to protect Mormon cattlemen from the Indians. The fort was never attacked, but instead became the center of a large cattle operation. Water from the natural spring was piped through the "cheese" room, keeping that room cool enough to store dairy prod-ucts. Cheese and butter were made at the fort and transported to St. George, Utah. Pipe Spring was a major stopover along the Honeymoon Trail. This route extended from St. George to far eastern Arizona and earned its name from Mormon couples traveling the wagon route to be married in the St. George Temple.

KEYHOLE SINK

location: *northern Arizona (Flagstaff area)*
directions: *From Flagstaff, travel west on I-40 to exit 178, Park's Rd. Drive north 0.4 mile on Park's Rd. to Historic Route 66 and turn left, heading west for 4.2 miles. A brown sign on the right marks the Oak Hill Snow Play Area; the parking lot is on the left just past the sign. The trailhead starts across the highway from the parking lot. The sign says the hike (one way) is a mile, but other sources say it is 0.6 mile. Either way, it is an easy hike, going and coming back on the same trail. Remember, the elevation is 7,000 feet. If you are not used to the high country, take it slow. Children should wear a pair of old shoes because it is usually muddy near the waterhole.*

This keyhole-shaped box canyon eroded from an ancient lava flow that erupted from the Flagstaff Volcanic Field to the east. Surrounded by gray-colored basalt, a natural waterhole holds water in all but the driest years. A variety of animals including deer, elk, coyote, and possibly bear and mountain lion visit this sink. It isn't hard to imagine ancient hunters waiting for animals here.

The basalt cliffs are 30 to 40 feet high with two main rock art panels, possibly made by Ancestral Puebloan people. Have you found the image of a deer herd entering the canyon? If you keep your eyes open, you might just see a *real* deer herd coming in for water, too.

On the main panel, the glyphs are crowded together, some incised on top of older ones. Notice the circle with rays? Do you think this is meant as a sun figure?

The tall white-barked trees are aspens. Usually, around the end of September, they turn a brilliant gold. Notice the wild rosebushes down in the canyon.

Sidelight

On your way to Keyhole Sink, you passed a section of Historic Route 66. Known as the Mother Road, the route started in Chicago, Illinois and ended at the ocean in Santa Monica, California. Many people traveled this road to the promised land of California during the Great Depression. I-40 replaced Route 66, but since then, the road has developed a following of fans. If you are interested in Route 66 memorabilia, stop in Seligman and take the longest remaining stretch of Route 66 from Seligman to Kingman.

ROCK ART RANCH

location: *north-central Arizona (Winslow and Holbrook area)*
fee charged; reservations required
directions: *Traveling east on I-40 from Winslow, take exit 252 (I-40 business loop) to AZ 87 and turn right. Continue on*

under a railway overpass and to a left turn at AZ 99. Stay on AZ 99 to Territorial Rd. and turn left. Continue on to the Rock Art Ranch sign, where you turn right and go on to the ranch house. The ranch is about 13 miles from Winslow. Or, traveling west on I-40 from Holbrook, take exit 266. Go south on AZ 77 and turn right on McLaws Rd. (the first road on the right after a large bridge over the Little Colorado River). The road takes some sharp corners, so watch for signs. It is the main paved road, and you'll end up going west. Stay on McLaws Rd. for

approximately 8 miles. The road will fork. Take the dirt road straight ahead. (The paved road leads to Joseph City.) At the Rock Art Ranch sign, turn left and go to the ranch house. Rock Art Ranch is 6.4 miles from the fork, a total of approximately 15 miles from Holbrook. It is a short, easy hike except for the steep climb in and out of Chevelon Canyon. There are uneven steps, but you can hold on to the handrail. At the bottom of the canyon, a dirt path winds from panel to panel. Bring a lunch and plenty of water. There is a shaded picnic area with toilets at the trailhead. Rock Art Ranch can accommodate groups up to 30. Visitors drive their own vehicles on several miles of dirt road to reach the trailhead. Open every day (weather permitting) except Sundays and major holidays. Make reservations by calling 928-288-3260 or writing to Brantley Baird, P. O. Box 244, Joseph City, AZ 86032.

Brantley Baird, owner of Rock Art Ranch, is a real cowboy, and Rock Art Ranch is a real cattle ranch. Baird's tanned skin, slow drawl, Levi's, and Stetson hat all attest to his years on the range. Ranch foreman Clem Rogers is just as authentic. Plan to spend at least an hour enjoying Baird's personal museum of Indian artifacts, petrified wood, pioneer machinery, and old cowboy equipment, and also his cactus garden, before you head down to Chevelon Canyon. Be sure to notice the unusual square Ancestral Puebloan pot among his collection.

This cattle ranch hides a surprising asset—pristine paleo-art in Chevelon Canyon. Chevelon Creek runs year-round, and people have gathered in this secluded canyon for thousands of years. Wild grapevines and black walnut trees must have made this a favorite spot. Here, you'll find hundreds of petroglyphs, some possibly over 4,000 years old. Most of the figures, though, date from the late Ancestral Puebloan period around A.D. 1100–1450. These pre-Columbian figures feature unusual motifs and are very well preserved.

One of the most unusual glyphs is the 4-foot-tall image of a woman giving birth. The whole figure is pecked, not just an outline, and hair whorls adorn each side of her head. Below her legs is a small baby-like figure. Also on this panel is a series of wavy lines, dots, human-like figures, extra-large hands, and a bear claw. Other zoomorphs are not so easily identified.

Across the creek (there is a small bridge), a variety of images are incised on a buff-colored sandstone wall coated with especially dark desert varnish. The contrast in colors makes the glyphs highly visible. The scene is dominated by a 2-foot figure with a large triangle-shaped body, small head, and square shoulders. His body is decorated with wavy and straight lines. There are at least 13 other ceremonial figures among the animals and geometric shapes.

It seems like every nook and cranny holds an image, and judging by the degree of repatination on some of the glyphs, it is obvious that these motifs are very old. A strange figure is tucked into one crack. The round head has facial features of eyes and mouth. He has a neck, but his body is just a square, with two sharp points forming his legs. Another unique design resembles a pyramid, and another looks like a big crab.

The canyon itself is beautiful, with light and dark sandstone walls, a small stream, wild rosebushes, and black walnut trees. Among the birds that flit in and out of the canyon, you'll see tiny hummingbirds.

The glyphs line both walls of the canyon until it narrows up and the water is wall-to-wall. One 2-foot figure is carved on a ledge above the water. Because of the way the image is situated it looks like his knees are bent. His square head tops a skinny neck and square-shaped body (fashionably nipped in at the waist), and he appears to be wearing some kind of skirt. The head is solidly pecked, while the body is dotted. Oddly, he has legs with feet, but no arms.

Archaeologists come to the Rock Art Ranch to study the glyphs and Baird's personal collection of artifacts, but the casual visitor will also enjoy this site, especially Baird's cowboy explanation of all this wonder about him.

Sidelight

The Rock Art Ranch is part of the original Aztec Land and Cattle Company, also known, by its brand, as the Hashknife. In the late 1800s, the Hashknife Outfit was one of Arizona's largest cattle ranches, grazing thousands of cattle across northern Arizona. The last remaining Hashknife bunkhouse is at the Rock Art Ranch. The original Hashknife chuckwagon is on display at the Courthouse Museum in Holbrook.

PALATKI

location: *north-central Arizona (Sedona area)*

reservations may be required

directions: *Take AZ 89A 9 miles southwest of Sedona to FR 525. This is a very scenic route and, though passable in passenger car, can be very rough and is best avoided in wet weather. Follow signs north on FR 525 (left) approximately 6 miles on unpaved dirt road. Take FR 725 (right) for 1.5 miles to the entrance gate. A parking pass may be required. Call Sedona (Red Rock District) Ranger Station, 982-282-4119, for up-to-date information. The Rock Art Trail is ⅙ mile and rated moderate with an 8.3 percent maximum grade. Another trail leads to the Palatki Ruins. Dating from A.D. 700, they are some of the largest in the Verde Valley.*

Palatki, appropriately meaning "red rock house," is built against a red rock cliff in an amazingly beautiful area. Here, well over 1,000 pictographs have been painted in red, black, and white on alcove walls. Many of the designs are faded, but a number are still recognizable. Palatki is one of the largest and most important concentrations of pictographs in central Arizona. It documents the entire passage of human occupation in the Verde Valley, from the Archaic Period, approximately 5,000 years ago, through the Southern Sinagua people of A.D. 600–1400, the prehistoric Yavapais and Apaches of A.D. 1300–1900—all the way to the earliest Anglo settlers of the early 1900s. Palatki rock art is located in four sites, all close together.

Grotto Site contains a seep, providing water most of the year. Most of the pictographs here are probably from the Archaic Period and consist mainly of rakes, squiggles, and patterns of dots. Stylized snakes are also common images and are often associated with water. Examine the smoke-stained rock wall for animal figures that are solid black. These were probably white at one time, but fire oxidized the pigment, turning them black.

Follow the trail on past the alcove, and you're in for a surprise. Here the first settler, Charles Willard, walled up an alcove to make a home. He lived here around 1925, and after he built another home down in the valley, he used this room for fruit storage.

Can you find the group of bears near the top of the roof in Bear Alcove? Yavapai or Apache people living here between A.D. 1583 and 1875 probably made these animal figures. A man on horseback in the center alcove was fashioned after 1583, when horses were brought in by Antonio de Espejo, the first European to arrive in the valley.

Also visible is a circle and half-moon design. Experts differ as to the meaning of this symbol. Some hold that it represents the supernova explosion of A.D. 1054, while others suggest the figures represent the moon and Venus, a common story theme among the western Pueblo people.

Under the next overhang is the Spring Area. Here a spring produced enough water to irrigate Willard's crops below. When farmers tried dynamiting the spring to increase the flow, the water dried up. The large, circular rock alignment is a water catchment made by Willard to catch rain runoff. Look closely at the end of the alcove for two faint designs that look like suns or a pair of shields.

The last stop is the Roasting Pit Site. Many of the native Southwestern peoples roasted the hearts of agave cacti. The harvested agave was placed in a pit on top of hot rocks, covered with leaves and dirt, and roasted for several days. The resulting gooey mass was either eaten immediately (it tastes somewhat like molasses) or dried for later use. If you look around you might see a "quid," the tough fibers of the agave leaves that were spat out after the roasted leaves were chewed. If you find one, you may pick it up and look at it, but please do not remove it from the site.

Sidelight

Charles Willard settled here in 1924. He routed water to his orchards, where he grew more than 2,000 fruit trees including peaches, apples, pears, plums, apricots, persimmons, pomegranates, almonds, and figs. Other crops included peanuts, watermelons, grapes, and blackberries. The farm was sold in 1933 to a rancher, and most of the trees died from lack of attention. You can still spot a few of them, however.

HONANKI

location: *north-central Arizona (Sedona area)*
reservations and permits may be required
directions: *Honanki is 4 miles past the Palatki Rock Art site. Take AZ 89A southwest of Sedona to FR 525. This is very scenic graded dirt road but can be very rough. Avoid it in wet weather. Turn left on FR 525 and follow the signs for Palatki 6 miles. At the junction of FR 525 and FR 795, follow FR 525 northwest (left) for 4 more miles. The road will pass through private land so be sure and stay on the road. There is not an official visitors center at this site, but usually someone is there to answer questions. Honanki is an easy quarter-mile hike with several stone steps. Contact the Sedona (Red Rock District) Ranger Station, 982-282-4119, for information and directions.*

Honanki, which means "bear house" in Hopi, is a pictograph site with red, black, and white designs painted on Sedona's famous red rock cliffs. This is an active archaeology site, and more pictographs are being identified all the time. If you look closely in the niches and under ledges you can see designs secreted away in all sorts of nooks and crannies. Some experts estimate that as many as 2,000 pictographs once adorned these cliffs, although many have faded away with time.

Honanki is great to visit because the pictographs and the cliff dwelling are at the same site. This village once contained about 60 rooms and represented one of the largest population centers in the Verde Valley. A tree-ring sample taken from a wooden window lintel dates back to A.D. 1271, so archaeologists estimate the pueblo was occupied from A.D. 1100 to 1300. "Honanki Phase" refers to the period of Southern Sinagua prehistory when Honanki and many of the other cliff dwellings in the Red Rock/Secret Mountain Wilderness were occupied.

The pictographs here cover several design styles and were probably created over a long period of time dating from the Archaic Period (3,000–8,000 years ago), long before the cliff dwelling was built. It is believed Southern Sinagua people (A.D. 900–1300) were responsible for most of the pictographs, though some are attributed to the Yavapais and Apaches and date from a slightly more recent 1400 to 1875.

Look along the cliff to the right of the main ruin. Can you find the white shield/circular figure above the room with a filled-in doorway? Notice the human and animal figures in red just below the shield. As you walk along, keep an eye open for the row of human figures with their arms in the air.

Plan to spend plenty of time at Honanki and see just how many pictographs you can spot tucked away in the cliff. If you are lucky, you might get to watch archaeologists at work.

Sidelight

Most of the pictographs at Honanki are red, black, or white. In other locations, blue, yellow, and gray are used. The red comes from iron oxides, white from kaoline, yellow from limonite, black and grays from charcoal, and the blue from ground turquoise. Sometimes you can spot small indentations in the rock floor where these naturally occurring pigments were ground into a fine powder to be mixed with saliva, urine, water, or even blood. The designs were sometimes painted with a finger or with a brush, probably made from yucca. Pictographs are fragile and often survive only in caves, under ledges, or in well-protected places.

V-BAR-V RANCH PETROGLYPH SITE

location: *north-central Arizona (Sedona/Camp Verde area)*
fee charged
directions: *Take exit 298 off I-17 between Flagstaff and Phoenix (closest towns are Sedona and Camp Verde). Turn east on FR 618 (paved), go approximately 2.5 miles. Turn right at the sign just past the Beaver Creek Bridge. This is an easy walk and good for children. Visitors center, gift shop, and restrooms. For times and fees, call the Sedona Forest Service Office, 928-282-4119.*

It is easy to see why the Sinagua people chose this site for their petroglyphs. A large, red sandstone wall covered with dark desert varnish provides a perfect backdrop for the nearly 1,100 individual images chipped into 13 separate panels. This is the largest known petroglyph site in the Verde Valley, and archaeologists refer to this clustering of rock art as a "bulletin board."

The V-Bar-B Ranch site has several unique elements. Instead of being a

compilation of different styles, only Sinagua (Beaver Creek style) is present here. The Sinaguas entered the Verde Valley around A.D. 650 and reached their occupation peak between A.D. 1150 and 1300. Notice there are very few petroglyphs pecked on top of other designs here.

Look for a number of heron-like water birds. While these figures are found at other sites in the Verde Valley, the V-Bar-V panels contain an unusual number of them. Also, at this site image elements tend to be paired. Do you see the pair of horned toads or the two herons?

Watch for the palm tree-like figure. So far, this is the only known example of a palm tree-like glyph anywhere in the Southwest. See the stick figures with what appears to be lumps each side of the head? These are thought to be young girls with hair whorls, similar to what historic Hopi maidens wore. Notice all the wavy lines that connect many of the figures? The frequency of this "connectivity" is another notable feature of the V-Bar-V site. How about the deer with a cougar-like animal on its back? Is this the depiction of an attack or just a chance placement of figures?

Most of these glyphs were probably made by using a pointed stone chisel and striking it with a hammer stone. They are finely executed and have another novel characteristic: Most of the animal and human figures have indentations drilled near their hearts or heads. These depressions were probably made soon after the original glyph, because they seem to have weathered at the same rate. There are other sites with these small hollows, but only the V-Bar-V site has so many of them.

Sidelight

The V-Bar-V Ranch was one of five working cattle ranches and three dude ranches that flourished along Wet Beaver Creek between the 1930s and 1960s. The name comes from the ranch's brand, the V—V. The house was built by Bruce Brockett in 1930 and torn down in 1990. The chimney still stands near the visitors center. It is made from gray river rock with the V-Bar-V brand highlighted in red sandstone.

PUERCO PUEBLO

location: *east-central Arizona (in Petrified Forest National Park, Holbrook area)*
wheelchair-accessible
directions: *Puerco Pueblo is located along Park Rd. in Petrified Forest National Park, about halfway between the north and south entrances. For the north entrance,*

take exit 311 off I-40 northeast of Holbrook and travel 11 miles in the park. The south entrance can be reached by taking US 180 east from Holbrook for 19 miles to the park entrance, then 17 miles to Puerco Pueblo. Petrified Forest National Park, P.O. Box 2217, Petrified Forest, 928-524-6228.

Puerco Pueblo is the easiest spot to see rock art in Petrified Forest National Forest. It is found right along Park Road, the main road through the park, and has a paved path. Plan extra time to enjoy Puerco Pueblo, a partially stabilized 100-room site. Built around A.D. 1250, the large pueblo housed as many as 1,200 people and was one of the last occupied villages in the park. For some reason, Ancestral Puebloans lived in the pueblo from A.D. 1100 to 1200, then abandoned it—only to move back again from A.D. 1300 to 1400. Most of the petroglyphs in the park were probably created by the Ancestral Puebloans between A.D. 1000 and 1350, but earlier human habitation here may date back 10,000 years.

Signs at the Puerco Pueblo parking lot give directions to the different petroglyphs. Be sure to find the bird motif. This unusual image depicts a large bird (it even has knees and toes) with a long beak. Do you see the image at the end of its beak? Is that a human figure? Any idea why this bird would have a human impaled on the tip of its beak?

The Petrified Forest has a number of solar calendars, and others are also being discovered throughout the Southwest. A small, nondescript spiral forms a summer solstice sign at the Puerco Pueblo. The spiral, pecked on the side of a boulder, has an interpretive sign nearby. At 9 a.m. on June 21, sunlight passes through a crack in a nearby rock, producing a shaft of light about 18 inches long and 2 inches wide, which in turn points to the exact center of the spiral glyph. It's possible to view the light shaft around 9 a.m. from approximately June 14 to 28, but the light hits the exact center of the spiral on the summer solstice, June 21.

To reach many solar calendars, visitors must climb to remote spots, but Puerco Pueblo's marker is at the end of a paved walk, and during the two weeks that it is visible, a ranger explains the whole process. It's the lazy man's way to view an authentic, ancient solar calendar.

Other glyphs at this site include lizards, human forms, and handprints. Some of the best geometrics are at a nearby site known as Newspaper Rock. Unfortunately, the large rock slid down a slope several years ago, and the glyphs are now visible only through a viewing tube or with binoculars.

Sidelight

Solar calendars often mark the summer and winter solstices. The Ancestral Puebloan people used these dates to time their ceremonies. Modern Puebloans still hold ceremonies during the solstices. Spirals and circles are often used for solar calendars, but not every spiral and circle constitutes a solar marker. Only by watching the interaction between the glyph and sunlight throughout the year can an observer determine if a glyph is indeed a solar calendar. If the rocks haven't been moved, most solar calendars are as accurate today as they were a thousand years ago. Archaeo-astronomy, a combination of archaeology and astronomy, is the science that studies this interesting phenomenon.

HOMOLOVI RUINS STATE PARK

location: *east-central Arizona (between Holbrook and Winslow)*
wheelchair-accessible
directions: *Located between Holbrook and Winslow. From I-40 take exit 257 (AZ 87) north 1.3 miles to the park entrance. Turn north and follow the road to the visitors center. Open daily except for Christmas Day. Homolovi Ruins State Park, 928-289-4106, e-mail homolovi@pr.state.az.us.*

Homolovi Ruins State Park, located along the Little Colorado River near Winslow, once contained seven pueblos, occupied during the thirteenth and fourteenth centuries. It is believed the Ancestral Puebloans lived here before they completed their "migration journey" to join the people living on the Hopi mesas to the north. The region has signs of human habitation dating back 11,000 years.

The Hopi people still consider this site part of their homeland, although it is not on the Hopi Reservation. Homolovi (ho-MOLE-oh-vee) means "place of the little hills." The residents raised cotton, squash, corn, and beans in the fertile soil along the river. Three of the seven Homolovi sites are open to the public. Homolovi II, the largest site, contains 1,200 rooms, three plazas, and forty kivas. Only a portion of the site has been reconstructed, and the site has interpretive signs.

Homolovi became a state park to protect the site from vandals. Pothunters were looting the site, particularly the burial grounds, and selling the artifacts. The park is especially careful of vandals, and Tsu'vo Loop Trail is the only advertised rock art site open to the public. *Tsu'vo* is a Hopi word meaning "path of rattlesnakes," so watch for them. One interpretive sign thoughtfully points out a boulder where rattlesnakes are often seen.

The petroglyphs along Tsu'vo Loop Trail are quite faint. The trail brochure available at the visitors center will help you locate the images. Bear paws, stick figures, and a katsina (also sometimes spelled kachina) are all depicted here, but the glyphs are easier to pick out during late afternoon.

The trail passes a golden eagle/raven nest and midden. Built on a ledge along a small bluff, the large nest is constructed from sticks. Debris from older nests (midden) can be found at the base of the cliff. In spring, you might be lucky enough to spot chicks in the nest.

There are other rock art sites in the park, but park personnel want to control visitation. If you want further information to these other sites, just ask at the visitors center.

Sidelight

The Navajo guides for nineteenth-century anthropologists and archaeologists referred to the ancient people that once lived in the Four Corners area as Anasazi, meaning "ancient ones" or "enemies of our ancestors." The Hopi prefer the name Hisat'sinom or "long-ago people." Most archaeologists now refer to the ancient people as Ancestral Puebloans.

LYMAN LAKE STATE PARK

location: *east-central Arizona (St. Johns area)*
directions: *Located 11 miles south of St. Johns on US 191. Open year-round; campground. P. O. Box 1428, St. Johns, 928-337-4441.*

Early Ancestral Puebloan people lived along the Little Colorado River long before European settlers arrived. In 1912, the river was dammed, forming Lyman Lake, with the water used for irrigation in nearby St. Johns. There are several petroglyph sites and a partially excavated pueblo along the lake.

The Ultimate Petroglyph Trail is the best place to see unusual and very distinct petroglyphs at Lyman Lake State Park. This ranger-led tour is reached by pontoon boat only. Tours are available through the Ranger Station on a seasonal basis and are very reasonably priced. Contact the park for day and time. The 1-mile round-trip hike is steep in portions and climbs 500 feet over 0.5 mile. In general, the rock art at this site dates from A.D. 700 to 1275.

Along the trail you'll see exceptional geometric and animal figures as well as traditional Hopi clan symbols. Notice the two women figures with knobs on each side of their heads? These are believed to represent the hair whorls traditionally worn by unmarried Hopi women. Also note the large geometric design with "waves." This may portray the symbol for the Hopi Water Clan.

The Ultimate Petroglyph Trail ends at what else but the Ultimate Rock—covered with petroglyphs representing six different time periods. Some experts believe the 24- inch bird figure represents a turkey, while others think it is an eagle, thunderbird, or possibly a katsina figure. Look for the 18-inch-long animal with his tail curled over his back. Is it a mountain lion or a coyote? Look again at the claws on its feet. Note also the male figure with unusually large hands and feet. This is thought to represent the Hopi deity Ma'saw.

The Peninsula Petroglyph Trail is a quarter-mile hike that starts at the campground. This is a self-guided walk, open during daylight hours all year long. Rangers also take visitors to the Rattlesnake Point Pueblo, an archaeological site containing eighty to ninety rooms.

Sidelight

The rock art at Lyman Lake is still important to the Hopi Tribe. *Tutuveni* is the Hopi word for petroglyphs and means "clan marks of the Hopi people." The Hopis believe their clans emerged from below and then went on a migration journey before settling on the Hopi mesas. Each clan has its own story of their journey.

Side Trip

Apache County Historical Society Museum, 180 W. Cleveland, P.O. Box 146, St. Johns, 520-337-4737. The small museum houses an eclectic collection including 24,000-year-old Columbian mammoth tusks found in a nearby gravel pit. Handmade quilts are next to mud-worm fossils, and a prehistoric camel leg competes with a collection of women's hats. Ancestral Puebloan artifacts are mingled with a photo of the longhaired Apache County Sheriff, Commodore Perry Owens, whose fast gun helped tame northeastern Arizona.

POLIMANA

location: *east-central Arizona (Heber area)*

directions: *The Polimana rock art site is a stop along the Black Canyon Journey Through Time Auto Tour. Start the route by taking Black Canyon Road (the last road on the left heading west out of Heber). A beautiful drive, this trip between Heber and Black Canyon Lake is best made from May to October because snow may close the road during winter. A tour brochure with numbered stops and directions can be picked up at local Forest Service offices, including Black Mesa Ranger Station on AZ 260 in Overgaard (928-535-4481). The auto tour highlights the beauty and history of the region. Starting at the junction of AZ 260 and Black Canyon Road in Heber, it is 3.2 miles to the Polimana rock art site (Stop #2 in the brochure). The marked site is on the right side of the road, with an interpretive sign at the start of the trail.*

Follow a short, but steep, climb up the narrow trail to a limestone overhang. Look underneath the ledge to find the pictographs, which are red figures painted on the light-colored limestone. Have you found the spiral yet or the animal with horns? Look for the man figure with his arms pointed downward.

These pictographs are from the Mogollon Culture, the earliest people known to have lived in Black Canyon. If you follow the road another 1.5 miles you'll find the Rock Shelter site (Stop #3). Again you'll need to follow a steep trail.

The Mogollon people used this location about 900 years ago. Look above the rooms on the ceiling of the shelter. Do you see the red figures?

The Polimana and Rock Shelter are the only two rock art sites, but the rest of the drive is beautiful, following Black Canyon up to the top of the Mogollon Rim. The road is paved in spots, and the rest is a well-maintained dirt road. Be sure to stop at Stop #6, the Baca Ranch. The Bacas had seven pretty daughters and one son. Something of a social center in its day, the homestead hosted many all-night dances, with families and cowboys coming from miles around. You'll find the Baca Family Cemetery just past the ranch site.

Sidelight

Have you noticed the red stain on the limestone rocks and the burned trees? The stain is fire retardant dropped by airplanes when the Rodeo-Chedeski fire (the largest forest fire in Arizona history) blazed through a portion of Black Canyon in the summer of 2002. Approximately 468,000 acres of the Apache-Sitgreaves National Forest, White Mountain Apache tribal forests, and private lands burned, with 467 homes lost and 30,000 people evacuated.

K5 HIGH COUNTRY ADVENTURES

location: *east-central Arizona (Springerville area)*
reservations required
directions: *Roxanne Knight of K5 High Country Adventures (the family brand is K5) leads guided hikes or horseback rides to various rock art sites in northeastern Arizona. (She also offers horseback rides or cattle drives in the White Mountains.) K5 High Country Adventures, 800-814-6451, 928-333-4323, k5reeds@cybertrails.com, www.k5reeds.com.*

Roxanne Knight, a lifelong resident of the Springerville area, leads guided hikes to rock art sites in the White Mountains. On her Discovery Hikes, Roxanne takes visitors to locations where rock art might be found and lets them help discover sites. The paleo-art along the Little Colorado and its tributaries is extensive and includes both petroglyphs and pictographs, so there is a good chance you'll see sites that are seldom visited or perhaps even discover an undocumented site. Much of the rock art is on private land or in difficult-to-reach areas, so it is much easier to go with Roxanne. She also has permits to take guided trips on to U.S. Forest Service land.

We hike with Roxanne to the Coyote Creek site on her own ranch. Coyote Creek starts high on Escudilla Mountain (the nearly 11,000-foot

mountain you see off to the southeast) and meanders its way north to merge with the Little Colorado. It is a moderate hike to a buff-colored, sandstone ridge east of Springerville. Various sun symbols stand out here, especially one with an "L" in the middle. Another figure resembles a salamander, while several others appear to be either eagles or thunderbirds. Animal, human, and abstract elements are carved into the light-colored sandstone and, as the sun starts to set, the glyphs become even clearer.

The Ancestral Puebloan and Mogollon cultures didn't totally disappear from this region as they did in much of the Southwest. Both cultures overlapped in the area and some groups possibly migrated to the Hopi and Zuni Pueblos. Roxanne has spent time with both Zuni and Hopi elders, listening to their interpretation of the rock art. As she lends insight into possible meanings of the different glyphs, she says tribal elders explain that the many spiral and maze designs found here symbolize the emergence portion of their creation story. They signify "migration markers" left by the clans as they traveled the Southwest before settling permanently in their pueblos.

Very knowledgeable in geology, Roxanne explains that much of the sandstone in the area formed during the mid-to-late Cretaceous Period when the region was covered with water. A lava flow from Coyote Hills, a shield volcano in the Springerville Volcanic Field, has left a thick cover of black rock on top of the older sandstone. In Springerville, the Casa Malpais ruins are built into the edge of the volcanic flow.

Sidelight

The Little Colorado River starts high in the White Mountains, flowing northward until it enters the Colorado River in the Grand Canyon. Early peoples lived and farmed along the waterway and, today, several small farming communities still line the river. Below Springerville, Lyman Lake Dam prevents flooding along the lower Little Colorado River and provides irrigation water for the town of St. Johns.

SIPE WHITE MOUNTAIN WILDLIFE AREA

location: *east-central Arizona (Springerville area)*
directions: *From Springerville, take US 191 south for 2 miles. At the top of the hill on the right, look for the turnoff sign for Sipe White Mountain Wildlife Area. Follow the well-maintained dirt road 5 miles. No food or gasoline is available, and no overnight camping is permitted in the wildlife area (although you may camp in the nearby national forest). Bring a lunch for a picnic on the tables in the orchard. Managed by Arizona Game and Fish Department, Pinetop Regional Office, 928-367-4281.*

With its running stream and plenty of wildlife, you can see why long-ago people were drawn to this meadow. The petroglyphs are nestled on the south-facing basalt cliffs north of the information center. Follow the High Point Trail through the orchard, over Rudd Creek, up to the top of the cliffs, and then down to the petroglyphs. The trail makes a 1-mile loop and, though rated easy, it is steep in spots. Climb down carefully. The glyphs are scattered among the boulders. There are resting benches along the way, so you can take it easy and enjoy the view.

Can you find the bowlegged man? There are also snake motifs—a warning that snakes still sun themselves on these black rocks. Looking around, you can find more scattered images, including a frog with his feet and toes splayed, assorted footprints, and lizard designs.

From the top of the bluff, look across the creek and to your right. You'll see the remains of the Rudd Creek Pueblo. From the information center, an

easy 0.5-mile walk along a dirt road leads to the ruin. The Ancestral Puebloan and Mogollon cultures overlapped here, but it is believed that Ancestral Puebloans built the site, starting around A.D. 1225. The village consisted of approximately 50 rooms and two great kivas. Notice the intricate rock work on the walls. Unusual in this region, these walls, with their alternating patterns of large and small stones, are very similar to rock work at Chaco Canyon, New Mexico. A fire destroyed the pueblo while it was still inhabited, and the people moved on after only 75 years. They may have migrated north to the Hopi and Zuni villages there. When archaeologists excavated a portion of the site, they uncovered kivas, rooms, pots, and more, but no sign of burials. It is not known where these people buried their dead.

Sidelight

Sipe White Mountain Wildlife Area is 1,362 acres of grasslands, riparian areas, and forest, a popular area to view birds and wildlife. It is open year-round, but snow usually blankets the area in the winter. The information center/museum is open from May 15 to October 15. Indian artifacts, animal information, and a hands-on room for children make this a worthwhile stop.

Hiking, biking, and horseback riding are favorite activities, along with hunting in season. The location was formerly a cattle ranch and farming area, and the meadow is still irrigated, with the grass baled and stored in the red barn. During winter months, the hay is scattered on the meadow for the area's elk, deer, and antelope. About 800 elk winter here. Feeding the elk during the winter keeps these large animals from overgrazing nearby cattle ranches.

Place to Visit

Renee Scharf Cushman, the only daughter of well-known European artist Victor Scharf II, once owned the ranch at Sipe White Mountain Wildlife Area. The Springerville Ward of the Church of Jesus Christ of Latter-day Saints (Mormons) was surprised to learn they had inherited her family art collection, which dated from the Renaissance to the early twentieth century. Containing paintings, furniture, tapestries, French and German glass, and other unique items, the collection is housed in the Cushman Museum (built as a wing onto the LDS church building). The museum pieces are protected with temperature and security controls, and the collection is open to the public by appointment. Contact the Springerville Chamber of Commerce for information, 928-333-2123.

BLUE RIVER

location: *east-central Arizona (Springerville area)*
wheelchair-accessible
directions: *From Springerville, take US 191 south through Alpine to just past milepost 240. Turn left (east) on Forest Service Road 567 (Red Hill Road) and go approximately 12 miles to Blue Crossing Campground on the left, along the Blue River. Another way to reach the campground is to turn east in Alpine on US 180, then go 4 miles to Blue River Road. Turn right (south), following the Blue River and crossing it several times. If the river is not running too high, you will need to go over it on a cement crossing to reach the campground. Both of these roads are slow and winding. The campground has camping shelters, picnic tables, fire pits with grills, and toilets. Go through the gate at the north end of the campground to see the petroglyphs and pictographs left by Mogollon people.*

The designs here are etched on the large, lichen-covered rocks. An interpretive sign explains that the figures are between 700 and 900 years old. Notice the bear paw designs. Even today there are many bears in the area. Can you see the human footprint between the bear paws? Do you think the hunter was tracking the bear, or was the bear following the man? There are more glyphs here depicting deer, stick figures, and circles. Have you found the painted handprints yet? Most of the images are located in this one area. It seems that the ancient Mogollon people enjoyed the beauty of Blue River, too.

The 173,762-acre Blue Range Primitive Area is still one of the more remote sections of Arizona. Visitors who do venture here come for the solitude, beauty, and wildlife. Hunting is allowed in the primitive area, so you may encounter more traffic during hunting season.

Sidelight

This remote area is home to a variety of wildlife, including bear, coyote, deer, and elk. If you are here in the late fall during the rut, you may hear bull elk bugling for a mate. As you walk along Blue River, notice the trees that have been gnawed by beavers, and keep your eyes open for a beaver dam. Mexican wolves, extinct from the area for half a century, were reintroduced in the 1990s, causing controversy between government officials and local cattlemen. The wolves, approximately the size of adult German shepherd dogs, are adapting well.

HIEROGLYPHIC POINT

location: *east-central Arizona (in Salt River Canyon, between Show Low and Globe)*

directions: *This easy-to-reach site between Globe and Show Low is right alongside US 60 between mileposts 290 and 291. Sometimes it is even marked with a "Hieroglyphic Point" sign, but likely as not, the sign has been stolen. There is a pull-off, and cement steps lead down to the rock art.*

At the bottom of the steps, look closely on the black diabase boulders for petroglyphs. Someone with a can of spray paint has "decorated" the boulders but, fortunately, has missed most of the rock art. Hunt for the unusual hand and forearm design. How about the fish designs? If you can't make them out, here's a hint: Below the stairs on the right, a flat white rock stands out among the black boulders. There you will find a life-sized forearm and hand, chiseled into the rock. Just above the hand is the fish. You don't see fish often in Arizona rock art, and so this image may have something to do with fishing in the Salt River below.

About 25 feet to the left of the steps, study the black boulders. Can you see the dog-like animals with tails curled over their backs? One even has his nose pointed in the air. They may represent coyotes or wolves. Wolves once roamed the area and have been reintroduced into the White Mountains near the New Mexico border.

To the right of the stairs is a reddish boulder with green lichen. It holds several lizard-like figures. If you are lucky, you might find a live lizard basking next to symbols of his ancestors. Also, on the right, look for a boulder nearly hidden by bushes. It has several petroglyphs. Hint: It is right before the dirt trail turns to white. The trail leads a short distance to a point providing a spectacular view of the Salt River, nearly 2,000 feet below.

Salt River Canyon marks a blending point of cultures. Artifacts from Ancestral Puebloan, Hohokam, and Mogollon peoples have been found in the caves and overhangs of this rugged area. There are several major ruins in the canyon and most of these are referred to as Salado (Spanish for salt) sites. They are nearly inaccessible and are on the Fort Apache Indian Reservation. The best place to see a Salado site is at Tonto National Monument near Roosevelt Lake northwest of Globe.

Sidelight

Salt River Canyon is so beautiful it could be a national park or monument. This stretch is known as the Upper Salt and descends at an average rate of 25 feet per mile. Rising in the White Mountains near 11,420-foot Mount Baldy, the fourth-highest mountain in Arizona, the river runs for 200 miles before it joins the Gila River just below Phoenix. Coronado, on his search for the fabled Seven Cities of Cibola, named the river Río de las Balsas (meaning "river of rafts"), suggesting early peoples built rafts to ford it. The Pima Indians called the river A'kimult (or "salty river"), and Padre Eusebio Francisco Kino, who traversed southern Arizona, followed their lead, calling it Río Salado, or "Salt River."

Early trappers James O. Pattie and Kit Carson followed the Salt, trapping beaver. The Apaches used the canyon as a hideout during the Apache Wars and rumors of gold mines and caves stashed with Spanish treasures in the area still abound.

Today, a portion of the Upper Salt is the boundary for the Fort Apache and San Carlos Indian Reservations. A bridge spans the river, and during the spring, whitewater rafting expeditions begin here. A dirt road follows along the north side of the river below the bridge, but a Fort Apache Reservation permit is required to travel this route. Fort Apache permits can be purchased at the small store/gas station north of the bridge. At the rest area south of the bridge, visitors can walk down to the river without a permit. The eastern Salt River upstream from the bridge is closed to non-tribal members.

Salt River Canyon is literally a wall of time. Rock layers stand out clearly, marking the various time periods. Some of the formations are from the Precambrian Era, the earliest geological era, and are believed to be 1,700 million years old. Limestone formations contain fossils and at one point have been altered to marble by the intrusion of hot igneous rocks.

HIEROGLYPHIC CANYON

location: *metro Phoenix area*

directions: *From Phoenix, take US 60 east to King's Ranch Rd. (this is the Gold Canyon Ranch housing development entrance). Turn left on King's Ranch Rd., then right on Baseline Rd. for a few hundred yards. Next turn left on Mohican and left on Valley View Rd. Valley View Rd. turns into Whitetail Rd., then turn right on Cloud Dr. At the end of Cloud Dr. is the parking lot. The trail starts at the north end of the parking lot. There are no facilities here, but it is a popular hiking spot, and the parking lot may fill up on weekends. The hike is rated easy but has loose rocks, so sturdy shoes are a must. At the end of the trail, expect to climb over and around boulders to get down to the water, but glyphs are visible from the top of trail without climbing down to the water. The trail is open year-round, though summer temperatures can reach over 100 degrees F. Spring flowers may be abundant if there were sufficient winter rains. The trail is approximately 3.5 miles round trip.*

Although this site is called Hieroglyphic Canyon, the figures here are not true hieroglyphics but rather petroglyphs. (Hieroglyphic is a system of writing using a character or symbol to represent a word, syllable, sound, or idea, and usually refers to ancient Egyptian writing. So far, petroglyphs have not been identified as a form of writing.) Located on the southwestern corner of the Superstitions Wilderness Area, this popular hike leads into a canyon where Hieroglyphic Spring and rain water feed a small series of waterfalls and pools. The pools usually contain some water year-round, but the stream and waterfalls depend on snowmelt and rain. At the entrance to the canyon, look for a

large panel of paleo-art with mountain sheep—a common rock art theme in the desert Southwest.

There are more motifs on all sides of the main panel. Try looking down two levels and to the left to see a large spiral. It is faint, probably worn away by water and exposure. Now, look on up the canyon several yards to locate a strange design resembling a face with a wavy one-line body. This figure is very mystifying.

On the next outcropping up the canyon is another panel with more sheep and geometric designs. The glyphs in Hieroglyphic Canyon are estimated to be between 200 and 2,000 years old and were probably made by the Hohokam people who farmed the Salt River and Gila River Valleys. Look for the man with an arch-shaped headdress. Most of the designs are on the east side of the canyon, but you will find a few stray figures and seven grinding holes located on the west side.

Geometric images are scattered along the canyon walls. Their meaning is unknown, but these same designs appear on Hohokam pottery. Can you find the large geometric pattern that resembles a maze? The shady canyon makes a great place to rest, especially if there is water in the pools. The small waterfalls make good "slide rocks." This seems more of a social center than a spiritual

place. The grinding stones indicate that women ground seeds here and the pools were probably popular with the children.

Sidelight

The Superstition Mountains are home to the legendary Lost Dutchman's Gold Mine. Jacob "Dutchman" Waltz supposedly made a fabulously rich gold strike but died in the early 1890s without revealing the mine's location. For more than a century, explorers have searched these rugged mountains, but no one has found the elusive treasure. The legend grew when prospectors started dying in the mountains. Rumors claimed the men died from Indian attacks, mysterious circumstances, or murder. Although there were a few murder victims, most probably died from thirst, exposure, or accident in these extremely rugged mountains.

DEER VALLEY ROCK ART CENTER

location: *metro Phoenix area*
wheelchair-accessible
directions: *From central Phoenix, go north on I-17 to exit 217B, then turn west on Deer Valley Rd. and go approximately 2.5 miles. At the fork in the road, stay to the right on Deer Valley Rd. and continue on into the parking lot. 3711 W. Deer Valley Rd., Phoenix, 623-582-8007, e-mail dvrac@asu.edu, www.asu.edu/clas/anthropology/dvrac. Closed Mon. and holidays.*

Deer Valley Rock Art Center (DVRAC) in northwest Phoenix is one of the best places to really learn about rock art. Over 15,000 visitors per year come to enjoy this largest concentration of rock art in the Phoenix area. Allow time to view the 40-minute video and study the artifacts and interpretive signs before you head out on the trail. This will help you understand the site much better. The DVRAC also offers children's story time, summer camps, guided tours, self-guided tours, and a gift shop. Children especially enjoy this site. They can pick up a clipboard, pencil, and sheet of motifs to identify on the walk. Bring your own binoculars to see the higher glyphs, or rent a pair at the front desk. A wheelchair is also available.

The 0.25-mile wheelchair-accessible path starts at the visitors center and passes close to the main display of rock art. A brochure explains numbered stops, and since DVRAC is also a nature preserve, plants are identified and birds are plentiful. At the start of the walk, a garden features native plants grown by early inhabitants. Visitors can try their hands at grinding corn on the stone metates. You will need to get the corn from the front desk, though. They can't leave it out, or the pesky ground squirrels carry it away!

This location, officially known as Hedgpeth Hills, is on the National Register of Historic Places. Over 1,500 glyphs, scattered on 600 boulders in the 47-acre preserve, represent three cultures: Archaic, Hohokam, and Patayan. The exact age of the paleo-art is unknown, but it's possible these designs range from 700 to 10,000 years old.

Ninety percent of the visible motifs are between stops #6 and #9. At #6, look for the "kissing deer." The image shows two deer with their noses touching and is the petroglyph DVRAC uses for its logo. The longer you look around, the more designs you will notice.

Between #6 and #7, look halfway up the hill to see two prominent human-like figures. Of the more than 1,500 glyphs on Hedgpeth Hills, only about 100 symbols represent animals. The rest are human figures or geometric designs.

At #9 you can use a viewing tube to see wavy-line motifs, the highest glyph visible from the trail. Keep in mind that there are 1,571 documented designs here. On your way back, you will see even more rock art, because now your eyes are better trained to look for them.

Sidelight

Early peoples came to Hedgpeth Hills to quarry volcanic basalt to fashion into grinding tools. The glyphs may even have

served as boundary markers, designating areas used by different cultures. Basalt is ideal for making large *metates* and the small grinding stones called *manos*. River rocks were used to shape the basalt into tools. Basalt has another advantage—it doesn't get dull as fast as most stone.

WHITE TANK MOUNTAIN REGIONAL PARK

location: *central Arizona (Phoenix area)*
partially wheelchair-accessible; fee charged
directions: *White Tank Mountain Regional Park is located west of the Phoenix metro area, near the small town of Waddell. From I-10, take exit 124 north onto AZ 303. Turn left (west) on Olive Ave., which goes directly into the park. 13025 N. White Tank Mountain Rd., Waddell, 623-935-2505, www.maricopa.gov/parks/white_tank/. Petroglyphs are on Waterfall Canyon Trail off Waterfall Canyon Rd.*

White Tank Mountain Regional Park, covering nearly 30,000 acres, is the largest park in Maricopa County. The steep White Tank Mountains divide the Salt River Valley from the Hassayampa Plain. The name is derived from tanks (*tinajas*) scoured out of the white granite by floodwaters. The catchment basins have provided water for travelers from ancient times through the present historic period.

There are 24 miles of hiking trails in the park, but the easiest way to see the petroglyphs is to follow Waterfall Canyon Trail. The first 0.25 mile of the trail, to Petroglyph Plaza, is wheelchair-accessible through desert vegetation. The images are cut into desert varnish along 25 feet of 4-foot-high boulders. Look directly behind the panels for more scattered glyphs. Most of the motifs are geometrics with squiggles and circles. Do you notice the centipede-like creature? Hint: Look at the center of the panel and about halfway up. On the first row of rocks behind the main panel and to the far right is a series of lines. I counted 13. How many can you see?

There are two styles of paleo-art in the park—Archaic and Hohokam. The Archaic people lived in the Southwest from 5000 B.C. to about A.D. 300. These are the oldest glyphs and are usually repatinated, and sometimes newer designs are superimposed over the older images. The Hohokam people lived in southern Arizona from A.D. 300 to 1450, and most of these glyphs are Hohokam style.

From Petroglyph Plaza, keep following the trail. It is not wheelchair-accessible from the plaza on, but is easy except for the last 300 yards, where you must climb around boulders. The complete Waterfall Canyon Trail loop is approximately 2 miles.

As you walk, check out the rocks along the path for random glyphs. About three-quarters of the way up the trail you will see a large metal water tank, then a large boulder almost completely covered with rock art. You can sit and scrutinize the motifs closely from a convenient bench. Can you find the daisy-like design near the highest point on the rock? Follow the trail around the boulder to see even more elements.

As the hike gets rockier, the petroglyphs become more frequent. Watch carefully (right before some rock stairs) for images on both sides of the trail. One the left side of the trail, look for especially vivid curly lines with *X*'s on the ends.

The canyon then narrows, with the trail ending at a water pool. The walls are white and steep, and if it has rained recently, there will be a waterfall pouring into this cool and shady pool—a pleasant resting spot for desert people. There are more glyphs here. Do you see them? Hint: Stand at the water hole and face back down the trail. Look up on the right just as the canyon widens to find an 18-inch multi-legged creature.

Another rock art trail is the Black Rock Trail. The first half-mile is hard-surfaced and winds around a dark outcrop of rock. Signs point out the petroglyphs. If you want to make the complete loop and connect with the Waterfall Trail, it is a 2.5-mile hike.

Sidelight

The Sonoran Loop Competitive Track, located in the park, is for high-speed, competitive bike racers. It is also available (when no races are scheduled) for those who just want to ride it for fun. The trail is nearly 10 miles long and includes long, short, and technical segments. There are also other hiking trails, as well as mountain bike and horseback trails, in the park.

PAINTED ROCKS PETROGLYPH SITE

location: *south-central Arizona (Gila Bend area)*
wheelchair-accessible
directions: *About 12.5 miles west of Gila Bend on I-8, take exit 102 (Painted Rock Dam Rd.). Follow the paved road 10.7 miles to Rocky Point Rd. (dirt). Painted Rocks Petroglyph Site is 0.6 mile west of Painted Rocks Dam Rd. on Rocky Point Rd. No water is available, but you will find picnic tables, barbecue grills, and vault toilets near the parking area. A campground host is on site Oct.–May. Temperatures may reach 120 degrees F in the summer. Formerly an Arizona State Park; now managed by BLM, Phoenix Field Office, 623-580-5500. The site is still listed on many road maps as Painted Rocks State Park.*

At Painted Rocks Petroglyph Site, hundreds of figures from the Hohokam culture (A.D. 300 to 1450) are pecked into the volcanic outcropping. Motifs range from geometric figures to solstice markers, animals (zoomorphs) and human forms (anthropomorphs.) Local Indian tribes, including the Tohono O'odham (Papago), the Hia Ced O'odham (Sand Papago), Maricopa, Yuman, and Akimel O'odham (Pima), all claim this as an ancestral site.

At the start of the trail, watch for a strange animal symbol with a long neck, six legs, and horns. Down the trail is a large boulder with many glyphs,

including a "stink bug" and turtles. Do you think the one design on the boulder represents a coyote chasing two deer? Watch for a bighorn sheep image that isn't pecked solid, or another image that is almost certainly that of a javelina (collared peccary) running with its mouth open.

In front of the large boulder is a smaller rock with a scorpion image. Hint: It is to the right of the cross. The site contains numerous petroglyphs illustrating lizards, Gila monsters, horned lizards, turtles, and even one resembling a newt with a large head and front legs that look like hands. Up at the top of the hill sits a rock with a checkered design. The crack through that rock is supposedly aligned with the North Star.

This natural pathway served as a route for later travelers too, and it's possible to locate inscriptions left by visitors from more recent historic periods. This is a portion of the Juan Bautista de Anza National Historic Trail. In 1775,

Anza noted in his journal that he stopped here on his way to California. The Butterfield Overland Mail and the Mormon Battalion also passed this way. Have you found the etching "T. D. Quinn 1879 AD," or "AAA 1907"?

Sidelight

The evergreen bushes growing in the desert are creosote. The most widespread desert shrub, it grows from California to Texas. One of the most pleasant desert smells is creosote during a rainstorm. The bush spreads from its root system and is possibly one of the most

ancient and longest-lived plants on Earth—a single root crown can create new clone shoots over a period of several thousand years. The native peoples used the plant like a medicine chest. Creosote helped with infections, pain, constipation, cramps, tuberculosis, and rheumatism, and it added seasoning to food and made a glue to mend pots.

BOUSE FISHERMAN (also known as FISHERMAN INTAGLIO)

location: *west-central Arizona (Quartzsite area)*
directions: *Take AZ 95 north from Quartzsite for about 6 miles to Plomosa Rd. Follow Plomosa Rd. northeast for about 5 miles. Watch for a parking lot on the north side of the road. Follow the trail about 500 feet to the fenced site. BLM, Yuma Field Office, 928-317-3237.*

Although its official name is Fisherman Intaglio, locals call this unusual form of paleo-art the Bouse Fisherman, because it is near the small town of Bouse. This design is an intaglio or geoglyph made by the removal of the small, dark surface rocks (sometimes called "desert pavement," not to be confused with desert varnish), revealing the lighter earth underneath. Intaglios are generally very large and usually recognizable only from the air. Pilots flying over the Colorado River canyons discovered the Bouse Fisherman in 1984. About 30 feet long, it is small for a geoglyph, which makes it easier to see from the ground.

The Bouse Fisherman also has more elements than most geoglyphs. It is a male figure that appears to be animated—running or dancing—across water. The

water beneath his feet is represent by a series of waves, much like a child's drawing. Can you see the other symbols in the intaglio? Look for the sun symbol. Do you think the curvy line above the fisherman and to the left is a snake or a bird?

There is a spear in the Fisherman's hand. The 2-foot-long spear point is filled in with pieces of white quartz, another unusual feature for intaglios. Now look down in the "water." Doesn't it look like the fisherman is trying to spear those two fat fish swimming below him?

There are several hypotheses about the meaning of the Bouse Fisherman. One theory is that the spear points the way to a spring near Parker, while another legend says the geoglyph represents the Creator carving the Colorado River with his spear.

It is difficult to tell the age of intaglios, not to mention who created them and why. There are a number of these geoglyphs in the Mojave Desert, and experts say the figures may range from as recent as 70 years old to as old as 5,000 years.

Sidelight

Jojoba (hoe-HOE-buh), a common evergreen desert plant, is grown commercially near Bouse. The seeds are also processed here into oil used for medicines, cosmetics, and machinery. The early pioneers in the area roasted jojoba seeds and used them as a substitute for coffee.

Side Trip

During World War II, the army used this desert area to train tank units, and the tank tracks are still visible on the dry desert surface. The tiny nearby town of Bouse contains a museum with artifacts, including a tank, from these training maneuvers.

ANTELOPE HILL

location: *southwestern Arizona (about 35 miles east of Yuma)*
directions: *Take exit 37 off I-8 east of Yuma and follow Antelope Hill Rd. Just before you reach the large metal bridge that crosses the Gila River, turn right toward a picnic table and information kiosk. Administered by BLM, Yuma Field Office, 928-317-3200.*

Antelope Hill, an isolated sandstone hill rising 575 feet above the valley floor, is hard to miss. The hill's outer rock made an excellent rock art canvas because of the dark patina covering it. Start at the kiosk and follow the trail. About 95 percent of the petroglyphs are on the northern portion of the hill. You'll notice

that most of the glyphs are human-like, with very few animal motifs. Have you found the 30-inch human-looking figure? Look closely—he has all five toes and sports two horn-like extensions on his head. His right arm is holding a circle and his left hand has a circle above the wrist. Now, look below the big figure's right hand, and note the similar figure, about 13 inches tall. He lacks the head decoration and has circles for feet.

Antelope Hill has another claim to fame. Experts think this is the largest and best-developed prehistoric milling quarry in the western United States. Members of many Indian tribes came to obtain sandstone for metates, manos, and pestles. These rocks were used to grind corn, grains, and beans. Native Americans used the stone pestles to pound hard seeds and mesquite pods in a wooden mortar, and then, using a *mano* (a flat grinding tool), they ground the flour even finer on a large metate. Can you imagine carrying those heavy grinding stones many miles back to your village?

Experts believe that Antelope Hill rock art was probably a combination of art, religion, and communication among the different groups. Some have speculated that the area was considered neutral ground, where groups met to get their milling equipment. Indian legends tell that Antelope Hill stone was created specifically for milling tools and didn't belong to any one tribe.

The Gila River was the main thoroughfare for prehistoric people; then came miners, settlers, stagecoaches, and even some outlaws. On the eastern slope of Antelope Hill, John J. Glanton carved his name on a boulder in 1850. Glanton earned his living as a scalp hunter before he came to Yuma. There he took over the ferry business until the Quechan tribe rebelled and Glanton and his gang were killed.

Sidelight

You can't help but notice the big rock quarry. In 1993, a 500-year flood occurred on the Gila River. More than a million cubic yards of rock were cut from the hill and used in an attempt to control the river. Considerable care was taken to avoid disturbing the rock art sites, so there was very little damage to cultural resources.

SEARS POINT

location: *southwest Arizona (Yuma area)*
directions: *Take I-8 east from Yuma for about 75 miles to Spot Rd. On the north frontage road, head east for about a mile to Ave. 76 E, then go north along the dirt road for about 7 miles. Park in the cleared area in front of the ridge. A high-clearance vehicle is advised because this road can be rutted, and the wash bottoms are sandy. Avoid this*

region during summer months, when temperatures reach more than 110 degrees F, and during wet weather. Camping is allowed, but there are no facilities. Bring plenty of water. Managed by the BLM, Yuma Field Office, 928-317-3200.

Sears Point is one of the most interesting sites along the Gila River. Located along a flat-topped volcanic outcrop over-looking the Gila floodplain, Sears Point has obviously been used for thousands of years. Not only are there hundreds of petroglyphs, but this site con-tains geoglyphs, rock shelters, rock alignments, sleeping cir-cles, and shrines.

It would take hours (or maybe days) to thoroughly explore this region, since the site stretches for 3 miles along the river. There are paths, but they are not maintained. Hiking boots are essential, and in some areas hiking is difficult due to loose gravel and rock boulders. Most of the glyphs take some hiking to reach, but many panels are visible from the ground. Binoculars are helpful.

It is thought that Sears Point might have been an "open site," where differ-ent cultures gathered for major ceremonials. There are elements of Archaic, Hohokam, and Patayan designs here.

Sign the trail register at the parking area, then look to your left. Petro-glyphs appear on scattered volcanic rocks along the hillside. The cliffs directly in front of the trail register also feature many panels. Follow this point around to the right and look up for even more panels. Many of the designs are abstract, their meanings lost over the centuries.

See the many motifs of rattlesnakes? This was rattlesnake country way back when—and it is *still* rattlesnake country, so be careful about sticking your hand into crevices. Lizards also like this rocky hillside, and you will see plenty of live ones here, along with lizard petroglyph figures. The centipede glyphs are a good warning sign, too. The trees along the floodplain form a mesquite bosque, providing a natural habitat for wildlife such as deer, javelinas, rabbits, and coyotes.

The petroglyphs seem to be clustered in certain areas, and it is not clear why their makers preferred one spot to another. The bird glyphs probably relate to the number of birds along the river. Before it was dammed, the Gila River was quite large. Note the image of a heron, complete with feet. Look on the cliff to the right of the parking area for another large bird with a fish in its mouth. Watch for the five birds in a row, resembling ducks flapping their wings. One "duck" has his bill open, as if he is squawking at the others.

This is a good place to play "find the petroglyphs," since many boulders have just one or two symbols. Most of the panels of glyphs clustered together are higher up on the bluffs. One of the glyphs shows a four-legged creature with a long tail up over its back. Experts usually refer to this design as a mountain lion. You will also find some sheep with their mouths open as though they are laughing, and one sheep even appears to be wearing tennis shoes.

Many petroglyphs that appear here are the same designs found on Hohokam pottery. Pieces of pottery are scattered on the ground—be sure to leave them where you find them. On top of the highest bluff you'll find a dozen grinding holes. It's possible here to see in all four directions, so women probably sat here to visit and grind food. It must have been a peaceful gathering place when the Gila River ran green and verdant through this valley.

Sidelight

Like Hohokam rock art, Hohokam pottery contained many different designs. Geometric forms were especially popular, and sometimes the design covered the inside of the pot as well as the outside. Red-on-buff was the most common color motif. Because many Hohokam villages were built along the Gila and Salt Rivers, birds were a popular design theme as well.

BABY JESUS RIDGE

location: *southern Arizona (Tucson area)*
reservations required
directions: *Sharon Urban, an archaeologist with the nickname of "Shurban," leads visitors to sites around Tucson. In the summer, this hike is hot, but when taken in fall and spring, the walk is beautiful. If you want to see some great rock art in the Tucson area, go with her. She is a personable guide and an expert on the rock art of the region.*
520-628-7648, surban@email.arizona.edu.

We asked Shurban to show us the "good stuff," and she took us to Baby Jesus Ridge in the foothills of the Santa Catalina Mountains. A series of small rolling hills covered with large granite boulders are studded with saguaros, cat-claw, prickly pears, and other thorny desert plants.

A tiny stream, draining snowmelt from the Santa Catalina Mountains, makes the most welcome sound in the desert—fresh running water. The site faces west, and in the winter the afternoon sun warms the boulders, making it a nice resting area. The spot is so serene it is easy to imagine children playing in the stream or hopping from boulder to boulder while their mothers grind wild seeds.

A large variety of petroglyphs are pecked into the boulders. Dating from the Archaic to the Hohokam period, some of the older glyphs are faded, but most motifs stand out starkly against the light-colored rocks. The rock art is not all in one panel but scattered on boulders for several hundred yards. One large boulder balanced atop another rock holds a 24-inch concentric circle glyph containing points and a "ruffle." The circle surrounds a softball-size natural rock protuberant. Below it is a four-legged animal with a long tail and also a bear print.

There are many "stick men" figures, some at least 30 inches high. Shurban tells us these Archaic-style motifs probably date between 6000 B.C. and A.D. 300. One particular stick figure catches our attention. Both legs and arms are turned up at the end, giving him a happy appearance, so we promptly nickname him "Court Jester." A 3-foot-long rattlesnake design is a more sobering image. Most of the petroglyphs are geometrics, probably from the Hohokam period. Many are repetitive designs, the motifs found on ancient textiles and pottery.

Sharon Urban has definitely shown us the "good stuff" (although no one seems to know how the site got its name), along with a wonderful view of the Sonoran Desert and a nice spring walk.

Sidelight

If you are lucky (or unlucky) you might meet up with a strange desert dweller called a javelina (hav-uh-LEE-na). Certainly no beauty, the javelina—official name collared peccary—resembles a pig, but peccaries are classified in a family of their own. Ranging from 35 to 60 pounds, javelinas roam the Chihuahuan and Sonoran Deserts. Some people think their name comes either from "javelin" or from *jabalina,* the Spanish word for spear (because spears were used to hunt them); more likely the name comes from *jabalí,* which is Spanish for wild boar. Javelinas like to chew on the pads of prickly pear cacti, so you may notice half-circles missing from the edge of some pads. Look in the sandy wash bottoms for javelina tracks, which resemble two lines about two inches long. The animals usually smell or hear you before they see you, because of their notoriously bad eyesight. Seldom aggressive, they usually run unless cornered. You might locate them by *their* smell. They just plain stink.

Learn More about Rock Art

If you want to become involved with the study and preservation of Tucson-area rock art, contact these organizations:

American Rock Art Research Association, Arizona State Museum, University of Arizona, Tucson, 888-668-0052, www.ARARA.org

Old Pueblo Archaeology Center, 1000 E. Fort Lowell Rd., Tucson, 520-798-1201, www.oldpueblo.org

SIGNAL HILL

location: *southern Arizona (in Saguaro National Park West, Tucson area)*
directions: *Saguaro National Park is divided into two sections—Saguaro East and Saguaro West, located on the east and west sides of the city and separated by about 30 miles. Together they preserve 91,327 acres of saguaro cacti and desert landscape. Saguaro East is the largest and more popular of the two districts, but Saguaro West contains Signal Hill picnic area—with petroglyphs. Take the Speedway exit off I-10 west to Gates*

Pass Rd. When Gates Pass Rd. meets Kinney Rd., turn right (north) toward the park. Watch for the sign to the Signal Hill picnic area. Summer temperatures from May to September may reach over 100 degrees F. The glyphs and the views are best seen in late afternoon. Saguaro West, 520-733-5158, www.nps.gov/sagu.

There are several petroglyphs sites in Saguaro West, but Signal Hill is the most publicized. (Ask at the visitors center for directions to other sites.) Signal Hill is a 0.25-mile walk from the parking/picnic area to where over 200 glyphs mark the black basalt boulders on the knoll. The trail is easy to follow, though it does involve climbing some stone steps. Watch to the left and you will see some of the best glyphs as you climb. If you've brought binoculars, you can get an even better view.

Stay on the trail, and if you have even the slightest temptation to crawl on the rocks, remember that those signs that say "Warning Rattlesnakes" are not lying. At the top you'll find an interpretive sign and a bench. Have you seen the three mountain sheep yet? Just right of the sheep is a large "sun" with rays, and next to it a circle of dots. What about the 18-inch spiral? This is the signature glyph of the park and is often seen in park publicity photos. Look for the circles. Some look like wheels, while others resemble flowers.

Hohokam people who lived in the area between approximately A.D. 450 and 1400 made these petroglyphs. Why they disappeared is a mystery, but some people theorize that perhaps irrigation raised the salinity of the soil, or overpopulation exhausted the resources. On the other hand, maybe they didn't disappear at all. The local Tohono O'odham people living in the region believe the Hohokam people are their ancestors.

As in many other Hohokam sites, there are some representational petroglyphs—human or animal figures—and many abstract glyphs that range from dots, nets, and squares to spirals and circles. Usually a site contains both representational and abstract figures. The abstract designs might portray part of a ceremony. Ethnological studies suggest that shamans used hallucinogenic plants like peyote or datura to elicit visions, and the designs might commemorate their experiences.

Sidelight

Saguaro cacti are the signature plant of the Sonoran Desert and grow no other place in the world. Growing extremely slowly, a year-old saguaro seedling may only be 1/4 inch high. The plant doesn't even bloom until it reaches about 30 years of age, and the first "arm" of the plant begins as a prickly nub after the saguaro reaches 75 years of age. Saguaros can live over 150 years, reach 50 feet high, and weigh 8 tons.

Places of Interest

The world-class Arizona–Sonora Desert Museum, south of Saguaro West, is one of the top ten zoos/museums in the country and is dedicated to the unique plants and wildlife of the Sonoran Desert. Here, in addition to viewing the region's unique animals in natural habitats, visitors enjoy wandering the paved pathways viewing the cacti, shrubs, and flowers, and spotting a surprising variety of birds. If you've never seen a mountain lion, coatimundi, javelina, or the infamous rattlesnake, be sure to stop here. 2021 N. Kinney Rd., 520-883-2702, www.desertmuseum.org

CALIFORNIA ROCK ART SITES
(Southeastern California)

Fish Slough Petroglyphs, Bishop Petroglyph Loop, California.

BISHOP PETROGLYPH LOOP

location: *east-central California (Bishop area)*

directions: *BLM publishes a Bishop Petroglyph Loop Brochure with directions to three petroglyph sites. Since the locations are considered sacred and ceremonials are still held there, the Owens Valley Paiute-Shoshone Indian Tribes ask that visitation be monitored. You may pick up a brochure for a self-guided tour at the Forest Service/BLM Inter-Agency Visitor Center, 798 N. Main, Bishop, 760-873-2500.*

Fish Slough Petroglyphs The Fish Slough petroglyphs are approximately 1,000 years old, but they are hard to date because the rock that holds them erodes easily. The lava cooled here in "waves," some of them several feet high. There are a few dozen glyphs at this site, and they are all geometric. These strange designs are sometimes referred to as "entopic patterns"—thought to be the patterns seen in the first stage of a shaman's altered state of consciousness. Other images may represent atlatls, sticks that aided in spear-throwing. These weapon images may indicate the shaman was praying for a successful hunt. Look also for the human stick figure. Hint: He is about 30 inches long. Some of the rocks containing petroglyphs also have grinding slicks where nuts and seeds were ground for food.

Chidago Petroglyphs A chain-link fence protects the Chidago site. There are about 100 petroglyphs at this location, including lizards and snakes, but the majority are geometric forms. Most of the designs are situated on a large group of boulders.

Red Rock Petroglyphs The Red Rock site is in a beautiful setting. There are many geometric forms here but also human and animal images. Can you locate the three human figures? What about

Red Rock

Chidago

the footprints? Do you think they identify a certain person, indicate a path, or perhaps represent a religious figure? Do you have your own theory?

Sidelight

The Bishop Petroglyph Tour is located on a 580-square-mile area known as the Volcanic Tablelands. A series of volcanic ash-flows from the eruption of Long Valley Caldera, 760,000 years ago, formed the Bishop Tuff, a rock layer between 12 and 600 feet deep.

Side Trip

Paiute-Shoshone Indian Cultural Center, 2301 W. Line Street, Bishop, 760-873-4478. Here you can learn about heritage of this culture and see baskets, tools, and a depiction of a Paiute camp. Open daily except for major holidays.

AYERS ROCK

location: *southeastern California (Ridgecrest area)*

directions: *From Ridgecrest, follow US 395 north, then turn off to the east at Coso Junction Rest Area on Coso Rd. Head east 3.7 miles, north (left) on a smaller dirt road for 4.3 miles to a locked gate. Follow another small dirt road on the left 0.3 mile to the parking lot. The marked trail leads approximately 0.25 mile to the site. BLM, Ridgecrest Field Office, 300 S. Richmond Rd., Ridgecrest, 760-384-5400.*

At the end of a 0.25-mile dirt path sits an immense granite boulder surrounded by Joshua trees. Look on the northeast side of the rock and at ground level to see the pictographs. Painted in red and orange, they are believed to have been made by the Coso Shoshone. Can you see the two handprints, one red and one orange, in the rock depression?

Try to find the two large shaman-like figures. One is red and more vivid, but directly to the left is a paler orange one. The red paint seems to have withstood the elements better. Both pictographs have headdresses and large circles in the center of their bodies. Now, look farther to the left for a smaller human-like figure with strange feet. To the right of the two shaman figures is a red animal with a pointed nose and a long tail, which almost resembles a skunk.

Go on around the boulder to the west, where more animals and human figures are again portrayed in red and orange. A few "rattlesnakes" in white may have been added later. Look closely on the left to what first appears to be a series of vertical lines. These are actually human-like figures with their arms uplifted.

Keep circling the boulder on around to the south. Find a small enclave and you'll see the figure of a foot-long black lizard. On the north side you'll find more colors—orange, black, and green—but these aren't man-made. They are lichen, a type of algae and fungus growing together as a unit on the rock.

Sidelight

According to the BLM, Bob Rabbit, the last Coso rain shaman, might have painted Ayers Rock. Living in the southern Sierra Nevada, he traveled to the Coso Mountains to perform rain-making rituals that required elk and bighorn sheep spirit helpers. If Rabbit made these paintings, he would have completed them in the early 1900s, and they might represent the last example of rain-making ceremonies in the region.

LITTLE PETROGLYPH CANYON

location: *southeastern California (in the Coso Mountains, Ridgecrest area)*
fee charged; reservations required
information: *Maturango Museum tours. Carpooling required. Proof of U.S. citizenship (only U.S. citizens allowed) and photo ID required for those over 16. No children under 10; no pets. Expect complete search of vehicles. Reservations must be made in person, by fax, or by mail (no phone or e-mail reservations accepted). For complete instructions, contact Maturango Musem, 100 E. Las Flores, Ridgecrest, 760-375-6900. A very helpful book is* Following the Shaman's Path: A Walking Guide to Little Petroglyph Canyon Coso Range, *California, by David S. Whitley. You may purchase it at the museum gift shop.*

If you want to see one of the largest concentrations of rock art in the United States, you're going to have to get up early and bring your lunch. You will also need a prior okay from the government, since Little Petroglyph Canyon is in China Lake Naval Air Weapons Station, a restricted area. The tours offered on spring and fall weekends by the Maturango Museum are the easiest way to access the petroglyphs. Call the museum directly for dates and tour request

forms. Availability may vary depending on Navy security.

The tour starts at 6:30 a.m. with a video explaining naval procedure and a history of the petroglyphs, then visitors load into cars (carpooling required), and the caravan enters the naval base, where every car is carefully inspected. The rules include no cameras or binoculars until you are within Little Petroglyph Canyon itself and no cell phones or pets. No smoking in the canyon, please, since it is considered a sacred site.

The 90-mile round trip heads up into the Coso Mountains, a volcanic desert range known by the Shoshone Indians as the "Mountains of Fire." The remote region is between Death Valley and the Sierra Nevada Range, where the Mojave and Great Basin Deserts overlap. The walk down Little Petroglyph Canyon, an arroyo cut through Wild Horse Mesa, is approximately a 3-mile round-trip at 5,000 feet of elevation. Although the trail is not rated as strenuous, you will be doing some scrambling and walking through sand, over cobblestones, and around boulders. Wear hiking boots, hat, and clothing appropriate for the weather. Bring water and a lunch, and a hiking stick is handy to maintain balance. There are plenty of rock art figures near the parking area and at the beginning of the trail, if you think you're not up to the whole hike. You must stay with the escorts from the museum at all times (this is a strict Navy rule); but you will be glad you did, because the guides can point out glyphs you might miss and will offer a variety of sidelights and information.

Another word of advice: Bring twice as much film as you think you'll need. You're not going to believe the rock art you'll see here. It is estimated the Coso Mountains contain over 100,000 petroglyphs, and Little Petroglyph Canyon contains thousands. The exact age of the glyphs depends on which

expert you talk to, but most agree they range from very old (some Coso motifs are estimated to be as much as 16,000 years old!) to as recent as 100 years. Most of the designs were probably created between 1,000 and 2,000 years ago, yet only a few of the pictographs have faded.

Experts also disagree on the meanings of the glyphs. Popular theories include: shamans on vision quests, tokens of hunting magic, representations of group rituals and rites of passage, boundary markers, and visual aids for storytellers reciting oral traditions.

Many human-like figures are wearing "shirts"—possibly ritual shirts worn by a shaman during ceremonies. If you look closely at the designs, you will discover that no two shirts are alike. Do you see the bags resembling purses with fringe? Many experts refer to these as "medicine bags" used to carry special or sacred objects.

It is not known why there are so many images of atlatls, or spear throwers, each depicted as a circle bisected by a line. Use of the atlatl made the spear go farther. Prehistoric Native Americans used the atlatl until about A.D. 500, when bow and arrow replaced the ancient hunting tool. Some experts take this to mean the atlatl signs are over 1,500 years old, and the figures with bows and arrows more recent.

There are also many geometric designs. These are thought to be figures or impressions seen during a trance. Have you seen the ladder-like motifs? These motifs are another unknown, because it is generally believed that the people in this region did not make the two-pole type ladder. The guides will point out many of the more unusual glyphs, including two men shooting bows and arrows at each other. Look closely at the largest figure. He has splayed feet with six toes.

Here you can also find many unusual bighorn sheep designs. One, nearly 5 feet long, is being shot by a man with a bow and arrow. Another panel contains fourteen sheep, and another glyph shows a two-headed sheep, with a head at each end. Some theories suggest this is a sheep giving birth. One sheep even appears to be laughing. Have you found the large sheep on its back, legs in the air, with a spear sticking out of its chest? This is near the end of the canyon, on the right side and about eye level.

The farther down the canyon you go, the narrower and deeper it gets. At one point, you climb down what would be a waterfall if there was any water. Flash floods have scoured the walls of designs, but don't give up. The canyon widens again and many more glyphs await you. Just be careful. Those zigzag signs might mean rattlesnakes, and a picture of a scorpion with his tail curled back over his body is a daunting reminder of desert wildlife.

At the fence, look on the right side of the canyon, about halfway up, directly above the fence. Can you see the line of dancers? The figures extend along a rock, around the corner, and onto another outcropping.

There is very little vandalism in Little Petroglyph Canyon, due to the Navy's excellent protection of the site. One exception is an $E=MC^2$—at least, we *hope* this a modern carving!

When your guides remind you that it is time to turn back, don't be too disappointed. On the return, you'll see glyphs that you missed on the way down. Little Petroglyph Canyon is the Disneyland of rock art, making other sites seem like the county fair.

Side Trip

Take time to really enjoy the Maturango Museum in Ridgecrest. The theme of the museum is, of course, petroglyphs. Outside, petroglyph figures adorn the building, including six steel shaman figures, each about 8 feet high. Exhibits highlight the natural and cultural history of the area, featuring desert plants, mining, Indian artifacts, and a brief history of the Navy at China Lake. A children's discovery area allows for hands-on learning, and the Sylvia Winslow Exhibit Gallery contains fine-art exhibits that change monthly. There is even a state-of-the-art telescope available for stargazers. Open daily except for major holidays. 1000 E. Las Flores Ave., 760-375-6900, www.maturango.org

SHEEP SPRINGS

location: *southeastern California (Ridgecrest area)*
directions: *Head south from Ridgecrest on China Lake Blvd. to intersection with US 395. Watch carefully for Randsberg-Inyokern Rd. heading west across from the intersection. Follow Randsberg-Inyokern Rd. past the Ridgecrest gunnery range and on past another gunnery range. Turn south, following the western edge of the second gunnery range. The dirt road is narrow and rocky in spots (high-clearance vehicles are recommended). Be sure you have fuel, supplies, and good tires. Do not attempt in wet*

weather. BLM, Ridgecrest Field Office, 300 S. Richmond Rd., Ridgecrest, 760-384-5400.

Sheep Springs petroglyph site is located near a spring on the northwest end of the El Paso Mountains. Kawaiisu people probably made these designs, since this is their historical territory. The road forks after approximately 5 miles. Stay to the right. You will see a brown post with road number EP 26, which leads downhill to a small campsite. There are a few faint glyphs on the scattered boulders on both the north and south sides of the wash, but the best images are ahead.

Down the road you should see four white poles. Stop here. The petroglyphs extend for approximately 500 feet along the side of the hill. There are some glyphs on top, along with some milling stations and grinding slicks A hiking stick comes in handy here because of the uneven ground. See if you can locate the double circle with a cross in the middle. It has a line over the top, connecting it with another abstract glyph.

There are a number of bighorn sheep symbols. Sheep designs are common throughout the Southwest, especially in the desert. Images that appear to represent animals are called zoomorphs. Many of these designs, though, are abstract geometric or free-form designs that are especially difficult to interpret.

Most of the glyphs are among the boulders on the side of the ridge. Can you find the ten lines about 18 inches long? There are few human forms

here, but one boulder in particular bears a spectacular glyph. It is approximately 40 inches long and human-like. Three circles seem to form his head, and he has horns. His body is one straight line covered with a wavy pattern. Doesn't this look like a drawing someone tried to scribble out? Look at his left hand. It has a small object resembling a prize ribbon.

Sidelight

If you are at Sheep Springs between February and July, notice the green plant with the small purple flowers. This is filaree. It only grows about 15 inches tall and about the same width. It was brought to California by the Spanish and has spread throughout the Southwest, becoming a food source for wildlife, sheep, and cattle.

STEAM WELLS PETROGLYPH SITE

location: *southeastern California (Ridgecrest area)*
directions: *From Ridgecrest, take China Lake Blvd. to US 395 and turn south. Between Johannesburg and Red Mountain, watch for the Trona Rd. exit and turn northeast, then take BLM Route RM 1444 east. About 4.1 miles from Trona Rd. you will*

come to another dirt road on your left. It is closed to vehicles, so hike north on this road about 0.4 mile. At this point, take another intersection left for about 0.2 mile. The Steam Wells area was once an active mining region. The petroglyphs are on all sides of the small knoll. BLM, Ridgecrest Field Office, 300 S. Richmond Rd., Ridgecrest, 760-384-5400.

Kawaiisu people or Southern Paiutes probably made the Steam Wells petroglyphs. A permanent spring made this a valuable and possibly sacred place. You will see a cistern and remains of a building.

Take your time in climbing the small rocky knoll, and watch for glyphs. Most of the designs are geometric, and some possibly may be entopic (images perhaps seen by a shaman during a trance). You will find some human figures and bighorn sheep images.

It is not understood why some boulders are crowded with glyphs while others have only a single element. The motifs extend all the way around the hill and on the back side of the knoll, where there are some bird figures.

Circles are a favorite image. Have you found the boulder with several designs made out of circles? One of the older-looking petroglyphs shows four connected circles. Did you see the figure with two connected circles for a body and forked lines at each end?

Another favorite element of this paleo-art is the "rake" figure. It is depicted as a horizontal line with a number of short vertical lines below it. Experts on the Ancestral Puebloan culture of the Four Corners area explain this as a rain design, but it is not known what it means in Kawaiisu rock art. There is also a foot figure with four toes. It is unclear if this is supposed to be a human or animal foot.

Sidelight

The Kawaiisu people occupied this region during prehistoric times. They now live farther west. They are members of the Southern Paiute language group, which includes the Chemehuevis (near the Colorado River) and the Koso people.

BLYTHE INTAGLIOS

location: *southeastern California (Blythe area)*

directions: *Located 15 miles north of Blythe on US 95, then 0.5 mile west on a dirt road. Look for a historical marker along US 95 near the turnoff, indicating "Giant Desert Figures." Managed by BLM, Yuma Field Office, 928-317-3200.*

George Palmer, a local pilot, discovered the Blythe intaglios in 1931. In North America, intaglios, also called geoglyphs, are mainly found in the Mojave and Sonoran Deserts of California, Arizona, and northern Mexico. Most of the known geoglyphs are along the Colorado River and were discovered from the air. Because these earth glyphs are so fragile, few of them are open to the public, but the ones around Blythe are probably the best known and easiest to reach.

The six intaglios are located in three sites on the mesa tops and include mystical human-like figures along with geometrics and animal figures. The largest man-like figure is 171 feet long. The first figures you'll see are enclosed by fences to protect them. The human figure's head points toward the south. He is 102 feet from head to toe, with an arm span of almost 65 feet. It is thought he might represent Mastamho, the creator of all life, in the local desert cultures. Possibly, ceremonial dances were once held here.

About 120 feet away is another fenced area enclosing two figures. The animal's body is 54 feet long and 7 feet wide, with legs extending 26 feet. It is unclear what type of animal this is. What is your guess? Some experts think it might be a cougar that represented a spirit helper for the human figure. Below the animal is a geometric spiral with a line ending in a circle. Is it a spiritual sign, or does it indicate a trail to water?

Experts disagree vastly on the age of intaglios. Some of the glyphs in the surrounding desert might be as old as 5,000 years, while some may be only 70 years old. The Blythe Intaglios are believed to date from 1,100 years ago. It is still a mystery why these figures are so immense. Maybe they were made to be viewed by the gods. The other three figures are on down the dirt road. What remains of an ancient trail to the Pacific Coast can still be seen in the desert. Can you tell where recreational vehicles have made marks in the desert? Because of the extremely dry conditions here, tire tracks can remain for hundreds of years.

Sidelight

Notice the dark rocks that seem to cover the hilltops. The wind blows the soil away, leaving only the rocks, and over a long period of time, manganese and other elements turn the stones a jet-black color known as desert pavement. Early peoples created the intaglios by scraping away the desert pavement to reveal lighter soil. The rocks that were removed were used to outline the figures.

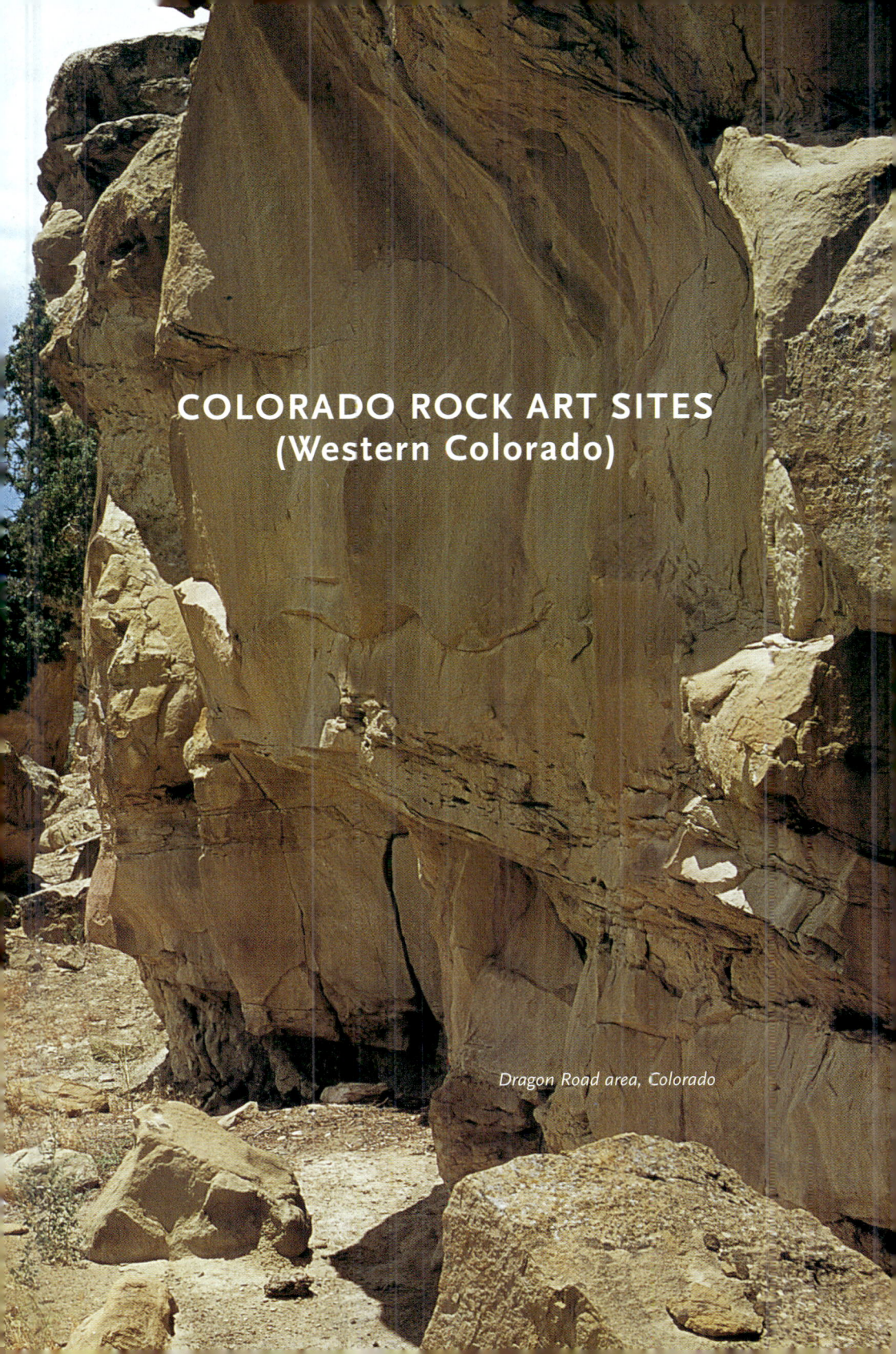

COLORADO ROCK ART SITES
(Western Colorado)

Dragon Road area, Colorado

CAÑON PINTADO NATIONAL HISTORIC DISTRICT

location: *northwestern Colorado (Rangely area)*
some of these sites wheelchair-accessible
directions: *The Rangely area offers a chance to see both pictographs and petroglyphs. Two drives, both starting in Rangely, are interesting and well marked, and both allow children a chance to explore. In its map/brochure, the town of Rangely promotes 16 rock art sites for public visitation. For this book, we've chosen our favorites, starting with sites in the Cañon Pintado National Historic District, followed by sites along Dragon Road. The map/brochure can be obtained at the Rangely Outdoor Museum (970-675-2612) or Rangely Chamber of Commerce (970-675-5290), www.rangely.com/area_map.html. Information is also available at the BLM, White River Field Office, 970-878-3601, www.co.blm.gov. There are eight sites along this route (sites 5–12 on the brochure), heading south from Rangely on CO 139 into the Douglas Creek Valley.*

East Fourmile Site (#7 on brochure, milepost 61.3) Pull over at the parking area near milepost 61.3. You'll find a picnic table, pit toilet, and interpretive sign here. Cross over the large draw that faces east, where a loop trail starts. We took the righthand trail first. The petroglyphs are on the northern cliffs. Can you find the red and white circles in a niche? This is thought to be a solar site, because on June 21 (the summer solstice) at about 10 a.m. Mountain Daylight Time, the shadow from the overhanging ledge bisects all three circles at the same time. Both the winter and summer solstices (shortest and longest days of

the year) were important ceremonial occasions, and the Pueblo people of the Southwest still mark the solstices with special ceremonies. On the facing ledge is a shaman figure with hornlike protrusions.

On down the path is a cowboy's line shack built up against the cliff. Cowboys stayed in these random cabins when herding cattle. Line shacks usually contained a stove, some food supplies, and, if the cowboy was lucky, a bed where he could roll out his blankets.

Farther along the trail is a petroglyph panel with corn figures. Corn was very important to the Pueblo people, and corncobs are commonly found in their archaeological sites. The Fremont people also raised corn, but strangely, archaeologists seldom find corn in Fremont archaeological digs. Look up from the panel and to the left for the petrified log protruding out of the cliff.

The final stop along the trail is a nice panel of rock art etched through the desert varnish. Notice the foot and hand on the far right. How about the bullet holes above the panel? Vandals have used the site for target practice.

Cañon Pintado Site (#11 on brochure, milepost 56.0) From the parking area, look across the road to the cliff face. The red pictograph, approximately 5 feet high, is a humpbacked figure interpreted as a Kokopelli symbol. Often portrayed as a flute-player, Kokopelli is a common motif in the Ancestral Puebloan culture of the Southwest. It is difficult to identify this particular glyph as a Kokopelli, but if it is, it is one of the northernmost instances of a Kokopelli and indicates a tie with the southern cultures. The exact purpose of the Kokopelli is unclear, but he has been labeled as a fertility symbol, trader with a pack on his back, roving storyteller, trickster, magician, rain priest, and even a seducer of young maidens.

Keep looking around. Can you locate the "centipede" to the left of Kokopelli? How about the stalks of corn, two deer, stick men, and the man with the horns? The cable keeps the rocks from sliding off.

Waving Hands Site (#12 on brochure, milepost 53.5) Pull over at milepost 53.5 and look for some red pictographs on the cliff face. Notice the two white arms with hands. Then look for what appear to be two white humps to the right of the hands. What do you think they are? Could this be a bird, or maybe represent two mountains?

Follow the other gravel trail to the right and look straight up at the stunning red icon. Known as "the Guardian," this design probably represents a transitional style, because the pictograph doesn't fit fully into either the classic Fremont or Barrier Canyon styles. If you look closely, you will be able to find the smaller red human-like figure on the left, further down. Also look for the nests located above the Guardian. These belong to rock swallows.

DRAGON ROAD SITES

location: *northwestern Colorado (Rangely area)*
some of these sites wheelchair-accessible
directions: *Follow the map/brochure from the Rangely Chamber of Commerce (970-675-5290), www.rangely.com/area_map.html. This drive starts by turning south at the one and only stoplight in Rangley. After 2.5 miles, the paved road turns to a well-maintained gravel road suitable for cars.*

Fremont Ridge Site (#14 on brochure, milepost 9.7) At milepost 9.7, watch for a dirt road to the east at the top of a small hill. A high-clearance vehicle is required on this side road. Go 1.3 miles, then take the left fork for 0.6 mile. The road ends at the top of a hill, where you will see a BLM sign. Across the road from the sign, follow the footpath, steep in places, around the base of the cliff for 250 yards. Watch for a petroglyph panel on the red sandstone about 6 feet above ground. The designs are quite faint and are more easily seen if you stand back. Can you pick out the triangular figures? There are at least six of them.

Crooks Brand Site (#15 on brochure, milepost 10.1) Turn west at milepost 10.1 (you should see a sign) and go 0.15 mile, turning right just before the well site. Follow the dirt tracks to the buff-colored cliffs directly in front of you. Park and walk to the right, along the cliffs, to find incised historic Ute

petroglyphs. There are several horses, a man in a top hat and coat, and arrows. Can you see the horse with a saddle and a brand? Hint: The brand is on the horse's left front shoulder. It is believed this is the brand of General George Crook (1828–1890). Crook was a general during the Indian Wars, but he also respected the Indians. After his retirement he campaigned for fair treatment of Native people.

Carrot Man Site (#16 on brochure, milepost 11.6) This is the best site along Dragon Road and is listed on the National Register of Historic Places. At milepost 11.6, turn west at the site sign and continue 0.3 mile. Park on the left and follow the footpath down into the wash. The trail is steep in places. There is a large rock shelter on your right, then an interpretive sign. Look up on the cliff and you'll see the 3-foot-high red carrot-shaped figures looking down on you. These mystical figures do not have legs but sport horns and white dots on their headgear. Just below the carrot men are some blue figures and some petroglyphs on the lower back wall of the rock shelter. These pictographs date from A.D. 800 to 1150, but some have been painted over older petroglyphs. It is unusual to see both petroglyphs and pictographs at the same site.

Sidelight

Cañon Pintado ("painted canyon" in Spanish) was named by Fathers Domínguez and Escalante in 1776. The expedition searched for a northern overland route from Santa Fe to the California missions. Although they failed to find a route to California, they did explore much of western Colorado and eastern Utah. Father Escalante's record of September 9, 1776, reads, "Halfway in this canyon towards the south there is a quite lofty rock cliff on which we saw crudely painted, three shields, or Apache shields, of hide and a spearhead. Farther down on the north side we saw another painting, which supposedly represented two men in combat. For this reason we named it El Cañon Pintado."

Side Trip

The small Rangely Outdoor Museum is worth the stop. It features fossils (and directions to spots where you can collect your own fossils), Native American artifacts, dinosaur footprints, and some history of the area. A 1950s-era home on the museum grounds, furnished in the same time period, will bring back memories. Museum hours vary, so contact the museum for exact information. Rangely Museum, Rangely, 970-675-2612, www.rangely.com, e-mail chamber@rangelygovt.com.

DEER CREEK

location: *western Colorado (Grand Junction area)*
directions: *Head south approximately 20 miles from Grand Junction on US 50. Turn right (west) onto the dirt road at milepost 52 on Bridgeport Rd. and go approximately 3 miles. The site is at the north side of Deer Creek, where it meets the Gunnison River. Easily navigated by car, it is a curvy drive following Deer Creek through some rugged scenery.*

From the parking lot, follow a faint footpath north across Deer Creek to the large boulders against the cliff. There are two groups of petroglyphs along the southwest side of the boulders. This paleo-art spans a long period of time and features several different cultures.

Have you found the deer and the bear claw? Notice the straight line with several short cross-lines? This is referred to as a pole ladder—a type of ladder used by the Indians to reach their high alcove homes. Look closely. These figures are darker (more repatinated) than the others. This probably means these images are older than the lighter glyphs.

Also note the horse and rider. Since horses did not appear in the West until after the Spaniards arrived, this image is probably Ute and one of the most recent specimens of rock art here. Did you notice the historic rock structure with a boulder forming one of its walls?

The Gunnison River is a major tributary of the Colorado River. It is responsible for the eroding of the Black Canyon near Delta, Colorado.

Sidelight

The green tree-like plants along the banks of the Gunnison River are tamarisks, sometimes called salt cedar. Brought first from the Mediterranean in the 1800s as an ornamental shrub, then planted by the Department of Agriculture along arroyos to stem erosion, the plant spread rapidly, becoming a nuisance along almost all waterways in the West.

The water-loving tamarisk's range expands about 12 miles per year, using a lot of precious water. It does not provide good habitat for birds or other animals, and its shade hinders the growth of native willow and cottonwoods. Massive efforts are being made to eradicate the plant, especially along the southern portion of the Colorado River. After tamarisk has been removed, it requires years of vigilance to stop new stalks from growing.

McDONALD CREEK CULTURAL RESOURCE AREA

location: *western Colorado (Grand Junction area)*
directions: *From Grand Junction, head west on I-70 for approximately 30 miles to exit #2 (Rabbit Valley). Turn left (south) at the stop sign, crossing the overpass and going over the cattle guard.*

Take the road straight ahead for about 2.5 miles. Watch for a very large rock that looks like a gumdrop or castle. When you reach this rock, you'll turn left (east) onto another two-track road, which follows the streambed about 0.3 mile to the parking area. (No vehicles are allowed beyond this point, not even mountain bikes.)

The hike is rated as easy, but getting there is not for the chicken-hearted. Although high-clearance vehicles are recommended, you really should have a four-wheel drive. The road has steep, narrow areas with blind corners, so drive slowly. Do not attempt this area during wet weather because the streambed is prone to flash floods. The best time to visit is March through November. There is a restroom here, but no camping or fires are allowed. This area is managed by the BLM. For information call 970-244-3000.

Colorful red-banded cliffs mark the route to this remote site. You won't find a marked trail or any signs pointing to rock art, so expect to do some exploring. The Fremont culture left both pictographs and petroglyphs down McDonald Creek about 1,000 years ago.

There are four panels, the first about 100 yards down from the parking area. Look on the west-facing wall. The red painted figures are approximately 15 feet up the wall. Can you find the image that looks like a sitting eagle with folded wings? Hint: It has round dots on its chest. Now try to find the geometric shape with dots and lines. You should also see a figure resembling a sunburst and one that looks like a turtle.

There are three more panels on down McDonald Creek, but our search was cut short when a BLM official arrived and told us to get out because flash floods were expected. Although the sun may be shining when you visit, it's a good idea to be aware of this possibility. In the West, rain many miles away can send water roaring down narrow streambeds in a matter of minutes.

According to the literature, the next three panels are all within 1.5 miles.

Two of the panels are about 0.5 mile down below the drop-off. On the east side of the canyon are some petroglyphs along with historic dates and names. On the west side is a painted panel. The final panel is high on the wall in an alcove, but you should not climb the rock ledge below the panel.

Sidelight

McDonald Creek, like many desert sites, was favored because of its water. Many plants used by the Fremont people grew here. Although they do not have a very appetizing name, skunkberry bushes provided sour berries, along with barberry and serviceberries. The Indians used these berries for food, and the plants attracted birds and deer, which made easy hunting for the residents.

UTE MOUNTAIN TRIBAL PARK

location: *southwestern Colorado (south of Cortez)*
fee charged; reservations required
directions: *The park covers 125,000 acres and borders Mesa Verde National Park. To protect the approximately 10,000 archaeological sites within the park, visitation is permitted only with a guide. Full-day tours start from the Ute Mountain visitors center*

22 miles south of Cortez at the junction of US 160 and US 491. Visitors must bring their own lunch and water, and use their own vehicles for transportation on 40 miles of dirt road. Be sure your gas tank is full. Best time to visit is spring or fall. It is very hot in the summer. Reservations should be made by calling 970-565-9653 or 800-847-5485. Visitors center 970-749-1452 (cell phone), www.mesaverdecountry.com.

The Ute Mountain Tribal Park is an archaeological gem seen by only about 3,000 visitors per year. The reservation was not opened to the public until 1982. Now, you may visit the sites, but must have a Ute Indian guide. The rock art is easy to view, but the ruins themselves are the true highlight of the park. Very similar to those seen in Mesa Verde National Park, these sites are not restored and look much the way they did when discovered, except that the artifacts have been removed.

This is a full-day trip and, if you go to the ruins, requires about 4 miles of hiking. Warning: If you are afraid of heights, visiting these ruins may not be for you. You will be following the old Ancestral Puebloan (Anasazi) trail, and you must climb ladders. Reaching the Eagle's Nest Ruin requires climbing a 40-foot wooden ladder, with a deep canyon below you!

Guides are very knowledgeable about Ute history. Some of the rock art is Ute and was painted by Chief Jack House in the 1920s and 1930s. These colorful portrayals of Ute people and symbols are tinted with red hematite and

yellow ocher. You'll notice a hogan at this site. Hogans are traditional Navajo homes, not Ute, but Jack House hired Navajos to herd his sheep, and they built the hogan. Jack House also proposed the Ute Tribal Park protecting these archaeological wonders.

Another stop is Kiva Point. Here petroglyphs date from A.D. 550 to 1300. There are bighorn sheep, deer, and shamanistic figures, some with V-shaped bodies. Some experts think the wavy line glyph might be a map of the Mancos River, a major trade route for Native Americans up to historic times.

The next stop is the ruins and some serious hiking. Climbing to a series of multi-story pueblos built in alcoves, we were amazed that many of the roof beams and ceilings are still intact, and paintings remain on the kiva walls. Granaries, tucked away in cracks, are still sealed with mud. A trip to Lion House, Eagle's Nest, Tree House, and other sites makes for an experience long remembered, both for the ruins and also for the climb up the ladders.

Sidelight

There are different bands of Ute tribes. In this area live the Ute Mountain bands. The large mountain northwest of the tribal park is Sleeping Ute Mountain. Can you see the sleeping Ute? The rocks at the southern end are his feet sticking up, and the northern end is his head, with a headdress laid out behind his head.

Side Trip

The Ute Indian Museum in Montrose, Colorado, offers a great place to learn about this Native American tribe. At one time the Nuche—the name the Utes call themselves—inhabited Colorado, Utah, and other parts of the West. Videos, old photos, beadwork, and a rare Cochetopa wickiup make the museum very interesting. You will find it 3 miles south of Montrose on US 550. Open 7 days a week from May 15 through September 30; 970-249-3098.

Valley of Fire State Park, Nevada

NEVADA ROCK ART SITES
(Southern Nevada)

RED ROCK CANYON NATIONAL CONSERVATION AREA

location: *southern Nevada (Las Vegas area)*
partially wheelchair-accessible
directions: *Red Rock Canyon National Conservation Area covers 197,000 acres and is administered by the BLM. Most visitors drive the 13-mile scenic one-way loop, stopping for short hikes along the way, while the more adventurous may hike the many back-country trails. From the northern part of Las Vegas, follow Charleston Blvd. (NV 159) northwest to the National Conservation Area. If you are coming from the airport or from the Strip, take I-15 south to NV 160 (Blue Diamond Highway). Exit west, drive 10 miles to the intersection of NV 159, then head north another 10 miles to the visitors center. Petroglyph Trail is wheelchair-accessible. Red Rock Canyon National Conservation Area, HCR 33, Box 5500, Las Vegas, 702-515-5350, www.redrockcanyon.blm.gov.*

Nearly a million people a year visit the spectacular scenery in Red Rock Canyon. A 13-mile, scenic one-way loop offers short walks to petroglyphs. Although there is probably much more paleo-art in the canyon, only a few sites are open to the public, and these are easily accessible.

Early Native Americans were drawn to this area by water—the real gold of the desert. There are more than 40 springs and many natural catchment basins in the area. The water also brings animals and allows for plant growth—both valuable assets for hunter and gatherer societies.

After enjoying the visitors center, stop at Calico Basin picnic area. A fenced area protects the alkali mariposa lilies. Follow the dirt path leading around behind the second fenced pond. The boulders at the cliff base have petroglyphs, and some of the elements are very clear. The dark figures that have repatinated are probably much older than the brighter glyphs.

Travel on to the Willow Springs picnic area. A short cement trail leads to a fenced area displaying six Ancestral Puebloan handprints, approximately 800

years old. There is also a roasting pit, where the residents roasted agaves and possibly other plants and animals. Roasted agave hearts have a taste similar to molasses, and roasting pits like this one were common throughout the Southwest. Some were as large as 27 feet across.

Next, you'll want to take the Petroglyph Trail, starting on the west side of the Willow Springs Picnic Area. This easy 0.1-mile-long walk is wheelchair-accessible. Cross over Lost Creek (usually dry) and study the rock wall for both petroglyphs and pictographs. You will find a red horse with a rider and, on the black area, another panel of figures. Check behind the scrub oak tree for two circles with a line through them. These are pictographs painted in burnt orange.

While Red Rock Canyon isn't the best place in the Southwest to see petroglyphs, it is easy to access, and the scenery is beautiful.

Sidelight

The alkali mariposa (which means "butterfly" in Spanish) lily protected behind fences at the Calico Basin area is becoming endangered because of increased recreation. It grows in these saline meadows and is easily trampled. In Clark County, Nevada, it is found only in the Red Rock Canyon National Conservation Area.

VALLEY OF FIRE STATE PARK

location: *southeastern Nevada (55 miles east of Las Vegas)*
directions: *Valley of Fire State Park is 55 miles east of Las Vegas via I-15 and SR 169. The closest town is Overton. A return loop trip leads from the park back west on SR 167 (Northshore Rd.), skirting the shores of Lake Mead and intercepting US 95 east of Boulder City, then northwest to Las Vegas. Spring and fall are the best times to visit, since summer daytime temperatures usually exceed 100 degrees F and may even reach 120 degrees F. Two campgrounds, plus picnic tables. Valley of Fire State Park, Overton, 702-397-2088.*

Valley of Fire, Nevada's oldest and largest state park, derives its name not from volcanic action but from fiery red rock formations. The park would be worth visiting just for the scenery, especially colorful during the late afternoon. Featured in both movies and commercials, the oddly shaped rocks seem painted red and white with a giant paintbrush. Many petroglyphs, dating from 300 B.C. to A.D. 1150, are scattered throughout the park, and most are believed to be from the Ancestral Puebloan culture.

Atlatl Rock is one of the most popular petroglyph sites in the park. Visitors climb stairs to view designs through a protective plexiglass cover. The site earned its name from the depiction of an atlatl, a prehistoric throwing stick that extended the distance a spear could be thrown. An atlatl-throwing competition is held annually in the park, sponsored by the World Atlatl Association.

A favorite viewing spot here is the Petroglyph Canyon/Mouse's Tank trail, a mile-long (round trip) walk down a sandy wash. Follow the cement steps from the parking lot down to the wash, where the glyphs start immediately. On the cliff to your left, you'll find hands, sheep, and other designs. Keep walking and checking the desert varnish for random images. As the canyon narrows, there is a large panel on your left. Up and slightly to the right are four figures holding hands. Noticed the large "turkey" tracks yet? There are hundreds of rock art images down this trail, mostly on the left side of the canyon. Have you seen the deer with very large antlers?

Many of the figures are nearly worn off by the wind and water that helped form the fantastic shapes in the park. How many designs do you think were once in this canyon? The early people were undoubtedly drawn to this spot for water and shade during the hot summers.

Mouse's Tank is not named for a small rodent. Legend claims that Mouse, a Paiute Indian, raided a woman's garden in July of 1897. To avoid the sheriff's posse, Mouse hid in this wild, inaccessible canyon. After 5 days, the posse sighted the fugitive and ordered him to surrender. Mouse refused to give up, and after an hour-long gun battle, he was killed.

Sidelight

Mouse's Tank is not a real "tank," but a stream-worn indentation in the rock that holds rainwater for up to 6 months after a storm. These formations are usually much smaller than Mouse's Tank and are called *tinajas*. Locations of tinajas were well-known by the local inhabitants, as they made it possible to live and travel in the desert.

Side Trip

The Lost City Museum is at Overton, about 15 miles north of Valley of Fire on SR 16. This wonderful museum showcases Ancestral Puebloan artifacts, excavated in the late 1930s when water from Lake Mead started covering sites. The museum is located on top of an ancient village known as Pueblo Grande de Nevada. Lost City Museum, 721 S. Moapa Valley Blvd., 702-397-2193, lostcity@comnett.net.

GRAPEVINE CANYON

location: *southern Nevada (Laughlin area)*
directions: *This is one of my favorite petroglyph sites in southern Nevada. The easiest and fastest access to Grapevine Canyon is from Laughlin. Follow NV 163 for 6 miles west to the Christmas Tree Pass turnoff on your right. Go approximately 2.5 miles to a small dirt road that takes off to the left. Follow this road about 0.25 mile to the end and a parking area. Trail signs lead west to the mouth of the canyon. If you plan to visit this spot in summer, go in the early morning or near dusk since summer temperatures are horrendous. Take plenty of water and watch for rattlesnakes.*

This hike begins along the edge of the wash, then it drops down and follows the wash itself. The trail goes about 0.5 mile to the mouth of the canyon, but here the visible trail ends and you are left to your own boulder hopping skills. Amazing petroglyphs are readily seen on both sides as you enter the canyon. You'll probably notice those up on the hill on the left side first.

At the entrance to the canyon, climb out of the wash and explore around the point on the right side until you see the design that looks like a large "H" turned on its side. There are hundreds of figures here, mainly geometric, along with some bighorn sheep and shamanistic figures. Some experts believe the symbols that look like bars with wavy lines hanging down might stand for rain.

As you head back to the mouth of the canyon, look across to the south side about halfway up. Do you see the five sheep in a row? This is the glyph most often associated with Grapevine Canyon. If you want to take pictures, it is somewhat easier to photograph the sheep from the north side of the canyon. The five sheep appear to have been made by the same artist. In addition, there are two other sheep below the main sheep, a sun image, and two male figures.

Head on down the canyon and search for more glyphs, keeping in mind that most of the designs occur near the entrance. On some rocks the desert varnish has worn off, but the figures were cut so deep that the pale designs are still visible on the light gray inner rock. There has been some speculation that the canyon has filled with sand over time and many more glyphs may lie buried under the sand.

If you want to walk up to the head of the canyon, follow the stream and animal trails. There is a spring at the top of the canyon adorned with grapevines, hence the name Grapevine Canyon. It is easy to see why prehistoric people chose this spot. Not only is there water here, but it is also shady in hot weather.

Side Trip

If you want to make this a longer trip, try the 16-mile Christmas Tree Pass scenic loop. The road you traveled to Grapevine Canyon loops around, rejoining US 95 a few miles south of Searchlight. High-clearance vehicles are recommended; take a detailed map and plenty of water.

TOPOCK GORGE

location: *this trip starts in southern Nevada, but the glyphs are actually in Arizona's Havasu Wildlife Refuge*

reservations required; fee charged

directions: *Contact River Jet Tours in Laughlin, 702-298-8363, 800-327-2386, to make reservations. Boats run year-round and are heated in winter. Best times to visit are mid-September to November and March to May.*

Take it easy while you look at rock art with the River Jet Tours 60-mile ride down the Colorado River between Laughlin, Nevada, and Lake Havasu City, Arizona. You'll spend time enjoying the London Bridge and Lake Havasu City, then make the 60-mile return trip. The tour departs Laughlin at 10:15 a.m. and arrives back at 4:30 p.m. All you have to do is relax and enjoy the ride.

The petroglyphs are in the Topock Gorge portion of the trip, where the Colorado River narrows up to labyrinths of canyons and arroyos slicing through the barren mountains to reach the river. Bighorn sheep thrive in these eroded mountains, much as they did thousands of years ago when desert people lived along the Colorado's banks.

Topock Gorge is within the Havasu Wildlife Refuge, which covers 37,515 acres of rugged mountainous terrain along the Arizona side of the Colorado River. The river snakes through 30 river-miles of refuge, but, with all the coves and inlets, it amounts to 300 miles of shoreline. This must have been a favorite hunting area for the ancient desert dwellers.

The boat stops at the petroglyphs in Topock Gorge on the return trip to Laughlin. The glyphs are easily seen from the boat. Geometric, human, and animal designs are carved into the dark coating on the south-facing rocks. Look down near the waterline to see a sunburst. If you are traveling in your own boat, tie up at Site #226 and hike around. There are more glyphs on the nearby hills and in the arroyos.

Some archaeologists estimate these motifs may be 5,000 years old, but no one is exactly sure. Early hunter and gatherer cultures used the Colorado River as a travel route, and later peoples farmed the fertile land along the banks.

Sidelight

Lake Havasu backs up behind Parker Dam, and the city on the shore (Lake Havasu City) is home to the world's largest antique—the London Bridge. City founder Robert P. McCulloch paid $2.5 million for the bridge itself and another $7 million to have it dismantled, shipped from London, and reconstructed over a channel on Lake Havasu.

NEW MEXICO ROCK ART SITES

Tsankawi portion of Bandelier National Monument, New Mexico

WATERFLOW

location: *northwestern New Mexico*
directions: *Located along US 64 between Shiprock and Farmington, directly across the highway from Big Rock Trading Post. Not recommended for small children because of nearby traffic.*

There are many more impressive rock art sites, but Waterflow is very easy to reach. Stop at the pullout on the north side of US 64 directly across from the Big Rock Trading Post. Walk east along the highway. (Although there is a guardrail between you and the road, it can be disconcerting when the cars speed by.)

The petroglyphs are carved into the reddish sandstone cliffs. Have you found the square divided into fourths with a design in each section? Look on the rock to the right of the square to discover a half circle of dots. Any idea what this could mean? Do you think it might be a trail or a method of counting? Look up to see swallow nests. Directly below the nests is a panel with a large animal figure that resembles a deer. Have you noticed that some of the images have been vandalized? It appears someone shot them.

Keep on walking east about 50 feet to see more panels with human-like forms, as well as a number of square and oval motifs. Another 50 feet onward is another set of petroglyphs, more faded due to weathering. Can you pick out the 18-inch human-like element, the spiral, and other geometrics? There are some additional glyphs to the west of the parking area, although they are quite faded.

Sidelight

Big Rock Trading Post is a historical trading post. In the 1800s, trading posts exchanged manufactured goods for Navajo blankets, jewelry, and other handmade crafts. The Navajos charged needed items, then paid their debts

when they sold wool or sheep. Jewelry was also pawned at the trading post. Today, many trading posts sell handmade Navajo rugs with an attached photo of the weaver so you will know the rug is authentic. You can usually find excellent silver and turquoise jewelry here, too, or quirky Navajo folk art, such as carved wood, brightly colored chickens, laughing horses, pickups, and other fanciful figures. Folk art is a relatively recent craft on the Navajo Reservation, and most pieces are humorous. This is a fun and inexpensive art form to collect.

CROW CANYON

location: *northwestern New Mexico*

directions: *The easiest way to learn about Crow Canyon (don't confuse this with Crow Canyon Archaeological Center in southwestern Colorado) is to visit Salmon Ruins just outside of Bloomfield (505-632-2013) and pick up the BLM brochure* Pueblitos of Dinetah. *From Bloomfield, head approximately 12 miles east on US 64 through Blanco and over the San Juan River, then watch for a well-maintained gravel road on your right On some maps this is CR 4462 and on others CR 4450. It heads southeast into Largo Canyon (or Cañon Largo). The road is soft dirt in places, especially where it crosses the frequent washes. Travel approximately 19 miles then watch for a BLM sign on the left for turnoff to Crow Canyon. From this turnoff it is 1.6 miles to a fork in the road. Follow the "Main Panel" sign to the left 0.3 mile to a parking area near an oil well. (You will be crossing the Largo Wash at Rock Crossing.) This is in the San Juan Basin oilfields, so watch carefully for trucks and pickups, especially going around corners. You should travel this road in a high-clearance vehicle, preferably 4-wheel drive, because you will be going through sandy areas.*

Crow Canyon is unique because it has both Navajo and Pueblo petroglyphs. In 1680, the local Pueblo people along the northern Rio Grande revolted

against the Spanish occupation, forcing the Spanish to relinquish northern New Mexico. In 1692, the Spanish returned, and many Pueblo people headed west to Navajo lands. This time in Native American history is referred to as the Gobernador Period, which lasted about 100 years. There was probably some intermarriage between Navajo and Pueblo people, along with a blending of architecture, religion, and traditions. By 1715, attacks from the Ute people forced the Navajos and Pueblos to build their homes in defensive areas now called *pueblitos* (little pueblos). Crow Canyon is one of these pueblitos and contains very impressive rock art.

Walk along the base of the cliff to the left of the parking lot to see panels carved on sandstone. The Navajo ceremonial images are exceptional. One of the first symbols you will notice is a motif resembling clothespins over a row of hourglasses. Have you found the line of men holding hands? I counted eighteen. Do you have any ideas about the circle divided in quarters?

Keep following the cliff around as the rock becomes redder and the petroglyphs clearer. Watch for the beautiful panel with many elements. See the two men on horseback? Do you think they are Spaniards brandishing swords? Directly below the two horses is another horned head. Look down to ground level and to the left of the horned figure to see something that looks like a sun with rays peeking out. The rays each have a tiny circle on the end. See the large

corn plant, complete with two ears of corn? Corn is important in both the Navajo and Pueblo religions. The figure between the spiral and the corn plant is probably a Yei, or Navajo deity.

Farther along, look for a figure with a headdress on only the left side of his head. He is holding a stick in one hand and a bow in the other.

His eyes appear square, and his body is divided into light and dark sections. This might illustrate the Navajo deity Monsterslayer, who made the earth safe for humankind by getting rid of all the monsters.

The geology here is unusual. Cracks and slot canyons are eroded into the cliff and some have petroglyphs just inside the openings. Most of the rock art is found before you reach the two freestanding rock formations.

Sidelight

Salmon Ruins is 2 miles west of Bloomfield. Once two stories high, the pueblo is believed to contain 150 rooms. This community was closely associated with the Chaco Canyon complex approximately 38 miles south of Salmon Ruins. The site is named for early homesteader George Salmon and his family, who protected the site for more than 90 years. The village was abandoned about A.D. 1285, along with many other sites in the Southwest. Salmon Ruins Museum and Research Library, 6131 US 64, Bloomfield, 505-632-2013.

BANDELIER NATIONAL MONUMENT

location: *northern New Mexico (48 miles northwest of Santa Fe)*
directions: *From Santa Fe, take US 285/84 north to Pojoaque, then west on NM 502 and south on NM 4. Most of Bandelier's petroglyphs are along Long House Trail, a 1.5-mile paved loop trail that is steep in spots and not wheelchair-accessible. This region is beautiful in the fall and gets quite cold in the winter. Bandelier National Monument, Los Alamos; visitors center 505-672-3861, ext. 517; recorded information 505-672-0343.*

Bandelier National Monument, named for Adolph Bandelier, an early anthropologist, is located in Frijoles (free-HOH-lace, meaning "beans") Canyon. A permanent stream here provided inhabitants with drinking water, while the fertile ground allowed for the cultivation of corn, beans, and squash.

The easiest place to view petroglyphs is the paved Long House Trail, leading to the ruins along the cliff base. Pick up a pamphlet at the visitors center called "Long House and its Rock Art" to help you locate some of the more weathered images. Only portions of the bottom story of this condominium-style pueblo remain today, but it runs for 800 feet along the cliff. Occupied during the fourteenth and fifteenth centuries, it was abandoned before the Spanish conquistadors arrived.

Do you see the small, round holes in lines? These were where *vigas* (VEE-gahs), or small roof beams, were anchored. You can count the number of rows of holes to see how many stories tall a particular room block reached.

Above rooms 166–170, according to the pamphlet, you'll find a panel with eight masks, as well as a cross inside two circles. From rooms 130 to 160 you won't see any rock art, but above room 127 you'll find seven katsina figures. According to Puebloan beliefs, katsinas are responsible for weather, especially bringing the rain.

Notice the red clay on the cliff at the back of some rooms. This probably was red plaster that lined the house walls. You'll find the most glyphs above rooms 65–111. Look closely to see the two turkeys above room 85 (this is the signature design of Bandelier National Monument). Look for a circle with a cross inside, then look directly up. The two turkeys are one above the other.

As you head west along the cliff you will find scattered designs including serpents, masks, and katsinas. People standing on the roof of the top-story room probably made the designs here at Long House. Near the west end is a red and white pictograph protected by plexiglass—the most spectacular of the Long House images. The geometric design, once on the wall of a second-story room, is a white zigzag on a red background.

Bandelier National Monument made a good location for the Puebloans because of nice summer weather. At this elevation it gets quite cold during the winter, but the cozy pueblo rooms could be kept comfortable with small fires.

Sidelight

This region is known as the Pajarito (pa-ha-REE-toe, meaning "little bird" in Spanish) Plateau and contains many Ancestral Puebloan sites. The cliff wall behind Long House is pocked with holes. This is because more than one million years ago Jemez (HAY-mess) Volcano erupted twice, depositing layers of ash up to 1,000 feet thick and covering 400 square miles. Each of the eruptions was 600 times as powerful as the Mount St. Helens eruption of 1980. The ash compacted, forming a rock called "tuff." This soft, crumbly rock weathers into natural caves that the residents used for storage and enlarged to make small rooms.

TSANKAWI LOOP TRAIL

location: *north-central New Mexico (Los Alamos area)*
directions: *Tsankawi is a detached portion of Bandelier National Monument (north of the main part of the monument), located 12 miles northeast of park headquarters on NM 4 near the town of Los Alamos. You may get a Tsankawi Trail guide brochure at park headquarters. This is a 1.5-mile loop trail with some narrow spots, high drop-offs, and three ladders, including one 12 feet high. You can view the petroglyphs on the Lower Cliff portion of the trail without climbing ladders, but it takes some rock scrambling. This isn't a trail for very young children. You should allow 2 hours to walk the entire route, and remember, this is at 6,600 feet of elevation. Wear sturdy shoes. You'll find a permit pay station, picnic tables, and pit toilets at the trailhead.*

If you are afraid of heights, you might want to avoid Tsankawi (SAN-ka-WEE) Trail. But if you have an adventuresome spirit, you'll find interesting rock art and a spectacular view of Española Valley and the Sangre de Cristo ("blood of Christ") Mountains. *Tsankawi* means "village between two canyons at the clump of sharp, round cactus," which is a mouthful! Much of the trail is on the original route used by residents as they climbed to their village. Portions of the path are worn 8 to 12 inches into solid rock. How would you like to carry your drinking water from the canyon bottom up to this pueblo?

Since we weren't too thrilled about climbing a 12-foot ladder in 30-mph winds, we went for the Lower Portion of the trail. The Upper Portion leads to the ruin and additional petroglyphs. Starting at the main parking lot, we scrambled over some boulders to pick up the Lower Trail. The area discussed here is between Markers 18 and 19.

Because this rock is tuff (compacted ash), some of the petroglyphs have dimmed with time, but many remain very distinct. The images you find will depend on the time of day, since light and shadow will work to reveal some of the fainter symbols. Remember, if you take only the Lower Trail, you will be following the trail guide directions backwards (looking for rock art between Markers 19 and 18).

Look for the man with the deep-cut eyes and mouth. Now, see if you can pick out the 18-inch male figure with a square head. When you reach an open area in the trail with light-colored sand, look up at the green lichen visible on the rock. Some of the images here are so old that the lichen has grown over them.

If you can find the three figures with headdresses, look straight above them about three feet to find a large deer image. This site seems to have more human-like deities and godlike images than animal designs. There are also several large spirals.

Although Tsankawi is part of Bandelier National Monument, the people at Tsankawi spoke Tewa, while those living in the pueblos at what is now the lower part of Bandelier National Monument spoke Keres. Their religious beliefs seem to have been similar, though.

Sidelight

There aren't any permanent water sources near Tsankawi, and the area receives an average 15 inches of precipitation yearly. Winters are cold, with freezing nights, sometimes extending into mid-May. The people probably planted their crops on the canyon floor to take advantage of the runoff from snowmelt or summer storms. The forest here is called a pygmy forest, consisting of piñon and juniper trees. The piñon trees produce a small nut used for food. High in calories and easy to store, it was an important food source. You can buy piñon nuts today in many local stores and sometimes from roadside vendors.

LA CIENEGUILLA

location: *north-central New Mexico (Santa Fe area)*
directions: *La Cieneguilla has just been opened to the public by the BLM. It is southwest of the Santa Fe airport on County Rd. 56. For more accurate directions call the BLM's Taos Field Office (505-751-4710). From the parking area it is short walk to the bottom of a rocky mesa. The petroglyphs are scattered along the mile-long mesa. To climb around on the rough lava rocks, wear sturdy shoes—and watch for snakes.*

Although known to the locals, La Cieneguilla (see-en-uh-GHEE-ya) is just being developed for the public. It is believed that there are over 4,000 glyphs here (carved in what archaeologists refer to as Rio Grande Style, mainly from the Ancestral Puebloan culture), but they seem to be scattered among the boulders. We had better luck finding them by going left along the mesa.

Around the point of the mesa on the south, watch high on the cliffs for a man-like glyph with his hand up. Now look above him for a lizard, and above that another figure, most likely a bird. Down lower on the cliff and to the left on a very dark rock is an image that resembles two figures kneeling and holding hands. This is a unique motif, rarely seen at other sites.

Keep on going around the mesa. The petroglyphs are there, but you need to train your eyes to spot them. We found one geometric design that covers an entire rock. It resembles a fish net—but in this high desert country a fish net seems unlikely. What do you think it means? When you walk back to the parking lot, you will notice more glyphs you had not seen when you first walked by.

Sidelight

La Cieneguilla is just a portion of the 3,556-acre La Cienega Area of Critical Environmental Concern (ACEC). The three major pueblos in the ACEC covered a time period of almost 900 years, giving experts a chance to see the development of different cultures. These pueblos were probably part of the turquoise trade, because turquoise was mined nearby. The stone was used in jewelry, as a ceremonial item, and for trade to villages as far away as northern Mexico.

PETROGLYPH NATIONAL MONUMENT

location: *Albuquerque area*
directions: *At Albuquerque, take I-40 west across the Rio Grande Bridge, then take the Unser Blvd. exit. Follow the signs to Petroglyph National Monument, 6001 Unser Blvd. NW. There are number of trails here, ranging from easy to strenuous. From the visitors center, it is a short drive to the two main trails, Rinconada and Boca Negra Canyon. No lodging in the park. Call for information on ranger-led hikes: 505-899-0205.*

Petroglyph National Monument, covering 17 miles along the West Mesa escarpment, is New Mexico's best-known site and easy to reach from Albuquerque. There are over 20,000 glyphs in this 7,236-acre park. Stop by the

visitors center to view the glyphs there and pick up trail guides. Many of the petroglyphs in the park were made by Ancestral Puebloans in the Rio Grande style, but experts believe the images range in date from 1000 B.C. until A.D. 1700. There are several trails in the park, but we will cover only the Boca Negra Canyon Trail.

Although there seems to be a large number of motifs along the Boca Negra Trail, they constitute only 4 percent of the petroglyphs in the park. Nevertheless, they are some of the best. Here at Boca Negra, there are four individual trails. The Mesa Point Trail is moderately strenuous. It takes about 30 minutes to walk, although you should allow longer if you are not used to the 5,280-foot elevation. The Cliff Base Trail is easy to moderate, and takes only about 15 minutes. Drive another 0.25 mile north past the main Boca Negra entrance to Upper Canyon Area. This hike is moderately strenuous, following a stairway down into the canyon.

The Macaw Trail is one of the most popular. Rated easy, it takes only a few minutes to walk but has some very interesting images. Have you come upon the first macaw parrot yet? It is about 18 inches high. Notice the long feathers on the bottom of the glyph. These feathers were prized for the headdresses used in ceremonial dances. We know the people who once lived here traded with people from present-day Mexico and Central America, because macaws live in rainforests and are not native to the Southwest.

Now look at the smaller macaw figure. It looks like it is in a cage. Perhaps these birds traveled all the way from Mexico in such cages. Keep your eyes open for a 30-inch human glyph with a headdress. Can you see that his nose is higher than his eyes? A few yards west is another man-like figure with a bird head. His body is a large circle with a design that might represent a shield.

Another distinct figure along the Macaw Trail looks like two half-circles with a long stem. This might portray yucca pods. The plant was widely used by the early residents and is still used by Pueblo people today. Many of the designs on the pottery sold in area gift shops are painted with tiny yucca paintbrushes.

Sidelight

Outside the visitors center you may see strings of red chile hanging along the porch. These are *ristras* and are common in the Southwest. Long green chiles—usually the Anaheim variety—turn red when mature. The chiles are then strung and hung on the walls. When needed for cooking, some of the chiles are taken down and ground into chili powder.

TOMÉ HILL

location: *central New Mexico (south of Albuquerque)*
directions: *From Albuquerque, take I-25 south to Los Lunas. Take exit 203 through Los Lunas (about 5 miles) to NM 47. Turn right on NM 47 for several miles to the town of Tomé. Follow the signs to Tomé Hill, where Tomé Hill Park is open from dawn to dusk. The trail to the summit is 0.25 mile long and quite steep, with an elevation gain of 1,200 feet. Elevation at the top is 5,223 feet. For information, contact the Belen Chamber of Commerce, 505-864-8091, or the Valley Improvement Association, 800-359-8186.*

Tomé Hill is volcanic in origin and rises as a landmark above the Rio Grande Valley. It is thought to have functioned as a spiritual site for Ancestral Puebloans. In 1945, the Penitentes (a Catholic religious group) erected the shrine of crosses on top of the hill. Every year on Good Friday, hundreds of people make the hike to the crosses. There are more than 1,800 documented petroglyphs on the hill, though many of them are, unfortunately, inaccessible. Some of the older circles may be 2,000 years old.

Climbing the hill is somewhat strenuous. The trail is steep and there are loose rocks, so be careful. About two-thirds of the way up, watch for spur paths (no signs) taking off to the right. On the east side of the jumble of basalt rocks you will see petroglyphs, including a mask with a square mouth and headdress. There is also a nice spiral on top of this rock with animal and feet images. Have you found the animals with horns? These symbols are in the Rio Grande style, most dating from A.D. 800 to 1600. You will probably notice several crosses incised on the rocks. These are Christian-style crosses, probably made by early Spanish shepherds or possibly by the Penitentes.

Sidelight

Tomé Hill is located along the Camino Real (Spanish for "royal road"). This route led from Mexico to northern New Mexico, bringing sixteenth-century Spanish armies and traders to the Pueblo and Spanish villages to the north. The large arch and metal figures at the parking lot commemorate the area's various cultural eras. You will find Indian dancers, Catholics bearing crosses, conquistadors, shepherds, and railroad workers. Tomé Hill is named for Tomé Domínguez de Mendoza, who farmed and ranched in the area around 1659.

EL MORRO NATIONAL MONUMENT

location: *west-central New Mexico (56 miles southeast of Gallup)*
directions: *From Gallup, take NM 602 south, then take NM 53 east. Or from Grants, take NM 53 west for 42 miles. Open daily except Christmas and New Years Day. Trails may be closed due to snow or bad weather. Bring bug repellent in the spring, since the "no-see-ums" can get vicious. 505-783-4226.*

PASÓ POR AQUI. This Spanish inscription carved into white sandstone translates to "passed by here," and for centuries Native American, Spanish, and

Anglo travelers have passed by El Morro, leaving over 2,000 inscriptions and petroglyphs carved into the massive 200-foot-high white sandstone cliff. Although the sandstone bluff provided a landmark and a great place to carve (it is also sometimes called Inscription Rock), it was water that brought travelers here. Except in extreme drought, annual snowmelt and rainwater form a pool about 12 feet deep here, holding about 200,000 gallons of water.

Pick up a trail guide at the visitors center and begin your own exploration of this fascinating rock wall. The trail goes all the way to the top, but nearly all the writings are along the base. See if you can pick out the zigzag line with hand and footprints. Some experts think this means "follow the hand and foot trail to the water." Now, look for the four mountain sheep walking in a line. Can you spot the bear claw? Could this be a warning that there are bears in these mountains, or is it a sign that the Bear Clan stopped here?

Intermingled among the petroglyphs are rudimentary carvings and elegantly embellished names left by later visitors. Of course, the petroglyphs are ancient, but Governor Don Juan de Oñate left the oldest *dated* inscription on April 16, 1605. The trail guide will help you translate the Spanish inscriptions. E. Pen Long of Baltimore elaborately carved his name in flowing script sometime between 1850 and 1862. P. Gilmer Breckinridge carefully chipped his name in block letters, and nearby you'll find the name Beale. (Read more about them in the accompanying Sidelight.)

The loop walk along the base of the bluff is about 0.5 mile long. If you feel more adventuresome, follow the trail to the top, but remember: elevation here is over 7,200 feet. At the top you will find two Ancestral Puebloan sites. A'ts'ina, the larger of the two ruins, was built around A.D. 1275 and has been excavated by archaeologists. It once stood several stories high and was home to 1,000–1,500 people. The deep square and round rooms are kivas—underground chambers used for ceremonies and possibly for informal gatherings. The pueblos were abandoned around A.D. 1400 for unknown reasons.

Sidelight

Remember the etching of P. Gilmer Breckinridge's name? His nickname was Peachy, and he was a member of Lt. Edward Beale's Army expedition that rested at El Morro in 1857. This group, the Camel Corps, brought along camels as part of the government's experiment to see how they would fare in the American Southwest. Peachy was in charge of 25 of these camels. The camels proved superior to horses and mules, and the Army might have switched means of transportation if the Civil War hadn't terminated the great camel experiment. When the camels reached Los Angeles, they were auctioned off, but a few escaped. As late as the early 1900s, travelers reported seeing feral camels in the desert. Peachy returned to Virginia and was killed in a battle at Kennon's Landing, Virginia, in 1863.

THREE RIVERS PETROGLYPH SITE

location: *south-central New Mexico (Tularosa area)*
fee charged
directions: *Three Rivers Petroglyph Site in southern New Mexico is located 17 miles north of Tularosa and 28 miles south of Carrizozo on US 54. Turn east at Three Rivers onto the paved Country Rd. B 30 and travel 5 miles, following the signs. There is a small fee, and overnight camping is permitted; picnic tables and toilets are available. The site is open 24 hours daily, year-round. The trail to the shade canopy is a 1-mile round trip, rated easy to moderate with some low stairs. The hike from the shade*

area to the end of the trail is another 1-mile round trip and is more difficult. A short trail on the east side of the picnic area goes to a partially excavated village. Allow several hours to enjoy all that's available. This site is administered by the BLM, Las Cruces Field Office, 1800 Marquess, Las Cruces, 505-525-4300.

Three Rivers gets my vote as the best rock art site to visit in New Mexico. Though it can be very hot in the summer, it's one of the largest sites in the state and is easily accessible. Visitors are not required to stay on the trail, but can explore all over the 50-acre site, "discovering" rock art images and motifs. Please do not climb on rocks containing glyphs—and, as always, do not touch or deface the designs.

These images are from the Jornada Mogollon (hor-NAH-da muggy-OWN), a branch of the Mogollon culture occupying southwestern New Mexico, southeastern Arizona, and northern Chihuahua, Mexico, from approximately A.D. 600 to 1200. (The Mimbres Mogollon group lived in the mountains, while the Jornada Mogollon populated the desert.)

You'll start spotting petroglyphs within the first 100 feet of the trail. Can you see the hand on the first group of boulders to the right? All told, there are 21,000 designs here at Three Rivers.

Another 50 yards on the right, you'll find a stair-stepped pyramid design. Some experts associate this with clouds or rain. Have you noticed that many of the designs face west? At most rock-art sites, the symbols face south or east. Fifty feet beyond the pyramid, look to the left at the bird glyph, usually

referred to as an eagle.

Why do you think there are so many symbols at this site? No one knows for sure, but the mountain might have been a lookout or a religious site, or maybe it was just a tradition among the Native peoples to add new designs to the ones already here.

At Marker #1 you'll find an expertly etched circle divided into quarters and surrounded with dots. Watch for many of these unusually clear figures along the trail. Any ideas on what they might mean?

The Sacramento Mountains, which can be seen off to the east, stretch for about 60 miles; the highest peak is 11,973 feet high. At the trail fork, go right to Marker #2. Look directly behind the sign at the Jornada mask. Notice the almond-shaped eyes that are typical of the Jornada Mogollon culture.

Stop at Marker #3. Can you see where the artist used a natural nodule in the rock for an eye in the animal glyph? Look below and to the left to find another mask with those almond eyes. Have you noticed faint side trails? These usually lead to interesting rock art.

Between Markers #3 and #4, the images aren't quite so numerous, but there are more ahead. Watch for the nice geometric form, right along the trail. Marker #4 is near the top of the ridge. Look west about 15 feet and you'll see a drawing of a bighorn sheep. Its body consists of wavy lines.

Marker #5 indicates an animal shot with an arrow. What kind of animal do you think it is? See the bear claw below the animal's tail? At the fork, go right and look for Marker #6. It is off the trail on the left. Behind the sign, to the left on a south-facing rock, are two tracks. Experts think these might be turkey or roadrunner tracks.

Directly behind Marker #7 is a petroglyph of a large bighorn sheep shot with three arrows—the symbol most often associated with the Three Rivers site.

To find what's waiting at Marker #8, you'll need to climb up to the sign. Can you find the mask? Hint: It is on a corner of a rock, giving it a three-dimensional look with the nose sticking out. Look around to find the circle with dots and a portion of another bighorn sheep. There is another mask at Marker #9. This one appears to be wearing earrings.

A thunderbird design can be found at Marker #10 if you look carefully. Hint: It is not the lizard straight ahead. At Marker #11, notice the animal with its ears laid back (or are they horns?). Its body is made up of a checkerboard design and what look like circles hanging from the nose and tail.

At this point, you will have reached the shade canopy, the end of the official trail. The trail that leads down and to the south of the canopy will take you to a nice panel with large geometric designs. Look for lizard, bird, and fish images. If you are accustomed to hiking, have sturdy shoes, and like rock scrambling, continue on. The trail is not maintained and in some places is faint. There aren't as many petroglyphs along the way, but you'll find some great ones at the end.

Notice more of those spirals or circles with dots around them. Watch carefully for glyphs, as they aren't as visible along this route. At the end of the trail, in some large basalt boulders, someone has scratched "The End."

It's *not* the end, though, if you're not afraid of heights. Carefully go around the hill to the west and about halfway down. Keep circling around to the north and look up; you'll see many panels with unusual designs. Have you spotted the geometric blanket design? Near the top of the rocks to the right of the blanket design is a strange creature image that resembles a rhinoceros beetle, along with a number of masks and more of those circles with dots.

It's time to turn around and backtrack to the parking lot. You won't be bored, though, because you are sure to spot any number of petroglyphs that you missed on the way up. If you're really good, you'll be able to count all 21,000 glyphs. Or maybe fewer…

Sidelight

The large valley to the west of Three Rivers is the Tularosa (Spanish for "red reed") Basin. At the southern end is White Sands National Monument, home to the world's largest (275 square miles) gypsum dune field. The White Sands Missile Range encompasses 3,200 square miles. At the northern end of the Missile Range is the famous Trinity Site. Here the first atomic bomb was detonated at 5:29 a.m. (Mountain War Time) on July 16, 1945.

GILA CLIFF DWELLINGS NATIONAL MONUMENT

location: *southwestern New Mexico (44 miles north of Silver City)*
wheelchair-accessible
directions: *From Silver City, take NM 15 north, or from the Mimbres area take NM 35 north to NM 15 and continue north on 15. Both routes are very curvy and slow, so plan at least 2 hours' driving time. The suggested route for recreational vehicles and trailers over 20 feet long is NM 35 from Mimbres. There is no public transportation to the site. Open every day except Christmas and New Year's Day. 505-536-9361.*

Between A.D. 1270 and the early 1300s, people from the Mogollon Culture built dwellings in five of the seven caves in Gila Cliff Dwellings National Monument. Like many other sites in the Southwest, the Gila Cliff Dwellings were abandoned in the 1300s for unknown reasons. Although there are a few pictographs up in the main ruins, the best and easiest place to view images is at Lower Scorpion Campground, on the north side of NM 15, about 0.25 mile before you get to the visitors center.

The Trail to the Past starts at the campground, with pictographs at the end of a short, paved, wheelchair-accessible walk. The images are painted in red on a cliff close to the highway. Known as Mogollon Red style, the pictographs here are larger and more elaborate than other Mogollon Red sites.

Probably the first image you will spot is the triangle-patterned, red blanket design. Have you found the figure of a man with outstretched arms? Shapes hang from his arms. Do you think they are meant to be feathers, or do you have some other idea? Remember, your interpretation might be as good as anyone else's, since rock art images aren't completely understood. To the left is another pictograph resembling a feathered shaft and then another human-like figure. You'll find a bench here so you can rest and just enjoy the images.

On the other side of the large rock are grinding slicks, where the early inhabitants ground seeds and nuts. Double back to where the remainder of the Trail to the Past heads up the canyon to a two-room cliff dwelling.

Sidelight

Silver City is so interesting and quirky that you might want to stay at a downtown B&B and wander the historic district. Billed as the "Town Built to Last," it boasts one of the largest concentrations of Victorian homes anywhere in New Mexico. This is because when the original mining town burned, new regulations required that all buildings be built of masonry. The downtown historic area is an eclectic collection of antique stores, studios, museums, and cafes.

Side Trip

Western New Mexico University Museum in Silver City contains the largest permanent exhibit of Mimbres pottery, plus natural history and Hispanic folk art. Mimbres bowls have large figures painted on the inside bottoms of the pots. Many of the pots have a single hole made through the figure. One theory is that the hole was made after the owner died, to release his spirit. The museum is located at 1000 W. College (end of 10th St.), 505-538-6386

Horseshoe Canyon, Canyonlands National Park, Utah

UTAH ROCK ART SITES

NINE MILE CANYON

location: *central Utah (Price area)*

directions: *Head southeast from Price on US 191/6 approximately 3 miles and turn left (north) on Soldier Creek Rd. (There is a large Chevron station on the northwest corner of the intersection.) Be sure you have plenty of fuel and water, as there are no services between Wellington and Myton. Nine Mile Canyon is a National Backcountry Byway. Cottonwood Glen Picnic Area and Daddy Canyon Complex have vault toilets. You'll find an information kiosk about Nine Mile Canyon at the turnoff to Soldier Creek Rd. After about 12.8 miles, the pavement turns to gravel road, climbing up through a pass then down to Minnie Maude Creek. The bridge doesn't have a sign but is about 21.5 miles from US 191/6. Reset your odometer at the bridge. All mileage given will be from this point, although odometers may vary a bit. A BLM sign explaining Nine Mile Canyon is 0.5 mile past the bridge. A brochure with mileage information for the sites is available from Castle Country Travel Council in Price, 800-842-0789.*

Nine Mile Canyon just might be the world's longest art gallery. Nine Mile is a misnomer, though, since the canyon is actually 40 miles long. There are thousands of petroglyphs and a few pictographs scattered along its length. Many are easily seen, some are visible only with binoculars, while still others are tucked away out of sight. There is some private land along the road, so please respect the "no trespassing" signs.

There are a number of sites listed in the Nine Mile Canyon Brochure, but we will cover just the highlights here. Reset your odometer when you cross the small bridge over Minnie Maude Creek. Proceed slowly along this scenic and interesting route. Other travelers will be watching for rock art, too, and you may encounter cattle and deer on the road. It is better if you have a driver and a navigator, because most sites aren't signed and you have to watch for them. All sites are on the left side of the road.

The first group of petroglyphs lies 4.9 miles from the bridge. There is a yellow sign 500 feet before the pullout. The glyphs are on the left, behind a rail fence, and include a man with a bow and arrow and sheep at ground level. About halfway up the cliff, images include men with horned headdresses. Look to the far left of the upper panel for a tall skinny man with a bird next to him.

You will have to watch carefully for the rest of the sites, because they are not signed. At 7.7 miles the glyphs are 100 feet up, under a ledge. You'll need to park around the bend for a site at 7.8 miles. The glyphs at 8.5 and 9.4 miles are Ute (or possibly Navajo), portraying horses.

One of the best sites, the Bolo Man, is at 10.7 miles. Park around the curve, and walk back to a footpath between two trees. Follow this short path to the base of a cliff and look at the area covered with dark varnish. Can you see the Bolo Man? He is pecked solid, has horns and curved legs, and seems to be swinging bolas (weighted ropes that are swung and used to capture animals). Also here are images of a large sheep and a design that resembles a spiderweb. Watch for other figures such as the dancers and the man with a bow and arrow

In less than 0.5 mile, you will see the Harmon Canyon sign. On the side of the road opposite the sign, look up at the dark ledge to see a number of petroglyphs stretching for about 100 yards. Binoculars are helpful. You can actually see more glyphs from the road, because if you make the steep climb, you are too close to see them clearly. Some of the images are faint. They may be older or perhaps just more weathered. Can you find the line of deer or the other animals that resemble buffalo? There are even a few red pictographs, but you will have to look closely to find them among the hundreds of glyphs along this panel. Have you seen the mountain lion and shaman figures yet?

There are glyphs at 12.9 miles, but you need binoculars to see them clearly, and there is another panel at 13.5 miles. The one at 14.3 miles is a good site. Look here for the long "snake skin" with two birds directly above it.

To see the petroglyph panel most often associated with Nine Mile Canyon, go to 23.7 miles and turn right, up Cottonwood Canyon. At 25 miles you will notice the "hunting scene." Look for the large, armless figure in the middle of the line of bighorn sheep. Do you see the man with a bow and arrow that looks like he is shooting the first sheep? Hint: He is at the far right. There are more sites listed in the brochure, and if you watch closely, you'll find even more glyphs

Sidelight

Nine Mile Canyon, a main tributary of the Green River, is actually 40 miles long. There are several versions of exactly how Nine Mile received its name, but they are all somewhat similar. One story is that topographer F. M. Bishop, with the 1869 John Wesley Powell exploring expedition, made a 9-mile triangulation drawing, and Nine Mile Creek earned its name from this. Another version is that the creek is 9 miles from a certain point, while yet another story says John Wesley Powell placed a stake 9 miles from the entrance to the canyon. Powell is famous for leading the first group of explorers through the Grand Canyon, braving the Colorado River in wooden boats and barely surviving.

SEGO CANYON (also known as Thompson Wash site)

location: *east-central Utah (east of Green River)*
directions: *From Green River, go east approximately 25 miles on I-70, then take exit 185. Head north for less than a mile to Thompson Springs, then cross the railroad tracks and go north on the paved road. You'll find a parking area on the left, 4 miles west of Thompson Springs.*

Very large pictographs make Sego Canyon (also known as Thompson Wash) a favorite rock art site. The site also is easy to reach from I-70, the main east-west route across Utah. Interpretive signs help visitors understand the paleo-art and give insight into their meanings. First reported in 1883 by G. K. Gilbert of the U.S. Geological Survey, Sego Canyon is one of the earliest recorded rock art sites in Utah.

Sego Canyon has three distinct styles covering at least 1,000 years: Barrier Canyon, Fremont, and historic Ute. The Ute glyphs are the most recent, and

they include horse figures as well as buffalo and shields. Although there is a trail of sorts, it is very difficult to get to the Ute images, which are actually much easier to observe from the parking lot.

To see some older images, take the marked trail from the parking lot to the end of a protruding bluff, where you'll find both petroglyphs and pictographs. These glyphs have been pecked over earlier painted symbols. Do you see the figures with necklaces? How about the bighorn sheep that looks as if it is wearing tennis shoes?

Just around the corner is a beautiful panel of 19 red figures in Barrier Canyon

style. These larger-than-life (6 to 7 feet tall) anthropomorphs do not have arms or legs, just vertical body marking. These impressive depictions have large vacant eyes, antennae, and earrings. They may have had ceremonial or ritual meanings. Have you found the man with snakes, who has circles on each side of his head? Notice the smaller figure on the far right Why do you think he is the only dark green figure? Now look to the far left to find an orange figure. Images like these at Sego Canyon have given rise to a myth claiming that aliens visited the earth.

One theory is that this canyon was a retreat for shamans, and the large red figures might have warned others not to enter. As at many other sites, it is a mystery why some walls have clusters of elements and other walls have none.

Go across the road near the corral to see several more panels containing both petroglyphs and pictographs. The glyphs include animals and human-like figures. Can you see the little footprints? The painted panel is at ground level and has a 7-foot-high shamanistic image.

Look up and to the left of the tall red figures. Can you see two more trapezoidal figures, a white circle, and a small elk? Modern engravings date from the 1800s, and the man with hair is also probably a modern addition.

Sidelight

Directly across the road from the parking lot is an unusual geologic feature. Water has eroded a large rock to make a bridge.

TEMPLE MOUNTAIN WASH

location: *east-central Utah (near Goblin Valley State Park)*

directions: *Temple Mountain Wash lies about halfway between Hanksville and I-70, about an hour southwest of Green River. Going south on UT 24 from I-70 just west of Green River, take the Goblin Valley State Park turnoff (sometimes listed as Temple Mountain Rd.) west. In about 5 miles you'll reach a junction. The left turn goes to Goblin Valley State Park, but you should go straight about a mile to Temple Mountain Wash. Several hundred yards inside the canyon mouth is a small dirt road on the right. It leads a short distance to the base of the large cliff. Although it's not part of Goblin Valley State Park, you can get information on this site by calling the park at 435-564-3633.*

Temple Mountain Wash is in a remote, scarcely inhabited section of eastern Utah, so take plenty of water and a full tank of gas. This makes a nice side trip on a visit to Goblin Valley State Park.

Look up to see the red pictographs on the cream-colored cliff walls of the canyon's north side, about 40 feet above ground level. In spots, the heads of the man-like figures—possibly shamans—appear to have slid off, but the bodies remain. Have you found the large headless figure holding a snake? To the left are two dog-like animals. The larger one has a vertical white stripe just behind its shoulder, while the smaller one has a horizontal stripe. Look for a smaller figure with the upper half remaining. Hint: The body has white dots on the red paint and the figure sports horns.

At this site we find both Barrier Canyon style and Fremont style figures. Can you see the broad-shouldered Fremont image superimposed over an older Barrier Canyon style? Hint: The man-like motif has strange eyes. There are more elements on the surrounding walls, but natural exfoliation has destroyed some of the figures. Look around and you will find paint remnants.

Sidelight

The San Rafael Swell is a large uplift on the western side of US 24. This 70 by 40-mile area contains some of the most beautiful canyons in Utah. Around the

edges of the swell you will see a ring of upturned wildly eroded strata known as the San Rafael Reef. Angled nearly vertically, it is steepest and widest on the eastern slopes. Mesas, buttes, and canyons provide days of backcountry hiking in this rugged region. A magnitude-5.3 earthquake occurred along the San Rafael Swell in 1988. Since the area is so remote, relatively little harm was done. Goblin Valley State Park, on the eastern slopes of the San Rafael Swell, contains many fanciful shapes of eroded sandstone.

GREAT GALLERY, HORSESHOE CANYON

location: *southeastern Utah (in Canyonlands National Park, south of Green River)*
directions: *From I-70 west of Green River, take UT 24 south for 29 miles. On your right will be the turnoff to Goblin Valley State Park. Just past the state park sign, a dirt road will take off to your left (east). The dirt road can usually be traveled by passenger car but may become impassable during wet weather. After 25 miles, the road forks. Take the left fork for 5 miles to Horseshoe Canyon campgrounds, on the right down a short dirt road. You may camp here on the edge of the west rim. There is a toilet but no water. No pets are allowed in the canyon. Horseshoe Canyon is open year-round, but in summer, the hike can be very hot, so be sure to take plenty of water. The hike to the pictographs is a 6.5-mile round trip and includes a 750-foot elevation change going into and out of the canyon. The canyon bottom is flat but sandy. A detached unit of Canyonlands National Park, this site is monitored by rangers. Hans Flat Ranger Station, Canyonlands National Park, 435-259-2652.*

Horseshoe Canyon contains absolutely spectacular pictographs. There are several sections of rock art in the canyon, but the most significant is the Great Gallery. Although it contains both pictographs and petroglyphs, most visitors make the hike to see the painted figures. In fact, many serious rock art lovers consider the hike to the Great Gallery in Horseshoe Canyon to be a pilgrimage. The artwork is ethereal and the setting spiritual. This region contains some of the best examples of Barrier Canyon style. Experts estimate that human habitation in Horseshoe Canyon may date back as far as 9000–7000 B.C. Most of the rock art seems to be from 2000 B.C. to A.D. 500, although the pictographs may be much older. Clay figures, found in a side canyon, are remarkably similar to the pictographs and may date to 4700 B.C.

The Great Gallery is 200 feet long and 15 feet high, and contains dozens of red and white pictographs. There are 20 life-size figures here. These mummy-like figures lack arms and legs and seem to hover on the walls, giving the gallery a sense of reverence. One pictograph of a 6-foot-tall white figure surrounded by six red attendants stands out among the rest. Named the "Holy Ghost," its enormous eyes and looming presence overshadow all the other painted symbols. Is he a spirit or supernatural being or a revered ancestor? No one knows. Note also the smaller animal figures around the heads and shoulders of some of the mummy-like figures. Most experts refer to them as shaman's spirit helpers.

Many of the pictographs are elaborately decorated. Different methods such as finger-painting, incised wavy lines, dots, and splatter-painting were used to make the rich textural designs.

Ancient people were not the only ones to use this canyon. When ranchers arrived, they made livestock trails into the canyon for water. Prospectors searched for, but didn't find, minerals and oil in the region.

Sidelight

The black crust covering portions of the ground is called cryptobiotic soil. This biological soil crust is made mainly of cyanobacteria but includes lichens, mosses, green algae, micro-fungi, and bacteria. When wet, cyanobacteria move through the soil and help bind rock or soil particles together, providing stability and helping to prevent erosion. Don't walk on this extremely fragile crust. Stay on the trails and roads.

MOAB ROCK ART TOUR GOLF COURSE SITE

location: *eastern Utah (Moab area; site #1 on the Moab Area Rock Art Auto Tour)*
wheelchair-accessible

directions: *The Moab Information Center provides a Moab Area Rock Art Auto Tour brochure, giving a brief background on the prehistory of the area and driving directions to each site. The tour offers five different drives, some with several sites along the route. A few stops are wheelchair-accessible, while others require a short walk or climb. You will need to follow directions exactly to find this first spot, as the route goes through a residential area. From the intersection of Main and Center in downtown Moab, go south approximately 4 miles on US 191. Watch for a golf course sign and turn left on Spanish Trail Rd. There is a large gas station or the southeast corner of the intersection. Go approximately 1 mile to a traffic control circle. Take Westwater Dr. out of the traffic circle (straight across the road). Proceed approximately 0.5 mile to a small pullout on the left side of the road next to a private entrance with a large arched sign. Do not block the driveway. The golf course is on the right side of the road. Moab Information Center, Center and Main, Moab, 435-259-8825, 800-635-MOAB, www.discovermoab.com.*

The petroglyphs at the golf course site reach up about 30 feet from ground level and extend approximately 90 feet. There are a number of figures here, including a row of bighorn sheep. Start at the left side of the panel, where there are just a few glyphs, and keep walking to the right. The Fremont-style man has long earrings and a forked-antler headdress, triangle-shaped body, and fingers. Look at the human figure to the right. Now look again. Does he have four legs?

About 15 feet to the right, look carefully for a 4-foot human-like petroglyph. The image is hard to see, because it is so old it has repatinated. The head is small with horns on top, earrings, square shoulders, and hands with fingers.

Another 10 feet to the right, you will find a large white sandstone outcropping with two men with "bubble" bodies. Directly below them is some kind of animal figure that appears to be running. Higher up, near where the white sandstone ends, you'll see another man figure with horns, but he lacks earrings. If you search, you will also be able to see the "reindeer and sled." The petroglyphs extend to the end of the fence.

Sidelight

The Moab region was first known as Spanish Valley, named after the Old Spanish Trail that once passed through here. It was later called Grand Valley after the Grand River. (The Grand River became officially known as the Colorado River in 1921.) Other names for the settlement have included Elk Mountain Mission and Mormon Fort. William Pierce suggested the name Moab from the Ute word *mohapa,* which means "mosquito water." This is Utah's only town built right along the banks of the Colorado River.

KANE CREEK BOULEVARD SITES

location: *eastern Utah (Moab area; site #2 on the Moab Area Rock Art Auto Tour)*
directions: *In Moab, turn west at Main and Kane Creek Dr. (McDonald's is on the southwest corner). Go 0.8 mile to the intersection of Kane Creek Dr. and 500 West. Stay left, following Kane Creek Dr. There are three sites along this route. Moab Information Center, Center and Main, Moab, 435-259-8825, 800-635-MOAB, www.discovermoab.com.*

Moon Flower Canyon (wheelchair-accessible) Moon Flower Canyon site, the easiest to find and view, is a good place for children. From the intersection of Kane Creek Dr. and 500 West, go 2.3 miles to the mouth of Moon Flower Canyon. Watch for a large pullout and rail fence on the left side of the road. There are large cottonwood trees here and a small campground.

The petroglyphs are at the south end of the parking area, conveniently shaded by a big tree and protected by a fence. Chipped in the Barrier Canyon style, they range from the Archaic Period to modern graffiti. Starting at the far right end, images include sheep, snakes, and a six-toed foot. To the left is a mysterious "ghost" figure with two horns. This site has many initials and dates. Do you see the 1903 date?

More animals and human elements are to the left around the rock point. Notice the "fence" (or maybe it is a grill). There are two such images, both near ground level. Next to these glyphs is a man with long arms extended over his head. Look just above him for two bighorn sheep. There is a 1900 date. Can you find any older dates?

To the left of the BLM interpretive sign is a figure with three long sticks in the top of his head. The largest image is square-headed with two straight horns, a large striped triangular body, and short legs.

At the end of the fence is a long vertical crack in the rock. Several notched logs are inside the crack. Locals and probably prehistoric people used these logs to climb up to higher areas.

Unnamed site This small panel is 1.2 miles down Kane Creek Blvd. The site is unsigned and hard to see, although it will be more visible on your return

(you will be coming back the same way you went in). The petroglyphs are on the left side of the road past the Kane Creek Campground. (If you reach the end of the pavement, you have gone too far.) The pullout is very small, but the images are near the road and at ground level, so you can easily view them from your car.

Can you find the trail of deer tracks going up the center of the panel? Notice the bowlegged figure. It doesn't have a head, just a straight line going off to the left. The topmost figure seems to be a human image with an antenna on its head.

Another unnamed site At 1.7 miles from the previous site (5.3 miles from the intersection of Kane Creek Dr. and 500 West), on the gravel portion of the road, watch for two small pullouts and park here. Walk approximately 75 feet west of the pullouts and downslope to a large boulder. The petroglyphs are on all four sides of the rock. Look on the road-facing side and in the lefthand corner of the rock. Can you see the birthing scene? Notice that the baby's feet are emerging first. Have you found the centipede or the bear paws?

Sidelight

In the late 1800s, Moab was a Wild West town. Outlaws such as Butch Cassidy and the Wild Bunch used the canyons and remote country around Moab for hiding out.

COURTHOUSE WASH SITE

location: *eastern Utah (Moab area; site #3 on the Moab Area Rock Art Auto Tour)*
directions: *From the Junction of US 191 and Scenic Byway 128, follow US 191 across*

the Colorado River and Courthouse Wash to a parking lot on the right side of the road. There will be an interpretive sign here. Take a gravel trail back across Courthouse Wash. There is a walled walk across the highway bridge. Do not go down into the wash, but go straight to the cliffs and watch for cairns. Steep trails go up the

talus slope. Pictographs and petroglyphs can be found on the smooth portion of the cliff. The trail is about 0.5 mile long, but pictographs can be viewed from halfway up. Take binoculars for better viewing if you do not plan to make the full climb. Moab Information Center, Center and Main, Moab. 435-259-8825, 800-635-MOAB, www.discovermoab.com.

The Courthouse Wash site is a part of Arches National Park near Moab. The panel stretches for 52 feet along the cliff and measures 19 feet high. The large red images are in typical Barrier Canyon style, with triangular bodies and headdresses. Look at the different styles of heads on these figures—triangle-shaped, large oblong, and no head at all. Most of them, though, do seem to have some sort of headwear, ranging from elaborate to a simple set of horns.

In the upper right corner of the panel are black, white, and red figures. These are referred to as polychrome designs because they contain more than two colors.

Notice the white one with black squares and rectangles decorating his body. Several others appear to be tightly wrapped like mummies, and other figures appear with long skinny arms, or holding objects. There are some animals, including sheep, and geometric designs mixed among these shaman-like images.

Images of shields are superimposed over the older pictographs and were probably made by Ancestral Puebloan or Ute people. The junction of Court-house Wash and the Colorado River was part of a popular route for many ancient peoples. If you climb up the steep slope, you will find additional petro-glyphs near the base of the cliff.

Someone tried to scrub these paintings off the wall in 1980, using a stiff brush and a harsh cleaner and badly vandalizing the site. The Park Service restored the site, but the colors will never be as bright as before. The vandals were never apprehended.

Sidelight

Moab is one of only three places in Utah where a bridge crosses the Colorado River. The other two sites are south of Cisco and at Hite. The bridge at Moab was built in 1911.

POTASH ROAD SITES (Potash Road is also called Utah Scenic Byway 279)

location: *eastern Utah (Moab area; site #4 on the Moab Area Rock Art Auto Tour)*
directions: *From US 191 just north of Moab, take Utah Scenic Byway 279 (Potash Rd.) south along the west side of the Colorado River. Moab Information Center, Center and Main, Moab, 435-259-8825, 800-635-MOAB, www.discovermoab.com.*

Site #1 Potash Road follows the Colorado River through an especially scenic area. Drive slowly—the cliffs next to the road are a popular rock-climbing area. After 5 miles, start watching for the "Indian Writing" sign. The pullout is on the left side of the road and the petroglyphs are on the right side. Be watch-ful of children, because there is no guardrail between the pullout and the high-way. The figures are best viewed from the parking area.

The panel extends for 125 feet along the red cliff. Notice the round holes on the left side of the panel. These anchored roof beams for a building. The artists must have stood on the roof to make these images, which are now 25 to 30 feet above ground level. Starting at the left, find the series of men with headdresses. Since they are in typical Fremont style, they were probably pecked by Fremont people between A.D. 600 and 1300. One figure is impres-sively large, with two figures with spirals at the ends of their right arms.

Move on to the next panel. Do you see another figure holding a spiral? Notice that it is in his left hand this time, perhaps indicating that he was left-handed. Immediately to the right and lower down is a string of figures holding hands. They look a little like paper dolls.

The glyphs continue on to the right, where you will find three "bubble men." Instead of the usual triangle-shaped bodies, they have circles. Look on the next panel to the right. The figures here seem to hold shields, some using their left hands and others their right.

What do you think the large "U" with lines on the next panel means? Have you found the "rake" design yet? Experts think this might signify rain falling from a cloud. What is your opinion?

Site #2 The second site is about 200 feet farther down Potash Road and is also marked with an "Indian Writing" sign. The parking area is on the left side of the road. These glyphs are very faint and have been vandalized, but you can still find the "Moab Bear." First, find the big rock jutting out of the Colorado River. Now, look back behind you at the cliff directly across the road from the rock. Slightly to the left, near the bottom of the panel, is a large bear—the signature glyph of this route. There are some more images, along with some dinosaur tracks, approximately 0.75 mile farther down the road. Viewing tubes help you spot the dinosaur tracks, but you will need binoculars to see the rock art.

Site #3 Go another 7.5 miles to a sign that says "Dinosaur Tracks and Poison Spider Trail." If you want to hike to the tracks and rock art, take the dirt road

off to the right and park. The images are on the big rock slab, balanced on the side of the hill, across the gully from the toilet. It is a steep hike. An easier way to see the figures is to park in the small pullout, on the right side of Potash Road, immediately past the sign. Hidden behind the bushes, about 12 feet from the gravel, is a viewing tube, through which you can see more dinosaur tracks. The petroglyphs are alongside the dinosaur tracks, but they are indistinct through the viewing pipe. Binoculars would be helpful here as well.

Sidelight

The Moab Valley may have been inhabited by early cultures for as long as 10,000 years. The town of Moab itself sits on the ruins of an eleventh- and twelfth-century Ancestral Puebloan farming village. After the Ancestral Puebloans left in the 1300s, Ute people sporadically used the area.

WOLFE RANCH, ARCHES NATIONAL PARK

location: *eastern Utah (Moab area; site #5 on the Moab Area Rock Art Auto Tour)*
directions: *Once you're in the park, follow the signs to Wolfe Ranch and Delicate Arch (same trailhead) about 14 miles from the park entrance. From the parking lot, walk east about 600 feet along the trail (past Wolfe Ranch and over the wash). The panel is on the cliffs to the left. Moab Information Center, Center and Main, Moab, 435-259-8825, 800-635-MOAB, www.discovermoab.com.*

The path to the Wolfe Ranch petroglyph site is on the Delicate Arch Trail. The side trail to the petroglyphs takes off to the left immediately after crossing a bridge over the small wash. A short walk on a dirt trail leads to a Navajo sandstone cliff, where buff-colored rock is coated with black desert varnish.

The petroglyphs here—very stylized and very clear—were fashioned by Utes sometime between 1650 and 1850. Can you find all five men on horseback? Remember, horses were introduced in the West after the Spanish arrived in the 1500s.

There are also six bighorn sheep figures along with three smaller animal symbols that resemble dogs.

Sidelight

The trail to the petroglyphs passes the Wolfe Ranch, settled in the late 1800s by John Wesley Wolfe and his son Fred. John was from Tennessee but fought with the North during the Civil War. Although he participated in many battles, he was never wounded in combat, but his leg was injured while he was lifting a large gun out of the mire during the siege of Vicksburg. He never walked without a crutch again.

After the Civil War, John moved West, hoping the dry climate would ease the pain in his leg. His wife refused to raise her children in such a primitive land, and she stayed behind. Only his adventuresome son Fred came along. In 1906, John's daughter, Flora Stanley, moved to the ranch with her husband and children, and John helped educate his grandchildren. They learned to read and write in both English and Dutch, which John spoke fluently.

CAVE SPRING

location: *southeastern Utah (in Canyonlands National Park, north of Monticello)*
directions: *Cave Spring is located in the Needles District of Canyonlands National Park. Enter Needles District from UT 211. Past the Roadside Ruin sign, the road forks; the left fork (there is a sign) heads to the Cave Spring Trail. The paved road lasts for approximately 0.5 mile, then the last mile of the road is good gravel. The trail is 0.6 mile, and there are ladders, but you can see the pictographs before you reach the ladders.*

In the slickrock country of Canyonlands, water is scarce. The water here at Cave Spring first attracted early peoples, and much later, cattlemen. From the parking lot, follow the path clockwise for a few hundred feet to Cave Spring Camp. Cowboys from the late 1800s camped here while working on the ranches, and the alcove is furnished much as it was back then. John Albert Scorup, an early cattleman, established the Scorup-Sommerville Cattle Company in 1926. Between 7,000 and 10,000 head of cattle ranged the 1,800,000 acres of the largest cattle ranch in Utah. Although Arches came under the national parks system in 1929 and became a full-fledged national park in 1971, this camp was still used until 1975, when cattle ranching was discontinued here.

Follow the trail approximately 100 yards to the second large alcove (you will pass several small ones). Here a park service sign says "Water To Live By." The red pictographs are on the wall directly behind the sign. Can you see the three human-like figures? They are 12 to 18 inches tall and quite distinct. The other splotches of red paint are probably remnants of worn pictographs.

Look to the right of the red figures. Can you see the three black handprints surrounded by white? Notice the black ceiling, darkened by the soot of centuries of campfires. The fern at the back of the cave is called maidenhair.

Outside the far end of the alcove you'll find a hackberry tree on the left side of the trail and a piece of iron railing protecting a flat sandstone rock. The three oblong indentations in the rock are grinding slicks, used long ago to grind seeds and grains.

Sidelight

The spring in Cave Spring has long been a godsend for wildlife as well as humans. Do you notice how much cooler it is inside the alcove? Look carefully in the mud to see if any wild animal visited the water during the night. You will probably find bird tracks, especially those of the raven. These large, black birds like to hang around spots where there are people. Their loud "caw" is often heard echoing in canyon country. Extremely curious and highly intelligent, they like to gather small objects to tuck away in various hiding spots.

NEWSPAPER ROCK STATE HISTORICAL MONUMENT

location: *southeastern Utah (Monticello area)*

wheelchair-accessible

directions: *Newspaper Rock is on UT 211 about 12 miles west of US 191, north of Monticello. This is the access road to Needles District of Canyonlands National Park. Camping is available, and the site has a pit toilet. Managed by BLM, San Juan Field Office, 435 N. Main, Monticello, 435-587-1500.*

Newspaper Rock State Historical Monument, located in Indian Creek Canyon, is a large panel of petroglyphs etched into dark desert varnish. The images are believed to be approximately 2,000 years old and cover cultures from the Archaic period to more recent Navajo, Ute, and historic figures.

Early Anglo settlers gave Newspaper Rock this name, and the Navajo name for it means "rock that tells a story." Hundreds of elements are protected by the large sandstone overhang, which also makes it very easy to photograph. One of the dominant designs, on the right side of the panel, about two-thirds of the way up, looks like a wheel. Since these early peoples didn't use wheels, where do you suppose that form came from?

Look above the wheel to the big foot with six toes. Six-toed foot glyphs are found at many sites, but it is not known why they were depicted. There are several six-toed feet at Newspaper Rock. How many can you find?

Directly right of the wheel, there is a row of little footprints. To the left of the wheel are horned figures that are especially clear. See the men on horseback? These historic glyphs were chipped by either Navajos or Utes.

What do you think about the "flying squirrels" on the top left side? One theory is that they are pelts staked out to dry. See how many buffalo you can find. Hint: One of the larger ones is in the center of the panel. To the left of the center buffalo you can find a shaman with horns on his head, a spear in his hand, wavy lines coming out of his ears, and fringe on his leggings.

Sidelight

Newspaper Rock is located along Indian Creek. With water and large shade trees, this site is as much a favorite camping spot today as it was centuries ago. Probably once a main travel route, Indian Creek certainly must have made a welcome resting spot in the dry, sandstone region of Canyonlands.

Side Trip

The museum at Edge of the Cedars State Park in nearby Blanding contains an excellent display of Ancestral Puebloan artifacts. The highlights of the collection are a beautiful sash made of macaw feathers and an original kiva ladder. Outside, a walking trail leads to a partially restored pueblo. Although the trees in the area are known as "cedars," they are really Utah junipers. 435-678-2238, www.stateparks.utah.gov.

PAROWAN GAP

location: *southwestern Utah (Parowan area)*

directions: *From Parowan, go north on Main to 400 North. Turn west (left) for 10.5 miles. The parking area is on the right near milepost 19. The road is paved. Parowan Visitor Information: 435-477-8190. From Cedar City, take UT 130 north 13.5 miles, then turn east (right) for 2.5 miles. BLM, Cedar City Field Office, 435-586-2401.*

The soaring sandstone walls of Parowan Gap form a natural summer solstice marker and may be the reason for some of the paleo-art in this area. During the summer solstice, on June 21, the sunset aligns with the huge gap. The dark patina on the cliffs made for a nice artist's canvas. The Parowan Gap Petroglyph Site is listed on the National Register of Historic Places.

The petroglyphs are on the right side of the road and are protected behind a chain-link fence. It is thought that the rock art here covers at least 1,000 years and was made by different cultures, including Archaic, Fremont, and Southern Paiute people. The first site on the east end of the gap contains the image known as the Big Zipper and resembles just that, a partially opened zipper. This is the motif most often associated with the site.

Can you find the large circle with three other solid circles hanging from it? Hint: Look above and to the left side of the zipper. Any idea what this could mean? There are also geometric designs on this panel, some superimposed over older elements.

Keep on walking until you come to a large snake. No, not a live snake, but a 4-foot-long snake symbol. At this panel there is a shaman with horns and many zigzag lines. This site shows very little sign of vandalism, a pleasant surprise in a spot so easy to reach. Have you found the "comb" with its line of dots? This is near the left end of the fence. There are more scattered images on into the gap, but be sure to stay inside the guardrail.

At the other end of the gap (at the end of the guardrail) is another pullout for vehicles and a fenced area with a smaller site. Here most of the figures are clustered on one boulder and are primarily geometric designs.

Sidelight

Parowan Gap is a classic wind gap. This unusual 600-foot-deep landform occurs where an ancient river once carved a deep notch. Eventually, the region's climate became more arid, drying up the river, until now only the rain and wind continue the gap's erosion.

ROCHESTER ROCK ART PANEL (also known as Rochester Creek site)

location: *central Utah (north of Emery, 2 miles south of Moore)*

directions: *From Emery, go north on UT 10 for 3.5 miles. Take the Moore turnoff (UT 1612) east for 0.6 mile to the Rochester Rock Art Panel sign; the trail begins on the east side of the parking area. The petroglyphs are a 0.5-mile walk above Muddy Creek. If you visit in the spring, bring bug spray; the cedar gnats are vicious.*

The Rochester site is well known for its unique designs. It is not certain who made these glyphs, since the site lies within the Fremont culture area but the images resemble Barrier Canyon style. Located at the confluence of Rochester and Muddy Creeks, this very complex panel has many elements crowded close together. Follow the 0.5-mile trail, then stop and gape at this wonderful panel. You'll probably notice the 3-foot arch made with a series of lines. Some shorter lines (maybe rain symbols?) hang from the top of the arch. This image—the signature petroglyph of this site—is called the Rainbow, even though its exact meaning is unknown.

To the left of the Rainbow and up is a bighorn sheep-like animal that has a head at both ends, and inside the arch is what appears to be an elk with a set of large antlers. There are many shamanistic figures here, some of them 2 feet tall.

Look to the left of the Rainbow and clear to the top. What do you think that creature is meant to be? Does it look like a hippopotamus to you? Now look left of the "hippo" creature, to a long narrow animal with "spines" on its back. Could this be a crocodile? Hardly likely in the arid Southwest, but certainly strange. Directly under the hippo is an animal that appears to be running. Maybe the strange animal directly behind it is chasing it. Have you found the 20-foot-long line, just right of the hippo's nose, that goes through the whole face of the rock?

Can you find the long squiggly line that ends at the heel of a foot? Hint: It is in the far left, upper corner of the panel. Could it be a symbol for a foot trail? Look down and slightly to the right of the "footpath" for a figure sitting inside a circle. It has horns and feather-like extensions from its arms.

You will notice designs here that are seldom seen at other sites, especially in such a large number. You will want to spend plenty of time studying these images and making your own interpretations of the unusual engravings. Look carefully—you'll probably even notice a few sexually explicit motifs.

Sidelight

The Old Spanish Trail passes close to the Rochester Site. This 1,120-mile trade route led from Santa Fe, New Mexico, to Los Angeles, California. A large section of the trail travels through central and southern Utah before turning south to reach Los Angeles. The route went north from Santa Fe to avoid the Grand Canyon and other large obstacles of the Colorado Plateau. Explorer John C. Fremont traveled the route in the 1840s, and, assuming that the Spanish laid it out, he named it the Spanish Trail. Actually, the route was well-known by prehistoric Native Americans.

FREMONT INDIAN STATE PARK

location: *central Utah (Richfield area)*
wheelchair-accessible
directions: *Fremont Indian State Park is located 20 miles southwest of Richfield. From I-70, take exit 17 and follow the signs approximately 1 mile to the visitors center. May through September is the ideal time to visit. 11550 Westclear Creek Canyon Rd., Sevier, 435-527-4631, www.stateparks.utah.gov.*

Pictoglyphs—a rare third type of rock art, along with petroglyphs and pictographs—make Fremont Indian State Park a favorite for rock art lovers. Pictoglyphs are first pecked into the surface, then painted, forming a combination of the other two rock art styles. There are only nine known pictoglyphs in Utah, seven of them in Fremont Indian State Park.

Several different trails lead to rock art sites and places of interest in the park, so stop by the visitors center to pick up brochures for each of the walks. The easiest is the 0.3-mile Parade of Rock Art. This paved, wheelchair-accessible trail starts at the museum and passes several rock art scenes. At stop #2 on the brochure, you'll find the petroglyphs closest to the trail. The lines that resemble a ladder are thought to represent the reed grass the Paiute people used to climb out of the Underworld, according to their creation story. Stop #5 depicts hunting scenes containing mainly bighorn sheep. Strangely, the excavation of nearby archaeological sites revealed that their inhabitants' meat more commonly came from deer, waterfowl, and rabbits. It is speculated that maybe the bighorn sheep were what the hunters *wished* they could kill or that maybe the images were mean to make the sheep easier to hunt.

Children will especially enjoy the Cave of a Hundred Hands walk. The round-trip hike is only 0.5 mile and crosses Clear Creek (yes, you can fish here) and goes under the freeway. Look up when you go under the second freeway bridge to see the swallow nests. Despite the name, the cave contains only 31 hands painted reddish orange, ox-blood red, and mustard orange. It seems a number of people made the hands. Fourteen are from the right hand, 16 from the left, and on one hand you can't tell! The cave is 23 feet wide, 7 feet high, and 10 feet deep, with bars to prevent entrance. Located near a spring, it seems a logical place for early Native people to have visited.

You can drive to the Arch of Art, where 61 panels of rock art are visible, including one panel with a wide assortment of blanket designs. Rest on the bench and use the brochure to pick out the blanket pictoglyph—the only one of its kind known to exist.

The Sheep Shelter walk is a mile long and passes by a 16 x 4-foot pictograph of an Indian blanket, located on the far wall of the canyon about 150 feet up from the canyon floor. The cave at Sheep Shelter, which people have used since at least 3700 B.C., has petroglyphs, too. On the outside of the cave, other panels seem to tell part of the Hopi emergence myth.

The Rim Trail viewpoints are a short, easy walk about 0.7 miles west of the visitors center. The trail includes Newspaper Rock Viewpoint, the most spectacular rock art panel in the park, containing over 250 elements. The Rim Trail itself includes 1,164 rock art elements, but it is a dangerous hike and is closed except for staff-led hikes with previous permission. Call the park for information.

The Court of Ceremonies Trail is only 0.5 mile long, but is steep in places, both uphill and down. The Canyon of Life Trail starts 0.5 mile west of the visitors center, and the trail is only 0.25 mile long. The site is considered sacred because the rock formations and rock art are believed to help tell part of the early Native people's creation stories.

This park has nice facilities, camping, fishing, an ATV trail, and interesting geology. Plan on at least half a day here or, even better, spend several days.

Sidelight

During construction of I-70, it was deemed necessary to remove an outcropping called Spider Woman Rock. Considering the site sacred, a Hopi religious leader cursed the Utah Department of Transportation through Spider Women and her daughter Salt Woman, who controls weather. In 1983 the UDOT was plagued with problems. A slide on Billies Mountain blocked US 50, flooding railroad tracks and the town of Thistle. Waters rose in both Utah Lake and Great Salt Lake, covering interstates. Two bridges have never completely settled, and workmen say that all the concrete poured after the curse cracked in the pattern of a spiderweb. The Hopi leader clipped the newspaper articles and sent them to UDOT as proof of the revenge of Spider Woman.

Side Trip

The museum at Fremont Indian State Park visitors center holds the Fremont culture artifacts unearthed at Five Finger Ridge during the construction of I-70. This is Utah's only museum devoted exclusively to the Fremont culture, and artifacts excavated here are either on display or housed in climate-controlled storage at the museum. Notice the painted clay figures, bone tools, and shell necklace. The large black corrugated pottery jar was found upside down, covering a variety of tools.

SAND ISLAND RECREATION AREA

location: *southeastern Utah (Bluff area)*
directions: *An easy-to-reach site on the north bank of the San Juan River, 3 miles west of Bluff, off US 163. Near milepost 22, turn south toward the river at the BLM sign. Follow the paved road downhill to the river, where another BLM sign directs you to turn west (right) for the rock art. The dirt trail starts at the right end of the pullout. The short trail requires some climbing and is rocky in spots. There are camping areas, picnic tables, toilets, and a boat-launch area. Area managed by BLM, 435-587-1500.*

The Sand Island petroglyph panel is on the cliff next to the parking lot, behind the fenced area, and extends for about 100 yards. To the right of the

immense boulder you can find a number of images. Some of the elements are so old they have repatinated, but do you see the man on horseback? That is probably a historic Ute or Navajo glyph. Look to the upper right to see a very clear figure with wavy forked horns. His long arms are holding something—perhaps rattles or corn plants? Did you notice that he has no legs?

Go back left past the large rock. You will notice that someone scratched some graffiti here—this time in 1963. Look closely up and to the right of the 1963 for a faint animal figure. From this figure keep looking up (much higher) to see an unusual motif. It is three semi-circles, one on top of the other. Any ideas what this might represent?

Approximately 20 feet down the trail, on the left, you'll find the Kokopelli panel—the signature motif for this site. There should be five Kokopellis, though we only found four. To the left of the Kokopellis is a line of animals all facing west. Directly below these figures is another series of animals, also heading west. Perhaps this represents a migrating herd. Look above the animals and to the left for a big animal with antlers. Above the antlered figure is a strange image. Do you think this is a frog or a man figure or something else?

Have you noticed the W. S. graffiti? Above it are some shamanistic figures. Look to the top of the panel slightly right of the shaman figures. Do you see three images with striped bodies? Although there are a few more random glyphs toward the end of the fence, this is the end of the main panel.

Sidelight

Mormons settled Bluff, the first white settlement in San Juan County. They were "called" (strongly requested by church leaders) to found the San Juan Mission. They farmed along the San Juan River and helped develop friendly relations with the local Ute and Navajo people.

Side Trip

At the far eastern end of Bluff is an unusual rock formation known as the Navajo Twins. Two massive sandstone spires touch at the top, and the Twin Rocks Café and Gift Shop stands at the base of these rocks.

WOLFMAN SITE

location: *in Butler Wash, southeastern Utah*

directions: *From the junction of US 163 and US 191 (3 miles west of Bluff), head west on 163 for less than a mile. Directly across the road (north) from the airport turnoff is a dirt road with a closed metal gate. There may or may not be a sign noting Butler*

Wash Rd. Go through the gate and shut it. This road is rough, and a high-clearance vehicle is recommended. Do not attempt in bad weather. After you get through the gate a sign says "San Juan County Rd. 262, Lower Butler Wash." Head north for 0.8 mile to the cattle guard. Turn left (west) onto the dirt road along the fence line. There is a parking area after 0.2 mile. You can see where the road goes on across the slick rock for 0.1 mile to the edge of the canyon. Attempt this only with high-clearance or 4-wheel drive, and careful driving. Let someone know where you are going, wear good hiking shoes, and carry plenty of water. This hike is not for small children, older children with nervous mothers, or those afraid of heights. Area managed by BLM, 435-587-1500.

Wolfman Site is located in Butler Wash, the Holy Grail for rock art lovers. A deep, rugged wash that cuts through sandstone on the east side of Comb Ridge, Butler Wash was home to native peoples for thousands of years. Remains of pueblos, villages, camps, and rock art sites are clustered along the entire length of the wash. Sites must be reached by hiking or horseback riding, and Western outfitters often lead groups into the area. The Wolfman Site is one of the easiest to reach without a guide.

Follow the directions above to the road's end, and walk toward the canyon edge, watching for small cairns that mark the faint trail heading south. The path leads down through an 18-inch crack in the rock (plan on some rock-scrambling) to a ledge about halfway down the canyon wall. Follow the wall south several hundred yards to an alcove.

Inside the alcove are remains of walls, some grinding slicks, knife-sharpening slashes, and a water seep. The petroglyphs are not in the alcove, and those strange images on the wall are not actually pictographs but natural rock colorations. Look down and you will notice a faint trail along the bottom of the alcove. Follow this path on south just past the alcove and look up.

At first the motifs are the usual sheep and geometrics—then you see the "wolfman." He is about 18 inches tall, with a rectangular body, square shoulders, and big feet. Look at his hands: each one has five claw-like extensions. This is a nice glyph, but the best are yet to come.

The desert varnish is so smooth it appears sanded and painted. Etched into this natural canvas is a 2-foot-high mask, complete with horns and eyes. The mouth is just an indentation in the lower face. Next is an unusual glyph over 3 feet high, which looks like a houseplant in a triangular pot. Could it represent a corn plant?

See the magnificent shield with a multi-pointed star in the center? A skilled artist incised this 30-inch glyph. Portions of this shield are solidly pecked and appear light-colored, while the black star in the middle retains the original desert varnish. Continue several more yards to a 4-foot-tall shaman figure, two large birds, other glyphs, and two large, haunting designs. The meaning of these identical designs is unknown, and they are difficult to describe. They resemble two large, oblong keyholes side-by-side. The solid black circle in the center is not chipped.

The petroglyphs at this site are so beautifully worked, it seems likely that a single, very gifted artist probably made them. The motifs are seen much better from below. It is dangerous to try to walk the narrow ledge in front of the glyphs, and you can't really appreciate the designs from there, because you are too close to them.

Sidelight

Butler Wash drains from the north, dumping snowmelt and rainwater into the San Juan River, the major drainage of the Four Corners region. Most of the year, the wash contains at least some water, and the large sandstone overhangs were favorite building spots for Ancestral Puebloan people. The quality of rock art at this site is superb.

OTHER SITES TO VISIT

Thousands of petroglyphs exist on public land throughout the Southwest. Although most of these sites are open because they are on public land, the agencies in charge prefer that directions to unprotected sites not be published, to avoid vandalism. By contacting the BLM, Park Service, or Forest Service office, you might receive directions to some sites. If you happen to stumble across rock art while hiking in a remote area, contact the agency in charge to see if they have documented the site.

Also, the status of sites does change. You can always contact the agency in charge again at a later date to check current status and accessibility. Many agencies will give private individuals directions to locations. Local museums and archaeological societies often lead group tours to sites and sometimes welcome help in recording sites. You can also check with outfitters for 4-wheel drive tours, float trips, hikes, or horseback rides that may be licensed to remote sites.

ARIZONA

Agua Fria National Monument, central Arizona, BLM, 623-580-5500

Canyon de Chelly National Monument, northeastern Arizona, National Park Service, 928-674-5500

Casa Malpais, east-central Arizona, City of Springerville, 928-333-5375

Eagle Tail Mountains, central Arizona, BLM, 928-317-3200

Garden Canyon, Fort Huachuca (U.S. Army post), southeastern Arizona, Sierra Vista Convention and Visitors Bureau, 800-288-3861

Wupatki National Monument, Arizona

Grand Canyon National Park, north-central Arizona, National Park
Service, 928-638-7888

Laws Spring, north-central Arizona, Kaibab National Forest, 928-635-5600

Little Black Canyon, northwestern Arizona, BLM, 435-688-3200

Muuputs/Owl Canyon, northwestern Arizona, Kaibab-Paiute Tribe,
928-643-7245

Petroglyph Discovery Trail (Pueblo Grande Museum tour),
central Arizona, Pueblo Grande Museum, 602-495-0901

Petroglyph Discovery Trail (Sierra Vista), southeastern Arizona, BLM,
520-439-6400, or Sierra Vista Convention and Visitors Bureau, 800-288-3861

Nampaweap, northwestern Arizona, BLM, 435-688-3200

Navajo National Monument, northeastern Arizona, National Park Service,
382-672-2700

South Mountain, central Arizona, Phoenix Parks Department, 602-495-0222

Wupatki National Monument, north-central Arizona, National Park Service,
928-679-2365

CALIFORNIA (southeastern)

Anza-Borrego State Park, California State Parks, 760-767-5311

Black Canyon, BLM, 760-252-0651

Corn Springs, BLM, 760-251-4800

Death Valley National Park, National Park Service, 760-786-3200

Fossil Falls, BLM, 760-384-5400

Joshua Tree National Park, National Park Service, 760-367-5500

Mojave National Preserve, National Park Service, 760-733-4040

Petroglyphs Point, BLM, 760-384-5400

Red Mountain Springs, BLM, 760-384-5400

COLORADO (western)

Canyon of the Ancients National Monument, southwestern Colorado, BLM,
970-882-5600

Mesa Verde National Park, southwestern Colorado, National Park Service,
970-529-4461 and 970-529-4465

Sandrocks Nature Trail, northwestern Colorado, Town of Craig, 970-824-5689

Chaco Culture Historical Park, New Mexico

NEVADA (southeastern)

Keyhole Canyon, BLM, 702-515-5000

Sloan Canyon National Conservation Area, BLM, 702-515-5000

NEW MEXICO

Apache Creek, west-central New Mexico, U.S. Forest Service, 505-533-6231

Carlsbad Caverns National Park, southeastern New Mexico, National Park Service, 505-785-2232

Chaco Culture National Historical Park, northwestern New Mexico, National Park Service, 505-786-7014

Rio Bonito National Petroglyph Trail, southeastern New Mexico, BLM, 505-627-0272

Salinas Pueblo Missions National Monument, central New Mexico, National Park Service, 505-847-2585

UTAH

Black Dragon Canyon, southeastern Utah, BLM, 435-636-3600

Buckhorn Wash, central Utah, BLM, 435-636-3600

Calf Creek Falls (Grand Staircase–Escalante National Monument), south-central Utah, Escalante Interagency Visitor Center, 435-826-5499

Canyonlands National Park, southeastern Utah, National Park Service, 435-719-2313

Capitol Reef National Park, south-central Utah, National Park Service, 435-425-3791

Cold Springs, southeast Utah, BLM, 435-587-1500

Dinosaur National Monument, northeastern Utah, National Park Service, 435-781-7700

Dry Wash Petroglyphs, central Utah, BLM 435-636-3600

Grand Gulch Primitive Area, southeastern Utah, BLM, 435-587-1500

Head of Sinbad, central Utah, BLM 435-636-3600

Hovenweep National Monument, southeastern Utah, National Park Service, 970-562-4282

Monarch Cave, southeast Utah, BLM, 435-587-1500

Monument Valley Tribal Park, southeastern Utah, Navajo Nation, 435-727-5870

Natural Bridges National Monument, southeastern Utah, National Park Service, 435-692-1234

Paria Canyon, south-central Utah, BLM, 435-688-3200

GLOSSARY

abstract Designs that may be geometric, free form, or non-representational images.

Anasazi Navajo word meaning "ancient ones" or "enemies of our ancestors." Used to describe the ancient culture of the Four Corners Region. Ancestral Puebloan or Hisat'sinom are now the preferred terms for this culture. See the Introduction for more information on Ancestral Puebloan culture.

anthropomorphs Images portraying human characteristics.

Ancestral Puebloan (Anasazi) style Rock art made by the Ancestral Puebloan culture, possibly from 100 B.C. to A.D. 1450. Located mainly in the Four Corners Region. Previously termed Anasazi style.

archaeo-astronomy The astronomy of ancient cultures. A field of science that studies solar calendars and other relationships between ancient cultures and the sky. A combination of archaeology and astronomy.

Barrier Canyon style A rock art style most common in eastern Utah. Dating is uncertain, but possibly from 1000 B.C. to A.D. 500. Includes anthropomorphic figures that appear supernatural or shamanistic and are elaborately decorated. Includes both petroglyphs and pictographs.

blanket designs Images that resemble patterns on textiles.

BLM Abbreviation for Bureau of Land Management.

dendrochronolgy The use of tree rings to establish date of wood found in dwellings.

desert pavement Small dark stones that cover the ground. Geoglyphs were formed by scraping away the dark rocks to reveal the lighter earth underneath.

desert varnish The dark patina that slowly forms on a rock surface. It is the result of weathering and microbial/chemical alterations. Many petroglyphs are chipped through the desert varnish to reveal the lighter stone underneath.

geoglyph See *desert pavement* and *intaglios.*

geometric Description of rock art that is abstract or non-representational.

entopic Representing images presumably seen during a shaman's trance. Usually abstract designs.

Fremont style Ranging from western Utah to western Colorado. Believed to have been made between A.D. 400 and 1500. Anthropomorphs are usually square shouldered and roughly trapezoidal in shape. Often overlaps with Barrier Canyon style. See the Introduction for more on Fremont culture.

Hisat'sinom Name preferred by the Hopi tribe to describe the Anasazi culture.

historic rock art Made after European arrival in the Americas. Often depicts horses, which were not known until after the Spanish arrival in the 1500s.

intaglios Also known as geoglyphs. Large designs formed on the ground and usually discernable only from the air.

migration journey In the creation story of the Ancestral Puebloan Culture, the people emerged from the Fourth World and were told to travel in four directions. Each clan was to find its "center place."

patina Also known as desert varnish. A dark surface formed very slowly by weathering and microbial/chemical alterations. (Also see *repatination.*)

paleo-art Art relating to early cultures.

petroglyphs Images pecked, chipped, abraded, or incised into a rock surface.

pictoglyphs Rare rock art figures that are both pecked and painted.

pictographs Designs painted onto a rock surface with natural pigment.

quadrupeds Animal figures with four legs.

repatination The slow reforming of patina or desert varnish over a glyph. Used as a means of estimating the age of rock art. Figures that have repatinated are considered older.

rock art Any form of imagery on rocks. Includes petroglyphs, pictographs, pictoglyphs, and geoglyphs. Does not denote a language but is a record of ideas and images.

shaman Holy leader. May go into trances as part of ceremonials or to receive guidance.

solar calendars Images, often circles and spirals, used to determine a specific date such as the summer or winter solstice.

spirit helper Usually a spiritual animal that was the shaman's helper. Many times a depiction of a shaman will have a smaller animal figure (spirit helper) nearby.

styles Categories used to describe rock art from different cultures and different time periods.

textile design Rock art images resembling designs found on ancient textiles and pottery.

zoomorphs Rock art imagery that appears to represent animals.

SUGGESTED READING

Cheek, Lawrence W. *Kokopelli.* Tucson, AZ: Rio Nuevo Publishers, 2004.

Cole, Sally J. *Legacy on Stone: Rock Art of the Colorado Plateau and Four Corners Region.* Boulder, CO: Johnson Books, 1990.

Harris, Rick. *Easy Field Guide to Rock Art Symbols of the Southwest.* Phoenix, AZ: American Traveler Press, 1995.

Kelen, Leslie, and David Sucec. *Sacred Images: A Vision of Native American Rock Art.* Layton, UT: Gibbs Smith Publishers, 1996.

Malville, J. McKim, and Claudia Putnam. *Prehistoric Astronomy in the Southwest.* Boulder, CO: Johnson Books, 1993.

McCreery, Patricia, and Ekkehart Malotki. *Tapamveni: Rock Art Galleries of the Southwest.* Petrified Forest, AZ: Petrified Forest Museum Association, 1994.

Noble, David Grant. *Ancient Ruins of the Southwest.* Flagstaff, AZ: Northland Publishing, 2000.

Patterson, Alex. *A Field Guide to Rock Art Symbols of the Greater Southwest.* Boulder, CO: Johnson Books, 1992.

Schaaf, Gregory. *Ancient Ancestors of the Southwest.* Portland, OR: Graphic Arts Center Publishing Company, 1996.

Schaafsma, Polly. *Indian Rock Art of the Southwest.* Albuquerque, NM: University of New Mexico Press, 1986.

———. *Rock Art in New Mexico.* Santa Fe, NM: Museum of New Mexico Press, 1992.

———. *Rock Art of Utah.* Salt Lake City, UT: University of Utah Press, 1994.

Schaafsma, Polly, with photographs by David Muench. *Images in Stone.* San Francisco, CA: BrownTrout Publishers, 1995.

Schneider, Joan S., and Jeffrey H. Altschul, eds. *Of Stones and Spirits: Pursuing the Past of Antelope Hill.* Tucson, AZ: Statistical Research Press, 2000.

Slifer, Dennis. *Guide to Rock Art of the Utah Region: Sites with Public Access.* Santa Fe, NM: Ancient City Press, 2000.

Welsh, Elizabeth. *Easy Field Guide to Southwestern Petroglyphs.* Phoenix, AZ: American Traveler Press, 1995.

Welsh, Liz, and Peter Welsh. *Rock-Art of the Southwest.* Berkeley, CA: Wilderness Press, 2000.

INDEX

Page numbers in *italic* type indicate
   illustrations.

agave, 24

American Rock Art Research
   Association, 57

Ancestral Puebloan. *See under*
   cultures and tribes

Anasazi. *See* cultures and tribes:
   Ancestral Puebloan

Antelope Hill, 51-53

Apache. *See under* cultures and tribes

Apache County Historical Society
   Museum, 34

Archaic. *See under* cultures and tribes

Arches National Park. *See* Wolfe
   Ranch

Arizona-Sonora Desert Museum, 59

Arizona Strip, 18-19

Ayers Rock, 63-64

Aztec Land and Cattle Company
   (Hashknife Outfit), 22

Baby Jesus Ridge, 55-57

Baca Ranch, 35

Baird, Brantley, 21

Bandelier National Monument,
   94-95, 99-100

Barrier Canyon. *See under* cultures
   and tribes

basalt, 45-46

berries, 83

Big Rock Trading Post, 97

Bishop Petroglyph Loop, *60-61,* 62

Blue Ridge Primitive Area, 40

Blue River, 39-40

Blythe Intaglios, 72-73

Bouse, Arizona, 51

Bouse Fisherman, 50-51

Breckinridge, P. Gilmer, 108-109

Butler Wash, 145

calendars, solar, 30

Camel Corps, 109

Camino Real, 107

Cañon Pintado National Historic
   District, 76-78, 79

Cañon Pintado site, 77

Carrot Man site, 79

Cave Spring, 132

Chaco Culture Historical Park, *148*

Chidago petroglyphs, 62

Christmas Tree Pass, 92

Courthouse Wash Site, 126-128

Coyote Creek site, 35-36

Coyote Pass Hospitality Bed and

Breakfast, 16

creosote, 49-50

Crook, Gen. George, 79

Crooks Brand site, 78-79

Crow Canyon, 97-99

cryptobiotic soil, 123

cultures and tribes

Ancestral Puebloan, 10, 22, 29-32, 36, 38, 41, 77, 89, 100-101, 103, 105-106, 108, 127, 130, 134, 145

Apache, 23, 26

Archaic, 10, 23, 26, 45, 47, 54, 56, 125, 135

Barrier Canyon, 118-122, 125, 127, 136

Fremont, 10, 77, 82, 118, 120, 123, 128, 135, 141

Hohokam, 10-11, 41, 43, 45, 47-48, 54-55, 56-57, 59

Hopi, 33

Kawaiisu, 69, 71-72

Mogollon, 11, 34-36, 38-39, 41, 110, 112

Navajo, 11, 97-98, 117, 133, 142

Paiute, Southern, 71, 135, 138

Paleo-Indian, 11, 21

Patayan, 45, 54

Pueblo, 77, 97-100

Shoshone, Coso, 64-66

Sinagua, Southern, 23, 26-27

Ute, 11, 80, 85, 117-118, 127, 131, 133, 142

Yavapai, 23, 26

Cushman Museum, 39

dating methods, 12, 17

Deer Creek, 80-81

Deer Valley Rock Art Center, 44-45

dendrochronology, 17

desert pavement, 50, 73, 149

desert varnish, 12, 50, 149

Douglass, A. E., 17

Dragon Road Sites, 74-75, 78-79

Edge of the Cedars State Park, 134

El Morro National Monument, 107-108

filaree, 70

fire retardant, 35

Fish Slough petroglyphs, 62

Fisherman Intaglio. See Bouse Fisherman

folk art, 97

Fourmile site, East, 76-77

Fremont. See under cultures and tribes

Fremont Indian State Park, 138-141

Fremont Ridge site, 78

geoglyphs, defined, 12

Gila Cliff Dwellings National Monument, 112-113

Glanton, John J., 53

Grapevine Canyon, *8*, 91-92

Great Gallery, Horseshoe Canyon, *114-115*, 121-122

grinding holes, 55

Hashknife Outfit (Aztec Land and Cattle Company), 22

Havasu Wildlife Refuge, 93

Hedgpeth Hills, 45-46

Hieroglyphic Canyon, 42-44

Hieroglyphic Point, 40-41

Hohokam. *See under* cultures and tribes

Homolovi Ruins State Park, 30-31

Honanki, 25-27

Honeymoon Trail, 19

Hopi. *See under* cultures and tribes

Horseshoe Canyon. *See* Great Gallery

House, Jack, 84-85

Indian Creek, 134

javelina, 57

jojoba, 51

Juan Bautista de Anza National Historic Trail, 49

Kawaiisu. *See under* cultures and tribes

K5 High Country Adventures, 35-37

Kanab Creek Wilderness Area, 18

Kane Creek Boulevard Sites, 124-126

Keyhole Sink, 19-20

Knight, Roxanne, 35-37

Kokopelli, 77

La Cienega Area of Critical Concern, 104

La Cieneguilla, 102-104

lily, alkalai mariposa, 89

Little Colorado River, 37

Little Petroglyph Canyon, 65-68

London Bridge, 93

Lost City Museum, 91

Lost Dutchman's Gold Mine, 44

Lyman Lake State Park, 32-33

manners, rock art and back road, 13

Maturango Museum, 65, 68

McDonald Creek Cultural Resource
Area, 81-83

Moab Rock Art Tour Golf Course
Site, 123-124

Moab, Utah, 126, 128, 130

Mogollon. *See under* cultures and
tribes

Moon Flower Canyon, 124-125

Mormons, 142

Mouse's Tank, 90

Navajo. *See under* cultures and tribes

Navajo Twins, 142

Newspaper Rock State Historical
Monument, 133-134

Nine Mile Canyon, 116-118

Nuche. *See* cultures and tribes: Ute

Old Pueblo Archaeology Center, 57

Old Spanish Trail, 138

Painted Cave, 16-17

Painted Rocks Petroglyph Site, 48-49

Paiute-Shoshone Indian Cultural
Center, 63

Paiute, Southern. *See under* cultures
and tribes

Pajarito Plateau, 100-101

Palatki, 23-24

Paleo-Indian. *See under* cultures and
tribes

Palmer, George, 72

Parowan Gap, 135-136

Patayan. *See under* cultures and tribes

Penitentes, 106

Petrified Forest National Forest,
29-30

Petroglyph National Monument
104-105

petroglyphs, defined, 11

pictographs
defined, 11
pigments, 27

pictoglyphs, 12, 138

piñon nuts, 102

Pipe Spring National Monument, 19

Polimana, 34-35

Potash Road Sites, 128-130

pottery
Hohokam, 55
Mimbres, 113

Powell, John Wesley, 118

Pueblo. *See under* cultures and tribes

Puerco Pueblo, 28-30

quarries, 52-53

Rabbit, Rob, 64
Rangely Outdoor Museum, 80
Red Rock Canyon National Conser-
    vation Area, 88-89
Red Rock petroglyphs, 62-63
ristras, 106
River Jet Tours, 93
Rochester Rock Art Panel (Rochester
    Creek Site), 136-137
Rock Art Ranch, 20-22
rock art types, 11-12
Route 66, 20
Rudd Creek Pueblo, 37-38

saguaro cactus, 59
Saguaro National Park, *14-15*
Salmon Ruins, 99
Salt River Canyon, 41-42
San Rafael Swell, 120-121
Sand Island Recreation Area,
    141-142
Sears Point, 53-55
Sego Canyon, 118-119
Sheep Springs, 68-70
Shoshone, Coso. *See under* cultures
    and tribes

Signal Hill, 57-59
Silver City, New Mexico, 113
Sinagua, Southern. *See under* cultures
    and tribes
Sipe White Mountain Wildlife Area,
    37-38
Sleeping Ute Mountain, 85
soil, cryptobiotic, 123
Sonoran Loop Competitive Track,
    48
Spider Woman Rock, 140
Steam Wells Petroglyph Site, 70-71
Superstition Mountains, 44

tamarisks, 81
Temple Mountain Wash, 119-120
Thompson Wash Site. *See* Sego
    Canyon
Three Rivers Petroglyph Site, 109-112
Tomé Hill, 106-107
Topock Gorge, 93
trading posts, 97
tree-ring dating, 17
Trinity Site, 112
Tsankawi Loop Trail, 101-102
Tsosie, Will, 16-17
Tularosa Basin, 112

Ultimate Petroglyph Trail, 33

Urban, Sharon, 55-57

Ute. *See under* cultures and tribes

Ute Indian Museum, 85

Ute Mountain Tribal Park, 83-85

V-Bar-V Ranch Petroglyph Site, 27-28

Valley of Fire State Park, *86-87*, 89-90

Volcanic Tablelands, 63

Waterflow, 96

Waving Hands site, 77-78

Western New Mexico University Museum, 113

White Sands National Monument and Missile Range, 112

White Tank Mountain Regional Park, 46-48

Willard, Charles, 24-25

Wolf, John Wesley and Fred, 131

Wolfe Ranch, Arches National Park, 130-131

Wolfman Site, 142-145

Wupatki National Monument, *146*

Yavapai. *See under* cultures and tribes